PMP® in 28 Days

Copyright © 2015
First Edition
All rights reserved.

ISBN: 978-0-9861914-0-4

No part of this publication may be reproduced, stored in a retrieval system or transmitted in any form or by any means, electronic, mechanical, photocopying, recording, scanning or otherwise, except under the terms of the Copyright, Designs and Patents Act 1988 or under the terms of a license issued by the Copyright Licensing Agency Ltd.

Legal Disclaimer

The publisher and the author make no representations or warranties with respect to the accuracy or completeness of the contents of this work and specifically disclaim all warranties, including without limitation warranties for a particular purpose. No warranty may be created or extended by sales or promotional materials. The advice and strategies contained herein may not be suitable for every situation.

Neither the publisher nor the author shall be liable for damages arising here from. The fact that an organization or website is referred to in this work as a citation and/or a potential source of further information does not mean that the author or the publisher endorses the information the organization or website may provide or recommendations it may make. Further, readers should be aware that internet websites listed in this work may have changed or disappeared since this book was written.

PMI®, PMP® and The PMBOK® Guide are trademarks of The Project Management Institute, Inc. PMI® has not endorsed and did not participate in the development of this study guide.

PMP® in 28 Days

Exam Preparation Guide

TABLE OF CONTENTS

PREFACE	9
ABOUT PMI® ARAB GULF CHAPTER (PMI-AGC) WWW.PMIAGC.ORG	11
CHAPTER 1: INTRODUCTION	**12**
THE PMP® EXAM	13
WHAT'S EXPECTED OF YOU	13
PMP® Eligibility Requirements.	*13*
The Application Process	*13*
WHAT YOU CAN EXPECT	14
CHAPTER 2: THE BASICS	**16**
THE PMBOK® GUIDE	16
DEFINING A PROJECT	16
RELATIONSHIPS AMONG PORTFOLIOS, PROGRAMS AND PROJECTS	17
DEFINING PROJECT MANAGEMENT	17
DEFINING PROGRAM MANAGEMENT	18
DEFINING PORTFOLIO MANAGEMENT	18
PORTFOLIO, PROGRAM & ORGANIZATIONAL MANAGEMENT: HOW ARE THEY RELATED?	18
LINKS BETWEEN PROJECT & OPERATIONS MANAGEMENT, ORGANIZATIONAL GOVERNANCE AND ORGANIZATIONAL STRATEGY OPERATION	21
ORGANIZATIONS AND PROJECT MANAGEMENT	22
BUSINESS VALUE	23
THE PROJECT MANAGER'S ROLE	23
TEST WHAT YOU'VE LEARNED	24
CHAPTER 3:	**26**
ORGANIZATION INFLUENCES & PROJECT LIFE CYCLE	**26**
ORGANIZATIONAL INFLUENCES ON PROJECT MANAGEMENT	26
ORGANIZATIONAL CULTURES AND STYLES	26
ORGANIZATIONAL STRUCTURES	26
ORGANIZATIONAL PROCESS ASSETS	29
ENTERPRISE ENVIRONMENTAL FACTORS	30
PROJECT STAKEHOLDERS & GOVERNANCE	31
PROJECT SUCCESS	33
PROJECT TEAM	34
PROJECT LIFE CYCLE	34
TEST WHAT YOU'VE LEARNED	38
CHAPTER 4: PROJECT MANAGEMENT PROCESSES	**40**
PROJECT MANAGEMENT PROCESS GROUPS	40
Initiating Process Group	*42*
Planning Process Group	*44*
Executing Process Group	*46*
Monitoring and Controlling Process Group	*47*
Closing Process Group	*49*
PROJECT INFORMATION	50
ROLE OF THE KNOWLEDGE AREAS	51
TEST WHAT YOU'VE LEARNED	53
CHAPTER 5: PROJECT INTEGRATION MANAGEMENT	**55**
DEVELOPING A PROJECT CHARTER	55

    Inputs *56*
    Tools & Techniques *59*
    Outputs *59*
  DEVELOPING A PROJECT MANAGEMENT PLAN 59
    Inputs *60*
    Tools & Techniques *61*
    Outputs *61*
  DIRECTING & MANAGING PROJECT WORK 63
    Inputs *64*
    Tools & Techniques *65*
    Outputs *66*
  MONITORING & CONTROLLING PROJECT WORK 67
    Inputs *68*
    Tools & Techniques *70*
    Outputs *71*
  PERFORMING INTEGRATED CHANGE CONTROL 72
    Inputs *74*
    Tools & Techniques *75*
    Outputs *75*
  CLOSE A PROJECT OR PHASE 76
    Inputs *77*
    Tools & Techniques *77*
    Outputs *77*
  TEST WHAT YOU'VE LEARNED 79

CHAPTER 6: PROJECT SCOPE MANAGEMENT 81

  PROJECT SCOPE MANAGEMENT 81
  PLAN SCOPE MANAGEMENT 81
    Inputs *81*
    Tools & Techniques *82*
    Outputs *82*
  COLLECT REQUIREMENTS 83
    Inputs *84*
    Tools & Techniques *85*
    Outputs *88*
  DEFINE SCOPE 89
    Inputs *90*
    Tools & Techniques *90*
    Outputs *91*
  CREATE WBS 92
    Inputs *93*
    Tools & Techniques *94*
    Outputs *96*
  VALIDATE SCOPE 96
    Inputs *97*
    Tools & Techniques *98*
    Outputs *98*
  CONTROL SCOPE 99
    Inputs *99*
    Tools & Techniques *100*
    Outputs *100*
  TEST WHAT YOU'VE LEARNED 102

CHAPTER 7: PROJECT TIME MANAGEMENT 104

  PLAN SCHEDULE MANAGEMENT 105

    Inputs *105*
    Tools & Techniques *106*
    Outputs *106*
DEFINE ACTIVITIES 107
    Inputs *107*
    Tools & Techniques *108*
    Outputs *109*
SEQUENCE ACTIVITIES 109
    Inputs *110*
    Tools & Techniques *111*
    Outputs *114*
ESTIMATE ACTIVITY RESOURCES 114
    Inputs *115*
    Tools & Techniques *116*
ESTIMATE ACTIVITY DURATIONS 118
    Inputs *118*
    Tools & Techniques *120*
    Outputs *122*
DEVELOP SCHEDULE 122
    Inputs *123*
    Tools & Techniques *124*
    Outputs *127*
CONTROL SCHEDULE 129
    Inputs *130*
    Tools & Techniques *131*
    Outputs *132*
TEST WHAT YOU'VE LEARNED 133

CHAPTER 8: PROJECT COST MANAGEMENT 135

PLAN COST MANAGEMENT 135
    Inputs *136*
    Tools & Techniques *137*
    Outputs *137*
ESTIMATE COSTS 138
    Inputs *139*
    Tools & Techniques *140*
    Outputs *142*
DETERMINE BUDGET 142
    Inputs *143*
    Tools & Techniques *144*
    Outputs *144*
CONTROL COSTS 145
    Tools & Techniques *147*
TEST WHAT YOU'VE LEARNED 153

CHAPTER 9: PROJECT QUALITY MANAGEMENT 155

PLAN QUALITY MANAGEMENT 157
    Inputs *157*
    Tools & Techniques *158*
    Outputs *166*
PERFORM QUALITY ASSURANCE 167
    Inputs *167*
    Tools & Techniques *168*
    Outputs *169*
CONTROL QUALITY 170

- *Inputs* *171*
- *Tools & Techniques* *171*
- *Outputs* *172*
- TEST WHAT YOU'VE LEARNED 173

CHAPTER 10: PROJECT HUMAN RESOURCE MANAGEMENT 175

- PLAN HUMAN RESOURCE MANAGEMENT 175
  - *Inputs* *176*
  - *Tools & Techniques* *177*
  - *Outputs* *181*
- ACQUIRE PROJECT TEAM 182
  - *Inputs* *183*
  - *Tools & Techniques* *183*
  - *Outputs* *185*
- DEVELOP PROJECT TEAM 185
  - *Inputs* *186*
  - *Tools & Techniques* *186*
  - *Outputs* *193*
- MANAGE PROJECT TEAM 193
  - *Inputs* *194*
  - *Tools & Techniques* *195*
  - *Outputs* *196*
- TEST WHAT YOU'VE LEARNED 197

CHAPTER 11: PROJECT COMMUNICATIONS MANAGEMENT 199

- PLAN COMMUNICATIONS MANAGEMENT 199
  - *Inputs* *200*
  - *Tools & Techniques* *201*
  - *Outputs* *202*
  - *Inputs* *204*
  - *Tools & Techniques* *204*
  - *Outputs* *205*
- CONTROL COMMUNICATIONS 205
  - *Inputs* *206*
  - *Tools & Techniques* *207*
  - *Outputs* *207*
- TEST WHAT YOU'VE LEARNED 208

CHAPTER 12: PROJECT RISK MANAGEMENT 210

- PLAN RISK MANAGEMENT 211
  - *Inputs* *212*
  - *Tools & Techniques* *212*
  - *Outputs* *212*
- IDENTIFY RISKS 214
  - *Inputs* *215*
  - *Tools & Techniques* *217*
  - *Outputs* *218*
- PERFORM QUALITATIVE RISK ANALYSIS 219
  - *Inputs* *219*
  - *Tools & Techniques* *220*
  - *Outputs* *222*
- PERFORM QUANTITATIVE ANALYSIS 222
  - *Inputs* *223*
  - *Tools & Techniques* *223*
  - *Outputs* *227*

- **PLAN RISK RESPONSES** ... 228
  - *Inputs* ... 228
  - *Tools & Techniques* ... 229
  - *Outputs* ... 231
  - *Inputs* ... 233
  - *Tools & Techniques* ... 233
  - *Outputs* ... 234
- **TEST WHAT YOU'VE LEARNED** ... 236

CHAPTER 13: PROJECT PROCUREMENT MANAGEMENT ... 238

- **PLAN PROCUREMENT MANAGEMENT** ... 239
  - *Inputs* ... 239
  - *Tools & Techniques* ... 243
  - *Outputs* ... 243
- **CONDUCT PROCUREMENTS** ... 246
  - *Inputs* ... 247
  - *Tools & Techniques* ... 247
  - *Outputs* ... 248
- **CONTROL PROCUREMENTS** ... 249
  - *Inputs* ... 250
  - *Tools & Techniques* ... 251
  - *Outputs* ... 251
- **CLOSE PROCUREMENTS** ... 252
  - *Inputs* ... 253
  - *Tools & Techniques* ... 254
  - *Outputs* ... 254
- **TEST WHAT YOU'VE LEARNED** ... 255

CHAPTER 14: PROJECT STAKEHOLDER MANAGEMENT ... 257

- **IDENTIFY STAKEHOLDERS** ... 257
  - *Tools & Techniques* ... 259
  - *Outputs* ... 260
- **PLAN STAKEHOLDER MANAGEMENT** ... 260
  - *Inputs* ... 261
  - *Tools & Techniques* ... 261
- **MANAGE STAKEHOLDER ENGAGEMENT** ... 262
  - *Inputs* ... 263
  - *Tools & Techniques* ... 263
  - *Outputs* ... 264
- **CONTROL STAKEHOLDER ENGAGEMENT** ... 264
  - *Inputs* ... 265
  - *Tools & Techniques* ... 265
  - *Outputs* ... 266
- **TEST WHAT YOU'VE LEARNED** ... 267

APPENDICES ... 269

- **APPENDIX A. PROJECT MANAGEMENT FORMULAS** ... 269
- **APPENDIX B: CHAPTER QUIZ ANSWER KEY** ... 270
- **APPENDIX C: SAMPLE EXAM ONE** ... 278
- **APPENDIX D: ANSWER KEY/ SAMPLE EXAM ONE** ... 313
- **APPENDIX E: SAMPLE EXAM TWO** ... 317
- **APPENDIX F: ANSWER KEY/ SAMPLE EXAM TWO** ... 354

INDEX ... 359

Preface

Hashim Al Rifaai
President - PMI® Arabian Gulf Chapter

At Project Management Institute – Arabian Gulf Chapter (PMI-AGC) our motivation for writing this book "PMP® in 28 Days" was to provide the project management community an enabler to enhance their careers with Project Management Professional (PMP)® certification. More and more companies are now regarding project management as being mandatory for the survival of the business. Organizations that were opponents of project management are now advocates. Management educators of the past, who preached that project management could not work and would be just another fad, are now staunch supporters. Project management is here to stay.

The role of projects in organizations is receiving increasing attention. Projects are becoming the major tool for implementing and achieving the strategic goals of the organization. In the face of intense, global competition, many organizations have reorganized around a philosophy of innovation, renewal, and organizational learning to survive. This philosophy suggests an organization that is flexible and project driven. Project management has developed to the point where it is a professional discipline having its own body of knowledge and skills. Today it is nearly impossible to imagine anyone at any level in the organization who would not benefit from some degree of expertise in the process of managing projects. Colleges and universities are now offering graduate degrees in project management. Furthermore organizations are looking for a seasoned talent who can drive their projects and programs to deliver business outcomes and PMP certification is one such indicator of a capable and effective project manager in contemporary times.

In addition to this book being an enabler for certification, at PMI AGC, we also wanted to provide project management community a holistic view that focuses on how projects contribute to the strategic goals of the organization. The linkages for integration include the process of selecting projects that best support the strategy of a particular organization and that in turn can be supported by the technical and managerial processes made available by the organization to bring projects to completion. The goals for prospective project managers are to understand the role of a project in their organizations and to master the project management tools, techniques, and interpersonal skills necessary to orchestrate projects from start to finish

The material in the book is directly related to the subjects and knowledge areas associated with the Project Management Institute® Project Management Professional PMP® Exam and the Certified Associate Project Manager CAPM® Exam and will provide a sound framework for exam preparation. The book is designed to engage the students to provide practical application of the concepts of project management as described in the textbook and in PMI®' global standard *The Project Management Body of Knowledge* (*PMBOK® Guide*) – Fifth edition. This book is organized in such a way as to serve as an in-depth review for the PMP® exam for those with a strong foundation in project management, as well as for those who are new PMP® candidates. Each chapter covers a major aspect of the exam, with an emphasis on the "why" as well as the "how to" of project management.

Acknowledgements

It is important to note that the text includes contributions from numerous volunteers and colleagues, gleaned from professional conversations. We want them to know we sincerely appreciate their counsel and suggestions. We are been passionate about developing this book and we endeavor to launch the Arabic version of this book within next two quarters. Special gratitude is due to PMI – Arabian Gulf Chapter's Board Members, who deserve special accolades for putting in their effort to deliver this publication. We are indebted to the volunteers and reviewers who shared our commitment to elevating the instruction of project management. We thank our corporate sponsors who have supported us over the years and members who made thoughtful suggestions during our technical presentations for their invaluable support and making our book better.

Hashim M. Al-Rifaai

November 10, 2015

About PMI® Arab Gulf Chapter (PMI-AGC)
www.pmiagc.org

Project Management Institute (PMI®)-Arabian Gulf Chapter (AGC) is the regional segment of PMI®, the world's largest not-for-profit membership association for the project management profession. PMI is headquartered in the US and PMI-AGC operates in The Kingdom of Saudi Arabia, Kuwait, Qatar, Bahrain and Oman.

PMI has more than 700,000 members in nearly every country in the world. PMI-AGC boasts over 3,200 members, with a constituency of well over 8,500 professionals throughout the Arabian Gulf region. Members include business analysts, program managers, engineers, developers, and managers, including project managers.

PMI® helps members enhance their careers, improve their organizations' successes and further mature the Project Management profession. It provides relevant and high quality education, certifications, job referrals, and networking opportunities to members.

PMI-AGC nurtures and develops talents through project, program, and portfolio management certifications, trainings, and mentoring programs. It maintains a focus on fostering technical skills and leadership, equipping members with the necessary capabilities to deliver favorable business outcomes.

PMI-AGC is well-reputed for its progressive and innovative programs. The programs help fulfill PMI®'s goal to promote the profession of project management, by creating a culture and community that facilitates professional growth through networking, education, and volunteerism.
Its programs help organizations establish standardized Project Management practices that deliver value. In order to create high performers who provide business value with results-based talents, the institute develops and delivers internationally accredited mentoring programs.

PMI-AGC prides itself on its numerous competitive advantages. It is the sole regional provider of the comprehensive PMI Certification Suite, including CAPM®, PMP®, PgMP®, PfMP®, PMI-RMP®, PMI-ACP®, OPM3®, PMI-SP® and PMI-PBA® programs. Also, based on PWC market research, PMI®-based frameworks dominate the Middle Eastern segment. Its members also have the privilege of PMI®'s support directly from the USA. The PMI® Executive Council further leverages expert-level Project Management support from 70 of the *Forbes'* Fortune 500 Companies.

Chapter 1: Introduction

Hello and congratulations on your decision to get certified as a Project Management Professional (PMP®). You've worked on a number of projects already, as a member of a project team and perhaps even as the manager for some projects. Now you're taking the opportunity to put your knowledge, background and skills to the test and gain The Project Management Institute's (PMI®) renown certification to advance your career.

This study guide will help you to do that. Within these pages, you'll find the definitions of all of the project management-related concepts and guidelines for the use of the inputs, tools and techniques, and outputs associated with those concepts.

This book follows the same organizational pattern as *A Guide to the Project Management Body of Knowledge*, also known as the *The PMBOK® Guide (5th Edition)*. That is intentional; if you feel the need to double-check a fact or examine a topic in greater depth as you work your way through *PMP® in 28 Days*, you can easily locate the corresponding chapter in *The PMBOK® Guide*.

Including this introduction, there are 14 chapters covering all aspects of the project management process. So, the math is simple – each chapter should comprise 2 of the 28 days in your study period. If you feel you can cover a chapter in just one day, use the extra time to work with a study group, take trial tests and memorize the formulae found in the appendix.

Best of luck and let's get started!

The PMP® Exam

What's Expected of You

PMP® Eligibility Requirements.[1]

Educational Background	Project Management Experience *(gained within the 8 years prior to application submission)*	Project Management Education
Secondary degree (high school diploma, associate's degree or global equivalent) and Four-year degree (bachelor's degree or global equivalent)	Minimum five years/60 months unique, non-overlapping professional project management experience during which at least 7500 hours were spent leading and directing the project	35 contact hours of formal education
OR		
Four-year degree (bachelor's degree or global equivalent)	Minimum five years/60 months unique, non-overlapping professional project management experience during which at least 4500 hours were spent leading and directing the project	35 contact hours of formal education

You should have experience in all five process groups across all your project management experience submitted on the application; however, in terms of a single project, experience in all five process groups is not required.

The Application Process

To apply for the PMP® credential:

- Complete your PMP® application online at **www.pmi.org**. Keep in mind that once you begin your application, you have 90 days to complete it online.
- Submit your application for review. PMI® takes approximately five business days to review your application.

---

[1] *PMP® Credential Handbook*, 2015, p. 6.

- o Following approval of your application, you must submit payment of your credential fees (without payment, you cannot schedule your exam).
- o In case of an audit, once your application is initially accepted, you have 90 days to send your audit materials. PMI® will process those materials in 5 to 7 days.
- o You have one year from the date of application approval to take the exam, which can be taken up to 3 times within a 12 month period.
- o Once you are certified, the PMP® credential must be maintained by earning and reporting 60 Professional Development Units (PDU's) within each 3 year cycle. Your credential will be renewed after you have done so, in addition to remitting the renewal fee.
- o If you fail to submit your PDU's and pay your renewal fee, your credential will be suspended on the 3rd anniversary of the day you passed the exam.
- o If, at the close of your 1-year suspension period, you have not fulfilled the requirements toward credential maintenance and renewal, your credential will expire and you must reapply.

What You Can Expect

The PMP® exam is conducted in a formal, closely monitored environment. No talking is permitted and neither is the use of notes, books, cell phones, PDA's or calculators that you have brought yourself. You will be provided with scratch paper and many experts suggest that you immediately jot down the Earned Value, time management and communication channels formulas you'll be utilizing during the exam. Be prepared; you will complete the test while being recorded through both video and audio surveillance.

The exam comprises an opening tutorial followed by 200 multiple-choice questions, which include 25 beta questions that are not scored and are used to test the validity of questions that may be used in future tests.

You will have 240 minutes to complete the test, which includes any breaks you may feel the need to take. A quick calculation shows that you can devote 72 seconds to each question although, of course, some will require less time than that and some, considerably longer.

One strategy to consider when taking the test is to skim over the questions and answer the ones that you are the most sure about. Then come back and spend the remainder of your time on questions that you have to give more thought to. You are also able to mark the questions that you want to review later on during the exam.

The feedback I have received from the over 15,000 students I have trained in certification tracks globally is to split the exam into spurts with a quick break in between to revive your energy. For example, your strategy might be to tackle 50 questions and then take a quick 3 minutes break. While PMI® has not announced an official exam passing grade, most experts assume it to be in the range of 70%. Play it safe and aim for a minimum grade of 75%. Practice tests can help you consistently achieve a grade above 75% to ensure that you are well-prepared.

You will be notified of your score as soon as you complete the exam. Your scorecard will reflect your proficiency level by Domain.

Domains into which the questions fall include:

Initiation	13% of the exam questions
Planning	24% of the exam questions
Executing	30% of the exam questions
Monitoring and Controlling	25% of the exam questions
Closing	8% of the exam questions

Keep in mind that the PMP® exam is far more than a test of your ability to memorize terms and formulae. You must be able to analyze situations, recognize elements of scenarios and then correctly apply this knowledge to manage those situations. That's why, in addition to formal training and education, a significant amount of project management experience is also a prerequisite for certification.

Few of the exam questions will be straightforward – "what is this" or "what's the difference between this and this?" In addition to situational questions, you'll come upon those with multiple, seemingly correct answers. When you do, it's been suggested that you choose the option that, in terms of proper project management, would be the *first* thing you'd do in that situation.

Other questions can contain a great deal of information, which, at first glance, may all seem to be important. However, some of this is extraneous and can actually obscure rather than illuminate the correct answer. Before you lose yourself in all the data, try to figure out what the question is really asking and zero in on the facts and figures that will actually provide the correct answer.

This may come as a surprise, but those who prepare this exam occasionally include made-up terms in the questions they create. If you've studied very hard, have confidence in your knowledge. When you encounter a phrase in the exam that you've never heard of, chances are good that no matter how reasonable it may sound, it's not the right answer.

Some answers come in multiples, with more than one item in each possible choice. Dissect each answer, looking at the first item in each; if it's unlikely to be correct, discard that answer. Look at the second item in the remaining answers and repeat the process until there's only one choice in which every element is correct.

Some questions will be unnecessarily wordy; once again, discard the unnecessary, filter the content and find the correct answer by determining what it's actually asking.

One last suggestion: practice, practice, practice. As part of your 28 days regimen, once you have studied the content thoroughly, take as many practice tests as you can.

Chapter 2: The Basics

The PMBOK® Guide
Every job or profession, no matter how simple or complex, is done to a certain standard, a standard to which competent and responsible holders of those jobs or practitioners of those professions must adhere. That standard provides established norms, methods, processes and practices and, in the case of *The PMBOK® Guide*, emerged from the acknowledged good practices of those who work in the field of project management and who contributed to its development as a formal global standard from PMI®.

Defining a Project
A project is a temporary endeavor with the goal of creating a product, service or result that is unique and that may be tangible or intangible. Note that, in this context, the word *temporary* does not necessarily mean of a short duration, nor does it necessarily apply to the product, service or result the project produces. Instead, it's meant to indicate a project's engagement and longevity and that a project has a definite beginning and a fixed end, which is reached when:

- Its objectives have been met.
- It's determined that its objectives will not or cannot be met.
- The client, be they a customer, sponsor or champion, wants it to be terminated.
- A project differs from ongoing work in that the latter is commonly a process that is both repetitive and that adheres to an organization's existing flow of business. In addition, because projects are unique, their outcomes (products, services, or results) can be uncertain or different. Projects require focused planning because their intrinsic activities can be new to team members. Further, projects can commence at every level of an organization and can comprise a single or several individuals, organizational units or multiple organizational units from a number of organizations.

What can be created by a project?

- A product that can be either a component or an enhancement of another item, or an item unique unto itself.
- A service or a capability to perform a service, for example, a business function that supports production or distribution
- An improvement in a product or a service that already exists
- An outcome or a document, for example, a research project aimed at developing knowledge about trends, etc.

Relationships Among Portfolios, Programs and Projects

Portfolios, programs and projects are all concepts that are closely interrelated. A portfolio is a collection of projects, programs, subportfolios and operations that are coordinated and managed as a group to support strategic objectives. Whether an individual project is managed within or outside of a program, it is still thought to be part of a portfolio and while projects or programs within the portfolio may or may not be interdependent or directly related, they are connected to organizational strategies via that organization's portfolio. These strategies and priorities are associated and interrelated, both between portfolios and programs and between programs and individual projects. Organizations prioritize projects in terms of risk, funding, etc., issues that are relevant to those organizations' overall strategic plan, which can affect the management of resources and support.

Defining Project Management

Project management is the application of knowledge, skills, tools and techniques to project activities to meet the requirements of that project.[2] This is achieved through the use and integration of the 47 project management processes, which have been categorized into five Process Groups:

- Initiating
- Planning
- Executing
- Monitoring and Controlling
- Closing

Tasks related to managing a project frequently include (but are not limited to) identifying requirements, addressing stakeholders' needs, concerns and expectations when planning and executing that project. Active, effective and collaborative communication among stakeholders must be established, maintained and operationalized. Stakeholders must be managed in terms of meeting project requirements and creating project deliverables. There are numerous constraints to be balanced, comprising but not limited to scope, quality, schedule, budget, resources and risks.

Further, if one of these factors changes, it will affect at least one other factor. That being the case, the development of the project management plan is far from 'create once and be done'; it's an iterative journey that typically goes through rolling wave planning. As more detailed and specific information and more accurate estimates come to light, the plan can be progressively elaborated on throughout the life cycle of a project which, in turn allows a more exact definition of work and the more detailed management of that work. Components of a plan are said to go through a cone of uncertainty. The cone gets narrower and more clearly defined as the project progresses.

Project coordinators and project expeditors may also be relevant roles for some projects. A project coordinator has some delegated authority from the project manager. A project expeditor has no authority and acts only based on direction from the project manager.

---

[2] Project Management Institute, *A Guide to the Project Management Body of Knowledge (PMBOK® Guide)*, 5th ed., p. 5

Defining Program Management

A program is a group of related projects, subprograms and program activities managed and coordinated in such a way as to obtain benefits that would not be accrued if they were to be managed individually. Components of related work that are outside of the scope of the separate projects within the program may be included in that program and, while a project may or may not be part of a program, a program will always encompass related projects.

Logically, program management itself is "the application of knowledge, skills, tools, and techniques to a program in order to meet the program requirements and to obtain benefits and control not available by managing projects individually."[3]

If the projects within a program are not related through a common outcome or a collective capability and if their relationship is only that of a shared client, seller, technology or resource, they should be managed as a portfolio of projects instead of being handled as a program.

Hence, the projects within a program are interdependent and the work of the program manager centers on these interdependencies to determine the best approach to managing them.

Defining Portfolio Management

We've already discussed the definition of a portfolio; portfolio management is the centralized management of one or more portfolio with the goal of achieving strategic objectives. As a portfolio manager, your focus will be on reviewing one or more portfolios to prioritize allocation of resources and to ascertain that their management is consistent with and aligned to the strategies of your organization.

Portfolio, Program & Organizational Management: How Are They Related?

There are both similarities and differences between portfolio, program and project management. Further, each of them relate differently to organizational project management (OPM), which is "a strategy execution framework utilizing project, program, and portfolio management as well as organizational enabling practices to consistently and predictably deliver organization strategy producing better performance, better results, and a sustainable competitive advantage."[4]

---

[3] Ibid., p. 9
[4] Ibid., p. 7.

Figure 2.1. **Portfolio, Program and Organizational Management**

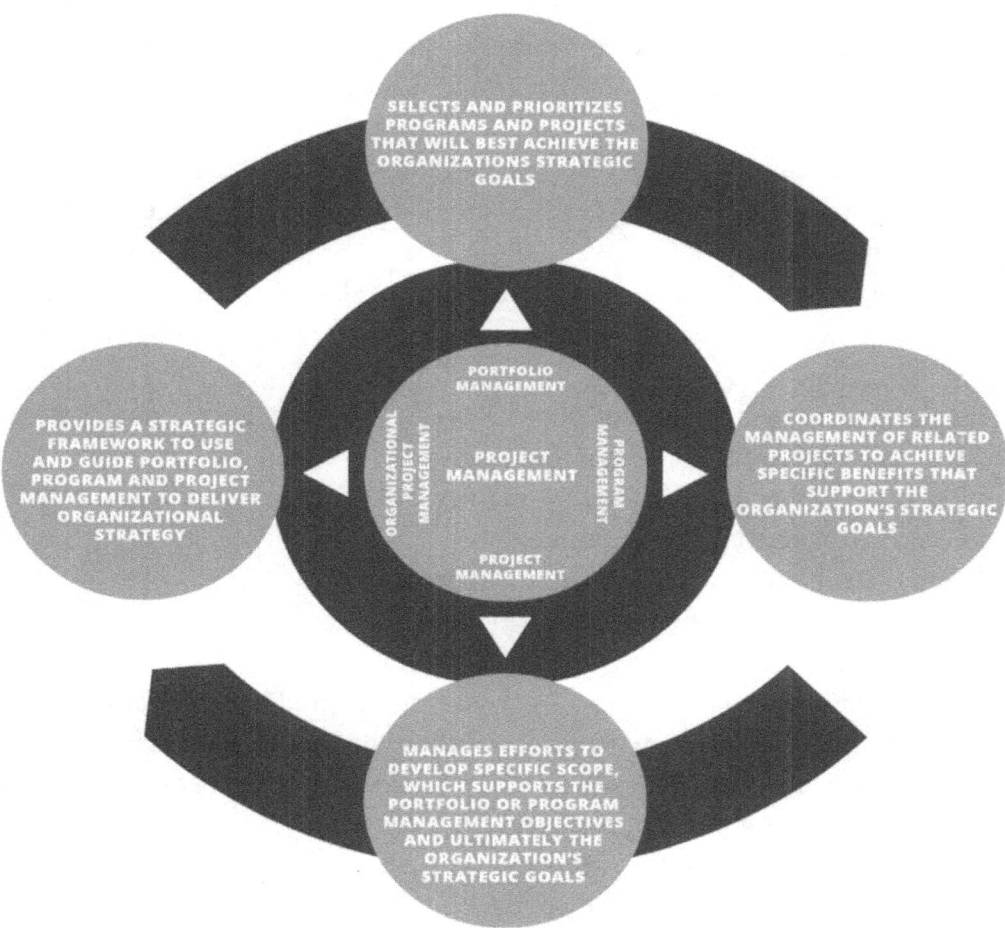

Comparing elements of the three forms of management:

- o Scope
    - ✓ Projects have defined objectives and scope is progressively elaborated throughout the project.
    - ✓ Programs have a larger scope and offer more significant benefits.
    - ✓ Portfolios have an organizational scope that varies along with the organization's strategic objectives.
- o Change
    - ✓ Change is expected by project managers, who are required to implement processes to keep those changes managed and under control.
    - ✓ Program managers also anticipate change that is both internal and external to the program and are ready to manage it.
    - ✓ Portfolio managers monitor change in the wider internal and external environment on a continuous basis.
- o Planning
    - ✓ Project managers progressively expand high-level information into detailed plans throughout the course of the project's life cycle.

- ✓ The development of the overall program plan and creation of high-level plans to direct detailed planning at the component level are the tasks of program managers.
- ✓ The creation and maintenance of processes and communication relative to the aggregate portfolio are the responsibility of the portfolio manager.
- o Management
    - ✓ Project managers manage the project team with the goal of meeting the project objectives.
    - ✓ Providing vision and overall leadership, program managers manage the program staff and the project managers.
    - ✓ Portfolio management staff or program and project staff who may have the responsibility to report into the aggregate portfolio may be managed or coordinated by portfolio managers.
- o Success
    - ✓ In projects, success is measured by product and project quality, timeliness, compliance to budgets, and the degree of customer satisfaction.
    - ✓ In programs, success is measured by the degree to which the program satisfies the needs and benefits for which it was initiated.
    - ✓ The aggregate investment performance and benefit realization of a portfolio are the measures of its success.
- o Monitoring
    - ✓ Monitoring and control of the work of producing the products, services or results for which the project was undertaken are the responsibilities of project managers.
    - ✓ Program managers ensure that the program's overall goals, schedules, budget and benefits are met by monitoring the progress of program components.
    - ✓ Portfolio managers monitor strategic changes and aggregate resource allocation, performance results and risk of the portfolio.

The Project Management Office (PMO)

A PMO is not the room in which the project manager spends most of his time. Instead, it's a management structure intended to standardize project-related governance processes and facilitate sharing of resources, methodologies, tools and techniques; its assigned tasks include everything from providing project management support functions such as coaching, mentoring, training and oversight to integrating data and information from corporate strategic projects and evaluating the degree of fulfilment of higher level strategic objectives to being help responsible for the direct management of one or several projects. The PMO serves as the natural liaison between the portfolios, programs, projects and corporate measurement systems of an organization. In addition, it sometimes has the authority to function as an integral stakeholder and a key decision maker over the course of each project, making recommendations, terminating projects, etc., with the goal of maintaining alignment with business objectives.

There is no single type of PMO structure within organizations. PMOs can be:
- o Supportive:
    - ✓ Function in the capacity of a consultant, providing templates, best practices, training, access to information and lessons learned from other projects
    - ✓ Serve as a project repository

- ✓ Provide a low degree of control
- o Controlling:
  - ✓ Provide support and require compliance through adopting project management frameworks or methodologies using specific templates, forms and tools or conformance to governance
  - ✓ Provide a moderate degree of control
- o Directive:
  - ✓ Control projects by directly managing those projects
  - ✓ Provide a high degree of control

To compare project managers and PMOs, here are the key points:

- o Focus:
  - ✓ The focus of the project manager is on specified project objectives.
  - ✓ The PMO manages changes in program scope that may serve as opportunities to more fully achieve business objectives.
- o Use of resources:
  - ✓ Control of assigned project resources to best meet project objectives is with the project manager.
  - ✓ The PMO enhances the utilization of shared organizational resources across all project.
- o Management:
  - ✓ Project managers oversee the scope, schedule, cost, quality, etc. (constraints) of individual projects.
  - ✓ The PMO handles the methodologies, standards, overall risks and/or opportunities, metrics and interdependencies among projects.

Links between Project & Operations Management, Organizational Governance and Organizational Strategy Operation

The PMBOK® Guide makes it very clear that while operations and operations management fall outside the scope of formal project management, the two intersect at several junctures.

Those who work in the area of operations management oversee, direct and control the operations of a business. Those operations develop in ways that support the day-to-day business and are crucial to accomplishing the strategic and tactical goals of that business.

Projects, even if they are temporary, assist in the achievement of organizational goals if and when they are aligned with that organization's strategy; operational, product and systems changes are both developed and implemented through projects which, of course, brings to the forefront project management activities and skill sets.

In terms of the aforementioned intersections of operations and project management, they can occur at several points in a product life cycle; for example, at the close of each phase, when developing or upgrading a product or when outputs are being expanded, when improving operations or until the close of a product life cycle.

That being the case, those who perform and conduct business operations can be project stakeholders whose needs, particularly in projects that will affect their future work and endeavors, should be very carefully considered by project managers. They should be engaged, their needs identified via the stakeholder register and their positive or negative influence addressed as part of the risk management plan.

Organizations and Project Management

The connection between organizations and project management is quite straightforward:

- o The strategic direction determined by organizations via governance provides the purpose, expectations, goals and the actions necessary to achieve those goals and is aligned with business objectives.
- o In turn, project management activities are aligned with top-level business direction.
- o Changes in that direction require realignment of project objectives.
- o Those changes will affect both project efficiency and success.

Project-based organizations (PBOs) are organizational forms that create temporary systems to complete their work and can be functional, matrix, or projectized (more on this in Chapter 3). PBOs undertake the majority of their work as projects and/or provide project instead of functional approaches and can refer to either entire firms, multi-firm consortia or networks.

Organizational governance can have a strong impact on projects and programs. Both are launched with the goal of achieving strategic business outcomes; those outcomes can then become subject to formal organizational governance processes and procedures. In fact, the success or failure of a project may be judged according to how well its product or service supports organizational governance. That being the case, it is important that the project manager is cognizant of corporate/organizational governance policies and procedures related to that product, service or result.

Project managers must also be knowledgeable about organizational strategy; in fact, this goes in both directions. Organizational strategies should offer guidance and direction to project management since projects exist to support organizational strategies.

It sometimes happens that the project's goals conflict with an existing organizational strategy; when that occurs, the project manager must identify, document and notify key stakeholders of that conflict as soon as possible.

At other times, rather than a guiding principle, developing an organizational strategy can actually be the goal of a project and, when that is the case, it's crucial that the project define "what constitutes an appropriate organizational strategy that will sustain the organization."[5]

---
[5] Ibid., p. 15.

Business Value

Business value is not a singular concept but is instead unique to every organization and is defined as the total sum of all of its tangible (monetary assets, fixtures, stockholder equity, utility) and intangible (good will, brand recognition, public benefit, trademarks) elements. Organizations have the ability to increase their value and meet their strategic objectives through the effective use of portfolio, program and project management. In terms of business value:

- Portfolio management:
  - Aligns programs, projects or operations to the organizational strategy organized into portfolios or subportfolios.
  - Provides organizations an overall view of how the strategic goals are reflected in the portfolio and the ability to institute appropriate governance management and to allocate human, financial or material resources based on expected performance and benefits.
- Program management:
  - Gives organizations the ability to achieve optimal or integrated costs, schedule, efforts and benefits by aligning multiple projects.
  - Centers on project interdependencies with the goal of determining the best approach to manage and realize the intended benefits.
- Project management:
  - Gives organizations the ability to apply knowledge, processes, skills, tools and techniques to increase the likelihood of success.
  - Within programs and portfolios, projects can foster achievement of organizational strategies and objectives.

The Project Manager's Role

It's the responsibility of the project manager to meet activity, team and individual needs. However, in this increasingly strategic role, even understanding and applying the knowledge, tools and techniques that have been recognized as good practice are insufficient to functioning effectively. Beyond any area-specific skills and general management proficiencies required for a project, project managers must possess:

- Knowledge
  - What the project manager knows about project management
- Performance
  - What the project manager is able to accomplish while applying that knowledge
- Personal
  - How the project manager behaves during the performance of a project related activity
  - Includes attitudes, core personality characteristics and leadership, which provides an ability to achieve projects objectives and balance project constraints concurrently with guiding the team

Test What You've Learned

1) Which, if any, of these statements is true?
   a) Because a project is, by definition, temporary, it's always of relatively short duration.
   b) A project only comes to a close after its objective is met.
   c) The term "temporary" in the context of a project indicates that it has a definite beginning and fixed end.
   d) To improve an existing product, an organization must reopen/extend the project that created it.

2) A _____ is a collection of projects, programs, subportfolios and operations managed as a group to achieve strategic objectives.
   a) Compendium
   b) Anthology
   c) Omnibus
   d) Portfolio

3) Organizational planning affects projects in terms of _____.
   a) Project prioritization
   b) Risk categorization
   c) Strategic design
   d) Project portfolios

4) Competing project constraints do not include:
   a) Scope
   b) Budget
   c) Risks
   d) Communication

5) Projects within a program are related through:
   a) A shared client
   b) A common resource
   c) A common outcome
   d) A similar technology

6) Which, if any, of these statements is false?
   a) Projects/programs in a portfolio must be interdependent or directly related.
   b) Portfolio management is the centralized management of one or more portfolios.
   c) Through portfolio management, projects are reviewed to rank the allocation of resources.
   d) In utilizing portfolio management, organizations administer related projects as a single program.

7) A project management office (PMO) that has a low degree of control and serves as a consultant to projects is:
   a) Integrative
   b) Supportive
   c) Controlling
   d) Directive

8) The integration of data and information from corporate strategic projects is the task of:
   a) The portfolio manager
   b) The project manager
   c) The IT department of the organization
   d) The project management office

9) The focus of the _____ is on specified project objectives.
   a) The project management office
   b) The project manager
   c) The portfolio manager
   d) Operations management

10) Business value is:
    a) A similar construct in all organizations
    b) Unique to each organization
    c) Created via effective management of ongoing operations
    d) Both a) and c).

Chapter 3: Organization Influences & Project Life Cycle

Organizational Influences on Project Management

Needless to say, projects do not happen in a vacuum; project management is done in a larger and more complex environment than that of the project itself. That being the case, the organization within which the project is initiated and carried out has its own goals with which work must be aligned as well as established practices that can influence that work.

Organizational Cultures and Styles

Organizations are defined as "systematic arrangements of entities (persons and/or departments) aimed at accomplishing a purpose."[6] Naturally, accomplishing those purposes sometimes requires them to undertake projects. An organization also develops a distinct culture and style, which are shaped by the experiences of its members and which develop into cultural norms. It's important for project managers to understand and work within these norms because they include the ways in which the organization approaches the initiation and planning of projects, what is believed to be acceptable in terms of completing the work and who are considered to be the organization's decision makers.

Organizational Structures

Oganizations are structured in a variety of ways – functional, matrix (weak, balanced or strong) and projectized – and those structures can have an effect on both the resource availability and the ways in which projects are conducted.

Table 3.1. **Positive/ Negative Aspects of a Functional Organization**

PROS AND CONS FUNCTIONAL ORGANIZATION
BOTH PROJECTED AND OPERATIONAL WORK ARE PERFORMED BY RESOURCES WITHIN THE FUNCTIONAL DEPARTMENT

PROS	CONS
• FLEX ABILITY IN STAFF USE	• CLIENT IS NOT THE FOCUS OF ACTIVITY
• AVAILABILITY OF EXPERTS FOR MULTIPLE PROJECTS	• FUNCTION RATHER THEN PROBLEM ORIENTED
• GROUPING OF SPECIALISTS	• NO ONE FULLY RESPONSIBLE FOR PROJECT
• TECHNOLOGICAL CONTINUITY	• SLOW RESPONSE TO THE CLIENT
• NORMAL ADVANCEMENT PATH	• TENDENCY TO SUB OPTIMIZE
	• FRAGMENTED APPROACH TO THE PROJECT

---

[6] Project Management Institute, *A Guide to the Project Management Body of Knowledge* (*PMBOK® Guide*), 5th ed., p. 20.

Once again, to be effective, project managers must be fully cognizant about the structure within which they are functioning. The most common structures include:

- Functional
  - ✓ A hierarchy with each employee having one clear superior; staff members are grouped by specialty, which can be further subdivided into focused functional groups; work is done by departments independently from each other.
- Matrix
  - ✓ A blend of functional and projectized characteristics that can be further classified via the relative level of power and influence between functional and project managers:
    - ➤ Weak: Maintain many characteristics of a functional organization; project manager's role is more similar to that of a coordinator, who can make some decisions, has a degree of authority and reports to a higher-level manager or an expediter, who coordinates communications but cannot personally make decisions.
    - ➤ Balanced: Falls between weak and strong matrix structures; project manager lacks full authority over projects and project funding
    - ➤ Strong: Share many of the traits of projectized organizations; project managers are full-time and have both authority and a full-time project administrative staff.

Figure 3.1. **Elements of a Matrix Organization**

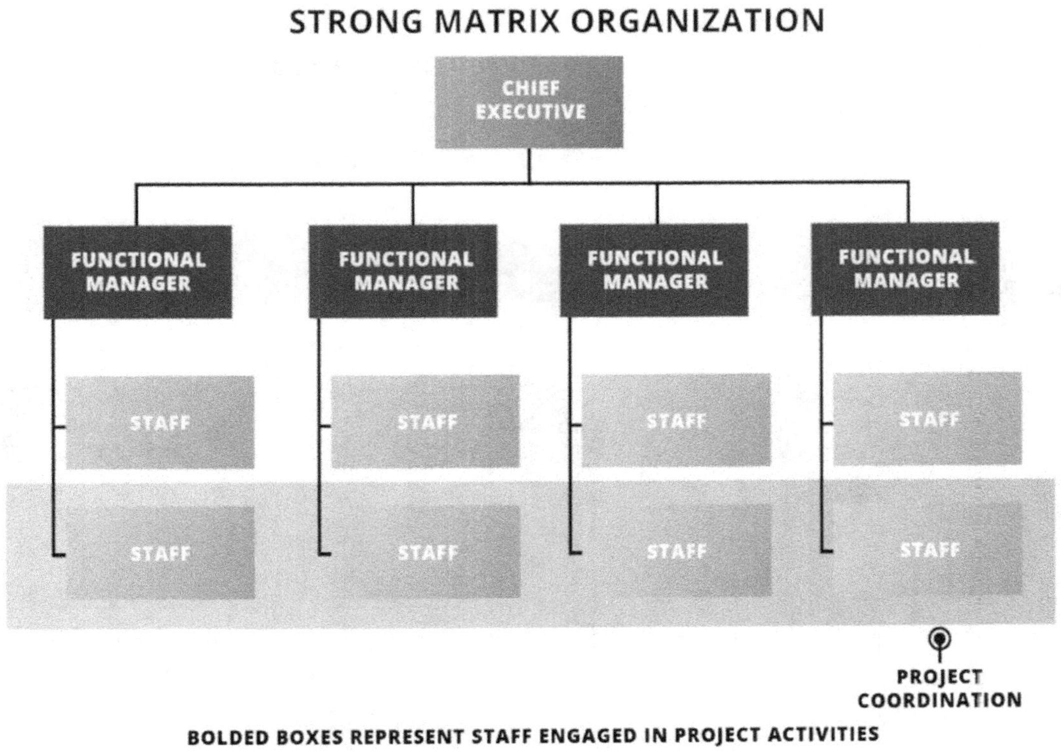

STRONG MATRIX ORGANIZATION

BOLDED BOXES REPRESENT STAFF ENGAGED IN PROJECT ACTIVITIES

Table 3.2. **Positive/ Negative Aspects of a Matrix Organization**

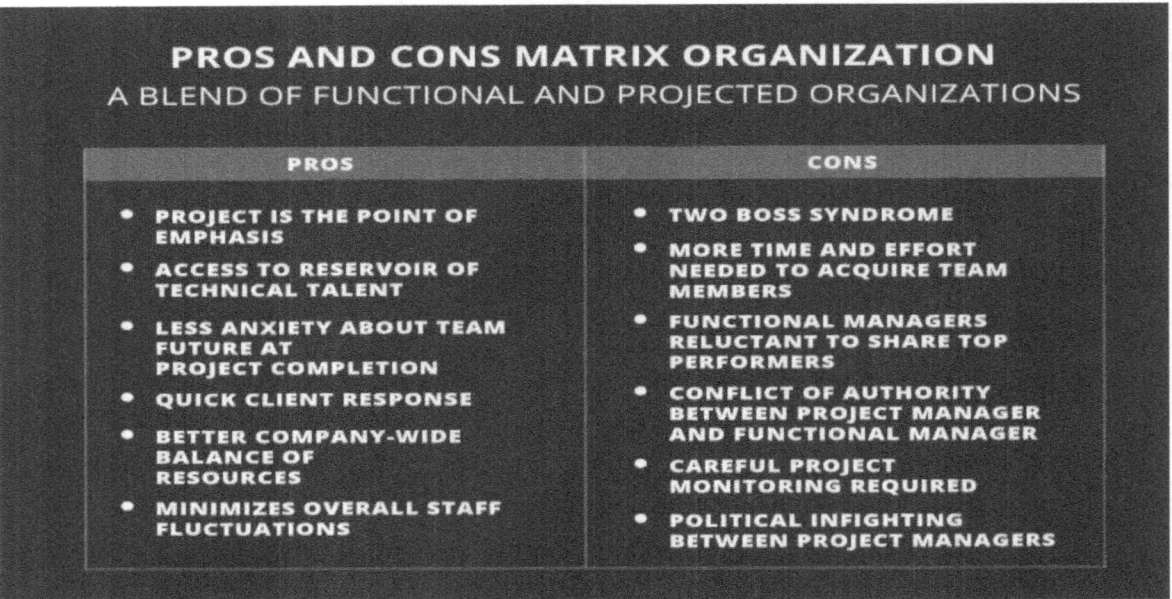

- o Projectized
  - ✓ Team members often colocated; most resources used for project work; project managers enjoy a great deal of independence and authority; contain organization units called departments which may report directly to the project manager or provide projects with support services. Note that colocation is also known as tight matrix.

Figure 3.2. **Elements of a Projectized Organization**

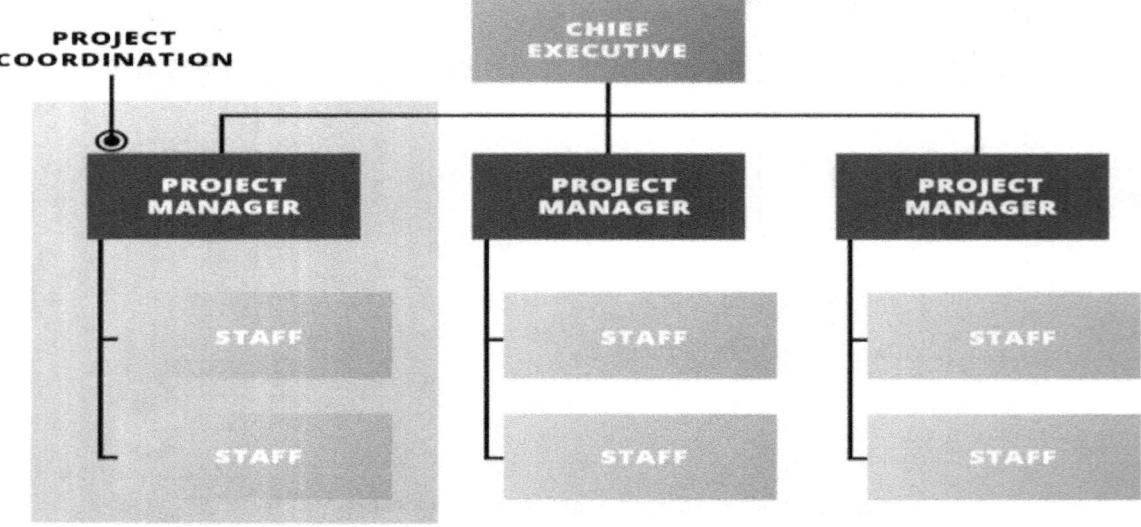

While there are a number of advantages of the projectized organizational structure vis-à-vis project management, there are some concerns as well.

Table 3.3. **Positive/ Negative Aspects of a Projectized Organization**

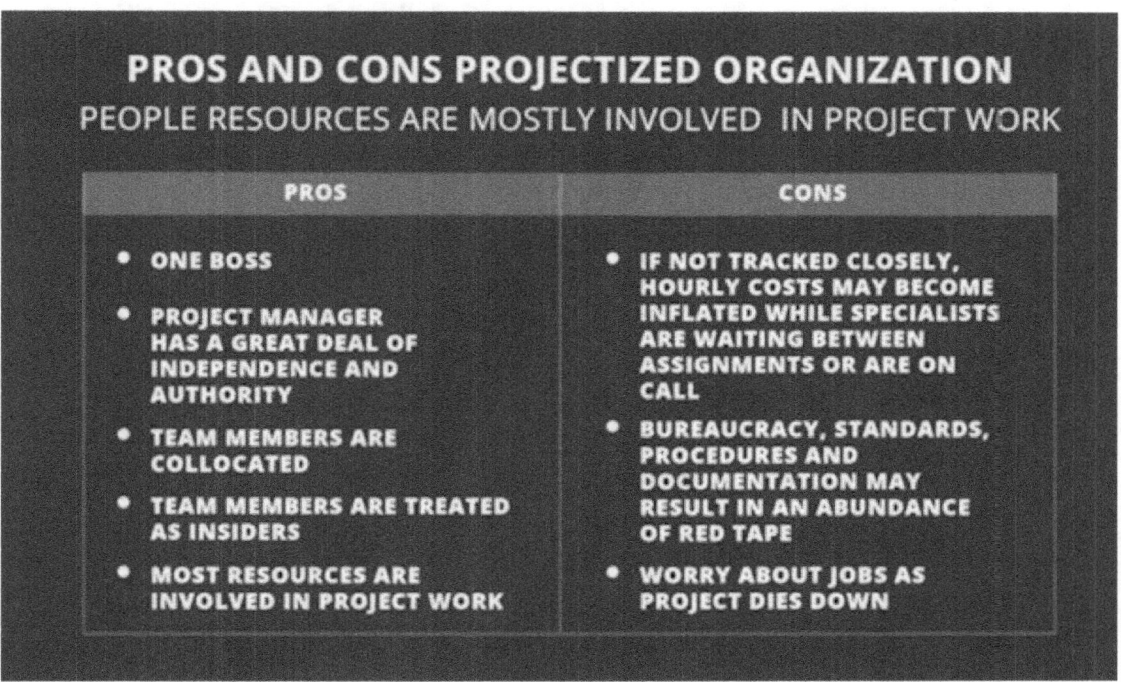

- o Composite
  - ✓ Involve all of these structures at various levels.

Further, organizational structures can have distinct levels: strategic, middle management and operational. As a project manager, you may interact with all three dependent on such issues as the project's strategic importance, the influence of stakeholders and the maturity of project management and organizational communication. Those interactions can govern your level of authority, what resources are available and how they're managed, who controls the budget, your overall role and who comprises your project team

Organizational Process Assets
The plans, processes, policies, procedures and knowledge bases that are specific to and utilized by an organization, including any artifact, practice or knowledge used to perform or govern a project, are considered to be that organization's process assets.

These are grouped into processes and procedures, and corporate knowledge bases:
- o Processes and procedures (include but are not limited to):
  - ✓ Initiating & Planning
    - ➢ Guidelines and criteria used to tailor standard processes and procedures to meet the specific needs of the project

- Policies such as those related to human resources, health/safety, ethics and project management, product and project life cycles, and quality policies and procedures such as process audits, improvement targets, checklists and standardized process definitions
- Templates such as risk register, work breakdown schedule, project schedule network diagram & contract templates
- ✓ Executing, monitoring and controlling
  - Change control procedures, which includes the ways in which performing organization standards, policies, plan and procedures as well as any project documents can be modified and how such modifications will be approved and validated
  - Financial controls procedures such as time reporting, required expenditure and disbursement reviews, accounting codes and standard contract provisions;
  - Issue and defect management procedures that define issue and defect controls, identification and resolution as well as action item tracking
  - Communication requirements
  - Procedures for prioritizing, approving and issuing work authorizations
  - Risk control procedures, which include risk categories and statement templates, probability and impact definitions, and probability and impact matrix; and
  - Standardized guidelines, work instructions and proposal evaluation and performance criteria
- ✓ Closing:
  - Guidelines or requirements for project closure, for example, lessons learned, final project audits, project evaluations, product validation and acceptance criteria

o Corporate knowledge bases (stores and retrieves information that include but are not limited to):
  - ✓ Versions and baselines of all performing organization standards, policies, procedures and any project documents
  - ✓ Labor hours, incurred costs, budgets and any project cost overruns
  - ✓ Historical information and lessons learned such as project records and documents, all project closure information and documentation, results of previous project selection decisions and project performance, and risk management activities
  - ✓ Issue and defect status, control information, issue and defect resolution and action item results
  - ✓ Available measurement data on processes and products
  - ✓ Project files from previous projects, including scope, cost, schedule, and performance measurement baselines, project calendars, project schedule network diagrams, risk registers, planned response actions and defined risk impact

Enterprise Environmental Factors

These are conditions not under the control of the project team that nevertheless influence, constrain or direct the project that are considered to be inputs to most planning processes, that may either augment or limit project management options and that can influence the outcome either positively or negatively. They vary a great deal in terms of type and nature and can include organizational culture, structure and governance, geographic distribution of facilities and resources, government or industry standards, infrastructure, available human resources, personnel administration, company work authorization systems, marketplace conditions, the risk tolerance of stakeholders, the political climate, the established communication channels of an organization, available commercial databases and the project management information system.

Figure 3.3. **Enterprise Environmental Factors**

Project Stakeholders & Governance

A stakeholder is "an individual, group or organization who may affect, be affected by, or perceive itself to be affected by a decision, activity or outcome of a project."[7] As such, they may or may not be actively involved in a project and can be either positively or negatively affected by the outcome of that project. With that in mind, their expectations, should they not coincide, can create conflicts; further, they can exert their influence on everything having to do with a project – the project itself, its deliverables and the project team – to achieve a particular set of outcomes aimed at satisfying objectives or other needs.

How is the project manager to successfully handle a diverse set of shareholders with equally diverse needs and expectations? "In many cases, managing stakeholder expectations while managing projects or programs within their constraints is as much an art as a science. It takes a balance of knowledge, tools, and "soft skills" on the part of the Program/Project manager, and an environment that is conducive to success."[8]

---

[7] Ibid., p. 30.
[8] Gareth Byatt, Gary Hamilton, & Jeff Hodgkinson, (19 December, 2012), "Tips on Shareholder Management," http://www.projecttimes.com/articles/tips-on-stakeholder-management.html

More specifically, what's required is project governance, the alignment of your project with stakeholders' needs or objectives, which is essential to successfully managing stakeholder engagement and achieving the objectives of an organization. It makes it possible for organizations to manage projects consistently, maximize the value of outcomes and allow projects to align with those organizations' strategies. It offers a framework within which both project managers and stakeholders can make decisions that meet both stakeholders' needs and hopes and the strategic objectives of the organization. It also facilitates addressing circumstances where the latter may not align.

It would be a mistake to assume that stakeholders' degrees of both responsibility and authority remain static throughout the life cycle of a project; they can vary over time, thus requiring the project manager's continual attention. Failure to do so can delay project completion, increase project costs and even lead to serious risks or cancellation.

In addition, managing stakeholder expectations can be difficult because they can conflict and must be balanced, even as the project manager and all members of the team remain both professional and supportive.

Examples of possible stakeholders include:
- Sponsor
    - A person or a group, either of which provides both resources and support for a project and is held accountable for its success. May be external or internal to the organization and works to promote the project from the start (initiation) to the completion (closure), serving as spokesperson to higher levels of management by promoting the value the organization will accrue via the project. Leads the project during the initiating process and takes a crucial role in initial scope and charter development. Also ensures the smooth transition of the deliverables of the project into the recipient organization's business
- Customers and users
    - The persons or organizations whose tasks are to approve and manage the product, service or result of a project are customers; users are those who will use that product, service or result. May be either internal or external to an organization and can also exist in multiple layers (physicians who prescribe a new medication, patients who use that medication and insurers who pay for it)
- Sellers
    - Vendors, etc. who are external companies entering into a contract to provide the components or services required by the product
- Business partners
    - External organizations that offer specialized expertise or provide services such as installation, customization, training or support
- Organizational groups
    - Internal stakeholders such as marketing and sales, human resources, legal, finance, operations, manufacturing and customer service who are both affected by the project team's activities and that support the business environment in which the projects are executed.

Interact closely with project team to achieve project goals, providing input on requirements and assisting in the smooth transition of products to production, etc.
- Functional managers
  - ✓ Take a management role with the administrative or functional area of a business. Are assigned permanent staff for ongoing work. May provide subject matter expertise or offer services to the project
- Other stakeholders
  - ✓ May include procurement entities, financial institutions, government regulators, subject matter experts, etc. with a financial interest in the product, who contribute inputs or have an interest in project outcome[9]

Figure 3.4. **Project Stakeholders**

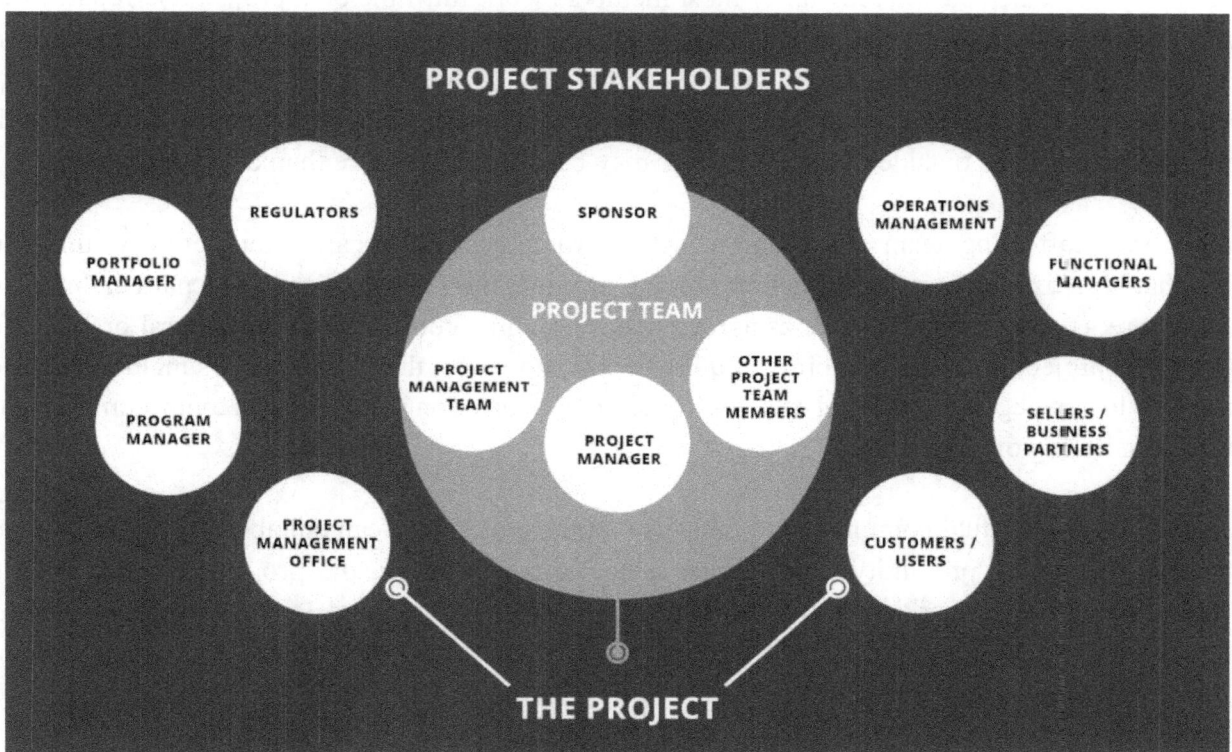

Project Success

What constitutes the success of a project? That can be gauged by its completion within the constraints of scope, time, cost, quality, resources and risk that had the approval of senior management at its inception, keeping in mind that everything must refer to the latest approved baselines as sanctioned by the authorized stakeholders.

---

[9] More information on both stakeholders and stakeholder engagement can be found in chapter 13.

Project Team

Who serves as part of a project team can depend on factors such as organizational culture, scope and location. Although projects always have a project manager, sometimes he or she is the team's line manager, having full authority over team members. On other occasions, because they are leading the project part-time or on a contractual basis, they may have little or no direct authority over team members.

Speaking of team members, they can include project management staff, a role that can be performed or supported by a PMO associate, project staff, supporting experts, user or customer representatives, sellers, business partner members and business partners.

A team may be dedicated whereby all or most members work full-time on a project and report directly to the project manager, which is frequently seen in projectized organizations. It can also be part-time, as is the case when projects are initiated as temporary additional work. This is common within functional organizations. In this scenario, both team members and the project manager usually continue to perform other duties outside of the project, or may be assigned to more than one project at a time.

Another issue affecting team composition is the structure of an organization; projects undertaken within that organization may be partnership-based, meaning they're established as a partnership, joint venture, consortium or alliance as agreed upon through a contract between several organizations. That type of project provides flexibility at a lower cost; however, the disadvantages include the project manager's lower degree of control and the requirement for strong methods for both communication and the monitoring of progress.

The availability of virtual communication means that team members can collaborate over considerable distances; geographic proximity is no longer a necessity. However, the project manager must take differences in culture, working hours, time zones, local conditions and language into consideration when forming and working with the project team.

Project Life Cycle

A project life cycle is "the series of phases that a project passes through from its initiation to its closure."[10]

Those phases are "collections of logically related project activities that culminate in the completion of one or more deliverable".[11]

Further, phases are:

- Usually sequential, with names and numbers determined by the management and control needs of the organization(s) involved in the project, its nature, and its area of application;

---

[10] Ibid., p. 38
[11] Ibid., p. 41

- Can be broken into functional or partial objectives, intermediate results or deliverables, which are specific milestones within the overall scope of work or the availability of financial resources;
- Usually time bound, with both a start and an ending or control point;
- Documented within a methodology; and
- Can be decided upon or shaped by the singular aspects of the organization, industry or technology utilized.
- Phase-to-phase relationships
  - ✓ Sequential, starting only when the preceding phase is complete. This approach reduces uncertainty but can eliminate the possibility of speeding up the overall process.
  - ✓ Overlapping, with one phase starting before the previous phase is complete; an example is fast tracking, which serves as a schedule compression technique. Requires additional resources, may increase risk and can require rework if all the data from the previous, as yet uncompleted, phase is not available.

Figure 3.5. **Overlapping Phases**

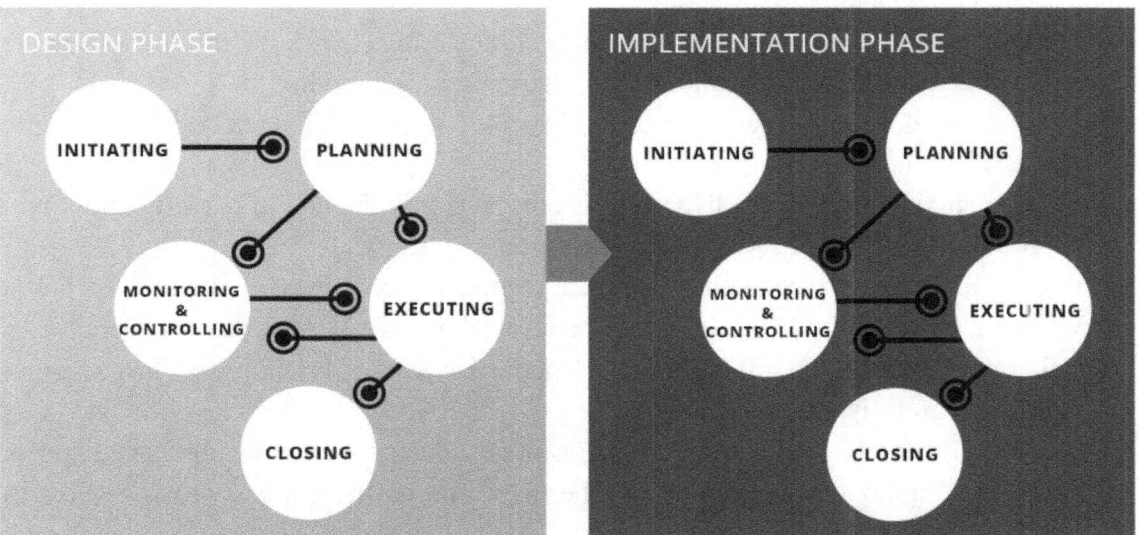

Although it's obvious that projects vary in terms of complexity and size, all of them can be mapped to a single life cycle structure: 1) starting the project, 2) organizing and preparing, 3) carrying out the project work, and 4) closing the project.

Other forms of project life cycles include those that are predictive, iterative and incremental and adaptive:

- Predictive life cycles
  - ✓ Also known as fully plan-driven

- ✓ Project scope and the cost and time to deliver that scope are decided upon as early in the life cycle as possible.
- ✓ Projects proceed through a series of sequential or overlapping phases, with each having a focus on a subset of activities and management processes. Work during each phase is different in nature from both the preceding and subsequent phases, causing required skills to vary from one phase to another.
- ✓ Focus at initiation is on delineating the product's overall scope, developing a plan to deliver that and any associated deliverables and, while remaining within the scope, moving through the phases to execute the plan.
- ✓ Any changes in scope must be managed carefully, requiring re-planning and gaining formal scope acceptance.
- ✓ Generally preferred when the deliverable is thoroughly understood, a substantial base of industry base exists or when the product must be delivered in full to have value to stakeholders.

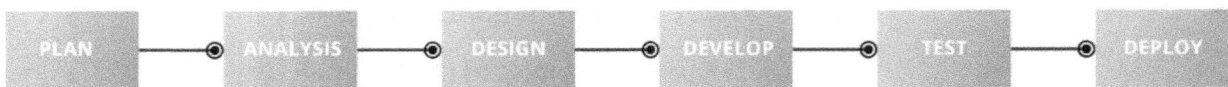

- o Iterative and incremental life cycles
  - ✓ Those in which project phases (iterations) purposefully repeat one or more project activities in the course of the team's gaining understanding of the product.
  - ✓ Product developed through a series of repeated cycles as functionality of the product is successfully increased in increments.
  - ✓ Either a single or a set of deliverables is completed by the end of each iteration, with future iterations enhancing deliverables or creating new ones.
  - ✓ When exit criteria for each phase are met, feedback can be incorporated by the project team.
  - ✓ While a high-level vision is developed for the overall undertaking, detailed scope is elaborated upon for each iteration and, once the work has commenced, any changes to that scope are carefully managed.
  - ✓ Usually preferred when the organization must manage changing objectives and scope, to limit the complexity of a project or when it would be helpful and provide value to one or more stakeholder groups to make a partial delivery of the product in a way such that there is no impact on the final deliverable.
  - ✓ Frequently used in large/complex projects to reduce risk by permitting the team to incorporate feedback and lessons learned between iterations.
- o Adaptive life cycles
  - ✓ Also known as change-driven or agile methods
  - ✓ Aimed at responding to high levels of change and ongoing stakeholder involvement
  - ✓ Although iterative and incremental, iterations are very rapid and fixed in both time and cost.
  - ✓ Overall project scope is decomposed into a set of requirements/work to be performed (product backlog).

- ✓ Initially, team will decide on the number of highest priority items on the backlog list that can be delivered within the next iteration, at which time, the product should be ready for customer review.
- ✓ Continuous engagement with sponsor and customer representatives provides feedback on newly created deliverables, ensuring that product backlog is reflective of their needs.
- ✓ Preferred when dealing with a rapidly changing environment, when it's difficult to define requirements and scope in advance and when defining small, incremental improvements that will provide stakeholders with value is possible.

Test What You've Learned

1) Which, if any, of the following is true?
    a) Organizational structures are always either functional or projectized.
    b) An organizational culture is formed by those who head that organization.
    c) Organizational communications capability has little influence on the ways projects are conducted.
    d) As an enterprise environmental factor, organizational structure can affect resource availability.

2) James only reports to one superior. Thus, he works within a _____ organization.
    a) Strong matrix
    b) Projectized
    c) Weak matrix
    d) Functional

3) A _____ structure intermingles functional and projectized characteristics and is classified by the relative level of power and influence between functional and project managers.
    a) Functional
    b) Projectized
    c) Matrix
    d) Coordinated

4) As a project expediter, Alicia:
    a) Serves as a staff assistant.
    b) Coordinates project funding.
    c) Can both make and enforce decisions.
    d) Has a great deal of authority over other project team members.

5) Tim is a project manager in a projectized organization and thus:
    a) Takes the role of a coordinator or expediter.
    b) Has some authority but reports to a higher-level manager.
    c) Works at a considerable distance from other team members.
    d) Has a great deal of independence and authority.

6) The Initiating and Planning process includes:
    a) Financial controls procedures
    b) Specific organizational policies such as those associated with human resources and safety
    c) Risk control procedures
    d) Project closure guidelines

7) Alan is trying to deal with an outdated project management information system, which should be considered to be a constraint imposed by _____.
   a) An enterprise environmental factor.
   b) His corporation's knowledge base.
   c) An organizational standard.
   d) Someone else's problem.

8) Enterprise environmental factors:
   a) Considered as outputs to most planning processes.
   b) Always have a positive effect on outcomes.
   c) Are limited to government or industry standards or the geographic distribution of resources.
   d) May either enhance or restrain project management options.

9) Issue and defect management procedures fall into the category of _____ processes:
   a) Initiating and Planning
   b) Executing, Monitoring and Controlling
   c) Closing
   d) Assets Processing

10) Stakeholders:
   a) May only be identified at the initiation of a project.
   b) Have needs and expectations that must align with each other.
   c) Maintain the same level of authority over the course of a project.
   d) Include both customers and sellers.

Chapter 4: Project Management Processes

Project Management Process Groups
The work of the project manager incorporates five process groups that 1) have clear dependencies, 2) are most frequently performed for every project and 3) are highly interactive with one another, which can be seen in the figure below.

Figure 4.1. Process Group Interaction

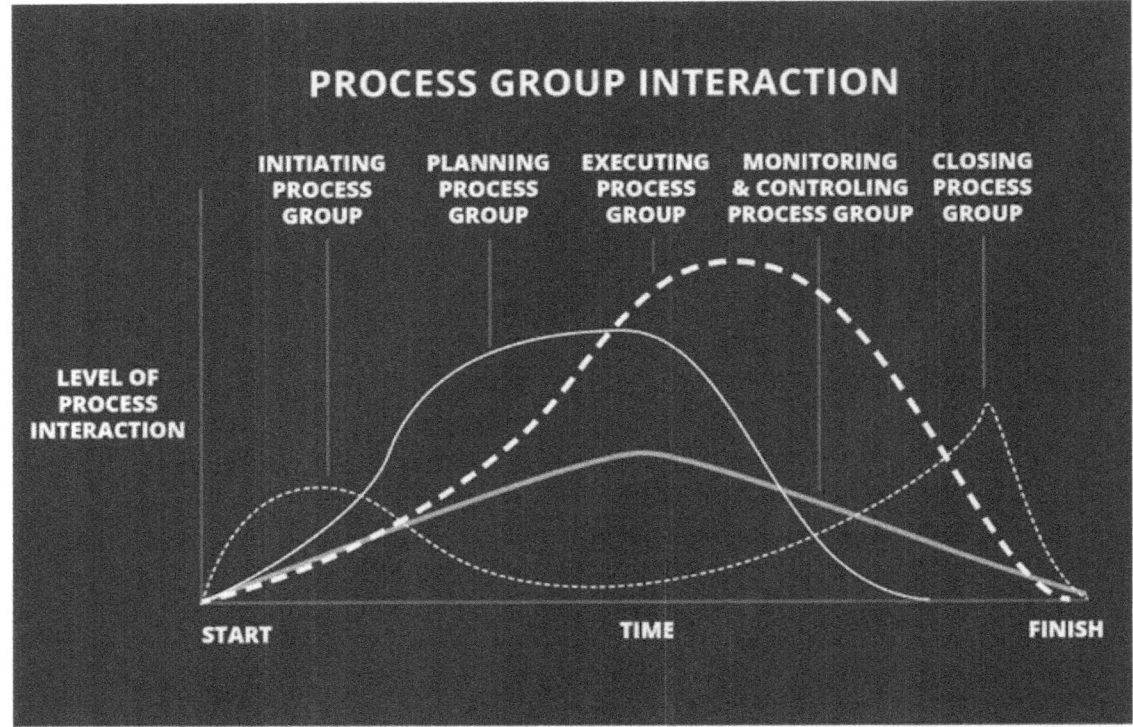

It must be kept in mind that the Process Groups are not the same as project life cycle phases. While these processes are interconnected by specific inputs and outputs, wherein the outcome of one process segues to being the input of another process, this does not indicate that this necessarily occurs within the same Process Group. It could happen that every Process Group is conducted within a phase. With projects being separated into distinct phases – concept development, feasibility study, design, prototype, etc. – all of the Process Groups would usually be reiterated for each phase.

At first glance, project management processes seem to function as separate elements that interface in a way that is logical and well-define. However, as those who work in the field of project management recognize, those processes overlap and intersect in myriad ways; thus, the required Process Groups and their incumbent processes serve more as guides to the application of project management knowledge and skills than as directives that control the ways in which that knowledge and those skills are utilized. In fact, the use of project management processes is iterative and you can anticipate repeating many of those processes throughout the course of a project.

Figure 4.2. **Project Management Process Groups**[12]

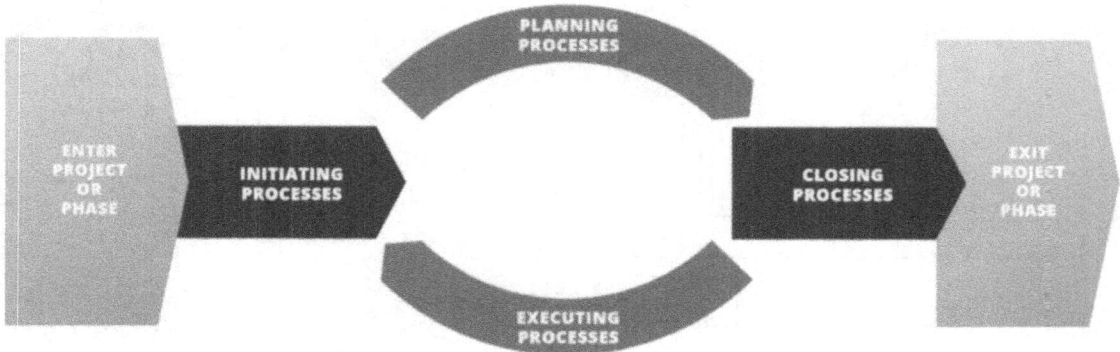

As can be seen in this figure, during all phases of a project, Monitoring and Controlling processes hover in the background, not merely interacting with the Initiating, Planning, Executing and Closing processes, but occurring simultaneously with them.

What else serves to link the various project management processes? Outputs – the output of one process usually serves as the input for another process or is actually the deliverable of the project, subproject or project phase, starting with the Planning Process Group, which provides the Executing Process Group with the project management plan (and project documents) and, over time, creates updates to that plan and its subsequent documents.

On the following page, in figure 4.3, you'll find a detailed figure showing each of these interactions, after which you'll learn a great deal more about each of these groups, the performance domains into which each fit, the tasks included in those domains and the knowledge and skills required to perform those tasks.

---

[12] Project Management Institute, *A Guide to the Project Management Body of Knowledge* (*The PMBOK® Guide*), 5th ed., p. 50.

Figure 4.3. Project Management Process Interactions

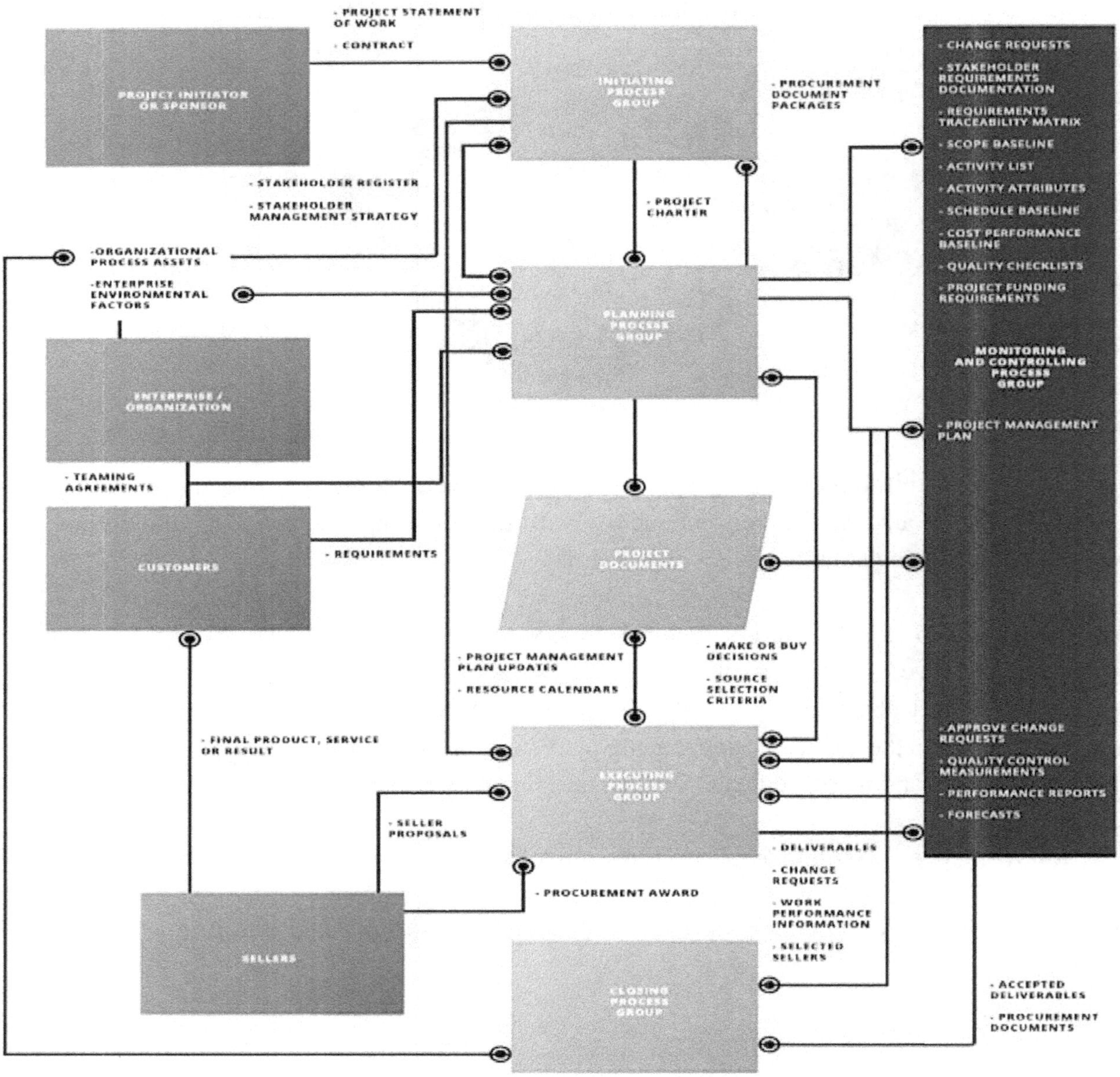

Initiating Process Group

The initiating process group is comprised of those processes "performed to define a new project or a new phase of an existing project by obtaining authorization to start the project or phase."[13]

Within those processes:

- o Initial scope is defined;
- o Initial financial resources are identified;
- o Internal and external stakeholders are ascertained; and
- o The project manager is selected (if not already assigned).

---

[13] Ibid., p. 54

All of this information is captured in the project charter; when it's approved, the project is officially authorized. It should be kept in mind that while the project team can assist in writing the charter, it is assumed that business case assessment, approval and funding are externally handled to the project boundaries (points in time at which either the initiation or completion of a project or project phase is authorized).

Aligning stakeholder expectations with the goal of the project, making its scope and objectives clearly visible, and demonstrating the way in which their participation in both the project itself and its associated phases can ensure achievement of their expectations are the key purposes for this Process Group.

If the project is large and complex, it should be divided into separate phases, with the Initiating process completed during each subsequent phase; this ensures that the overall project is kept on its original track and continues to focus on the need it was created to address. Once all aspects of the project are reviewed – criteria for success, stakeholders' influence, drivers and objectives – a decision can be made as to continuing, delaying or discontinuing the project.

Table 4.1. **Performance Domain I: Initiating**[14]

Domain I	Initiating — 7%
Task 1	Perform project assessment based upon available information, lessons learned from previous projects and meetings with relevant stakeholders in order to support the evaluation of the feasibility of new products or services within the given assumptions and/or constraints.
Task 2	Identify key deliverables based on the business requirements in order to manage customer expectations and direct the achievement of project goals.
Task 3	Perform stakeholder analysis using appropriate tools and techniques in order to align expectations and direct the achievement of project goals.
Task 4	Identify high level risks, assumptions and constraints based on the current environment, organizational factors, historical data and expert judgment in order to propose an implementation strategy.
Task 5	Participate in the development of the project charter by compiling and analyzing gathered information in order to ensure project stakeholders are in agreement on its elements.
Task 6	Obtain project charter approval from the sponsor in order to formalize the authority assigned to the project manager and gain commitment and acceptance for the project.
Task 7	Conduct benefit analysis with relevant stakeholders to validate project alignment with organizational strategy and expected business value.
Task 8	Inform stakeholders of approved project charter to ensure common understanding of the key deliverables, milestones, and their roles and responsibilities.
	Knowledge and Skills o Analytical skills,　　　　　　o Elements of a project charter,　　　　o Strategic management o Benefit analysis techniques,　o Estimation tools and techniques,

---

[14] *Project Management Professional (PMP)® Examination Content Online*, 2015, p. 5

Planning Process Group

The Planning Process Group is comprised of "those processes performed to establish the total scope of the effort, define and refine the objectives, and develop the course of action to attain those objectives."[15] Once again, this is far from a one and done exercise; project management can be very complex and hence may require repeated feedback loops for additional analysis. The more project information or characteristics that are gathered, the greater the need to revisit one or several Planning or even Initiating processes, which is termed "progressive elaboration."

Figure 4.4. **Planning Process Group Activities**

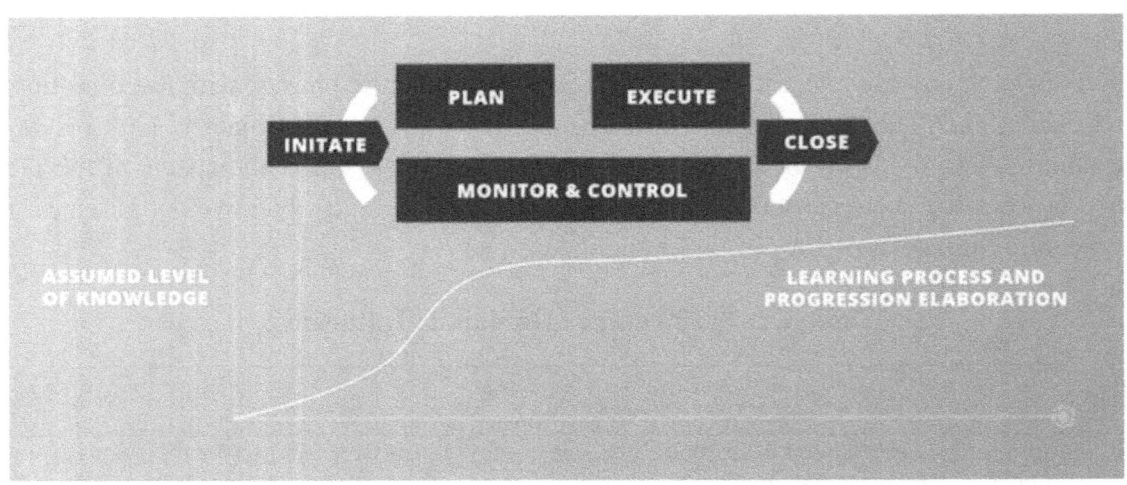

The most significant benefit of this Process Group is that it provides the delineation of the strategy and tactics, in addition to the course of action, required to successfully complete the project. When this is done well, stakeholder buy-in and engagement become much easier to acquire.

The outputs from the Planning Process Group include a project management plan and project documents that pertain to all aspects of the scope, time, cost, quality, communications, human resources, risks, procurements, and stakeholder engagement.

Approved changes that frequently arise during the Monitoring and Controlling processes (more specifically, during the Direct and Manage Project Work Process) can really impact areas of the project management plan and project documents.

Luckily, collecting feedback and refinement of the documents does not go on indefinitely; your organization will have procedures in place that will dictate the end of initial planning, procedures that are affected by the project's nature, established project boundaries, appropriate monitoring and controlling activities and the environment in which the project is undertaken and concluded.

---

[15] Project Management Institute, *A Guide to the Project Management Body of Knowledge (The PMBOK® Guide)*, 5th ed., p. 55.

Table 4.2. **Performance Domain II: Planning**[16]
(continued on following page)

Domain II	Planning — 24%
Task 1	Review and assess detailed project requirements, constraints and assumptions with stakeholders based on the project charter, lessons learned and by using requirement gathering techniques to establish detailed project deliverables.
Task 2	Develop a scope management plan, based on the approved project scope and using scope management techniques, to define, maintain and manage the scope of the project.
Task 3	Develop the cost management plan, based on the project scope, schedule, resources, approved project charter and other information, using estimating techniques to manage project costs.
Task 4	Develop the project schedule, based on the approved project deliverables and milestones, scope, and resource management plans, to manage timely completion of the project.
Task 5	Develop the human resource management plan by defining the roles and responsibilities of the project team members to create a project organizational structure and provide guidance regarding how resources will be assigned and managed.
Task 6	Develop the communications management plan, based on the project organizational structure and stakeholder requirements, to define and manage the flow of project information.
Task 7	Develop the procurement management plan, based on the project scope, budget and schedule, to ensure that the required project resources will be available.
Task 8	Develop the quality management plan and define the quality standards for the project and its products, based on the project scope, risks and requirements, to prevent the occurrence of defects and control the cost of quality.
Task 9	Develop the change management plan by defining how changes will be addressed and controlled in order to track and manage change.
Task 10	Plan for risk management by developing a risk management plan; identifying, analyzing, and prioritizing project risk; creating the risk register; and defining risk response strategies in order to manage uncertainty and opportunity throughout the project life cycle.
Task 11	Present the project management plan to the relevant stakeholders, according to applicable policies and procedures, to obtain approval to proceed with project execution.

---

[16] *Project Management Professional (PMP)® Examination Content Online*, 2015, p. 6.

Table 4.2. Performance Domain II: Planning[17]
(continued from previous page)

Task 12	Conduct kick-off meeting, communicating the start of the project, key milestones, and other relevant information in order to inform and engage stakeholders and gain commitment.
Task 13	Develop the stakeholder management plan by analyzing needs, interests and potential impact to effectively manage stakeholders' expectations and to engage them in project decisions.
	Knowledge and Skills o Change management planning o Cost management planning, including project budgeting tools and techniques o Communications planning o Contract types and selection criteria o Estimation tools and techniques o Human resource planning o Lean and efficiency principles o Procurement planning o Quality management planning o Requirements-gathering techniques such as planning sessions, brainstorming and focus groups o Regulatory and environmental impacts assessment planning o Risk management planning o Scope deconstruction (e.g., WBS, Scope backlog) tools and techniques o Scope management planning o Stakeholder management planning o Time management planning, including scheduling tools and techniques o Workflow diagraming techniques

Executing Process Group

The Executing Process Group comprises "those processes performed to complete the work defined in the project management plan to satisfy the project specifications," which involves "coordinating people and resources, managing stakeholder expectations, as well as integrating and performing the activities of the project in accordance with the project management plan."[18]

You should expect changes in areas such as anticipated activity durations, resource productivity and availability and unexpected risks during the course of project execution; emerging results and the analysis of those results may make it necessary to update plans and re-baseline. The project's budget will be expended to a large degree during the Executing Process Group phase of your project.

---

[17] *Project Management Professional (PMP)® Examination Content Online*, 2015, p. 6.
[18] Ibid., p. 56.

Table 4.3. **Performance Domain III: Executing**[19]

Domain III	Executing — 31%	
Task 1	Acquire and manage project resources by following the human resource and procurement management plans in order to meet project requirements.	
Task 2	Manage task execution based on the project management plan by leading and developing the project team in order to achieve project deliverables.	
Task 3	Implement the quality management plan using the appropriate tools and techniques in order to ensure that work is performed in accordance with required quality standards.	
Task 4	Implement approved changes and corrective actions by following the change management plan in order to meet project requirements.	
Task 5	Implement approved actions by following the risk management plan in order to minimize the impact of the risks and take advantage of opportunities on the project.	
Task 6	Manage the flow of information by following the communications plan in order to keep stakeholders engaged and informed.	
Task 7	Maintain stakeholder relationships in following the stakeholder management plan in order to receive continued support and manage expectations.	
	Knowledge and Skills o Continuous improvement processes o Contract management techniques o Elements of a statement of work	o Interdependencies among project elements o Project budgeting tools and techniques o Quality standard tools o Vendor management techniques

Monitoring and Controlling Process Group

The Monitoring and Controlling Process Group is comprised of processes "required to track, review, and orchestrate the progress and performance of the project; identify any areas in which changes to the plan are required; and initiate the corresponding changes."[20] This Group's most significant benefit is that it allows project performance to be regularly measured and analyzed and that appropriate events or exception conditions can identify variances from the project management plan.

In addition, the Monitoring and Controlling Process Group involves:

o The control of changes and recommendations for corrective or preventative action in anticipation of possible problems;

o Monitoring and comparing ongoing project activities against the project management plan and the performance measurement baseline; and

o Manipulating factors that could bypass integrated change control or configuration management so that only approved changes are actually implemented.

---

[19] *Project Management Professional (PMP)® Examination Content Online*, 2015, p. 6.
[20] Project Management Institute, *A Guide to the Project Management Body of Knowledge (The PMBOK® Guide)*, 5th ed., p. 57.

Thus, the Monitoring and Controlling Process Group goes beyond the work being done in that process group to monitor and control the entire project; in projects with multiple phases, those phases are coordinated to employ corrective or preventative actions with the goal of bringing the project into compliance with the project management plan.

Table 4.4. **Performance Domain IV: Monitoring and Controlling**[21]

Domain IV	Monitoring and Controlling — 25%
Task 1	Measure project performance using appropriate tools and techniques in order to identify and quantify any variances and corrective actions.
Task 2	Manage changes to the project by following the change management plan in order to ensure that project goals remain aligned with business needs.
Task 3	Verify that project deliverables conform to the quality standards established in the quality management plan by using appropriate tools and techniques to meet project requirements and business needs.
Task 4	Monitor and assess risk by determining whether exposure has changed and evaluating the effectiveness of response strategies in order to manage the impact of risks and opportunities on the project.
Task 5	Review the issue log, update if necessary, and determine corrective actions by using appropriate tools and techniques in order to minimize the impact on the project.
Task 6	Capture, analyze and manage lessons learned, using lessons learned management techniques in order to enable continuous improvement.
Task 7	Monitor procurement activities according to procurement plan in order to verify compliance with project objectives.
	Knowledge and Skills o Performance measurement and tracking techniques, e.g., EV, CPM, PERT, Trend Analysis o Process analysis techniques, e.g., LEAN, Kanban, Six Sigma o Project control limits, e.g., thresholds, tolerance o Project finance principles o Project monitoring tools and techniques o Project quality best practices and standards, e.g., ISO, BS, CMMI, IEEE o Quality measurement tools, e.g., statistical sampling, control charts, flow-charting, inspection, assessment o Risk identification and analysis techniques o Risk response techniques o Quality validation and verification techniques

---

[21] *Project Management Professional (PMP)® Examination Content Online*, 2015, p. 9.

Closing Process Group

As its title implies, the Closing Process Group is composed of "those processes performed to conclude all activities across all Project Management Process Groups to formally complete the project, phase, or contractual obligations."[22]

This is also true of projects that are closed prematurely, e.g., aborted or cancelled projects or those having a critical situation. In such a scenario, the project is said to have reached a kill point.

During project or phase closure, activities that may take place include:

- Obtaining customer/sponsor permission to formally close the project or phase;
- Conducting post-project or phase-end review;
- Recording impacts of tailoring to any process;
- Documenting lessons learned;
- Applying appropriate updates to organizational process assets;
- Archiving all relevant project documents in the project management information system as elements of historical data;
- Closing out all procurement activities thus ensuring termination of all relevant agreements; and
- Performing assessment of team members and releasing project resources.

Table 4.5. **Performance Domain V: Closing**[23]
(Continued on following page)

Domain V	Closing— 7%
Task 1	Obtain final acceptance of the project deliverables from relevant stakeholders in order to confirm that project scope and deliverables were achieved.
Task 2	Transfer the ownership of deliverables to assigned stakeholders in accordance with the project plan in order to facilitate project closure.
Task 3	Obtain financial, legal and administrative closure using generally accepted practices and policies in order to communicate formal project closure and ensure transfer of liability.
Task 4	Prepare and share the final project report according to the communications management plan in order to document and convey project performance and assist in project evaluation.
Task 5	Collate lessons learned that were documented throughout the project and conduct a comprehensive project review in order to update the organization's knowledge base.
Task 6	Archive project documents and materials using generally accepted practices in order to comply with statutory requirements and for potential use in future projects and audits.

---

[22] Project Management Institute, *A Guide to the Project Management Body of Knowledge (The PMBOK® Guide)*, 5th ed., p. 57.
[23] *Project Management Professional (PMP)® Examination Content Online*, 2015, p. 10.

Task 7	Obtain feedback from relevant stakeholders using appropriate tools and techniques and based on the stakeholder management plan in order to evaluate their satisfaction.
	Knowledge and Skills o Archiving practices and statutes o Compliance (statute/organization) o Contract closure requirements o Close-out procedures o Feedback techniques o Performance measurement techniques (KPI and key success factors) o Project review techniques o Transition planning technique

Table 4.5. **Performance Domain V: Closing**[24]
(Continued from previous page)

Project Information

Over the course of a project, a great deal of information is gathered, reworked and, in several formats, distributed to project team members and other stakeholders. These data are analyzed in the context from which they emerge, combined and transformed into project information throughout various Controlling processes.

It's important that terms are not used indiscriminately and are standardized to avoid confusion and misunderstandings among the stakeholders. With that in mind, the following are guidelines to appropriate terminology:[25]

- o Work performance data
    - ✓ Raw observations and measurements identified during activities performed to complete project work
    - ✓ Include reported percent of work physically completed, quality and technical performance measures, start and finish dates, numbers of change requests or defects, actual costs or durations, etc.
- o Work performance information
    - ✓ Performance data collected from various controlling processes, analyzed in context and integrated based relationships across areas
    - ✓ Include status of deliverables, implementation status for change requests, forecasted estimates to completion
- o Work performance reports
    - ✓ The physical or electronic representation of work performance information compiled in project documents that are intended to generate decisions or raise issues, actions or awareness

---

[24] *Project Management Professional (PMP)® Examination Content Online*, 2015, p. 10.
[25] Project Management Institute, *A Guide to the Project Management Body of Knowledge (The PMBOK® Guide)*, 5th ed., p. 59.

✓ Include status reports, memos, justifications, information notes, electronic dashboards, recommendations and updates

Figure 6. **Project Data, Information and Report Flow**[26]

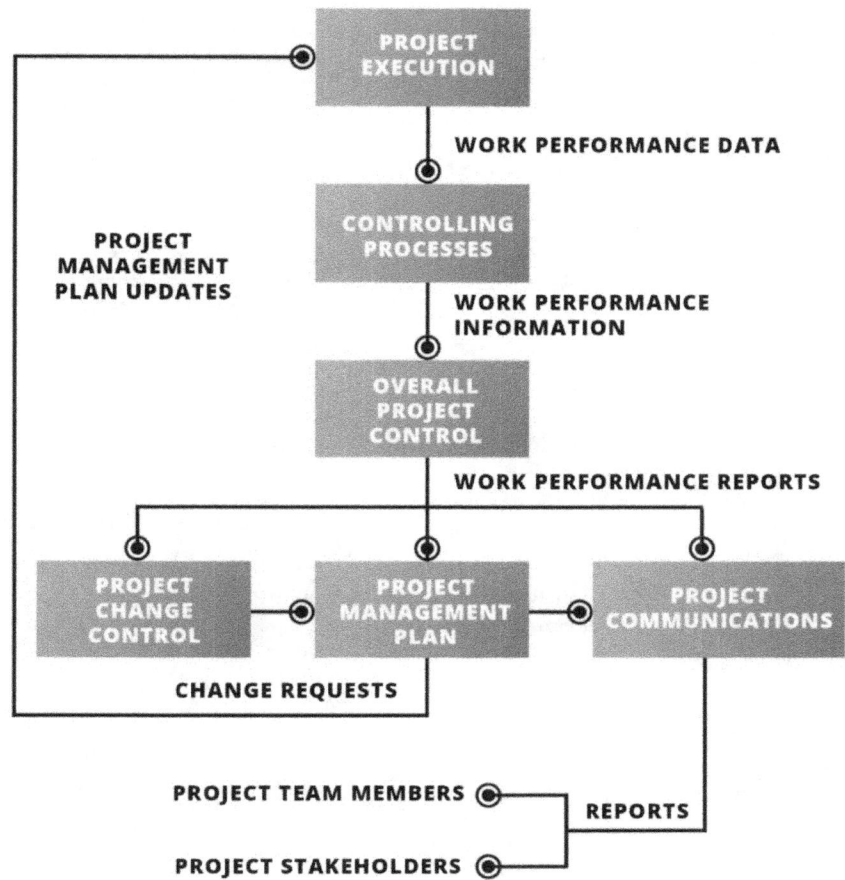

Role of the Knowledge Areas

A Knowledge Area denotes a complete set of concepts, terms and activities that comprise a professional field, project management field or area of specialization. *The PMBOK® Guide* identifies 47 project management processes that are additionally grouped into ten separate Knowledge Areas that project teams use as appropriate over the course of their specific project. These Knowledge Areas, as well as their respective processes, can be seen in table 4.6.

---

[26] Ibid., p. 59

Table 4.6. **Project Management Process Group and Knowledge Area Mapping**[27]

	\multicolumn{5}{c}{Process Groups}				
Knowledge Areas	Initiating	Planning	Executing	Monitoring & Controlling	Closing
Project Integration Management	Develop Project Charter	Develop Project Management Plan	Direct and Manage Project Work	Monitor & Control Project Work Perform Integrated Change Control	Close Project or Phase
Project Scope Management		Plan Scope Management Collect Requirements Define Scopes Create WBS		Validate Scope Control Scope	
Project Time Management		Plan Schedule Management Define Activities Sequence Activities Estimate Activity Resources Estimate Activity Durations Develop Schedule		Control Schedule	
Project Cost Management		Plan Cost Management Estimate Costs Determine Budget		Control Costs	
Project Quality Management		Plan Quality Management	Perform Quality Assurance	Control Quality	
Project HR Management		Plan Human Resources Management	Acquire Project Team Develop Project Team Manage Project Team		
Project Communications Management		Plan Communications Management	Manage Communications	Control Communications	
Project Risk Management		Plan Risk Management Identify Risks Perform Qualitative Risk Analysis Perform Quantitative Risk Analysis Plan Risk Responses		Control Risks	
Project Procurement Management		Plan Procurement Management	Conduct Procurements	Control Procurements	Close Procurements
Project Stakeholder Management	Identify Stakeholders	Plan Stakeholder Management	Manage Stakeholder Engagement	Manage Stakeholder Engagement	

---

[27] Ken Parker, 12 February, 2015, "Project Management – What is it and why do we care so much?", http://terratherm.com/blog/?p=1641

Test What You've Learned

1) Which, if any, of the following statements are true?
   a) Process Groups are much the same as project life cycle phases.
   b) Process Groups are interconnected by their inputs and outputs, with the output of one process becoming the input of another process.
   c) Processes in the Monitoring and Controlling Group occur at the same time as those in every other group.
   d) Both b) and c) are true.

2) What is/are not identified during the Initiating Process Group?
   a) Initial scope
   b) Project team members
   c) Initial financial resources
   d) Internal and external stakeholders

3) Reviewing and assessing detail project requirements, constraints and assumptions with stakeholders is a task related to:
   a) The Initiating Performance Domain
   b) The Planning Performance Domain
   c) All of the Domains
   d) The Executing Performance Domain

4) The coordination of people and resources, management of stakeholder expectations and the integration and performance of project activities takes place during the:
   a) The Initiating Performance Domain
   b) The Planning Performance Domain
   c) The Closing Domain
   d) The Executing Performance Domain

5) James is working within the Executing Process Group and has acquired and managed project resources and implemented the quality management plan. Which task, if any, has James skipped?
   a) Managing task execution by leading and developing the project team to achieve project deliverables.
   b) Maintaining stakeholder relationships
   c) Implementing approved changes and corrective actions
   d) Managing the flow of information by following the communication plan.

6) The widget being produced by Thomas' project, which has moved to the Closing phase, may or may not fit the customer's sprocket. What should Thomas do?
   a) Forge ahead with the project; it will probably fit.
   b) Suggest that the customer resize his sprocket.
   c) Return to the tasks of the Initiating Process Group to totally reorganize the project.
   d) Revisit task 1 of the Monitoring and Controlling Process Group.

7) Stakeholder buy-in and engagement are much easier to attain if:
   a) The delineation of strategy, tactics and a course of action is carefully done as part of the Planning Process Group.
   b) They are part of all aspects of the Initiating Process Group.
   c) They are well-informed as to results during project close.
   d) They are sent all raw data that emerges during the course of the project.

8) Knowledge and skills required in the Executing Process Group include:
   a) Quality standard tools and risk response techniques
   b) Continuous improvement processes and quality validation and verification techniques
   c) Compliance (statute/organization) and capture of lessons learned
   d) Managing flow of information and vendor management techniques

9) When closing a project, you must:
   a) Obtain provisional acceptance of the project deliverables
   b) Obtain feedback from team members
   c) Transfer ownership of deliverables to assigned shareholders
   d) Implement approved actions and corrective measures

10) _____ is performance data collected from various controlling processes, analyzed in context and integrated based on relationships across areas.
   a) Work performance data
   b) Work performance information
   c) Work performance reports
   d) Work performance statistics

Chapter 5: Project Integration Management

Project Integration Management encompasses many processes and activities aimed at identifying, defining, combining and coordinating everything that is involved within the Project Management Process Groups. In this book, as in *The PMBOK® Guide*, these project management processes are discussed individually as discrete actions that frequently and repeatedly interface. Thus, it should be kept in mind that they in fact overlap and interact in complex ways that must be understood by professional project managers, both for the exam and during the course of real life projects.

It is equally true that every project does not involve every process. However, although there is no single correct way to manage all projects, both project managers and teams must determine the right level of implementation for each process for their project and within their particular environment.

The iterative nature of project management can be observed in any complex project, as the outputs of each process become, in turn, the inputs on which the next process is founded, from the inception of the project, marked by the development of the project charter to its close, when the hoped for result is achieved.

Developing a Project Charter
Develop Project Charter is "the process of developing a document that formally authorizes the existence of a project and provides the project manager with the authority to apply organizational resources to project activities."[28]

Figure 5.1 features the inputs, tools and techniques and outputs of this process.

Figure 5.1. **Develop Project Charter: Inputs, Tools and Techniques, and Outputs**

Inputs	Tools & Techniques	Outputs
• Project statement of work • Business case • Agreements • Enterprise environmental factors • Organizational process assets	• Expert judgment • Facilitation techniques	• Project charter

---

[28] Project Management Institute, *A Guide to the Project Management Body of Knowledge* (*The PMBOK® Guide*), 5th ed., p. 66.

The project charter:
- o Prior to or during charter development (in which he/she should participate), the project manager is identified and assigned, with the charter providing that manager with authority to plan/execute the project.
- o Creates a partnership between the performing and requesting organizations
  - ✓ External projects - typically require a formal contract
  - ✓ Internal agreements - are set by the project charter
- o Formally initiates the project
- o Is authored by the sponsor or sponsoring entity
- o Validates alignment of the project to the organization's strategy and ongoing work.
- o Because no consideration/money promised or exchanged, is not considered to be a contract.

Inputs

Project Statement of Work

A project statement of work (SOW) is "a narrative description of products, services or results to be delivered by a project."[29] Internally, the SOW is provided by the project initiator or sponsor based on business needs, product or service requirements. For external projects, the SOW is part of the bid document or contract received from the customer.

The SOW should encompass:
- o Business need
  - ✓ Based on a market demand, technological advance, legal requirement, government regulation, or environmental concern
  - ✓ In addition to the cost-benefit analysis, is meant to justify the project
- o Product scope description
  - ✓ Documents features of the products, services or results the project is intended to create as well as their relationship to the business need addressed by that project
- o Strategic plan
  - ✓ Documents the strategic vision, goals and objectives of the organization to which the project should be aligned, an alignment that ensures that all projects coincide with the organization's overall objectives
  - ✓ May include a high-level mission statement

---

[29] Ibid., p. 68

The Business Case

Figure 5.2. **Benefits of the Business Case**

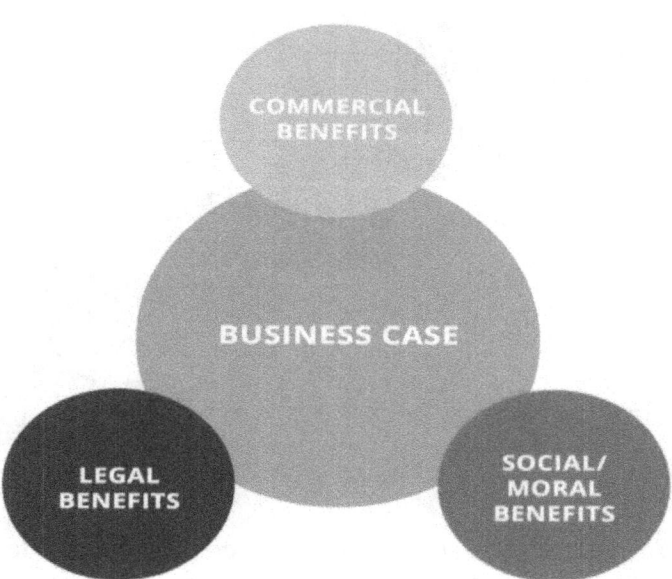

The business case outlines "the necessary information from a business standpoint to determine whether the project is worth the required investment"[30] and is most frequently utilized to assist managers and executives higher than the project level in their decision-making process. The business need and cost-benefit analysis (normally completed by a business analyst using input from various stakeholders) within the business case serve to justify and establish boundaries for the project. The sponsor also has a role, as their agreement with the scope and limitations of the business case is required.

Business cases can be based on a market demand, an organizational need, a customer request, a technological advance, legal requirement, ecological impact and/or social need. Like so many things affecting a multiphase project, because business cases may contain elements of risk, they should be occasionally reviewed to ensure the project has remained on a trajectory that will deliver the sought after benefits. Although, in a project's early stages, periodic review by the sponsor confirms that it remains aligned with the business case, it is the project manager who ensures that shareholder's requirements, as defined in the business case, as well as the organization's goals, are being met.

Organizations will typically conduct some analysis of the needs and wants for a project before the business case is even considered to be put together. For large scale projects, an organization might conduct a feasibility study to assess whether a project is viable of not. Among other things, a feasibility study is an analysis of whether a project is legally feasible, technically feasible, operationally feasible and economically justifiable.

---

[30] Ibid., p. 69

Figure 5.3. **Elements of a Feasibility Study**

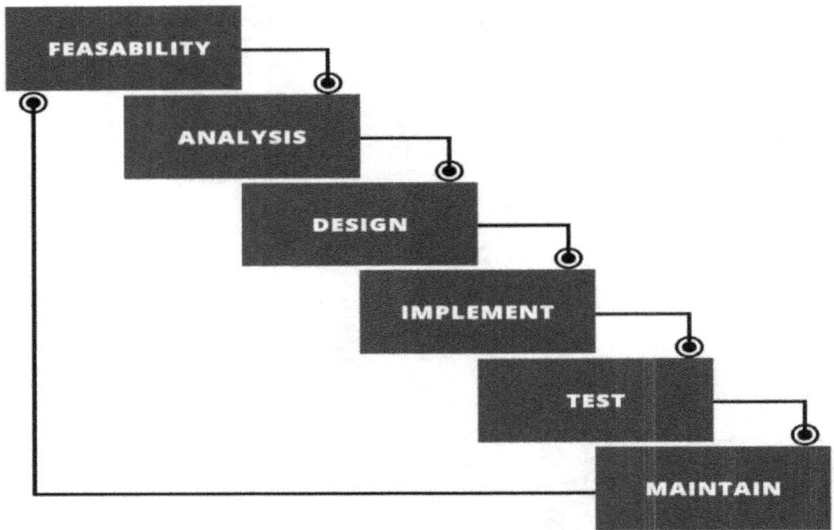

Back to the business case, several project selection methods are used. Many of these methods will forecast and try to quantify the financial benefits of the project investment. Some of the financial metrics that may arise in this analysis include Benefit Cost Ratio (BCR), Economic Value Add (EVA), Internal Rate of Return (IRR), Net Present Value (NPV), Opportunity Cost, Payback Period, Present Value (PV), Net Present Value (NPV), Return on Investment (ROI) and Return on Invested Capital (ROIC).

As the project progresses, the project manager will need to continue to monitor the relevant metrics to maximize the chances of project benefits realization. Benefits realization is a way of managing, as well as monitoring, how resources are invested by an organization to attain the desired and defined project goals.

Agreements
Utilized to define initial purposes for the project, agreements can be contracts (usually used for projects undertaken for external customers), memorandums of understanding (MOUs), service level agreements (SLAs), verbal agreements, emails or other written agreements.

Enterprise environmental factors
Enterprise environmental factors that can impact the Develop Project Charter process include, among others:

- o Governmental and industry standards or regulations (codes of conduct, quality standards, worker protection standards)
- o Organizational culture and structure
- o Marketplace conditions

Organizational process assets

Organizational process assets involved in the Develop Project Charter process include, among others:

- o Organizational standard processes, policies and process definitions
- o Templates
- o Historical information and lessons learned knowledge base

Tools & Techniques

Expert judgment

Expert judgment, frequently used to assess project charter inputs, is directed at all technical and management details and provided by those with specialized training or knowledge, including:

- ✓ Other units within the organization
- ✓ Consultants
- ✓ Key stakeholders (such as customers or sponsors)
- ✓ Professional and technical associations
- ✓ Industry groups
- ✓ Subject matter experts (SMEs)
- ✓ The project management office (PMO)

Facilitation techniques

Facilitation techniques guide project charter development and include brainstorming, conflict resolution, problem solving and meeting management.

Outputs

Project charter

As we're discussing the development of the project charter in this section, it's logical to assume that this activity's output consists of the project charter. In addition to providing formal authorization for the project and giving the project manager the authority to manage that project, the project charter verifies business needs, assumptions, constraints and the customer's needs and the new product, service or result intended to satisfy that need. These can include project purpose or justification, measurable project objectives and criteria for success, high-level requirements and/or risks, summary milestone schedule and budget, list of stakeholders, requirements for project approval, the project manager assigned to the project and his/her responsibility and authority level, etc.

Developing a Project Management Plan

Develop Project Management Plan is "the process of defining, preparing and coordinating all subsidiary plans and integrating them into a comprehensive project management plan,"[31] with the most significant benefit of creating a document defining the foundation of all work involved in the project.

---

[31] Ibid., p. 72

The project management plan:

- Defines the way in which the project is executed, monitored and controlled, and, ultimately, closed
- Content differs dependent on the project's area of application and complexity
- Developed via a series of integrated processes that result in a plan that's gradually expanded upon by updates
- Controlled and approved through the Perform Integrated Change Control process
- Should be developed in a manner consistent with the program management plan

Figure 5.4. **Develop Project Management Plan: Inputs, Tools and Techniques, and Outputs**

Inputs	Tools & Techniques	Outputs
•1 Project statement of work •2 Outputs from other processes •3 Enterprise environmental factors •4 Organizational process assets	•Expert judgment •Facilitation techniques	•Project management plan

Inputs

Project charter
As described previously, the Project Charter varies in size dependent on both the project's complexity and whatever information is available when it's created. At the least, it should define the high-level boundaries of the project and serves as the starting point for the Initiating Process Group.

Outputs from other processes
The process outputs used in this context, which will be thoroughly described in chapters 6 through 14, are integrated to form the project management plan, with any baselines and subsidiary plans that are outputs from other processes becoming inputs to this process. Further, if approved changes are made to those documents, updates to the project management plan will be necessary.

Enterprise environmental factors
Those factors that can affect the Develop Project Management Plan process include (but are not limited to):
- Governmental or industry standards
- Project management body of knowledge for vertical markets, such as construction, and focus area, such as environmental, safety, risk or development of agile software
- Project management information system (PMIS)

- o Structure, culture, management practices and sustainability of the organization
- o Existing infrastructure
- o Personnel administration, such as guidelines for hiring and termination, employee performance reviews, etc.

Organizational process assets
Those that can influence this process include (but aren't limited to):

- o Standardized guidelines, work instructions, proposal evaluation and performance measurement criteria
- o The project management template
    - ✓ Encompasses what is required to tailor the organization's set of standard processes intended to satisfy the project's specific needs and guidelines for project closure (product validation and acceptance criteria)
- o Change control procedures
- o Previous projects' files (scope, cost schedule and performance measurement baselines, calendars, schedule network diagrams, risk registers), historical information, lessons learned knowledge and configuration management knowledge bases.

Tools & Techniques

Expert judgment
Utilization of expert judgment is aimed at tailoring the process to meet project needs; developing technical and management details that will be included in the project management plan; determining necessary resource and skill levels; defining configuration management level to apply on the project; determining which project documents will be subject to the formal change control process; and prioritizing project work so that project resources are properly allocated as to work and time.

Facilitation techniques
As previously mentioned, brainstorming, conflict resolution, problem solving and meeting management are facilitators' key techniques as they assist both teams and individuals attain agreement in accomplishing project activities.

Outputs

Project management plan
The project management plan encompasses baselines that include (but aren't limited to) those involving scope, schedule and cost. In addition, subsidiary plans may include (but aren't limited to):

- o Scope management plan
- o Requirement management plan
- o Schedule management plan
- o Quality management plan
- o Process improvement plan
- o Human resource management plan

- Communications management plan
- Risk management plan
- Procurement management plan
- Stakeholder management plan

The project management plan may also include:

- ✓ The project life cycle and the processes to be applied to each phase
- ✓ Details of tailoring decisions specified by the project teams such as project management processes and their corresponding implementation levels
- ✓ Descriptions of the tools/techniques that will be used, the ways in which the selected processes will be utilized to manage the project and how work will be executed to attain project objectives
- ✓ Change management plan documenting the performance of configuration management
- ✓ How project baseline integrity will be maintained
- ✓ Requirements/techniques for shareholder communication
- ✓ Key management reviews for content, extent and timing to address open issues and pending decisions.

The project management plan may be either detailed or summarized and can be comprised of subsidiary plans. Keep in mind that once the project management plan is baselined, only the generation and approval of a change request via the Perform Integrated Change Control process can alter it.

Remember that the project management plan, while being one of the primary documents utilized in managing a project, is not the sole document involved; other project documents that are not part of that plan are used as well. Table 5.1 provides a representative list of the components of the project management components and project documents.

Table 5.1. **Differences Between the Project Management Plan and Project Documents**

Project Management Plan	Project Documents	
Change management plan	Activity attributes	Project staff assignments
Communications management plan	Activity cost estimates	Project statement of work
Configuration management plan	Activity duration estimates	Quality checklists
Cost baseline	Activity list	Quality control measurements
Cost management plan	Activity resource requirements	Quality metrics
Human resources management plan	Agreements	Requirements documentation
Process improvement plan	Basis of estimates	Requirements traceability matrix
Procurement management plan	Change log	Resource breakdown structure
Scope baseline (project scope statement, WBS, WBS dictionary)	Change requests	Resource calendars
Quality management plan	Forecasts (cost & schedule)	Risk register
Requirements management plan	Issue log	Schedule data
Risk management plan	Milestone list	Seller proposals
Schedule baseline	Procurement documents	Source selection criteria
Schedule management plan	Procurement statement of work	Stakeholder register
Scope management plan	Project calendars	Team performance assessments
Stakeholder management plan	Project charter, project funding requirements, project schedule, project schedule network diagrams	Work performance data, work performance information, work performance reports

Directing & Managing Project Work

Direct and Manage Project Work is "the process of leading and performing the work defined in the project management plan and implementing approved changes to achieve the project's objectives,"[32] the key benefit of which is that it delivers overall management of the project work.

Activities include (but are not limited to):
- Performing activities to accomplish project objectives
- Creating project deliverables to meet planned project work
- Providing, training and managing assigned team members
- Obtaining, managing and utilizing resources such as materials, tools, equipment and facilities
- Implementing planned methods and standards
- Establishing and managing both external and internal project communication channels
- Generating work performance data (cost, schedule, technical and quality progress and status to enable forecasting)
- Issuing change requests and adding approved changes to scope, plans and environment
- Managing risks, sellers, suppliers and stakeholders and implementing risk response activities

---

[32] Ibid., p. 79

- o Gathering and documenting lessons learned and executing approved process improvement activities.

Figure 5.3. **Direct and Manage Project Work: Inputs, Tools and Techniques, and Outputs**

Inputs	Tools & Techniques	Outputs
•Project management plan •Approved change requests •Enterprise environmental factors •Organizational process assets	•Expert judgment •Project management information system •Meetings	•Deliverables •Work performance data •Change requests •Project management plan updates •Project documents updates

This process also demands review of the impact of all project changes as well as the implementation of those changes once they're approved. This includes:

- o Corrective action, an intentional activity aimed at realigning the performance of project work with the project management plan
- o Preventive action, an intentional activity that ensures the future performance of the project work is aligned with the project management
- o Defect repair, another intentional activity that modifies a nonconforming product or component of a product

Inputs

Project management plan
We've already discussed the use of the project management plan as an input to several integration management processes. In this context, remember that it contains a number of subsidiary plans that will be described in much greater detail in the next chapters, including (but not limited to):

- o Scope management plan
- o Requirements management plan
- o Schedule management plan
- o Cost management plan
- o Stakeholder management plan

Approved change requests
Outputs of the Perform Integrated Change Control process, approved change requests are reviewed and their implementation approved by the change control board (CCB). In addition, they:

- o May be a corrective or preventative action or a defect repair
- o Are scheduled and implemented by the project team
- o Can impact any segment of the project of the project management plan
- o Can modify the policies, project management plan, procedures, costs, budgets and schedules

Enterprise environmental factors
The factors that can affect the Develop Project Management Plan process include (but are not limited to):
- o Culture and structure of performing/sponsor organization
- o Existing facilities and capital equipment that comprise the infrastructure
- o Personnel administration, including guidelines for hiring & firing, performance reviews and training records
- o Risk tolerances of stakeholders such as allowable cost overrun percentage
- o Project management information system, including automated tool suites, for example, a scheduling software tool, a configuration management system, an information collection/distribution system or internet interfaces to other online automated systems

Organizational process assets
The Direct and Manage Project work process can be affected by organizational process assets that include (but are not limited to):
- o Standardized guidelines and work instructions
- o Communication requirements that outline allowed communication media, records retention and security constraints
- o Issues and defects management procedures that define related controls, identification and resolution and action items tracking
- o A process measurement data base utilized to collect and make available data concerning processes and products
- o Project files from previous projects, including scope, cost, schedule, and performance measurement baselines, project calendars, project schedule network diagrams, risk registers, planned response actions and defined risk impact and documented lessons learned
- o Issues and defects management database(s) that comprise historical issues and defects status and resolution, control information and action item results.

Tools & Techniques

Expert judgment
Used to assess the inputs necessary to directing and managing the project management plan's execution, expert judgment and expertise are applied to all technical and management details during this process and are largely supplied by the project manager and the project management team. However, other sources of expertise may include:
- o Other units within the organization
- o Internal and external consultants and other subject matter experts
- o Key stakeholders
- o Professional and technical associations

Project management information system (PMIS)
The PMIS typically consists of automated tools to help track schedule, cost, performance, etc. It is an enterprise environmental factor since it plays an important role in the environment in which the project is being managed.

Meetings
Attendees at meetings may include the project manager, the team and any stakeholders involved in or affected by the subjects discussed, each of which should have a defined role to ensure participation that involves an exchange of information; brainstorming, option evaluation or design; or decision making.

Outputs

Deliverables
A deliverable is "any unique and verifiable product, result or capability to perform a service that is required to be produced to complete a process, phase or project."[33] Typically, these are tangible components completed to meet the objectives of a project, including project management plan elements. In the case of Direct and Manage Project Work process, deliverables include:

- Work performance data
    - Raw observations/measurements identified during the course of carrying out project work
    - Often considered to be the lowest level of detail from which information is derived by other processes
    - Gathered via work execution and passed on to the controlling processes for additional analysis
    - Examples include work completed, key performance indicators, technical performance measures, start/finish dates of scheduled activities, numbers of change requests and defects, actual costs and durations, etc.
- Change requests, which are formal proposals to "modify any document, deliverable or baseline" which, when approved, "will replace the associated document, deliverable or baseline and may result in an update to other parts of the project management plan."[34] These can be either direct or indirect, may be initiated internally or externally, can be optional or legally/contractually directed and might include:
    - Corrective action, an intentional activity done to realign project work performance with the project management plan
    - Preventive action completed to guarantee that future performance of project work is consistent with the project management plan
    - Defect repair done to modify a nonconforming product or a component of a product
- Updates, which are changes to formally controlled project documents, plans, etc. aimed at reflecting modified or additional ideas or content

---

[33] Ibid., p. 84
[34] Ibid., p. 85

- ✓ Project management plan updates, which may include changes to the scope, requirements, schedule, cost, quality, human resource, communications, risk, procurement and stakeholder management plans as well as the process improvement plan and project baselines
- ✓ Project documents updates, including (but not limited to) requirements documentation, project logs, risk register and stakeholder register.

Monitoring & Controlling Project Work

Monitor and Control Project Work is "the process of tracking, reviewing and reporting project progress against the performance objectives defined in the project management plan," the key advantage of which being that "it allows stakeholders to understand the current state of the project, the steps taken, and budget, schedule, and scope forecasts."[35]

Needless to say, monitoring, including the collection, measurement and distribution of performance information and assessment of measurements and trends to improve processes, is done throughout the course of a project. That provides insights into the health of the project and points out areas in need of special attention.

The concerns addressed in the Monitor and Control Project Work process include:

- o Comparing actual project performance against the project management plan
- o Assessing performance to determine if any corrective or preventative actions are warranted and then recommending those actions if necessary
- o Identifying new risks and analyzing, tracking and monitoring existing risks to ensure that they are identified, their status reported and that appropriate risk response plans are executed
- o Maintaining an accurate and timely information base centered on the project's product or products and documentation through project completion associated with them
- o Offering information that supports status reporting, progress measurement and forecasting
- o Providing forecasts that update current cost and schedule information
- o Monitoring approved changes' implementation as those changes occur
- o When the project is part of an overall program, providing program management with appropriate reporting on project progress and status

---

[35] Ibid., p. 86

Figure 5.4. **Monitor and Control Project Work: Inputs, Tools and Techniques, and Outputs**

Inputs	Tools & Techniques	Outputs
• Project management plan • Work performance reports • Change requests • Enterprise environmental factors • Organizational process assets	• Expert judgment • change control tools • Meetings	• Approved change requests • Project management plan updates • Project documents updates

Inputs

Project management plan
Because the monitoring and controlling project work process
encompasses every aspect of your project, subsidiary plans within the project management plan form the basis of that process. Those
plans and their baselines include (but aren't limited to):

- Scope management plan
- Requirements management plan
- Schedule management plan
- Cost management plan
- Quality management plan
- Process improvement plan
- Human resource management plan
- Communications management plan
- Risk management plan
- Procurement management plan
- Stakeholder management plan
- Scope, schedule and cost baselines

Schedule forecasts
Schedule forecasts are "estimates or predictions of conditions and events in the project's future based on information and knowledge available at the time of the forecast" that are "updated and reissued based on work performance information provided as the project is executed." Originating from progress against the schedule baseline and computed time estimate to complete (ETC), they are usually expressed in terms of schedule variance (SV) and schedule performance index (SPI). Variances against the anticipated finish dates and forecasted finish dates are provided for projects that are not using earned value management. The forecast may be utilized to learn if the project remains within defined tolerance ranges and to identify any necessary change requests.

Cost forecasts

Cost forecasts are "derived from progress against the cost baseline and computed estimates to complete (ETC)" and are "typically expressed in terms of cost variance (CV) and cost performance index."[36] A comparison between an estimate at completion (EAC) and the budget at completion (BAC) can reveal if the project has remained within tolerance ranges or if a change request is necessary. Variances against planned versus actual expenditures are provided for projects that are not using earned value management.

Validated changes

Approved changes emerging from the Perform Integrated Change Control process necessitate validation to certify that those changes were correctly implemented, the data for which is confirmed via a validated change.

Work performance information

Work performance information is the "performance data collected from various controlling processes, analyzed in context and integrated based on relationships across areas."[37] This is necessary as data itself is unusable in the decision-making process as it is out of context whereas the information gained from that data is both correlated and in context, thus providing a firm basis for project decisions. Examples include the status of deliverables, change request implementation status and forecast estimates that must be completed.

Enterprise environmental factors

Enterprise environmental factors affecting the Monitor and Control Project Work process include (but are not limited to):

- o Governmental or industry standards such as agency regulations, codes of conduct, and product, quality and workmanship standards
- o Organization work authorization systems
- o Stakeholder risk tolerances
- o Project management information system

Organizational process assets

Organizational process assets having an influence on the Monitor and Control Project Work process include (but are not limited to):

- o Organizational communication requirements
- o Financial controls procedures such as time reporting, required reviews of expenditures and disbursements, accounting codes and standard contract provisions
- o Issue and detect management procedures that define controls, identification and resolution and action item tracking
- o Change control procedures, including those for scope, schedule, cost and quality variances

---

[36] Ibid., p. 89
[37] Ibid., p. 90

- o Risk control procedures, which include risk categories, probability and impact definition and matrix
- o Process measurement database
- o Lessons learned database

Tools & Techniques

Expert judgment
Used in the Monitor and Control Project Work process to interpret the information provided via that process, expert judgment allows the project manager, in conjunction with the team, to determine what actions are necessary to guarantee that project performance matches expectations.

Analytical techniques
Founded on possible variations of project or environmental variables and their relationships with other variables, analytical techniques are utilized in project management to forecast potential outcomes. These include:
- o Regression analysis
- o Grouping methods
- o Causal analysis
- o Root cause analysis
- o Forecasting methods such as time series, scenario building, simulation, etc.
- o Failure mode and effect analysis (FMEA)
- o Fault tree analysis
- o Reserve analysis
- o Trend analysis
- o Earned value management
- o Variance analysis

Project management information system
The PMIS typically consists of automated tools to help track schedule, cost, performance, etc. It is an enterprise environmental factor and can include, among others, a work authorization system and a configuration management system.

Meetings
Meetings, which may include project team members, stakeholders and others involved in or affected by the project, may be face-to-face, virtual, formal or informal and can include user groups or review meetings.

Outputs

Change requests
If necessary following a comparison of planned to actual results, change requests may be made for the expansion, adjustment or reduction of project or product scope, quality requirements and schedule or cost baselines, which may require the collection and documentation of new requirements and that can affect the project management plan, project documents or product deliverables. Changes may include (but aren't limited to):

- Corrective action, an intentional activity aimed at realigning the performance of project work with the project management plan
- Preventive action, an intentional activity that ensures the future performance of the project work is aligned with the project management
- Defect repair, another intentional activity that modifies a nonconforming product or component of a product

Work performance reports
Work performance reports are "the physical or electronic representation of work performance information compiled in project documents, intended to generate decisions, actions or awareness, . . . that are a subset of project documents, which are intended to create awareness and generate decisions or actions."[38] Although work performance information can be communicated verbally, a physical/electronic representation of that information is necessary to record, store and, occasionally, distribute that information. Examples include status reports, memos, justifications, information notes, recommendations and updates.

Project management plan updates
Clearly, any changes identified during this process and after being processed through the appropriate change control process may very well affect the overall project management plan and lead to updates. Elements of the project management plan that may require updating include (but are not limited to) the:
- Scope management plan
- Requirements management plan
- Schedule management plan
- Cost management plan
- Quality management plan
- Scope baseline
- Schedule baseline
- Cost baseline

Project document updates
Schedule and cost forecasts, work performance reports and issue logs (and possibly others) are project documents that may be updated.

---

[38] Ibid., p. 93

Performing Integrated Change Control

Perform Integrated Change Control is "the process of reviewing all change requests; approving changes and managing changes to deliverables, organizational process assets, project documents, and the project management plan; and communicating their disposition."[39] Its most important benefit is that it permits the consideration of documented changes within the project in an integrated way while, at the same time, reducing project risk that can arise from changes that are made without considering overall project objectives or plans.

Figure 5.5. **Perform Integrated Change Control: Inputs, Tools and Techniques, and Outputs**

Inputs	Tools & Techniques	Outputs
• Project management plan • Work performance reports • Change requests • Enterprise environmental factors • Organizational process assets	• Expert judgment • change control tools • Meetings	• Approved change requests • Project management plan updates • Project documents updates

As with so many processes, the Performing Integrated Change Control process begins at the inception of the project and continues through its completion and is something for which the project manager is responsible. To ensure that only approved changes are incorporated into revised baselines, the project management plan, the project scope statement and other deliverables must be maintained via the careful and continuous management of changes, either by rejecting or approving them.

Any stakeholder can request a change and while this can be done verbally, changes must be recorded in writing and entered into the change management and/or configuration management system and are subject to the process outlined in those systems. Then, a responsible individual, most frequently the project sponsor or manager, must either approve or reject those documented change requests. When necessary, this process includes a change control board (CCB), a formally chartered group that is responsible for reviewing, evaluating, approving, delaying or rejecting project changes and for recording/communication their decisions. Once approved, change requests can become very complicated, necessitating new/revised:

- o Cost estimates
- o Activity sequences
- o Schedule dates
- o Resource requirements
- o Analysis of risk response alternatives

---

[39] Ibid., p. 94

These, in turn, will require adjustments in the project management plan and other project documents and the level of control that is utilized depends on the application and complexity of the specific project, contract requirements and the context and environment in which the project is performed.

Configuration control centers on both the deliverables' and processes' specifications; change control focuses on identifying, documenting and approving or rejecting changes to the project documents, deliverables or baselines. Configuration management activities[40] included in this process are:

- Configuration identification
    - ✓ Identification and selection of a configuration item to provide the basis for which the product configuration is defined and verified, products are labeled, changes are managed and accountability maintained.
- Configuration status accounting
    - ✓ Information is recorded and reported as to when appropriate data about the configuration item should be provided, which includes a listing of approved configuration identification, status of proposed changes to the configuration and the implementation status of approved changes.
- Configuration verification and audit
    - ✓ Certifies that the composition of a project's configuration items is correct and that corresponding changes are registered, assessed, approved, tracked and correctly implemented, which ensures the functional requirements defined in the configuration documentation have been met.

Figure 5.6. **Project Management Information System**

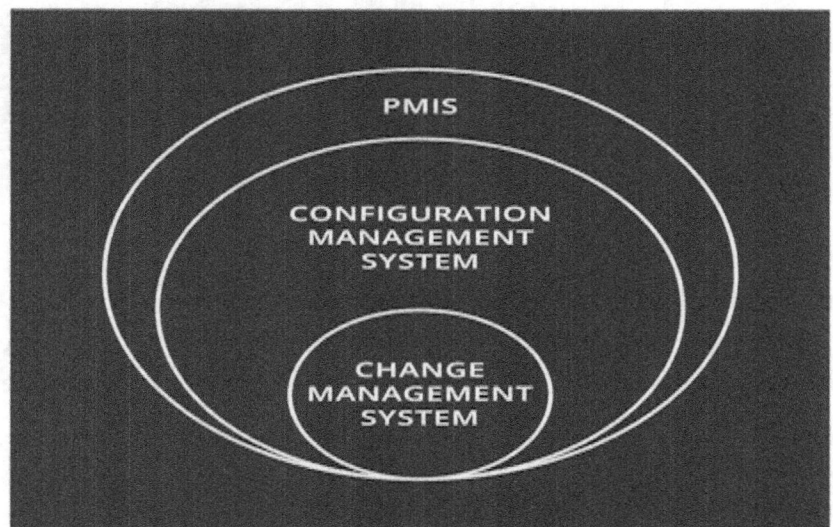

---

[40] Ibid., p. 96

Inputs

Project management plan

Elements of the project management plan utilized in this process comprise (but are not limited to):

- o Scope management plan containing scope change procedures
- o Scope baseline providing product definition
- o Change management plan providing the direction for managing the change control process and documenting the formal change control board

Work performance reports

Work performance reports of special interest here are resource availability, schedule and cost data, earned value management (EVM) reports and burnup or burndown charts.

Figure 5.7. **Burn Down/Burn Up Charts**

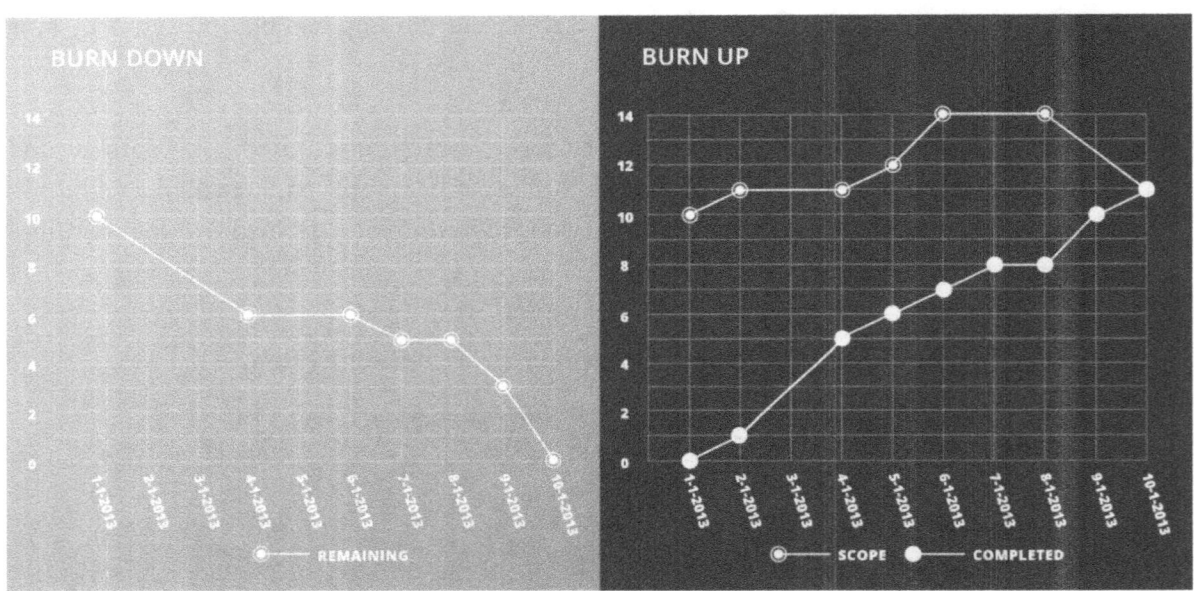

Change requests

Every Monitoring and Controlling process as well as the Executing processes have change requests as their outputs. While these may include corrective or preventative action or defect repairs, the first two normally do not affect project baselines, only the performance against those baselines.

Enterprise environmental factors

The sole enterprise environmental factor that can influence this process is the project management information system.

Organizational process assets

Organizational process assets that can affect the Perform Integrated Change Control process include (but are not limited to):

- o Change control procedures that include the steps involved in the modification of official organization standard, policies, plans and other project documents and the way in which any changes will be approved, validated and implemented
- o Procedures for approving and issuing change authorizations
- o Process measurement data utilized to collect and make available measurement data on processes and products
- o Project documents such as scope, cost and schedule baselines, project calendars and schedule network diagrams, risk registers, planned response actions and defined risk impact
- o Configuration management knowledge base comprising the versions and baselines of all official organization standards, policies, procedures and any project documents

Tools & Techniques

Expert judgment
As well as the team's expert judgment, stakeholders might be asked to provide their own expertise and to become part of the change control board (CCB), with that judgment and expertise being applied to any technical and management decisions. Further expertise may be provided by additional sources such as consultants, professional and technical associations, industry groups, subject matter experts and the project management office (PMO).

Meetings
Meetings in this context are usually referred to as change control meetings, which, when necessary, involve a change control board that is responsible for meeting and reviewing, approving or rejecting change requests as well as possibly reviewing configuration management activities. All CCB decisions are both documented and communicated to the stakeholders for information and follow-up actions.

Change control tools
Facilitation of configuration and change management may require the use of manual or automated tools, selection of those tools being based on stakeholders' needs, including organizational and environmental considerations and/or constraints.

Outputs

Approved change requests
The project manager, CCB or an assigned team member process change requests based on the change control system, with approved changes implemented via the Direct and Manage Project Work process. Whether approved or not, the disposition of all change requests are updated in the change log as part of project document updates.

Change logs
A change log is used to record changes occurring during a project and both the changes themselves and their impact as to time, cost and risk are communicated to the appropriate stakeholders. This includes capture on rejected change requests.

Project management plan updates
Any subsidiary plans and baselines that are subject to the formal change control process, as well as other possible elements, are updated. However, baseline changes should only show changes from the current time forward, which protects those baselines' integrity and past performance historical data.

Project documents updates
This is quite straightforward; every document subject to the project's formal change control process should be updated.

Close a Project or Phase
Close Project or Phase is the "process of finalizing all activities across all of the Project Management Process Groups to formally complete the project of phase."[41] Its primary benefit is that it affords lessons learned, the formal cessation of project work and the release of organization resources to allow the organization to undertake new endeavors.

During this process, the project manager ensures that all project work is completed and that the project has met its objectives by reviewing all prior information from the previous phase closures, as well as the scope baseline to confirm completion before the project is considered to be closed. In addition, this process establishes procedures to investigate and documents the reasons for actions taken if a project was, in fact, terminated prior to completion; to be successful, it is imperative that all appropriate stakeholders are engaged in the process. Planned activities necessary for the project or phase's administrative closure include:

- Actions and activities necessary to satisfy completion or exit criteria for the phase or project
- Actions and activities necessary to transfer the project's products, services or results to the next phase or to production and/or operations
- Activities needed to collect project or phase records, audit project success or failure, gather lessons learned and archive project information for the organization to use in the future

Figure 5.8. **Close Project or Phase: Inputs, Tools and Techniques, and Outputs**

Inputs	Tools & Techniques	Outputs
• Project management plan • Accepted deliverables • Organizational process assets	• Expert judgment • Analytical techniques • Meetings	• Final product, service or result transition • Organizational process assets updates

---

[41] Ibid., p. 100

Inputs

Project management plan
The project management plan transforms into the agreement between the project manager and project sponsor, thus serving to define what constitutes the completion of the project.

Accepted deliverables
Approved product specifications, delivery receipts and work performance documents are the accepted deliverables for the Close Project or Phase process; in the case of phased or cancelled projects, these sometimes include partial or interim deliverables as well. Accepted deliverables will be described in greater detail in the next chapter as part of the *Validate Scope* section.

Organizational process assets
These include (but are not limited to) project or phase closure guidelines or requirement (such as administrative procedures, project audits and evaluations, and transition criteria) and historical information and lessons learned knowledge base (such as project records and documents, all information and documentation pertaining to project closure, and information concerning the results of previous project selection decisions, project performance information and risk management activities).

Tools & Techniques

Expert judgment
Expert judgment applied to administrative closure activities ensures that these activities are performed to the appropriate standards and is available from a number of sources, including (but not limited to):

- Other project managers within the organization
- Project management office (PMO)
- Professional and technical associations

Analytical techniques
Analytical techniques used here include regression and trend analysis.

Meetings
No phase or process would be complete without meetings. In this process, meeting types include (but are not limited to) lessons learned, closeout, user groups and review meetings.

Outputs

Final product, service or result transition

Organizational process assets updates
These include (but are not limited to):

- Project files

- The close of a project requires a good deal of documentation of the activities undertaken over the course of the project:
  - The project management plan
  - Scope, cost, schedule and project calendars
  - Risk and other registers
  - Change management documentation
  - Planned risk response actions
  - Risk impact
- Project or phase closure documents
  - Formal documentation indicating completion of a project or phase and transfer of deliverables to others or to the next phase
  - With the goal of ensuring that project requirements have been completed, prior phase and customer acceptance documentation and, if applicable, the contract, are reviewed by the project manager. This would include documentation as to why a project was terminated in the case of those projects that were not completed and formal procedures concerning the transfer of the cancelled project's deliverables (both finished and incomplete) to others.

Historical information
Information on risks, techniques that worked well, and lessons learned

Test What You've Learned

1) Which, if any, of the following statements are true?
    a) Project managers are assigned following the development of the project charter.
    b) Project charters are considered to be firm contracts between the organization and the customer.
    c) The project statement of work is provided by the project sponsor.
    d) SOWs include a full description of any possible risks to the project.

2) What offers the information that will determine if undertaking a project is worth the investment it will require?
    a) The statement of work
    b) Enterprise environmental factors
    c) The project management plan
    d) The business case

3) Utilized throughout project integration process, _____ include(s) brainstorming and problem solving.
    a) Facilitation techniques
    b) Meetings
    c) Expert judgment
    d) The project management plan

4) _____ are scheduled and implemented by the project team and may be either corrective or preventative.
    a) Enterprise environmental factors
    b) Acknowledgements of defect(s)
    c) Approved change requests
    d) Organizational process assets

5) Standardized guidelines and work instructions are included in:
    a) Organizational process assets
    b) Project management information systems
    c) Work performance data
    d) Monitor & Control process deliverables

6) Which, if any, of the following statements are false?
    a) Preventative action is completed to realign project work performance with the project management plan.
    b) Work performance data are the raw observations made during the course of completing project work
    c) Project management plan updates can include the process development plan and project baselines.
    d) All of these statements are true.

7) Outputs of the Monitor and Control Project Work process include:
   a) Change requests
   b) Change log
   c) Change control tools
   d) Organizational process assets

8) _____ are updated and reissued based on work performance information provided as the project is executed.
   a) Project management plans
   b) Schedule forecasts
   c) Change requests
   d) Work performance reports

9) The Performing Integrated Change Control process is undertaken:
   a) At the beginning and end of a project.
   b) Only at the close of a project.
   c) Only at the inception of a project.
   d) Throughout the entire course of a project.

10) Which of these processes are in the order in which they are completed?
    a) Develop Project Charter, Develop Project Management Plan, Perform Integrated Change Control
    b) Develop Project Management Plan, Develop Project Charter, Monitor and Control Project Work
    c) Develop Project Charter, Develop Project Management Plan, Direct and Manage Project Execution
    d) Perform Integrated Change Control, Direct and Manage Project Execution, Close Project or Phase

Chapter 6: Project Scope Management

Project Scope Management

Project Scope Management comprises the processes necessary to ensuring the project includes all and only the work required to successfully complete that project and to prevent the incursion of scope creep or gold plating.

The PMBOK® Guide covers the terms product scope and project scope. Product scope is primarily the customer-centric features and functionality of a project's product, service or result. Project scope refers more to the work needed to be performed to deliver the project's product, service or result.

Plan Scope Management

Plan Scope Management is the "process of creating a scope management plan that documents how the project scope will be defined, validated, and controlled,"[42] the key benefit of which is that it offers guidance and direction as to the way in which scope will be managed over the course of the project.

Figure 6.1. Plan Scope Management: Inputs, Tools and Techniques, and Outputs

Inputs	Tools & Techniques	Outputs
• Project management plan • Project charter • Enterprise environmental factors • Organizational process assets	• Expert judgment • Meetings	• Scope management plan • Requirements management plan

Inputs

Project management plan

The project management plan was discussed in great detail in chapter 5. In the context of scope management, its approved subsidiary plans are utilized in the creation of the scope management plan and, in fact, have a strong influence on the tactics used to plan scope and manage project scope.

---

[42] Project Management Institute, *A Guide to the Project Management Body of Knowledge* (*The PMBOK® Guide*), 5th ed., p. 107.

Project charter
It is important to keep the project context in mind when creating the scope management plan; this is done through the use of the project charter, which provides the high-level project description as well as the characteristics of the product attained from the project statement of work.

Enterprise environmental factors
The Plan Scope Management process can be affected by enterprise environmental factors that include (but are not limited to):

- Organization's culture
- Infrastructure
- Personnel administration
- Marketplace conditions

Organizational process assets
Those assets that can impact the Plan Scope Management process include (but are not limited to) policies, procedures and the historical information and lessons learned knowledge base.

Tools & Techniques

Expert judgment
Experts with the right experience, knowledge and skills related to crafting scope management plans would be ideal candidates.

Meetings
The project manager, along with relevant stakeholders, may add value to developing the scope management plan via project meetings.

Outputs

Scope management plan
Just as the scope management plan is a component of either the project or program management plan, it comprises its own components, which include:

- The process aimed at preparing a detailed project scope statement
- The process enabling the creation of the WBS from the detailed project scope statement
- The process establishing the way in the WBS will be maintained and approved
- The process specifying the way in which formal acceptance of the completed project deliverables will be obtained
- The process that serves to control how changes to the detailed project scope statement are to be processed, which is directly connected to the Perform Integrated Change Control process.

Requirements management plan

A component of the project management plan describes the ways in which requirements will be analyzed, documented and managed. The most effective project relationship is typically chosen by the project manager, who documents this approach in the requirements management plan. Components include (but are not limited to):

- The way in which requirements activities are planned, tracked and reported
- Configuration management activities, for example,
    - ✓ How changes to the project will be initiated
    - ✓ How impacts will be analyzed, traced, tracked and reported
    - ✓ The authorization levels necessary to approving these changes
- Requirements prioritization process
- Product metrics used and the rationale for their use
- Traceability structure reflecting which requirement attributes will be captured on the traceability matrix.

Collect Requirements

Collect requirements is "the process of determining, documenting and managing stakeholder needs and requirements to meet project objectives,"[43] thus providing the foundation for defining and managing the project, and by extension, product scope.

Figure 6.2. **Collect Requirements: Inputs, Tools and Techniques, and Outputs**

Inputs	Tools & Techniques	Outputs
• Scope management plan • Requirements management plan • Stakeholder management plan • Stakeholder register	• Interviews • Focus groups • Facilitated workshops • Group creativity techniques • Group decision-making techniques • Questionnaires & surveys • Observations • Prototypes • Benchmarking • Context diagrams • Document analysis	• Requirements documentation • Requirements traceability matrix

This process demonstrates the importance of active stakeholder involvement in both the discovery and decomposition of needs into requirements and the care that must be taken in determining, documenting and managing what is required for the product, service or result of the project. Without this, no project will succeed.

---

[43] Ibid., p. 110

Those aforementioned requirements are comprised by the quantified and documented needs and expectations of the sponsor, customer and other stakeholders and must be sought, analyzed and recorded in sufficient detail to be included in the scope baseline and to be measurable following the inception of project execution. In time, requirements form the foundation of the WBS, specifically in terms of cost, schedule, quality planning and occasionally, procurement.

Requirements are frequently categorized into different types; examples include business (referring to stakeholder needs) and technical (referring to how those needs are implemented) solutions.

As requirements are expanded upon, they can be placed into classifications that allow for additional refinement and detail; these include:

- Business requirements
    - Describe the higher-level needs of the entire organization, e.g., business issues/opportunities and reasons for undertaking the project
- Stakeholder requirements
- Solution requirements
    - The product's, service's or result's features, functions and characteristics that will meet the business or stakeholder requirements
    - These can be further delineated into:
        - Functional requirements (processes, data and interaction with the product) that describe the product's behavior
        - Nonfunctional requirements that supplement those that are functional and describe the conditions or qualities necessary for the product to be effective (reliability, security, performance, safety, level of service, supportability, retention/purge, etc.)
- Transition requirements designate temporary capabilities (data conversion and training requirements) necessary to transitioning from the current "as-is" state to the future "to-be" state
- Project requirements describing the actions, processes or other conditions the project must meet
- Quality requirements capturing conditions and criteria needed to validate a project deliverable's successful completion or achievement of other project requirements.

Inputs

Scope management plan
This offers clarity in the way in which project teams will decide which type of requirements must be collected for the project.

Requirements management plan
This includes the processes to be utilized throughout the Collect Requirements process to define and document the needs of stakeholders.

Stakeholder management plan
To assess and adapt to the level of stakeholder participation in requirement activities, this plan is used to understand their communication requirements and their level of engagement.

Project charter
This provides product's, service's or result's high-level description to allow for the development of detailed requirements.

Stakeholder register
This register identifies stakeholders capable of providing information on the requirements and, in addition, captures stakeholders' major requirements and main expectations for the project.

Tools & Techniques

Interviews
By interviewing project stakeholders the project manager and his or her team are able to identify requirements and elicit other relevant information. Interviews can be conducted formally or informally with an individual or group of participants. Options include conducting interviews in person, over the phone, via email, or leveraging communications technologies such as VOIP.

Focus groups
Focus groups are guided by trained moderators and bring prequalified stakeholders and subject matter experts together to determine their expectations of and attitudes about a product, service or result that has been proposed. The discussion is interactive and is designed to be more conversational than a simple one-on-one interview. Focus groups enable the project team to gather requirements for a population by reaching out to a sample of the intended audience.

Facilitated workshops
These are focused sessions bringing key stakeholders together with the goal of defining product requirements and are thought to be a primary technique to define cross-functional requirements and to reconcile stakeholder differences. An increase in stakeholder agreement can be attained by building trust, fostering relationships and improving communication among the participants.

One example of a facilitated workshop that is particularly popular in agile software development projects is a joint application design/development (JAD) session. JAD sessions help resolve any difficulties or differences between the interested parties.

Another term typically associated with agile projects is user stories. User stories are concise descriptions written in business language of what a user does or needs from a project solution.

A popular facilitated workshop technique in the manufacturing world is Quality Function Deployment (QFD), originally developed by Dr. Yoji Akao in Japan in the 1960s. QFD focuses on converting qualitative requirements into quantitative characteristics for a new or existing product or service. In QFD, the voice of the customer (VOC) is initially gathered and then transformed into a prioritized list of objective characteristics.

Group creativity techniques
  - Brainstorming, where participants are encouraged to generate ideas spontaneously
  - Nominal group technique, which enhances brainstorming with a voting process that ranks ideas by usefulness, allowing them to be used for further brainstorming or for prioritization
  - Idea/mind mapping, through which ideas emerging from brainstorming sessions are consolidated into a single map reflecting commonality and differences and intended to generate new ideas

Figure 6.3. **Mind Mapping**

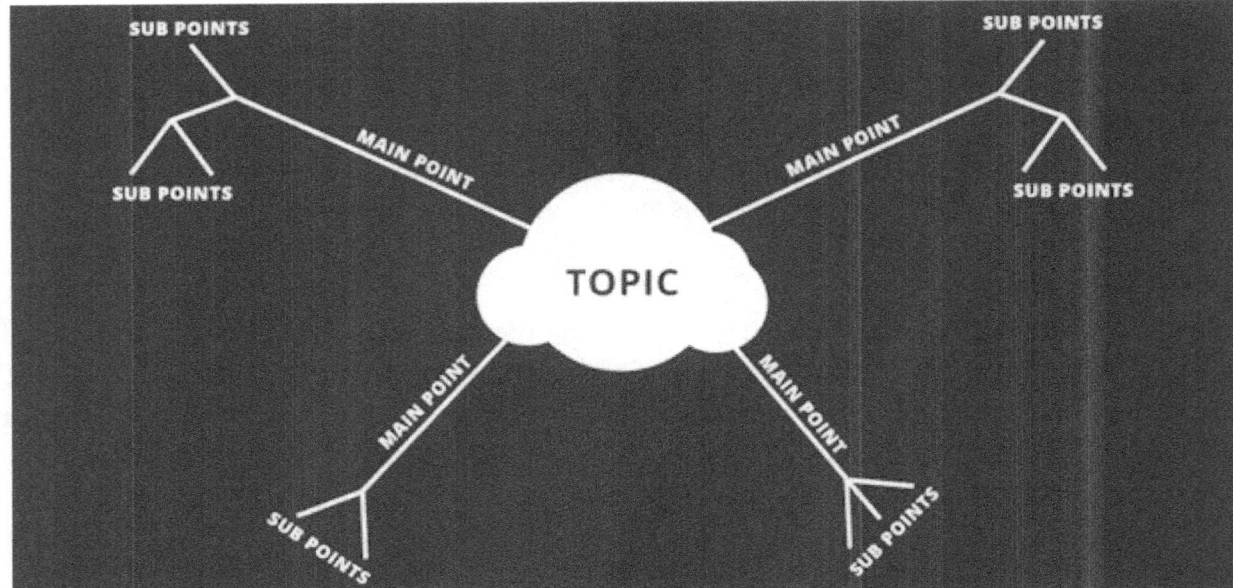

  - Affinity diagram, which permits large numbers of ideas to be classified into groups for review and analysis

Figure 6.4. **Affinity Diagram**

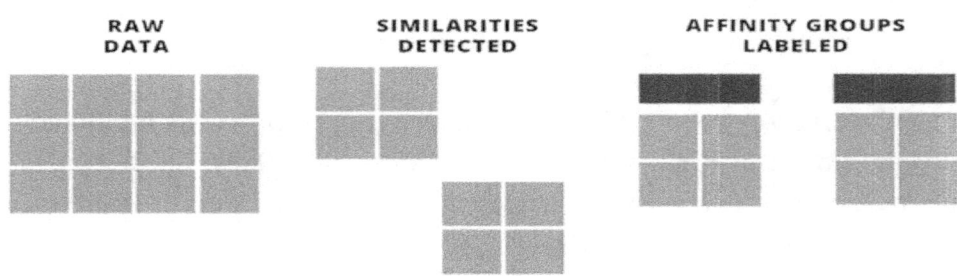

- o Multicriteria decision analysis, which utilizes a decision matrix with the aim of providing a systematic analytic approach to set criteria (risk levels, uncertainty, valuation) to evaluate and rank a number of ideas

Group decision-making techniques
These methods of reaching a group decision can be applied to the group creativity techniques and include:
- o Unanimity
- o Majority
- o Plurality
- o Dictatorship

Questionnaires and surveys
These are appropriate for use when the audience is varied, widely dispersed, a quick turnaround is necessary and wherein statistical analysis is appropriate. Questions can be open-ended or closed-ended.

Observation
Observations are valuable in understanding how a process currently works, as well as the current challenges that need to be overcome. It is also known as job shadowing.

Prototypes
Prototyping is a means of gaining early feedback on requirements via providing a working model of a product prior to it actually being constructed. This can also be done in the form of a storyboard, which is a prototyping technique showing a sequence or navigation through a series of images that is used in a variety of projects in industries such as film, advertising, instructional design and on agile and other software development projects.

Benchmarking
Benchmarking is comprised of comparisons of actual or planned processes to those of comparable internal or external organizations for the identification of best practices, generation of improvement ideas and to provide a basis for performance measurement.

Context diagrams
Context diagrams are examples of scope models and provide a visual depiction of the product scope by showing a business system (such as a process, equipment, etc.) and the way in which people and other actors (systems) interact with it.

Document analysis
This form of input is utilized to elicit requirements through analysis of existing documentation and the identification of information that is relevant to the requirements. Documents analyzed include (but are not limited to) business plans, marketing literature, agreements, requests for proposals, current process flows, logical data models, use cases, etc.

Outputs

Requirements documentation

This process output indicates the way in which individual requirements meet the project's business need, which may initiate at a high level and progressively become more detailed as more information about the requirements is known. Prior to being baselined, these requirements must be:

- Unambiguous (meaning they are both measureable and testable)
- Traceable
- Complete
- Consistent
- Acceptable to stakeholders

The acronym SMART can be used to establish clear objectives.

Figure 6.5. **Project Objective - "SMART"**

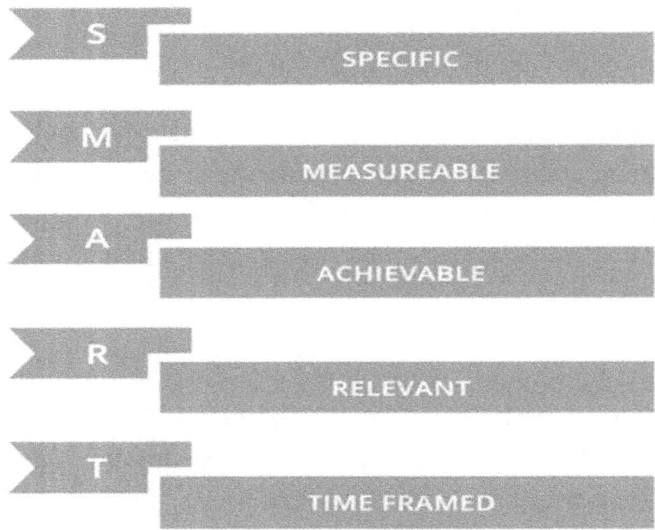

Formats can be simple, merely listing all the requirements categorized by stakeholder and priority, or more elaborate, including an executive summary, detailed descriptions and attachments.

Components include (but are not limited to):

- Business requirements (business/project objectives for traceability, rules for the performing organization and the organization's guiding principles)
- Stakeholder requirements (impacts to other organizational areas and to other internal or external entities, and stakeholder communication and reporting)
- Solution requirements (functional and nonfunctional, technology and standard compliance, support and training, quality, and reporting requirements)
- Project requirements (levels of service, safety, compliance, etc. and acceptance criteria)
- Transition requirements
- Requirements assumptions, dependencies and constraints

Requirements traceability matrix

This matrix is a "grid that links products requirements form their origin to the deliverables that satisfy them,"[44] implementation of which assists in ensuring that every requirement contributes business value by connecting it with the business and project deliverables. The traceability matrix also:

- o Provides a way to track requirements throughout the project life cycle, ensuring that, at the end of the project, approved requirements are delivered
- o Provides a structure for the management of changes to the product scope
- o Includes (but is not limited to) tracing requirements for:
    - ✓ Business needs, opportunities, goals and objectives
    - ✓ Project objectives, scope/WBD deliverables
    - ✓ Product design and development
    - ✓ Test strategy and scenarios
    - ✓ High-level requirements to more detailed requirements

Each requirements' attributes can be recorded in this matrix, including a unique identifier, a textual description of the requirement, rationale for inclusion, owner, source, priority, version, current status (active, cancelled, deferred, approved, assigned, completed) and status date, as well as those related to stakeholders' satisfaction, such as stability, complexity and acceptance criteria.

Define Scope

Define Scope is "the process of developing a detailed description of the project and product . . . by defining which of the requirements collected will be included in and excluded from the project scope"[45] following selection of the final product requirements from the requirements documentation gleaned from the Collect Requirements process.

This process is critical to project success, building on the major deliverables, assumptions and constraints documented at the time of project initiation. It is highly iterative. In iterative life cycle projects, a high-level vision is developed for the overall project first. Then detailed scope is established one iteration at a time with the detailed planning for the next iteration done as work progresses on the current project scope and deliverables. This is known as rolling wave planning.

Figure 6.6. **Define Scope: Inputs, Tools and Techniques, and Outputs**

Inputs	Tools & Techniques	Outputs
• Scope management plan • Requirements documentation • Organizational process assets	• Expert judgment • Product analysis • Alternatives generation • Facilitated workshops	• Project scope statement • Project documents updates

---

[44] Ibid., p. 118
[45] Ibid., p. 120

Inputs

Scope management plan
A component of the project management plan, this plan institutes the activities involved in developing, monitoring and controlling project scope.

Project charter
The project charter, besides being the formal authorization for the project, provides a high level description of the project's product, service or result. This charter is the foundation for the project scope statement.

Requirements documentation
The Define Scope process takes requirements documentation and expands it into a more detailed project scope statement.

Organizational process assets
Organizational process assets have an influence on the way in which scope is defined; some examples include policies, procedures and templates for a project scope statement, project files from previous projects and lessons learned from previous phases and projects.

Tools & Techniques

Expert judgment
Experts play a critical role in better understanding the information required to develop the project scope statement. Depending on the project scope, experts may come from a technical background, provide subject matter expertise, or other experts internal or external to the organization.

Product analysis
Product analysis is used as a tool only when the project deliverable will be a product rather than a service or a result. Techniques for product analysis include product breakdown, system or requirements analysis, systems or value engineering, reverse engineering and value analysis.

Alternatives generation
As the name suggests, alternatives generation involves the development of as many conceivable options as feasible with the goal of identifying a variety of approaches to the tasks of executing and performing project work. This can be accomplished through brainstorming, lateral thinking and analysis of alternatives, among others.

Facilitated workshops
Facilitated workshops helps a cross-functional group reach a common set of scope requirements.

Outputs

Project scope statement

This output provides a description of the project scope, the project's major deliverables, assumptions and constraints. It documents both the project and product scope. The project's deliverables as well as the work necessary to creating those deliverables are laid out in detail. Further, the project scope statement offers a common understanding of the project scope among stakeholders, possibly including specific scope exclusions that can be useful in managing stakeholder expectations.

The project scope statement facilitates the project team's ability to do more detailed planning, guiding their work during execution and providing a baseline for the evaluation of what, in terms of requests for changes or additional work, falls within or outside the project's boundaries.

Both the degree and level of detail used in the project scope statement to define the work performed or excluded will affect how well the project team controls overall project scope. The following outlines the information that is included in the project scope statement, directly or via reference to other documents:

- Product scope description
    - Adds progressively more detail to the characteristics of the product, service or result described in the project charter and the requirements documentation
- Acceptance criteria
    - The set of conditions that must be met prior to the deliverables being accepted
- Deliverable
    - As discussed previously, a deliverable, which, in this context, can be described at a summary level or in detail, is "any unique and verifiable product, result, or capability that is required to be produced to complete a process, phase or project"[46] and may include additional results, e.g., project management results and documentation.
- Project exclusion
    - Most frequently notes what is excluded from the project, thus assisting in the management of stakeholders' expectations
- Constraints
    - Limiting factors that will affect the execution of a project or process As identified in the project scope statement list, describe specific internal/external restrictions or limitations related to project scope, e.g., predefined budgets or any imposed dates or scheduled milestones set by the customer or performing organization
    - With an agreement in place, contractual provisions are generally constraints.
- Assumptions
    - Factors in a planning process considered to true, real or certain without a need for proof or demonstration which also describe those factors' potential impact should they prove to be false

---

[46] Ibid., p. 123

✓ May be listed in either the project scope statement or a separate log

It is important to understand that while the project charter and the project scope statement may be thought to be somewhat redundant, they differ in terms of their level of detail, with the project charter comprising high-level information and the project scope statement containing a detailed description of the scope elements.

A formal approved project scope statement is one step in mitigating scope creep. Scope creep can result in uncontrolled changes that may introduce significant risks to the project. The project scope statement also helps minimize gold plating. Gold plating refers to the addition of features and functionality by the project team beyond the approved project scope. To reduce confusion, table 6.1 provides the key elements found in each document.

Table 6.1. **Elements of the Project Charter and Project Scope Statement**

Project Charter	Project Scope Statement
Project purpose or justification	Project scope description (progressively elaborated)
Measureable project objectives and related success criteria	Acceptance criteria
High-level requirements	Project deliverables
High-level project description	Project exclusions
High-level risks	Project constraints
Summary milestone schedule	Project assumptions
Summary budget	
Stakeholder list	
Project approval requirements (what constitutes success, who decides it, who signs off)	
Assigned project manager, responsibility and authority level	
Name and authority of the sponsor or other person(s) authorizing the project charter	

Project documents updates
Project documents updated for the Define Scope process include (but are not limited to) the stakeholder register, requirements documentation and the requirements traceability matrix.

Create WBS
Create WBS is "the process of subdividing project deliverables and project work into smaller, more manageable components," with the key benefit being that its creation offers a structured vision of what is to be delivered by the project. As an hierarchical decomposition of the complete scope of the work necessary to accomplish project objectives and produce the deliverables required, this process both

organizes and defines the project's total scope and is representative of the work indicated in the current approved project scope statement. The WBS becomes an excellent communication tool for project stakeholders.

Work packages, which are the lowest level of WBS components and can be utilized to group activities whereby work is scheduled, estimated, monitored and controlled, contain the planned work. Remember that in this context, 'work' refers to work products and deliverables resulting from activities rather than the activities themselves.

Figure 6.7. **Create WBS: Inputs, Tools and Techniques, and Outputs**

Inputs	Tools & Techniques	Outputs
• Scope management plan • Project scope statement • Requirements documentation • Organizational process assets • Enterprise environmental factors	• Expert judgment • Decomposition	• Scope baseline • Project documents updates

Inputs

Scope management plan
As part of this process, the scope management plan explains the way in which the WBS is created from the detailed project scope statement and how it will be maintained and approved.

Project scope statement
The project scope statement gives direction on what is included, as well as excluded, in the project scope.

Requirements documentation
This outlines what requirements the project needs to deliver.

Enterprise environmental factors
To create the WBS, WBS standards specific to your industry and relevant to the nature of the project can serve as external reference sources.

Organizational process assets
In the context of the Create WBS process, relevant organizational process assets include (but are not limited to) policies, procedures and templates for the WBS and project files and lessons learned from previous projects.

Tools & Techniques

Decomposition

Decomposition is a "technique used for dividing and subdividing the project scope and project deliverables into smaller, more manageable parts,"[47] which are frequently work packages. Decomposition into work packages is usually comprised of:

- Identifying and analyzing the deliverables and related work
- Structuring and organizing the WBS
- Decomposing the upper WBS levels into lower-level detailed components
- Creating and assigning identification codes to those components
- Ascertaining that the degree of deliverable decomposition is appropriate

Expert judgment

- Frequently utilized to analyze the information necessary to decomposing deliverables into smaller components with the goal of creating an effective WBS
- Applied to the project scope's technical details to resolve differences in opinion as to the best way to break down the overall scope of the project
- Also available in the form of predefined templates, either industry- or discipline-specific, offering guidance as how common deliverables can be most effectively broken down

Structuring a WBS

There are several approaches to structuring a WBS; popular methods include the top-down approach, using organizational guidelines and the utilization of WBS templates. To integrate the subcomponents, a bottom-up approach can be used.

There are a number of forms by which this structure can be represented:

- Using phases of the project life cycle as the second level of decomposition, inserting the product and project deliverables at the third level
- Employing major deliverables as the second level of decomposition
- Integrating subcomponents that may be developed by organizations external to the project team, e.g., contracted work, with the seller then developing the supporting contract WBS as part of the contracted work

---

[47] Ibid., p. 128

Figure 6.8. **Structuring a WBS**

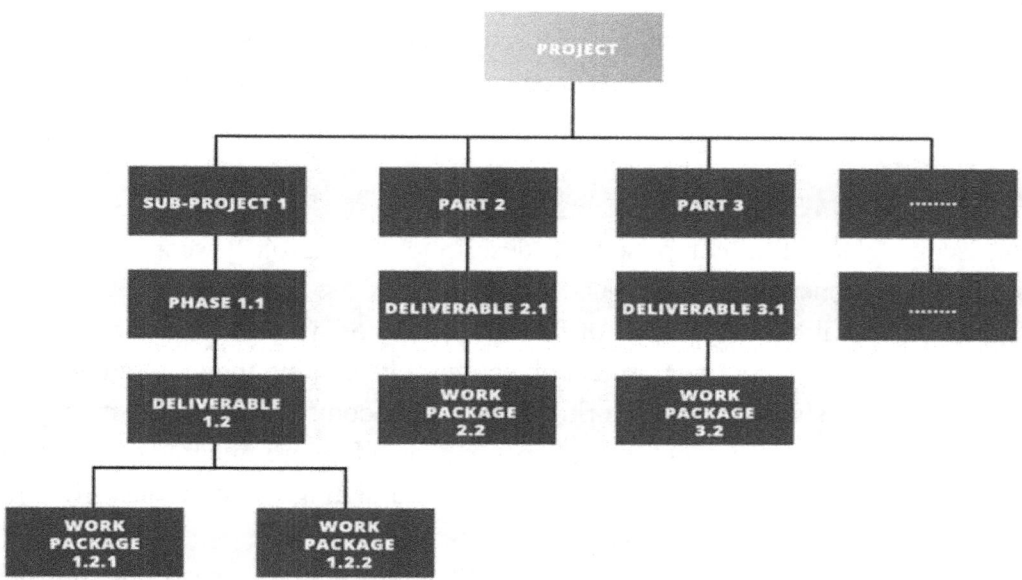

To decompose upper-level WBS components, the work must be subdivided into its most basic elements for each of the deliverables or subcomponents, whereby the WBS components represent verifiable products. To confirm that the decomposition is correct, be sure that the lower-level WBS components are both necessary and sufficient to complete the corresponding higher-level deliverables. Also keep in mind that different deliverables can have different levels of decomposition; arriving at a work package requires that work for some deliverables needs only to be decomposed to the next levels while others will require additional levels. While it is true that the decomposition of the work to greater levels of detail increases the ability to plan, manage and control the work, too much can lead to management effort that is nonproductive, a use of resources and performance of work that are inefficient and problems with aggregating data over different levels of the WBS.

Further, decomposition may be impossible for deliverables or subcomponents to be done in the future, with the project team usually waiting until agreement has been reached on the deliverable or subcomponent to allow the details of the WBS to be developed, which is sometimes called rolling wave planning.

Each work package should be assigned a unique identifier, known as a WBS ID or Code of Accounts.

Another issue involves what is termed the '100 percent rule,' meaning that since the WBS represents all product and project work (including that of the project manager and the project team), the "total of the work at the lowest levels should roll up to the higher levels so that nothing is left out and no extra work is performed."[48]

---

[48] Ibid., p. 131

Outputs

Scope baseline
The scope baseline is the "approved version of a scope statement, work breakdown structure (WBS), and its associated WBS dictionary."[49] Used as a basis for monitoring and control, it can only be altered by using formal change control procedures.

Its components include:
- Project scope statement, comprised of descriptions of project scope, major deliverables, assumptions and constraints
- WBS, a hierarchical decomposition of the total scope of work to be completed by the project team with the goals of achieving project objectives and creating the required deliverables
    - Finalized by assigning every work package to a control account (a management control point at which scope, budget, actual cost and schedule are integrated and assessed against the earned value for performance measure) and setting a unique identifier for that work package from a code of accounts
- WBS dictionary, a document providing detailed information concerning the deliverable(s), activity and scheduling for each component of the WBS, information that may include (but is not limited to):
    - Code of account identifier
    - Description of work
    - Assumptions and constraints
    - Responsible organization
    - Schedule milestones
    - Associated schedule activities
    - Required resources
    - Cost estimates
    - Quality requirements
    - Acceptance criteria
    - Technical references
    - Agreement information

Project documents updates
These updates may include (but are not limited to)) requirements documentation, updated to incorporate any approved changes.

Validate Scope
Validate scope is the "process of formalizing acceptance of the completed project deliverables,"[50] the key benefits of which are twofold in that it brings objectivity to the acceptance process and, by validating each deliverable, increases the possibility that the final product, service or result will be accepted.

---

[49] Ibid., p. 131

[50] Ibid., p. 133

Obtained via the Control Quality process, deliverables that have been verified are then reviewed with the customer or sponsor with the goal of ensuring they have been completed to their satisfaction and that the customer or sponsor have formally accepted them.

Validation and acceptance are based on outputs obtained via the Planning processes in the Project Scope Management Knowledge Area, e.g., the requirements documentation or the scope baseline, in addition to the work performance data gained from the Executing processes in other Knowledge Areas.

It is important to note that the Validate Scope process contrasts with the Control Quality process in that the former is largely concerned with the acceptance of deliverables whereas Control Quality centers on the correctness of those deliverables and meeting those deliverables' specified quality requirements. Control Quality is usually performed prior to Validate Scope (although they may be performed in parallel).

Figure 6.8. **Validate Scope: Inputs, Tools and Techniques, and Outputs**

Inputs	Tools & Techniques	Outputs
• Project management plan • Requirements documentation • Requirements traceability matrix • Verified deliverables • Work performance data	• Inspection • Group decision-making techniques	• Accepted deliverables • Change requests • Work performance information • Project documents updates

Inputs

Project management plan
The aspects of the project management plan that serve as inputs to the Validate Scope process include the scope management plan and the scope baseline.

Requirements documentation
Requirements documentation includes the acceptance criteria.

Requirements Traceability Matrix
Requirements traceability matrix keeps a trail of the source of each requirement. It also traces progress throughout the project life cycle.

Verified deliverables
Inputs are completed project deliverables, the correctness of which has been checked as part of the Control Quality process.

Work performance data
Work performance data serving as inputs to this process can consist of the degree of compliance with requirements, the number and severity of nonconformities, or the number of validation cycles performed within a period of time.

Tools & Techniques

Inspection
Sometimes referred to as reviews, product reviews, audits and walkthroughs (although, in certain application areas, the meanings of these terms are unique and specific), this tool includes such activities as measuring, examining and validating with the goal of determining if work and deliverables meet requirements and project acceptance criteria.

Group decision-making techniques
Along with the group decision-making techniques listed in Control Requirements, Delphi technique can also be used. The Delphi technique collects the opinion of experts in an anonymous manner to avoid the bandwagon effect (also known as the halo effect or groupthink).

Outputs

Accepted deliverables
As deliverables meet the acceptance criteria, they are formally signed off and approved by the customer or sponsor, after which formal documentation from the customer or sponsor that acknowledges formal stakeholder acceptance is forwarded to the Close Project or Phase process.

Change requests
Documentation must be done of the completed deliverables not formally accepted, in addition to the reasons for that non-acceptance. In that case, a change request for defect repair may be necessary and should be processed for review and disposition through the Perform Integrated Change Control process.

Work performance information
This includes information concerning project progress, e.g., which deliverables have begun, their progress, which have been completed and which have been accepted. This information should be forwarded to stakeholders.

Project documents updates
This includes documents that define the product or report the status of product completion and require approval from the customer or sponsor via signatures or signoffs.

Control Scope

Control scope is the "process of monitoring the status of the project and product scope and managing changes to the scope baseline,"[51] with the main benefit of allowing that baseline to be maintained over the entire course of the project.

This process guarantees that all of the requested changes and corrective or preventative actions that have been suggested are handled through the Perform Integrated Change Control process. In addition, Control Scope is utilized in the management of the actual changes as they occur and is integrated with the other control processes.

If scope is not monitored and regulated, scope creep and gold plating can occur. Scope creep and gold plating can result in the uncontrolled expansion of product or project scope without appropriate adjustments to constraints such as time, cost and resources. However, it should be kept in mind that change is unavoidable; that being the case, some form of change control process is vital to every project.

Figure 6.9. Control Scope: Inputs, Tools and Techniques, and Outputs

Inputs	Tools & Techniques	Outputs
• Project management plan • Requirements documentation • Requirements traceability matrix • Work performance data • Organizational process assets	• Variance analysis	• Work performance information • Change requests • Project management plan updates • Project documents updates • Organizational process assets updates

Inputs

Project management plan, including information concerning:

- o Scope baseline compared to actual results to learn if there are necessary changes to be made and/or corrective or preventive actions to be taken
- o Scope management plan
- o Change management plan
- o Configuration management plan, defining items that are configurable or that require formal change control and the process to control changes to those items
- o Requirements management plan

---

[51] Ibid., p. 136

Requirements documentation
Requirements documentation is used to identify any anomalies from the defined project scope.

Requirements traceability matrix
Requirements traceability matrix traces any changes from the scope baseline.

Work performance data, which can comprise:
- The number of change requests received and/or accepted
- The number of deliverables completed, etc.

Organizational process assets, which may include (but are not limited to):
- Existing formal and informal scope
- Control-related policies, procedures and guidelines
- Monitoring and reporting methods and templates to be utilized.

Tools & Techniques

Variance analysis
Variance analysis is a technique utilized in the determination of the cause and degree of difference between the baseline and actual performance. In the case of Control Scope, this includes establishing the cause and effect of variance relative to the scope baseline and determining if it is necessary to take corrective or preventative action.

Outputs

Work performance information
As part of the Control Scope process, correlated and contextualized information concerning the way in which project scope is performing as compared to the scope baseline is produced, which will serve as the foundation for making decisions about scope. This can include:

- Categories of the changes received
- The identified scope variances and their causes
- How those variances impact schedule or cost
- The forecast of the future scope performance

Change requests
These include change requests to the scope baseline or other project management plan components and can be the result of an analysis of scope performance. They can include requests to take preventive or corrective actions, defect repairs defects or enhancements. These are all processed for review and disposition as established by the Perform Integrated Change Control process.

Project management plan updates

These updates may include (but are not limited to):

- Scope baseline updates, which means that, due to the approval of change requests, revisions to the scope statement, the WBS and the WBS dictionary must be made and those items must be reissued, all through the Perform Integrated Change Control process
- Other baseline updates, required if the approved change requests affect the project beyond its scope and involve revision and reissuance of the corresponding cost and schedule baselines to reflect those approved changes

Project documents updates

These may include (but are not limited to) requirements documentation and the requirements traceability matrix.

Organizational process assets updates

These may include (but are not limited to) causes of variances, corrective action selected and the reasons for that choice and other types of lessons learned from Project Scope Control.

Test What You've Learned

1) The work performed to deliver a product, service or result with the features and functions that have been specified is the _____.
   a) Product scope
   b) Project scope
   c) Scope management
   d) Affinity diagram

2) Enterprise environmental factors that can affect the Plan Scope Management process include:
   a) Governmental and industry standards or regulations
   b) Project management information system
   c) Infrastructure
   d) Stakeholder risk tolerances

3) _____ provides the foundation for defining and managing the project, including product scope.
   a) Collect Requirements
   b) Plan Scope Management
   c) Document analysis
   d) Define Scope

4) Which, if any, of the following statements is true?
   a) Systems engineering is a technique used when the deliverable is a service.
   b) Product analysis involves the generation of as many options are available to execute a project.
   c) One element of the project scope statement is project exclusion, which helps to manage stakeholder expectations.
   d) In the context of project management, "work" refers to the activities involved in producing a deliverable.

5) _____ is the process of subdividing project deliverables and project work into smaller, easier to manage components.
   a) Work packaging
   b) Create WBS
   c) Decomposition
   d) Scope baselining

6) What is defined as a technique utilized to divide and subdivide project scope and deliverables into smaller, more manageable parts?
   a) Top-down approach
   b) Bottom-up approach

c) 100 percent rule
   d) Decomposition

7) Tools utilized in the Validate Scope process include:
   a) Requirements traceability matrix
   b) Work performance information
   c) Inspection
   d) Project documents updating

8) In the Control Scope process, work performance information includes:
   a) Forecast of future scope performance
   b) Control-related policies, procedures and guidelines
   c) Impact of variances on schedule and cost
   d) Change requests

9) Frequently, _____ is used in the analysis of information necessary to decomposing deliverables into smaller components when creating a WBS.
   a) Expert judgment
   b) Enterprise environmental factors
   c) Organizational assets
   d) Decomposition

10) Acceptance criteria is included in the:
    a) Project charter
    b) WBS dictionary
    c) Project scope statement
    d) Product analysis

Chapter 7: Project Time Management

As its title suggests, Project Time Management encompasses "all of the processes necessary to managing the timely completion of a project."[52] This includes establishing and controlling the project schedule, defining and sequencing activities, estimating activity resources and duration and developing and controlling the project ⁱschedule model and plan.

Figure 7.1. **Scheduling Overview**[53]

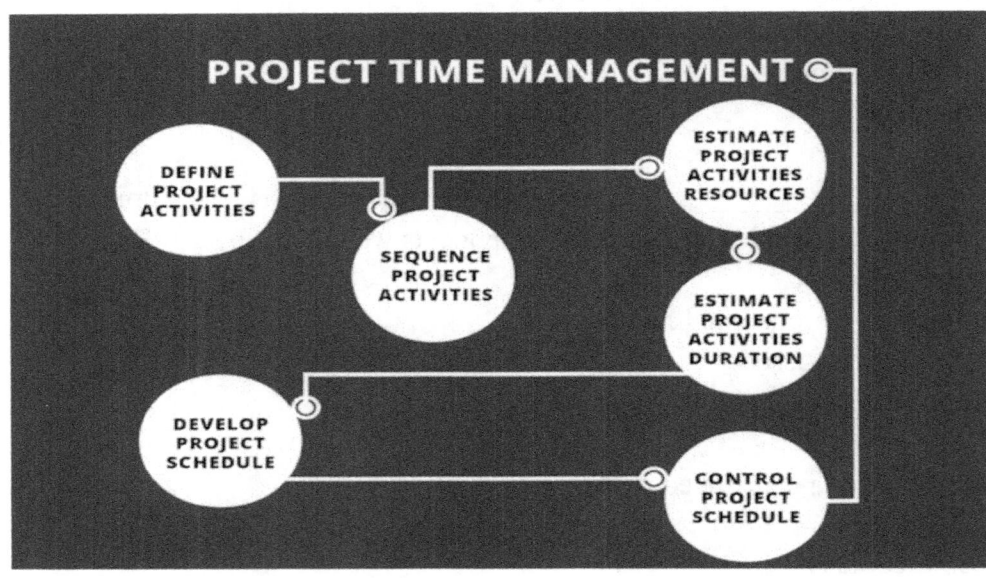

The PMBOK® Guide places great emphasis on differentiating between the project schedule presentation (schedule) and the schedule data and calculations that produce the project schedule. It notes that doing so is easier if one references the scheduling tool populated with project data as the schedule model. A schedule model is a "representation of the plan for executing the project's activities including durations, dependencies, and other planning information, used to produce project schedules along with other scheduling artifacts."[54]

All of the Project Time Management processes, along with their associated tools and techniques, are recorded in the schedule management plan, a subsidiary plan of and fully integrated with the project management plan via something we have already discussed, the Develop Project Management Plan process in the Project Integration Management Knowledge Area.

---

[52] Project Management Institute, *A Guide to the Project Management Body of Knowledge* (*The PMBOK® Guide*), 5th ed., p. 142.
[53] Kurt Englmeier, "Time, Cost & Quality Management," http://wiki.fh-sm.de/PmTimeCostQuality

[54] Ibid., p. 145

Plan Schedule Management

Plan Schedule Management is the "process of establishing the policies, procedures, and documentation for planning, developing, managing, executing, and controlling the project schedule,"[55] the key benefit of which is that it offers guidance and direction as to the way the project schedule will be managed over the course of the project.

As a component of the project management plan, the schedule management plan can be written in a variety of ways – formal or informal, highly detailed or in broad strokes – centered on the requirements of the project and including control thresholds appropriate to that project. The schedule management plan provides a definition of the way in which schedule contingencies will be reported and assessed. It can be updated if there is a change in how the schedule is managed. It also serves as a major input into the Develop Project Management Plan process.

Figure 7.2. **Plan Schedule Management: Inputs, Tools and Techniques, and Outputs**

Inputs	Tools & Techniques	Outputs
• Project management plan • Project charter • Enterprise environmental factors • Organizational process assets	• Expert judgment • Analytical techniques • Meetings	• Schedule management plan

Inputs

Project management plan

This input holds information used in the development of the schedule management plan, including (but not limited to) the scope baseline comprising the project scope statement, work breakdown structure (WBS) and WBS dictionary. These details are used to define activities, estimate duration, as well as other information concerning other scheduling-related cost, risk and communication decisions derived from the project management plan in the course of developing the schedule.

Project charter

In the case of this process, the project charter provides the definition of the summary milestones schedule and the project approval requirements that will affect project schedule management.

Enterprise environmental factors

These comprise (but are not limited to):
- o Organizational culture and structure

---

[55] Ibid., p. 145

- o   Availability of resources and skills
- o   Project management software, which provides the scheduling tool and alternative options for managing the schedule
- o   Published commercial information, e.g., resource productivity information that is frequently available from commercial databases
- o   Organizational work authorization systems

Tools & Techniques

Expert judgment
Expert judgment is valuable in providing guidance on how best to manage the schedule based on prior experience, historical information and industry trends.

Analytical techniques
Choosing strategic options with which to estimate and schedule the project may be part of the Plan Schedule Management process. These can include scheduling methodology, scheduling tools and techniques, estimating approaches, formats and project management software. Strategies such as fast-tracking or crashing the project schedule can be detailed in the schedule management plan. Of course, it should be kept in mind that these decisions may affect project risks and costs. Organizational policies and procedures may have a role in determining which scheduling techniques, which may include (but are not limited to) rolling wave planning, alternatives analysis and methods for reviewing schedule performance, are employed.

Meetings

Outputs

Schedule management plan
The schedule management plan may institute:
- o   Project schedule model development
    - ✓ Specifying the scheduling methodology and tool to be used to develop the project schedule model
- o   Level of accuracy
    - ✓ Range used to determine realistic activity duration estimates that is acceptable
    - ✓ May include an amount for contingencies
- o   Units of measure defined for each resource
- o   Organizational procedures links
    - ✓ Framework for the schedule management plan consistent with the estimates and resulting schedules provided by the WBS
- o   Project schedule model maintenance
- o   Control thresholds

- ✓ Specification of the variance thresholds for monitoring schedule performance that indicate an agreed-upon degree of variation allowable prior to action be required
- ✓ Usually expressed as percentage deviations form parameters set in the baseline plan
- o Rules of performance measurement
  - ✓ Set earned value management (EVM) or other physical measurement rules of performance measurement
  - ✓ May specify:
    - ➢ Rules for establishing percent complete
    - ➢ Control accounts at which management of progress and schedule will be measured
    - ➢ Earned value measurement strategies to be utilized, such as baselines, fixed formula, percent complete, etc.
    - ➢ Schedule performance measurements, e.g., schedule variance (SV) and schedule performance index (SPI) that will be used in determining the magnitude of variation to the original schedule baseline
- o Reporting formats
- o Process descriptions

Define Activities

Define Activities is the "process of identifying and documenting the specific actions to be performed to produce the project deliverables,"[56] the key benefit of which is to break down work packages – the deliverables at the lowest level in the WBS – into activities that will provide a basis to estimate, schedule, execute, monitor and control the project work.

Figure 7.3. **Define Activities: Inputs, Tools and Techniques, and Outputs**

Inputs	Tools & Techniques	Outputs
• Schedule managment plan • Scope baseline • Enterprise environmental factors • Organizational process assets	• Decomposition • Rolling wave technique • Expert judgment	• Activity list • Activity attributes • Milestone list

Inputs

Schedule management plan

The prescribed level of detail required to manage the work is the key input from the schedule management plan.

---
[56] Ibid., p. 149

Scope baseline
The scope baseline provides the project WBS, deliverables, constraints and assumptions that should be considered when defining activities.

Enterprise environmental factors
In this case, those factors include (but are not limited to) organizational cultures and structures, published commercial information from commercial databases and project management information system (PMIS).

Tools & Techniques

Decomposition
As mentioned previously, decomposition is utilized in dividing and subdividing the project scope and deliverables into reduced and hence more manageable parts. In the case of the Define Activities process, the final outputs are defined as activities.

Rolling wave planning
Rolling wave planning is one form of progressive elaboration in which planning occurs in 'waves' iteratively. While there is an overall high level long term plan, the near term work is planned in depth. This allows for proactively incorporating lessons learned within the project itself.

Figure 7.4. **Rolling Wave Planning**

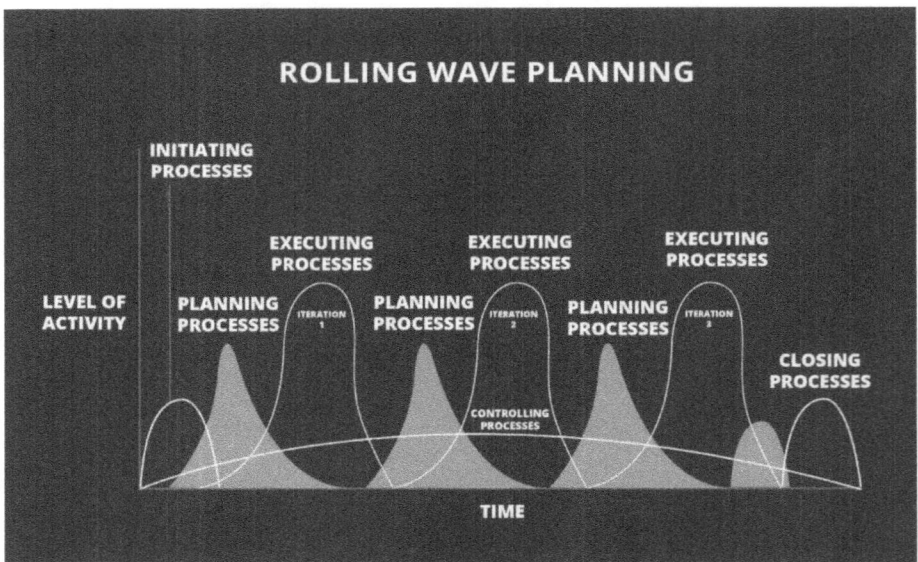

Expert judgment
Experts can provide direction on defining activities.

Outputs

Activity list
The activity list is comprehensive, including all required schedule activities titled in a way that describes its place in the schedule, the activity identifier, and a scope of work description of all activities written in enough detail that each team member understands what work is to be completed.

Activity attributes
Unlike milestones, activities have durations, periods during which the work is performed, and may also have resources and costs that are related to that work. Activity attributes expand on an activity's description by noting the multiple components associated with that activity.

These components evolve over time, initially including the activity identifier (ID), WBS ID, and activity label or name. When completed, they could include activity codes and descriptions, predecessor and successor activities, logical relationship, leads and lags, resource requirements, imposed dates, constraints and assumptions.

Activity attributes can be used to identify a number of aspects of a project:
- Person responsible for completing the work
- Geographic area or location at which the work must be performed
- Project calendar to which the activity is assigned
- Level of effort (LOE)
- Discrete and apportioned effort

Milestone list
A milestone marks a significant point or even in a project. A milestone list identifies all project milestones, specifying whether they are mandatory, i.e., required by contract, or optional, meaning that they are based on historical information. In addition, note that while milestones have some commonality with regular schedule activities, they have zero duration, representing a single moment in time.

Sequence Activities
Sequence Activities is the "process of identifying and documenting relationships among the project activities,"[57] with the greatest gain being its ability to determine a logical sequence of work that will attain the greatest efficiency, keeping all project constraints in mind.

In finish-to-start or start-to-start logical relationships, with the exception of the first and last, each activity and milestone should be coupled with at least one predecessor. In finish-to-start or finish-to-finish logical relationships, each should be connected to at least one successor. These logical relationships should be developed with the goal of creating a realistic project schedule, possibly

---

[57] Ibid., p. 153

requiring the use of lead or lag time between activities. Sequencing itself can be done through the use of project management software or manual or automated techniques.

Figure 7.5. **Sequence Activities: Inputs, Tools and Techniques, and Outputs**

Inputs	Tools & Techniques	Outputs
• Schedule management plan • Activity list • Activity attributes • Milestone list • Project scope statement • Enterprise environmental factors • Organizational process assets	• Precedence diagramming method (PDM) • Dependency determination • Leads and lags	• Project schedule network diagrams • Project documents updates

Inputs

Schedule management plan

During the Sequence Activities process, the schedule management plan serves to identify the scheduling method and tool that will be utilized by the project which, in turn, will offer guidance on the way in which the activities may be sequenced.

Activities list

This provides all of the schedule activities that are to be sequenced, as well as any dependencies and other constraints that can affect that sequencing.

Activity attributes

Attributes may include defined predecessor or successor relationships or other attributes that can indicate a necessary sequence of events.

Milestone list

There may be scheduled dates for specific milestones that must be kept in mind when sequencing activities.

Project scope statement

The project scope description found in the project scope statement will include characteristics of the product that could affect activity sequencing. In addition, the project scope statement contains project deliverables, constraints and assumptions, all of which can influence organizing the way in which activities are sequenced and although this same data often appear in the activity list, it is best to review the project scope statement to ensure accuracy.

Enterprise environmental factors
Factors that affect the Sequence Activities process include (but are not limited to) government or industry standards, the PMIS, scheduling tool and company work authorization systems.

Organizational process assets
The Sequence Activities process can be influenced by a number of these assets, including (but not limited to):

- Project files from the corporate data base such as those related to:
  - ✓ Scheduling methodology
  - ✓ Policies concerning existing formal and informal activity planning, procedures and guidelines like scheduling methodology utilized in developing logical relationships
  - ✓ Templates utilized for expediting preparation of project activities networks as well as additional descriptive information helpful when sequencing activities

Tools & Techniques

Precedence diagramming method
The precedence diagramming (PDM) is a "technique used for constructing a schedule model in which activities are represented by nodes and are graphically linked to one or more logical relationships to show the sequence in which the activities are to performed."[58] The method most often used by the majority of project management software packages is activity-on-node (AON).

Figure 7.6. **Precedence Diagraming**

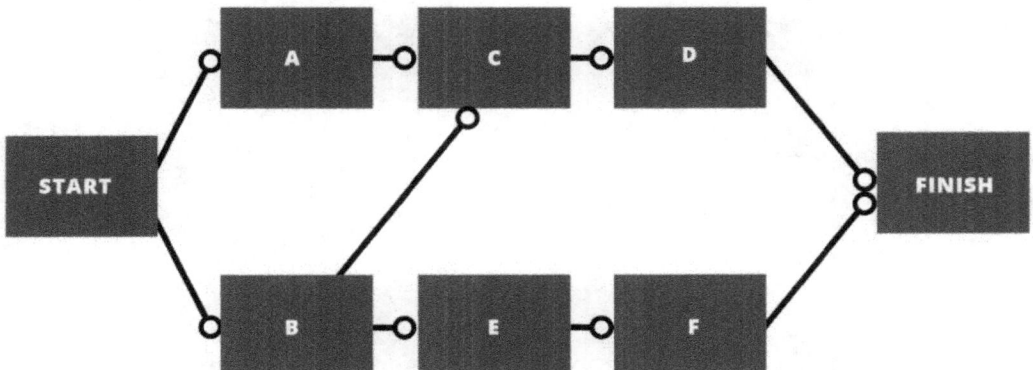

PDM is comprised of four types of dependencies (logical) relationships. The two types of relationships are quite easy to understand, with a predecessor activity being one that logically precedes a dependent

---
[58] Ibid., p. 156

activity in a schedule and a successor activity being one that logically follows another activity in that schedule. The most frequently used precedence relationship is finish-to-start, while the start-to-finish relationship is rarely utilized.

Here are the definitions of these relationships, followed by figure 7.7, in which they are illustrated:
- Finish-to-start (FS)
  - ✓ A successor activity cannot start prior to the finish of a predecessor activity. This is the most common precedence relationship
- Finish-to-finish (FF)
  - ✓ A successor activity cannot finish until a predecessor activity has finished
- Start-to-start (SS)
  - ✓ A successor activity cannot start until a predecessor activity has started.
- Start-to-finish (SF)
  - ✓ A successor activity cannot finish until a predecessor activity has started; this is usually the least common precedence relationship.

Figure 7.7. **Precedence Relationships**

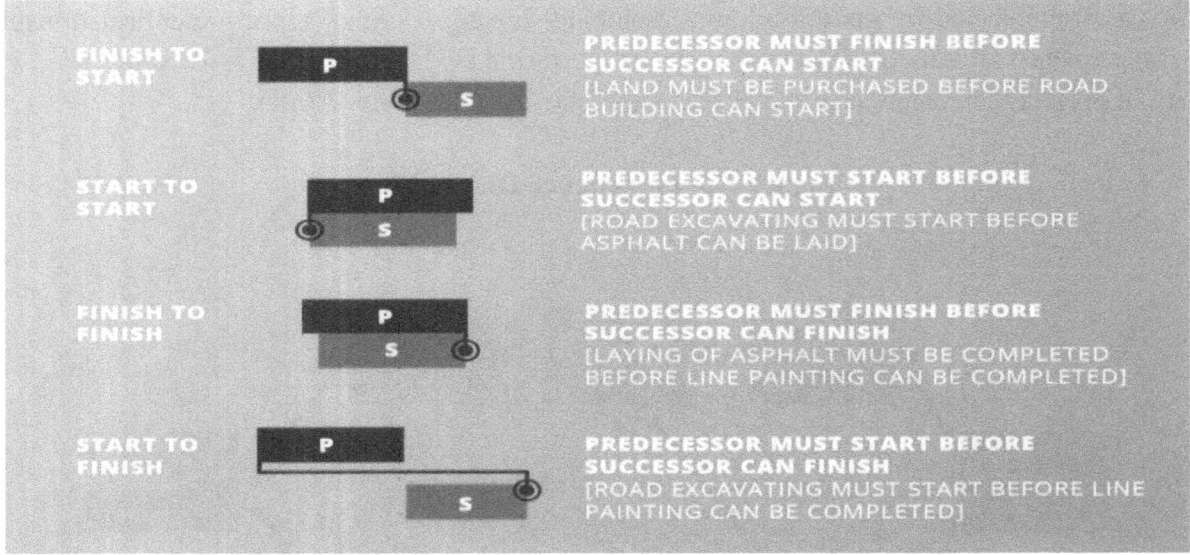

Dependency determination

Dependencies can be mandatory or discretionary and internal or external. Among each of these attributes, two can be simultaneously applicable as in mandatory external dependencies, mandatory internal dependencies, discretionary external dependencies and discretionary internal dependencies.
- Mandatory dependencies
  - ✓ Those that are legally or contractually required for or inherent to the nature of the project
  - ✓ Often involve physical limitations, e.g., one cannot build a house until the foundation has been laid or test an electronic device until a prototype has been completed
  - ✓ Sometimes referred to as hard logic or hard dependencies

- ✓ Whether or not a dependency is mandatory is determined during sequencing activities by the project team.
- ✓ Not to be confused with assigning schedule constraints in the scheduling tool
- o Discretionary dependencies
    - ✓ Sometimes referred to as preferred, preferential or soft logic
    - ✓ Established based on best practices knowledge within a certain application area or an uncommon aspect of a project in which a specific sequence is desired, despite there being other acceptable sequences
    - ✓ Must be fully documented as they can create arbitrary total float values, limiting later scheduling options
    - ✓ Should be reviewed for modification or removal if fast tracking techniques are utilized
    - ✓ The determination of which should be discretionary made by the project team as they sequence activities
- o External dependencies
    - ✓ Involve a relationship between project and non-project activities and are commonly outside the control of the project team
    - ✓ Determination of which are external done by the project team as they sequence activities
- o Internal dependencies
    - ✓ Involve a precedence relationship between project activities most commonly controlled by the project team
    - ✓ Determination of which are internal done by the project team as they sequence activities

Leads and lags

A lead, also known as a negative lag, is the "amount of time whereby a successor activity can be advanced with respect to a predecessor activity"[59] and is frequently represented by a negative number. In contrast, a lag is the "amount of time whereby a successor activity will be delayed with respect to a predecessor activity."[60] It is the project management team that determines which dependencies may require a lean or lag as they accurately define the logical relationship.

---
[59] Ibid., p. 158
[60] Ibid., p. 159

Figure 7.8. **Examples of Lead and Lag**[61]

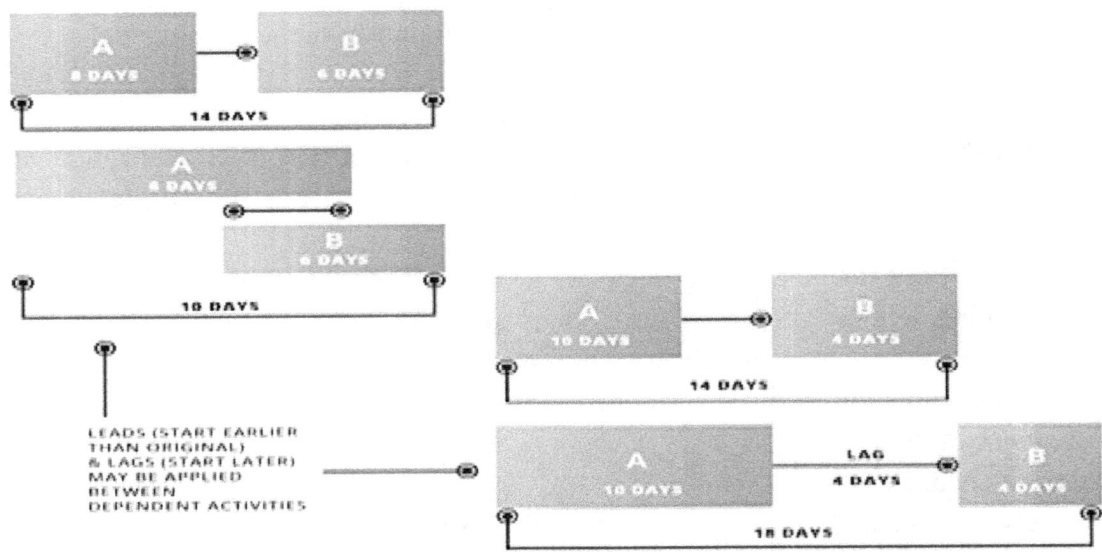

Outputs

Project schedule network diagrams

A project schedule network diagram is a "graphical representation of the logical relationships, also referred to an dependencies, among the project schedule activities"[62] that can be either produced manually or through the use of project management software and can include all of the details of a project or have one or more summary activities. In addition, the diagram can be accompanied by a summary narrative that outlines the basic approach utilized to sequence the activities and describes any unusual activity sequences within the network.

Project documents updates

Those project documents that can be updated include (but are not limited to) activity and milestone lists, activity attributes and the risk register.

Estimate Activity Resources

Estimate Activity Resources is the "process of estimating the type and quantities of material, human resources, equipment, or supplies required to perform each activity,"[63] its key benefit being that it provides identification of the type, quantity and characteristics of those resources that are necessary to complete the activity, allowing for cost and duration estimates that are more accurate. Not surprisingly, this process is closely coordinated with the Estimate Costs process.

---

[61] Firebrand, http://www.firebrandtraining.co.uk/learn/pmp/course-material/project-time-management/sequence-activities

[62] Ibid., p. 159

[63] Ibid., p. 160

Figure 7.9. **Estimate Activity Resources: Inputs, Tools and Techniques, and Outputs**

Inputs	Tools & Techniques	Outputs
• Schedule management plan • Activity list • Activity attributes • Resource calendars • Risk register • Activity cost estimates • Enterprise environmental factors • Organizational process assets	• Expert judgment • Alternative analysis • Published estimating data • Bottom-up estimating • Project management software	• Activity resource requirements • Resource breakdown structure • Project documents updates

Inputs

Schedule management plan

The schedule management plan identifies both the accuracy level and the units of measure for the resources that will be estimated.

Activity list

The activity list notes the activities that will require resources.

Activity attributes

Activity attributes offer the primary data input to be used to estimate the resources necessary to each activity in the activity list.

Resource calendars

A resource calendar is one that "identifies the working days and shifts on which each specific resources is available,"[64] information used to estimate resource utilization. Resource calendars specify at what time and for how long resources that have identified will be available over the course of the project and include consideration elements of attributes such as resource experience and/or skill level in addition to the various geographical locations the resources come from and when they are available.

Risk register

Information in the risk register is significant as risk events can affect resource selection and availability.

Activity cost estimates

Resource costs have an impact on the selection of resources.

---

[64] Ibid., p. 163

Enterprise environmental factors
Those that can affect the Estimate Activity Resources process include (but are not limited to) resource location, availability and skills.

Organizational process assets
The assets that can affect the Estimate Activity Resources process include (but are not limited to) policies and procedures concerning staffing and related to the rental/purchase of supplies and equipment and historical information about the resource types used for similar work on previously competed projects.

Tools & Techniques

Expert judgment
Stakeholders with experience and expertise in estimating and resource planning are good sources.

Alternative analysis
There are alternative methods to accomplish schedule activities, including utilizing several levels of resource capability or skills, machines of different sizes or types, hand vs. automated tools and make-or-buy decisions to be made about the resources.

Published estimating data
A number of organizations regularly publish updates on production rates and unit costs of resources for a broad range of labor trades, material and equipment for various countries and geographical locations within those countries.

Bottom-up estimating
Bottom-up estimating is a "method of estimating project duration or cost by aggregating the estimates of the lower-level components of the WBS."[65] If it is not possible to have a reasonable degree of confidence in those estimates, work within the activity must be decomposed into greater detail. Once resource needs are estimated, those estimates are combined into a total quantity for each resource of the activity. While there may or may not be dependencies between activities to affect resources' applications or uses, if there are, this resource usage pattern is reflected and documented in the activity's estimated requirements.

Project management software
Project management software vary from being very simple scheduling software, to being able to generate resource breakdown structures, resource calendars, and assist with resource optimization.

---

[65] Ibid., p. 164

Outputs

Activity resource requirements

These identify resource types and quantities necessary for each activity in a work package, with requirements then being combined to determine each work package's and work period's estimated resources. Detail and degree of specificity of these descriptions can differ by application area and the basis of estimate for each resource as well as assumptions made to determine which types of resources are to be applied, their availability and required quantities can be documented.

Resource breakdown structure

The resource breakdown structure is a "hierarchical representation of resources by category and type,"[66] with categories that include labor, material, equipment and supplies. Skill level, grade level or other information germane to the project can be included in resource types.

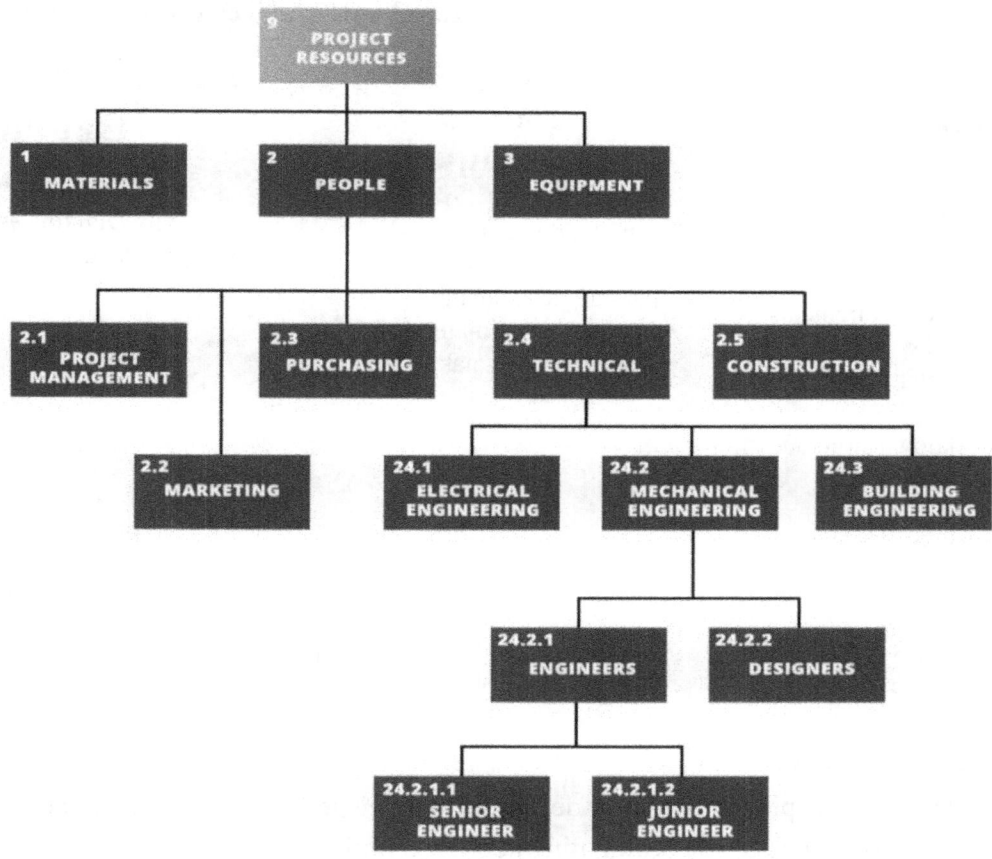

Figure 7.10. Resource Breakdown Structure

Project documents updates

These may include (but are not limited to) activity list and attributes and resource calendars.

---

[66] Ibid., p. 165

Estimate Activity Durations

Estimate Activity Durations is the "process of estimating the number of work periods needed to complete individual activities with estimated resources,"[67] the key benefit of which is that it provides a major input to the Develop Schedule process, i.e., the amount of time it will take to complete each activity, through the use of information on activity scope of work, required resource types and estimated quantities of those resources, and resource calendars.

The person or group on the project team who has the greatest familiarity with the nature of the work in the specific activity is expected to provide activity duration estimates which will be progressively elaborated on and, over the course of the process, the quality and availability of the input data will be considered, thus improving the accuracy of the duration estimates.

The estimation of the amount of work effort and available resources required for the completion of the activity is requisite to this process, with estimates utilized to assess the number of work periods (activity duration) necessary to completing the activity using the correct project and resource calendars. Documentation of all data and assumptions supporting duration estimating is required.

Figure 7.11. **Estimate Activity Durations: Inputs, Tools and Techniques, and Outputs**

Inputs	Tools & Techniques	Outputs
• Schedule management plan • Activity list • Activity attributes • Activity resource requirements • Resource calendars • Project scope statement • Risk register • Resource breakdown structure • Enterprise environmental factors • Organizational process assets	• Expert judgment • Analogous estimating • Parametric estimating • Three-point estimating • Group decision-making techniques • Reserve analysis	• Activity Duration estimates • Project documents updates

Inputs

Schedule management plan

The schedule management plan provides a definition of the method used and the accuracy level, in addition to other criteria necessary for estimating activity durations, including the project update cycle.

Activity list

This notes the activities in need of duration estimates.

---

[67] Ibid. p. 165

Activity attributes
This provides the primary data input for estimating the required durations for each activity in the activity list.

Activity resource requirements
The durations of activities will be affected by the estimated activity resource requirements because of the level to which resources assigned to those activities, e.g., if new or less skilled resources are assigned the task of completing an activity, completion may require increased communication, training and coordination, which can reduce efficiency and productivity, leading to a duration estimate that is considerably longer.

Resource calendars
As they reflect the availability of specific resources, types of resources and resources with specific qualities, resource calendars can affect the duration of schedule activities, e.g., if a skilled staff member can be assigned a task full-time, they will most likely complete the activity in less time than someone who is less skilled.

Project scope statement
Estimating activity durations requires the consideration of assumptions and constraints attained from the project scope statement. Assumptions can include (but are not limited to) existing conditions, information availability, and the length of reporting periods while constraints can include (but are not limited to) available skilled resources and contract terms and requirements.

Risk register
Risks can influence the schedule, so the list of identified risks are an important input.

Resource breakdown structure
The resource breakdown structure is a useful approach to communicating the breakdown of resources.

Enterprise environmental factors
Enterprise environmental factors affecting the Estimate Activity Durations process can include (but are not limited to) duration estimating databases as well as other reference data, productivity metrics, published commercial information and team members' location.

Organizational process assets
In this context, these include historical duration information, project calendars, scheduling methodology and lessons learned.

Tools & Techniques

Expert judgment
Duration estimate information or recommendations on maximum activity durations can be attained through expert judgment, guided by historical information. This is also the means of determining if one should combine estimating methods and the way in which to reconcile differences between them.

Analogous estimating
As its name implies, analogous estimating is "a technique for estimating the duration or cost of an activity or a project using historical data from a similar activity or project"[68] such as parameters related to duration, budget, size, weight and complexity. In terms of project duration, analogous estimating is dependent on the actual duration of previous, similar projects and is a gross value estimating approach which is occasionally adjusted for known differences in project complexity. Often, the technique is utilized in estimating project duration when detailed information about the project is limited.

It should be kept in mind that while analogous estimating is usually less costly and time consuming that other techniques, it is not as accurate; it is most reliable when past activities do not just appear to be similar but are in fact similar and when the necessary expertise is provided by the project team members.

Parametric estimating
Parametric estimating is "a technique in which an algorithm is used to calculate cost or duration based on historical data and project parameters."[69] A statistical relationship between that data and other variables is used to estimate activity parameters, e.g., cost, budget or duration.

A quantitative determination of activity durations can be found by multiplying the quantity of work to be performed by labor hours per unit of work. *The PMBOK® Guide* offers the example of the activity duration of a cable installation being estimated by multiplying the meters of cable by the number of labor hours per meter. Thus, if the assigned resource can install 25 meters of cable each hour, the duration of an activity involving the installation of 1,000 meters is 40 hours, i.e., 1,000 meters/25 meters per hour.

Three-point estimating
Keeping estimation uncertainty and risk in mind can increase the accuracy of single-point activity duration estimates, an idea that originated with the program evaluation and review technique referred to as PERT. With *t* equaling *time*, the three estimates PERT uses to define an approximate range for an activity's duration include:

- Most likely (tM), based on the activity's duration given the resources that will likely be assigned, their productivity, realistic expectations of availability for the activity, dependencies on other participants and interruptions

---

[68] Ibid., p. 170
[69] Ibid., p. 170

- Optimistic (*tO*), the activity duration based on an analysis of the best-case scenario for the activity
- Pessimistic (*tP*), the activity duration based on an analysis of the worst-case scenario for the activity

Expected duration, *tE*, can be found using a formula (dependent on the assumed distribution of values within the range of the three estimates), the most common of which are triangular and beta distributions.
- Triangular Distribution
  $tE = (tO + tM + tP) / 3$
- Beta Distribution (from the traditional PERT technique)
  $tE = (tO + 4tM + tP) / 6$

Duration estimates that are based on three points with an assumed distribution deliver an expected duration and clarification of the range of uncertainty around the expected duration.

Three-point estimating is favored over one-point estimating in which one estimate is provided per activity. One-point camouflages the level of uncertainty with the estimates. It also has the risk of forcing estimators to pad their estimates. In the long run, this leads to unreliable estimates. Padding is to be avoided for a number of reasons, including the negative effect of Parkinson's Law where work is known fill the time given to it.

Group decision-making techniques
We have already discussed the nature and type of these techniques. It is important to note that, in a group setting, those who are involved in the estimation process tend to be more committed to meeting the results obtained from that process.

Reserve analysis
Contingency reserves, also called time reserves or buffers, are included in duration estimates and are inserted into the project schedule to allow for schedule uncertainty. In addition, contingency reserves:

- Are the estimated duration within the schedule baseline allocated for identified, accepted risks and for which mitigation responses are developed
- Associated with the "known-unknowns" that may be estimated with the goal of accounting for this unknown amount of rework
- May be a percentage of the estimated activity duration
- Might be a fixed number of work periods
- Can be developed through the use of quantitative methods such as Monte Carlo simulation or Latin Hypercube sampling
- May be separate from individual activities and aggregated into buffers
- May be used, reduced or eliminated as more accurate information about the project become available

Management reserves, "a specified amount of the project duration withheld for management control purposes and . . . reserved for unforeseen work that is within the scope of the project"[70] are meant to address the "unknown-unknowns" that can have an effect on the project and are part of the overall project duration requirement, but are not part of the schedule baseline. In fact, dependent on the terms of the contract, using management reserves may require schedule baseline changes.

Outputs

Activity duration estimates

Clearly, after all this discussion about the tools used to estimate the duration of activities, one logical output of this process would be activity duration estimates. These are "qualitative assessments of the likely number of time periods that are required to complete an activity"[71] which do not include any lags and that may comprise indications of the range of possible results, e.g., '2 weeks ± 2 days,' indicating that, assuming a five-day workweek, it will take at least eight days and no more than twelve to complete the activity or '15% probability of the activity exceeding three weeks,' indicating a probability of 85% that the activity will be completed in three weeks or less.

Project documents updates

These include (but are not limited to) activity attributes and assumptions such as skill levels and availability made while developing the activity duration estimate in addition to a basis of duration estimates.

Develop Schedule

Develop Schedule is the "process of analyzing activity sequences, durations, resource requirements, and schedule constraints to create the project schedule model,"[72] the main benefit of which is that it generates a schedule model comprising planned completion dates for project activities by entering schedule activities, durations, resources and resource availability, and logical relationships into a scheduling tools.

The development of a suitable project schedule is frequently an iterative process that utilizes the schedule model to determine planned project activity start and finish dates as well as milestones based on the accuracy of the inputs.

Creating the project schedule model that will establish an approved project schedule serving as a baseline with which to track progress involves schedule development. This can equate to the review and revision of duration and resource estimates.

Usually, project staff assigned to the activities review their assignments, verifying that resource calendars or assigned activities related to other projects or tasks do not conflict with start and finish

---

[70] Ibid., 171
[71] Ibid., p. 172
[72] Ibid., p. 172

dates that have been determined and that those dates are still valid. Over the duration of the project and as work progresses, the project schedule model may require revising and maintaining to sustain a realistic schedule.

Figure 7.12. **Develop Schedule: Inputs, Tools and Techniques, and Outputs**

Inputs	Tools & Techniques	Outputs
• Schedule management plan • Activity list • Activity attributes • project schedule network diagrams • Resource calendars • Activity duration estimates • Project scope statement • Risk register • Project staff assignments • Resource breakdown structure • Enterprise environmental factors • Organizational process assets	• Schedule network analysis • Critical path method • Critical chain method • Resources optimization techniques • Modeling techniques • Leads and lags • Schedule compression • Scheduling tool	• Schedule baseline • Project schedule • Schedule data • Project calendars • Project management plan updates • Project documents updates

Inputs

Scheduling management plan
The scheduling management plan is used in the identification of the scheduling method and tool that will be utilized in the creation and calculation of the schedule.

Activities list
The activities list provides those activities included in the schedule model.

Activity attributes
Activity attributes provide additional details on each activity, which can be helpful when determining the schedule.

Project schedule network diagrams
These comprise predecessors' and successor' logical relationships to be utilized to arrive at the schedule.

Activity resource requirements
Activity resource requirements provide details on the categories and amount of resources needed per activity.

Resource calendars
Resource calendar assist with resource leveling since they have information on when resources are available.

Activity duration estimates
Depending on the various constraints, the activity duration estimates provide a forecast of how long each activity will take.

Project scope statement
In this context, the relevant section of the project scope statement outlines assumptions and constraints that may impact project schedule development.

Risk register
Risks have an influence on the schedule.

Project staff assignments
Project staff assignments ensure resources are assigned to each activity.

Resource breakdown structure
In the course of the Develop Schedule process, this offers the details needed to complete resource analysis and organizational reporting.

Enterprise environmental factors
During this process, relevant enterprise environmental factors include (but are not limited to) standards, communication channels and the scheduling tool that will be used to develop the schedule model.

Tools & Techniques

Schedule network analysis
Schedule network analysis is a technique for the generation of the project schedule model using several analytical techniques, including critical path and critical chain methods, what-if analysis and resource optimization techniques for the calculation of the early and late start and finish dates for portions of project activities not yet completed. Points of path convergence or divergence that are identifiable and can be used in schedule compression and other analysis are contained within some network paths.

Critical path method (CPM)
Critical path method, "a method used to estimate the minimum project duration and determine the amount of scheduling flexibility on the logical network paths within the schedule model,"[73] is a

---

[73] Ibid., p. 176

schedule network analysis technique calculating the early start, early finish, late start and late finish dates for all activities through the use of a forward and backward analysis through the schedule network without considering any resource limitations.

Figure 7.13. **Critical Path Diagramming Method**

Activity	
WBSID	
Duration	Float
ES	EF
LS	LF

→

Activity	
WBSID	
Duration	Float
ES	EF
LS	LF

The sequence of activities representing the longest path through a project is that project's critical path, determining a project duration that is as short as is possible. The resultant early and late start and finish dates do not necessarily comprise the project schedule. Utilizing the parameters for the activity durations, logical relationships, leads, lags and other known constraints that were included in the schedule model, they are indicative of the time periods in which the activity could be executed.

The amount of schedule flexibility on the logical network paths within the schedule model is calculated via the critical path method, indicating how long a schedule activity can delayed from its early start date without causing a delay in the project's finish date or creating a violation of a schedule constraint. This is called "total float." Float is also known as slack.

A CPM critical path is:

- The longest duration path
- Most frequently characterized by zero total float
- Can have a negative total float if a constraint on late dates is violated by duration and logic

Critical chain method

Critical chain method (CCM) is a "schedule method that allows the
project team to place buffers on any project schedule path to account for limited resources and project uncertainties."[74]

- Developed from the critical path method approach
- Takes into consideration influences of resource allocation, optimization and leveling and activity duration on the critical path arrived at via the critical path method
- Introduces the notion of buffers and their management
- Utilizes activities with durations that exclude safety margins, logical relationships and resource availability
- Aggregated activity safety margins at specific points on the project schedule path accounting for limited resources and project uncertainties comprise statistically determined buffers

---

[74] Ibid., p. 178

- Critical chain = resource-constrained critical path
- Centers on the management of remaining buffer durations against durations of chains of activities that remain

Buffers include:
- Duration buffers
  - Non-work schedule activities that manage uncertainty
  - Placed at the end of the critical chain, protect the target finish date from slippage occurring along that chain
- Feeding buffers
  - Located at each point at which a chain of dependent activities not on the critical chain feed into that chain, offering protection from slippage along the feeding chains
  - Buffer size accounts for uncertainty as to the chain of dependent activities' duration leading up to that buffer

Resource optimization techniques

As the term suggests, resource optimization techniques can be utilized to adjust the schedule model when required due to the demand and supply of resources. They include (but are not limited to):

- Resource leveling
  - A means by "which start and finish dates are adjusted based on resource constraints with the goal of balancing demand for resources with the available supply"[75]
  - Used when shared or critical resources' availability is restricted to certain times, when there is a limited supply, when they are over-allocated (assigned to two or more activities within the same timeframe or to maintain resource use at a constant level
  - Can frequently result in changes (usually increases) in the original critical path
- Resource smoothing
  - A means to adjust schedule model activities so that resource requirements do not exceed certain predefined limits
  - Unlike resource leveling, activities may only experience delay within their free and total float; hence, all resources may not be optimized.

Modeling techniques
- What-if scenario analysis
  - A process that involves the evaluation of scenarios with the goal of predicting their either positive or negative effect on project objectives
  - Can be utilized to assess project schedule feasibility under adverse circumstances and to prepare contingency/response plans to reduce risk in the event of unexpected situations
- Simulation
  - A process involving the calculation of multiple project duration using differing sets of activity assumptions

---

[75] Ibid., p. 179

- ✓ Commonly utilizes probability distributions constructed from three-point estimates to account for uncertainty
- ✓ Most common technique is Monte Carlo analysis, "in which a distribution of possible activity durations is defined for each activity and used to calculate a distribution of possible outcomes for the total project"[76]

Leads and lags
The schedule is adjusted for leads and lags to develop a more reliable schedule.

Schedule compression
- o Crashing
    - ✓ Adds resources with the goal of minimizing the schedule duration to the least incremental cost
    - ✓ Is limited to activities on the critical path for which the activity's duration will be shortened with additional resources
    - ✓ May increase risk and/or cost
- o Fast tracking
    - ✓ A schedule compression technique whereby, over at least a portion of their duration, normally sequential activities or phases are instead performed in parallel
    - ✓ Can result in rework and increase risk
    - ✓ Only feasible in cases of activity overlap

Scheduling tools
Based on activities, network diagrams, resources and activity durations and utilizing schedule network analysis, automated scheduling tools, sometimes in conjunction with other project management software, comprise the schedule model and accelerate the scheduling process by generating start and finish dates.

Outputs

Schedule baseline
As an output of the Develop Schedule process, baseline dates previously approved by appropriate stakeholders are compared to actual start and finish dates with the goal of noting any variances.

Project schedule
The outputs that emerge from a schedule model are schedule presentations while the project schedule is an "output of a schedule model that presents linked activities with planned dates, durations, milestones and resources" that minimally, comprises each activity's planned start and finish dates. Assignment of resources planned at an early stage must be confirmed and scheduled start and finish dates established before the project schedule moves from being preliminary to being set, a process that

---

[76] Ibid. p. 180

normally happens no later than the completion of the project management plan.
The project schedule presentation:
- May be in summary form (master or milestone schedule) or in detail
- More often, presented in graphically utilizing one or more formats classified as presentations
    - Bar charts
        - Also known as Gantt charts
        - Activities listed on the vertical axis, dates listed on horizontal axis, activity durations shown as horizontal bars placed according to start and finish dates
        - Hammock activity, which is broader and more comprehensive summary activity, used between milestones or spanning multiple interdependent work packages and displayed in bar chart reports

Figure 7.14. **Gantt or Bar Chart Example**

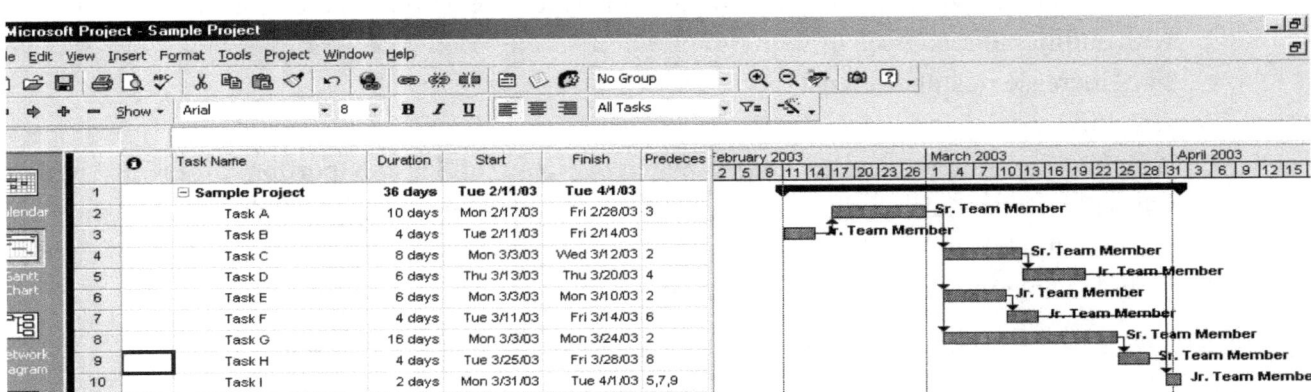

- Milestone charts
    - Similar to bar charts but differ in that they identify only major deliverables' and key external interfaces' scheduled start or completion

Figure 7.15. **Milestone Chart Example**

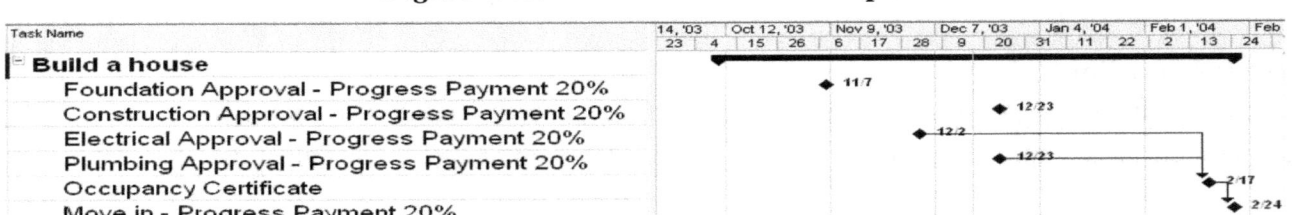

Project schedule network diagrams
- Graphical representations of the logical relationships among the project schedule activities
- Display activities and relationships without a time scale, usually presented in the activity-on-node diagram format (pure logic diagram) or in a time-scaled schedule network diagram (logic bar diagram)

Schedule data
For this process, schedule data, logically, comprise the information for describing and controlling the schedule and should at least include schedule milestones, schedule activities, activity attributes and documentation of all identified assumptions and constraints. Information often supplied as supporting detail includes (but is not limited to):

- o Resource requirements by time period (frequently in the form of a resource histogram)
- o Alternative schedules (best- or worst-case, resource-leveled or not resource-leveled, with or without imposed dates)
- o Contingency reserves scheduling
- o Cash-flow projections
- o Order and delivery schedules

Project calendars
A project calendar visually presents the schedule for all the activities planned.

Project management plan updates
These include (but are not limited to) schedule baseline and schedule management plan.

Project documents updates
These include (but are not limited to) activity resource requirements (particularly when resource leveling has been done as that can have a significant effect on preliminary estimates), activity attributes, calendars and risk registers to reflect opportunities/threats observed through scheduling assumptions.

Control Schedule
Control schedule is the "process of monitoring the status of project activities to update project progress and manage changes to the schedule baseline to achieve the plan,"[77] with the benefit of providing the means by which project managers and project teams can recognize any deviation from the plan and take the necessary corrective/preventative actions, thereby minimizing risk.

Being aware of the actual performance to date is required to update the schedule model and any changes to the schedule baseline must be approved via the Perform Integrated Change Control process. As a component of that process, Control Schedule centers on:

- o Ascertaining the project schedule's current status
- o Influencing the factors that create schedule changes
- o Learning if the project schedule has changed
- o Managing actual changes as they happen

When any agile approach has been used, Control Schedule centers on:

- o Comparing the total amount of work delivered and accepted against estimates of work completed for the elapsed time cycle to determine the project schedule's current status

---
[77] Ibid., p. 185

- Running scheduled reviews to record lessons learned or retrospectives with the goal of correcting processes and, if required, making improvements
- Reprioritizing backlog
- Determining the rates at which deliverables are produced, validated and accepted in a given time per iteration
- Determining if any changes in the project schedule have occurred and managing any that have actually occurred

Figure 7.16. **Control Schedule: Inputs, Tools and Techniques, and Outputs**

Inputs	Tools & Techniques	Outputs
• Project management plan • Project schedule • Work performance data • Project calendars • Schedule data • Organizational process assets	• Performance reviews • Project management software • Resource optimization techniques • Modeling techniques • Leads and lags • Schedule compression • Scheduling tool	• Work performance information • Schedule forecasts • Change requests • Project management plan updates • Project documents updates • Organizational process assets updates

Inputs

Project management plan
The schedule management plan and schedule baseline are included in the project management plan.

Project schedule
Activity schedules are controlled against the project schedule.

Work performance data
Work performance data provides data on progress. This helps identify variances.

Project calendars
Projects may contain more than one calendar to cover multiple work periods or multiple participating organizations.

Schedule data
Schedule data contains additional schedule information.

Organizational process assets
Those influencing this process include (but are not limited to) existing formal and informal schedule policies, procedures and guidelines related to the Schedule Control process.

Tools & Techniques

Performance reviews
Techniques for completing performance reviews include:
- Trend analysis
  - ✓ Used to look at project performance over time with the goal of determining improvement or deterioration
  - ✓ Valuable for gaining an understanding of performance to date and for comparison to future performance goals in the form of completion dates
- Critical path method
  - ✓ The process of determining schedule status can be assisted by a comparison of progress along the critical path
  - ✓ Variances directly impact the project end date.
  - ✓ Schedule risk can be identified via an evaluation of progress on near critical paths.
- Critical chain method
  - ✓ Schedule status can be determined by comparing the remaining amount of buffer to the amount necessary to protecting the delivery date.
  - ✓ Differences in the two can show if corrective action is appropriate.
- Earned value management
  - ✓ Magnitude of variation to the original schedule baseline can be assessed through the use of schedule performance measurements, e.g., schedule variance (SV) and schedule performance index (SPI).
  - ✓ Additional planning components such as total float and early finish variances are also essential to the evaluation of project time performance.
  - ✓ Crucial aspects of schedule control include:
    - ➢ Ascertaining cause/degree of variance relative to schedule baseline
    - ➢ Estimating those variances' implications as to future work to completion
    - ➢ Determining if corrective/preventative action is necessary

Project management software
Project management software helps track progress.

Resource optimization techniques
This involves resource leveling or resource smoothing.

Modeling techniques
Modeling techniques allow for what-if analysis.

Leads and lags
Leads and lags can impact the schedule.

Schedule compression
Crashing and fast tracking may be used to try and bring the schedule back on track.

Scheduling tool
Scheduling tools are helpful in analyzing and tracking progress.

Outputs

Work performance information
Work performance information includes SV and SPI time performance indicators for WBS components, with particular emphasis on the work packages and control accounts, which is documented and communicated to stakeholders.

Schedule forecasts
Schedule forecasts leverage Earned Value Management formulas to see what, if any, impact the current progress may have on the schedule.

Change requests
Change requests may arise based on a review of current progress. All changes have to go through Perform Integrated Change Control.

Project management plan updates
Updated elements of the project management plan may include (but are not limited to):
- Schedule baseline, changes to which are made in response to approved change requests as to project scope, activity resources or activity duration estimates, or those caused by schedule compression techniques
- Schedule management plan
- Cost baseline updates to reflect approved change requests or changes caused by compression techniques

Project document updates
Project document updates may include (but are not limited to) schedule data, project schedule and risk register (which may be altered due to use of schedule compression techniques.

Test What You've Learned

1) Where are the Project Time Management processes and the tools and techniques utilized in those processes documented?
   a) Schedule management plan
   b) Scope management plan
   c) Project schedule model
   d) Project scope statement

2) If you were working to complete a representation of the plan for executing the project's duration, dependencies and other planning information, what document would you be producing?
   a) Project scope statement
   b) Project schedule presentation
   c) Schedule model
   d) Project scope statement

3) Tools and techniques utilized in the Define Activities process include:
   a) Activity list, expert judgment and analytical techniques
   b) Decomposition, rolling wave planning and expert judgment
   c) Precedence diagramming and leads and lags
   d) Project management software and schedule compression

4) Which, if any, of the following statement is true?
   a) A schedule management plan includes the rules of performance measurement.
   b) Decomposition is a technique used in the Plan Schedule Management process.
   c) Milestone lists describe a necessary sequence of events or define predecessor or successor relationships.
   d) Mandatory dependencies are the same as the assignment of schedule constraints in the scheduling tool.

5) A/an _____ is the amount of time whereby a successor activity can be advanced with respect to a predecessor activity and a/an _____ is the amount of time whereby a successor activity will be delayed with respect to a predecessor activity.
   a) Lag, lead
   b) Delay, accelerate
   c) Lead, lag
   d) Efficiency, deficiency

6) _____ are included in duration estimates, are occasionally referred to as buffers and are used to account for schedule uncertainty.
   a) Parametric estimates
   b) Triangular distributions
   c) Reserve analyzes
   d) Contingency reserves

7) _____ utilizes most likely, optimistic and pessimistic estimates to describe an activity's duration's approximate range.
   a) Parametric estimating
   b) PERT
   c) Beta distribution
   d) Reserve analysis

8) Which, if any, of the following statements are false?
   a) There is little difference between the critical path and critical chain methods.
   b) Use of the critical path method allows project teams to provide an estimation of the minimum project duration.
   c) The critical chain method allows project teams to insert buffers on any project schedule path with the goal of accounting for limited resources and project uncertainties.

9) _____ are non-work schedule activities that are added to manage scheduling uncertainty.
   a) Feeding buffers
   b) Scheduling buffers
   c) Resource buffers
   d) Duration buffers

10) When a resource has been assigned to two or more activities during the same time period, _____ can be used to balance supply with demand.
    a) Resource smoothing
    b) What-if scenario analysis
    c) Resource leveling
    d) Crashing

Chapter 8: Project Cost Management

In business, as well as in life, remaining within a budget is of optimal importance. This chapter describes the means of doing so as a project manager, discussing in great detail "the processes involved in planning, estimating, budgeting, financing, funding, managing, and controlling costs so that the project can be completed within the approved budget."[78]

Keep in mind that the usually distinct cost estimating and budgeting processes are nevertheless closely connected and, in the case of projects having a smaller scope, can be combined and performed by one person over the course of a fairly short period. In *The PMBOK® Guide*, they are presented singly because of their differences in tools and techniques. *The PMBOK® Guide* also observes that early scope definition is crucial because, in a project's early stages, the ability to influence cost is greatest.

Stakeholder requirements for managing costs are of some concern during the Project Cost Management process, with different stakeholders measuring project costs in different ways and at different points in the process. In addition to its primary concern with the cost of the resources necessary to completing project activities, Project Cost Management must also keep the effect of project decisions on the ensuing recurrent cost of using, maintaining and supporting the project's product, service or result in mind.

With the goal of ensuring that performance of the processes will be both effective and coordinated, the work of cost management planning is done early in project planning, establishing the framework for each of the cost management processes.

Plan Cost Management
Plan cost management is the "process that establishes the policies, procedures, and documentation for planning, managing, expending, and controlling project costs,"[79] with the central benefit of, throughout the project, providing guidance and direction as the way in which project costs will be managed. All of the cost management processes as well as the tools and techniques associated with those processes are documented in the cost management plan, which is a project management plan component.

---

[78] Project Management Institute, *A Guide to the Project Management Body of Knowledge* (*The PMBOK® Guide*), 5th ed., p. 193.

[79] Ibid., p. 196

Figure 8.1. **Plan Cost Management: Inputs, Tools and Techniques, and Outputs**

Inputs	Tools & Techniques	Outputs
• Project management plan • Project charter • Enterprise environmental factors • Organizational process assets	• Expert judgment • Analytical techniques • Meetings	• Cost management plan

Inputs

Project management plan

The information contained in the project management plan is utilized in the development of the cost management plan includes (but is not limited to) the scope baseline, including the project scope statement and WBS details concerning cost estimation and management, the schedule baseline defining when project costs will be incurred and additional cost-related scheduling, risk and communications decisions.

Project charter

The project charter offers the summary budget used to develop detailed project costs and definitions of project approval requirements that will affect project costs management.

Enterprise environmental factors

These include (but are not limited to):

- o Organizational culture and structure
- o Market conditions, e.g., products, services and results attainable in the regional and global market
- o For project costs sources from multiple countries, currency exchange rates
- o Published commercial information and seller price lists
- o Project management information system offering alternatives for managing cost

Organizational process assets

Organizational process assets influencing the Plan Cost Management process include (but are not limited to):

- o Financial controls procedures
- o Time reporting
- o Required expenditure and disbursement reviews
- o Accounting codes
- o Standard contract provisions

Tools & Techniques

Expert judgment
In addition to that which is guided by available historical information, those providing expert judgment can offer suggestions as to ways to combine methods and to reconcile differences between those methods.

Analytical techniques
There are many decisions to be made when planning and managing project costs that may affect project schedule and risks. These include:
- Which funding options to use, e.g., self-funding, with equity or with debt
- How to finance project resources, e.g., making purchasing, renting or leasing

Techniques, which can be affected by organizational policies and procedures, include (but are not limited to):
- Payback period
- Return on investment
- Internal rate of return
- Discounted cash flow
- Net present value

Meetings
Project team meetings may be held to plan out cost management.

Outputs

Cost management plan
Items documented in the cost management plan include cost management processes and the tools and techniques associated with those processes; the plan itself can verify:
- Definitions of units of measure for each resource, e.g., time (staff hours, days, weeks), quantities (meters, liters, tons, kilometers, cubic yards) and currency
- Level of precision - degree of rounding up/down of activity cost estimates
- Level of accuracy - specification of acceptable range utilized for determining realistic activity cost (may include an amount for contingencies)
- Organizational procedures links - provided by the WBS, the framework for the cost management plan allows for consistent estimates, budgets and control of costs, with the WBS component called the control account, each of which is assigned a unique code/account number linking directly to the performing organization's accounting system
- Control thresholds - specified variance thresholds used to monitor cost performance that indicate an agreed-upon degree of variation allowable prior to action being taken and usually expressed as percentage deviations from the baseline plan

- o Rules of performance measurement - setting earned value management (EVM) rules of performance measurement. The cost management plan may:
  - ✓ Provide definitions of the points in the WBS at which control accounts' measurement will be performed
  - ✓ Establishment of the earned value measurement techniques (weighted milestones, fixed-formula, percentage complete, etc.) that will be employed
  - ✓ Specification of tracking methodologies and the earned value management computation equations used to calculate projected estimate at completion (EAC) forecasts to provide a validity check on the bottom-up EAC
- o Reporting formats - definitions of formats/frequency for various cost reports
- o Process descriptions
- o Additional details including (but not limited to) description of strategic funding choices, procedures for accounting for fluctuations in currency exchange rates and project cost recording

Estimate Costs

Estimate Costs is the "process of developing an approximation of the monetary resources needed to complete project activities,"[80] the main benefit of which is that it calculates the cost required to complete project work.

Cost estimates, which are qualitative assessments of the expected costs of the resources required to complete the activity, are based on the information that is known at a given point in time. These predictions comprise the identification and consideration of those costing alternative necessary to the initiation and completion of a project. To achieve optimal project costs, cost trade-offs and risks that include make versus buy, buy versus lease, and the sharing of resources must be taken into account.

Although, in some circumstances, units of measure such as staff hours or staff days are utilized for comparison, units of currency such as dollars, euros, yen, etc. are most often used to express cost estimates because it avoids the effects of currency fluctuations.

Cost estimates are not only done prior to beginning a project; they must be reviewed and refined over the project's course with the goal of reflecting additional detail as it becomes available and while assumptions are being tested, with accuracy increasing as the project passes through its life cycle. They can be presented at either the activity level or in the form of a summary.

Costs must be estimated for every resource charged to the project, including (but not limited to) labor, materials, equipment, services, facilities, inflation allowance and financing and contingency cost.

Project costs can be fixed or variable. The project team needs to also estimate direct, as well as indirect project costs.

---

[80] Ibid., p. 200

Figure 8.2. **Estimate Costs: Inputs, Tools and Techniques, and Outputs**

Inputs	Tools & Techniques	Outputs
• Cost management plan • Human resource management plan • Scope baseline • Project schedule • Risk register • Enterprise environmental factors • Organizational process assets	• Expert judgment • Analogous estimating • Parametric estimating • Bottom-up estimating • Three-point estimating • Reserve analysis • Cost of quality • Project management software • Vendor bid analysis • Group decision-making techniques	• Activity cost estimates • Basis of estimates • Project documents updates

Inputs

Cost management plan

The cost management plan provides definitions of the way in which project costs will be managed and controlled as well as the method to be utilized and the accuracy level required to estimate activity cost.

Human resource management plan

This will be discussed in more detail in chapter 10 but, in this context, keep in mind that the human resource management plan comprises staffing attributes, personnel rates and related rewards/recognition, all of which are vital components for the development of project cost estimates.

Scope baseline

The scope baseline includes the:

- Project scope statement
  - ✓ Assumptions applicable to the Estimate Costs process
    - ➢ Estimates will include direct project costs OR incorporate indirect costs as well.
    - ➢ The latter (costs that cannot be directly ascribed to a specific project) accumulate and are equally allocated over several projects via an approved and documented accounting procedure.
  - ✓ Constraints
    - ➢ Limited project budget
    - ➢ Requisite delivery dates
    - ➢ Availability of skilled resources
    - ➢ Organizational policies
- Work breakdown structure
- WBS dictionary
- Additional information found in scope baseline

- ✓ Contractual/legal implications
- ✓ Health and safety
- ✓ Security
- ✓ Environmental
- ✓ Insurance
- ✓ Intellectual property rights
- ✓ Licenses and permits

Project schedule

To understand the importance of the project schedule to the cost estimating process, remember the old saying that "time is money." The project schedule's key inputs to this process include:

- o Type and quantity of material and equipment and the time those resources must be used to complete the project
- o Availability of staff
- o Number of staff hours required
- o Activity duration estimates (can affect cost estimates that include time-sensitive costs, e.g., union labor with regularly expiring collective bargaining agreements or materials having variations in seasonal cost

Risk register

Threats and/or opportunities can impact activity and overall project costs. A negative risk event can cause an increase in the near-term cost of the project, while a potential opportunity can either reduce activity costs directly or accelerate the schedule.

Enterprise environmental factors

Enterprise environmental factors affecting the Estimate Costs process include (but are not limited to):

- o Market conditions - resource costs can be greatly influenced by regional and/or global supply.
- o Published commercial information - databases track skills and human resource costs as well as providing standard material and equipment costs. Other information can be obtained from published seller price lists.

Organizational process assets

Organizational process assets affecting this process include (but are not limited to) cost estimating policies and templates, historical information and lessons learned.

Tools & Techniques

Expert judgment

Analogous estimating[81]

To estimate costs, analogous estimating:

---

[81] Detailed information concerning analogous, parametric and three-point estimating as well as reserve analysis can be found in chapter 7.

- o Uses values such as scope, cost and budget or measures of scale like size, weight and complexity from previous, similar projects to estimate parameters or measurements for current project
- o Is a technique that relies on previous, similar projects' actual costs to estimate the current project's costs.
- o Is a gross value estimating approach that is sometimes adjusted for known project complexity differences
- o Often used in early project phases when limited detailed information is available at which point, historical information and expert judgment are utilized

Parametric estimating

To estimate costs, parametric estimating:

- o Utilizes a statistical relationship between relevant historical data as well as other variables
- o Greater accuracy can be produced dependent on the sophistication and underlying data built into the model
- o Can be applied to the entire project or its segments while incorporating other estimating methods, such as regression analysis, i.e., a scatter diagram) or by calculating a learning curve

Bottom-up estimating

Bottom-up estimating:

- o Is a means of estimating a component of work
- o Individual work packages' or activities' cost estimated to greatest level of specified detail after which, detailed cost is condensed ("rolled up") to higher levels for use in ensuing reporting and tracking
- o Individual activity's or work package's size/complexity usually influences the cost/accuracy of this form of estimating

Three-point estimating

- o Utilizing estimation uncertainty and risk as well as three estimates to define an approximate range for an activity's cost can improve on the accuracy of single-point activity cost estimates.
- o With slight modifications, triangular or beta distribution formulas similar to those discussed in chapter 7 that utilize the concepts of most likely (cM), optimistic (cO) and pessimistic (cP) can provide an expected cost and clarify the range of uncertainty around that cost.

Reserve analysis

Reserve analysis is needed to ensure that the reserve amounts being allocated for the project are in alignment with the project risks.

Cost of quality (COQ)

Assumptions about costs of quality (which will be discussed in greater detail in chapter 9) can be utilized in preparation of the activity cost estimate.

Project management software
Cost estimating can be simplified through the use of project management software applications, computerized spreadsheets, simulation and statistical tools.

Vendor bid analysis
Founded on the responsive bids from qualified vendors, an analysis of what a project should cost can be included among methods to estimate cost. When, using competitive processes, vendors are awarded projects, it may be necessary for the project team to undertake additional cost estimating work with the goal of examining the price of individual deliverables and deriving a cost supporting the final total cost of the project.

Group decision-making techniques
Those close to the work's technical execution can provide additional information aimed at estimates that are more accurate. Further, involving people in this process increases their commitment ot meeting the resulting estimates.

Outputs

Activity cost estimates
Activity cost estimates are compiled based on the estimates for all resources required.

Basis of estimates
As one might expect, documentation that offers a clear, complete understanding of the way in which a cost estimate was derived is a crucial output of this process. Supporting detail may comprise documentation of how the estimate was developed (its basis), all assumptions that were made and any known constraints as well as indications of both the range of possible estimates, for example, €10,000 (±10%) used to indicate that it is anticipated that the cost of an item will fall within a range of values, and the confidence level of the of the final estimate.

Project documents updates
These should include (but are not limited to) the risk register.

Determine Budget
Determine Budget is the "process of aggregating the estimated costs of individual activities or work packages to establish an authorized cost baseline,"[82] with the main benefit of determining the cost baseline against which monitoring and controlling project performance can be done.

---

[82] Ibid., p. 208

Figure 8.3. **Determine Budget: Inputs, Tools and Techniques, and Outputs**

Inputs
- Cost management plan
- Scope baseline
- Activity cost estimates
- Basis of estimates
- Project schedule
- Resource calendars
- Risk register
- Agreements
- Organizational process assets

Tools & Techniques
- Cost aggregation
- Reserve analysis
- Expert judgment
- Historical relationships
- Funding limit reconciliation

Outputs
- Cost baseline
- Project funding requirements
- Project documents updates

Inputs

Cost management plan
The cost management plan outlines how costs associated with the project are to be managed.

Scope baseline
The scope baseline includes the project scope statement, work breakdown structure and WBS dictionary.

Activity cost estimates
Activity cost estimates are compiled based on the estimates for all resources required.

Basis of estimates
Documentation that offers a clear, complete understanding of the way in which a cost estimate was derived is crucial.

Project schedule
The project schedule helps assess the budget per calendar period.

Resource calendars
Resource calendars assist with planning out when costs are expected.

Risk register
The cost of project risk responses need to be taken into account when calculating the budget.

Agreements
Relevant agreements pertain to information and costs that relate to those products, services or results that have been or will be purchased.

Organizational process assets
In this context, organizational process assets include (but are not limited to) existing formal and/or informal policies, procedures and guidelines related to cost budgeting.

Tools & Techniques

Cost aggregation
First and in accordance with the WBS, cost estimates are aggregated by work packages which are then grouped for the WBS's higher components' levels, e.g., control accounts, and finally, for the entire project.

Reserve analysis
Reserve analysis deals with quantifying the level of contingency reserve and management reserve that should be put aside for uncertainties associated with the project. There is no defined formula for calculating reserves since each project's risks levels and tolerances are unique.

Expert judgment
Experts, particularly the front line workers assigned the specific activities, should play a key role in determining the budget.

Historical relationships
Historical relationships resulting in parametric or analogous estimates involve the utilization of project parameters for the development of mathematical models to predict a project's total costs. Models may be simple or complex and there can be wide variations in their cost and accuracy.

Reliability is most certain when models are scalable, working equally well for large or small projects or phases of a project and are developed using accurate historical information and readily quantifiable parameters.

Funding limit reconciliation
Fund expenditures "should be reconciled with any funding limits on the commitment of funds for the project."[83] Rescheduling of work by placing imposed date restraints for that work into the project schedule may sometimes be necessary if a variance between funding limits and planned expenditures is found.

Outputs

Cost baseline
The cost baseline is the "approved version of the time-phased project budget, excluding any management reserves, which can only be changed through formal change control procedures and is

---

[83] Ibid., p. 212

used as a basis for comparison to actual results" that "is developed as a summation of the approved budgets for the different schedule activities."[84]

Activity cost estimates related to the various project activities plus those activities' contingency reserves are combined into their associated work package costs which, in turn, are aggregated into control accounts. It is the summation of those control accounts that comprises the cost baseline. Finally, management reserves are incorporated into the cost baseline to produce the budget. As changes making the use of management reserves necessary occur, approval to move applicable management reserve funds into the cost baseline must be attained through the Perform Integrated Change Control Process.

Figure 8.4. **Components of the Project Budget**

Total Amount →	Project Budget	Management Reserve			
		Cost Baseline	Control Accounts	Contingency Reserve	
				Work Package Cost Estimates	Activity Contingency Reserves
					Activity Cost Estimates

Project funding requirements

Total funding and periodic funding requirements, for example, those that are annual and those that are quarterly, stem from the cost baseline, which includes both projected expenditures added to anticipated liabilities. Characterized as steps because they may not be evenly distributed, funding frequently occurs in incremental, non-continuous amounts.

Project documents updates

These may include (but are not limited to) the risk register, activity costs estimates and the project schedule.

Control Costs

Control Costs is the "process of monitoring the status of a project to update the project costs and managing changes to the cost baseline,"[85] with the key benefit being that it provides the means to note variances from the plan and undertake corrective action, thus minimizing risk. Knowing what actual costs have been spent to date is necessary to update the budget and any increase to the budget that has been authorized can be approved solely through the Perform Integrated Change process.

---

[84] Ibid., p. 212

[85] Ibid., p. 215

It is crucial to remember that, beyond permitting the project team to remain within the authorized funding, merely monitoring fund expenditure without considering the value of the work being accomplished provides very little. Cost control comprises the analysis of the relationship between project fund consumption and the physical work being completed. What is key to effectively controlling costs is the management of the approved cost baseline and any changes to that baseline. This involves:

- Influencing those factors creating changes to the authorized cost baseline
- Making certain that all change requests are acted on in a timely manner
- Managing the actual changes when and as they happen
- Confirming that authorized funding is not exceeded by cost expenditures by period, by WBS component, by activity and in total for the project
- Checking cost performance with the goal of isolating and understanding variances from the approved cost baseline
- Comparing work performance to funds expended
- Providing information about all approved changes and their associated costs to appropriate stakeholders
- Bringing anticipated cost overruns within limits that are acceptable

Figure 8.5. Control Costs: Inputs, Tools and Techniques, and Outputs

Inputs	Tools & Techniques	Outputs
• Project management plan • Project funding requirements • Work performance data • Organizational process assets	• Earned value management • Forecasting • To-complete performance index (TCPI) • Performance reviews • Project management software • Reserve analysis	• Work performance information • Cost forecasts • Change requests • Project management plan updates • Project documents updates • Organizational process assets updates

Inputs

Project management plan

The information from the project management plan used to control costs includes the cost baseline as compared to actual results with the aim of deciding if a change, corrective or preventative action is in order.

Project funding requirements

These include projected expenditures as well as anticipated liabilities.

Work performance data

Data include which project activities have started, the progress made on those activities and which deliverables are finished as well as authorized and incurred costs.

Organizational process assets

Those that can affect the Control Costs process include (but are not limited to) formal and informal policies, procedures and guidelines related to cost control, cost control tools and methods to be utilized for monitoring and reporting.

Tools & Techniques

Earned value management

The most commonly used method of performance measurement for projects, earned value management (EVM) is a methodology used to assess project performance and progress through a combination of scope, schedule and resource measurements. Integrating the scope baseline with both the cost and schedule baselines, it assists the project management team in assessing and measuring project performance and progress.

This technique necessitates the formation of an integrated baseline against which teams can measure performance over the project duration and its principles are applicable to every project in every industry. Three key dimensions for each work package and control account can be developed and monitored through the use of EVM. These include:

- Planned value (PV)
    - ✓ The authorized budget assigned to scheduled work which is planned to be completed for an activity or work breakdown structure component
    - ✓ Although allocated by phase over the life of a project, defines the physical work meant to be accomplished at a given moment in time
    - ✓ Total sometimes called the performance measurement baseline (PMB)
    - ✓ Budget at completion (BAC) also refers to the project's total planned value.
- Earned value (EV)
    - ✓ A measure of work performed expressed in terms of the authorized budget for that work
    - ✓ Associated with completed, authorized work
    - ✓ EV being measured must be related to the PMB.
    - ✓ EV measured cannot exceed the PV budget authorized for a component.
    - ✓ Frequently utilized to determine the percent complete of a project
    - ✓ To measure work in progress, progress measurement criteria must be set for each WBS component.
    - ✓ Monitored both incrementally to discover current status and cumulatively to determine long term performance trends by project managers
- Actual cost (AC)
    - ✓ The realized cost incurred during a specified time period for work performed on an activity
    - ✓ Total cost incurred to accomplish work measured by the EV
    - ✓ Must correspond in terms of definition to both what was budgeted in the PV and measured in the EV, for example, direct hours or costs only or all costs, which includes those that were indirect
- ✓ Has no upper limit, measures whatever is spent to accomplish the EV Variances from the approved baseline are also checked, including:

- Schedule variance (SV)
  - Expressed as the difference between earned and planned value, is a measure of schedule performance
  - The amount by which, at a given point in time, the project is either ahead or behind the planned delivery date
  - Equals the earned value (EV) less the planned value (PV)
  - Ultimately will equal zero at project completion because all planned values will have been earned
  - Best utilized along with critical path methodology scheduling and risk management
  - *Equation*: SV = EV - PV
- Cost variance (CV)
  - The amount of budget deficit or surplus at a given point in time
  - Shown as the difference between earned value and actual cost
  - Upon the completion of a project, will be the difference between the BAC and the actual amount that was spent
  - As it is indicative of the relationship between physical performance to costs spent, it is especially significant
  - Often difficult for a project to recover negative CV
  - *Equation*: CV = EV - AC

To determine project status, its SV and CV values can be converted to efficiency indicators that reflect any project's cost and schedule performance, allowing comparison against all other projects or within a portfolio of project.

- Schedule performance index (SPI)
  - A measure of schedule efficiency shown as the ratio of earned to planned value that determines how effectively a project team is utilizing its time
  - Occasionally used in conjunction with the cost performance index with the aim of forecasting estimates of final project completion
  - Less than 1.0 = less work completed than planned
  - Greater than 1.0 = more work completed than planned
  - As it measures all project work, determining if a project will finish before or behind its planned finish date requires the analysis of the performance on the critical path.
  - *Equation*: SPI = EV/PV
- Cost performance index (CPI)
  - A measure of the budgeted resources' cost efficiency shown as the ratio of earned value to actual cost
  - Thought to be the most critical EVM metric, measuring the cost efficiency for the work completed
  - Less than 1.0 = a cost overrun for work completed
  - Greater than 1.0 = a cost overrun of performance to date
  - *Equation*: CPI = EV/AC

Monitoring and reporting the three parameters of planned and earned value and actual cost can be done on a period-by-period (usually weekly or monthly) or a cumulative basis.

Forecasting

Forecasting the EAC "involves making projections of conditions and events in a project's future based on current performance information and other knowledge available at the time of the forecast"[86] and is done when, because due to a new forecast for the estimate at completion (EAC) indicating a difference from the budget at completion (BAC), the BAC is clearly no longer viable. The EAC:

- Is commonly based on actual costs incurred for work, with the addition of an estimate to complete (ETC) work that is still to be done that must be completed by the project team using their experience to date
- Most frequently used approach is a manual, bottom-up summary building on actual costs and experience completed by the project manager and team.
- *Equation*: EAC = AC + Bottom-up ETC
- Easily comparable to a range of calculated EACs incorporating various risk scenarios
- Cumulative CPE and SPI values are usually utilized to calculate EAC values.
- Three common methods, each of which is "applicable for any given project and [that] will provide the project management team with an 'early warning' signal if the EAC forecasts are not within acceptable tolerances"[87] are:
    - ✓ EAC forecast for ETC performed at the budgeted rate:
        - ➢ Accepts the actual project performance to date (whether favorable or unfavorable) as shown by the actual costs
        - ➢ Predicts all ETC work done in the future will be completed at the budgeted rate
        - ➢ In situations in which actual performance is unfavorable, only accept the assumption that future performance will improve if it is supported by project risk analysis.
        - ➢ *Equation*: EAC = AC + (BAC - EV)
    - ✓ EAC forecast for ETC work performed at present CPI
        - ➢ Assumes project experience to date will continue in the future
        - ➢ Assumes that ETC work will be performed at the same cumulative cost performance index (CPI) as what was incurred to date
        - ➢ *Equation*: EAC = BAC/CPI
    - ✓ EAC forecast for ETC work utilizing both SPI and CPI factors
        - ➢ Performed at a rate of efficiency that takes both the cost and schedule indices into consideration
        - ➢ Of greatest value when the ETC effort is impacted by the project schedule
        - ➢ Method variations (utilized according to project manager's judgment) weight CPI and SPI at different values such as 80/20 or 50/50.
        - ➢ *Equation*: EAC = AC + [(BAC - EV)/ (CPI x SPS)]

---

[86] Ibid., p. 220

[87] Ibid., p. 221

To-complete performance index (TCPI)
The to-complete performance index (TCPI) is a "measure of the cost performance that is required to be achieved with the remaining resources in order to meet a specified management goal, expressed as the ratio of the cost to finish the outstanding work to the remaining budget."[88] That defined goal of management, for example, the BAC or the EAC, is met via the TCPI, which is a calculated cost performance index attained on the work that remains. Once it becomes clear that the BAC is not feasible, the forecasted EAC can be considered and, upon approval, the BAC may be replaced by the EAC in the TCPI calculation. As based on the BAC, the equation for the TCPI is (BAC - EV)/(BAC - AC).

To remain within the authorized BAC if the cumulative CPI falls below the baseline, all ongoing project work must be performed immediately in the range of the TCPI. A judgment call is required to decide if this performance level is attainable, which is based on issues such as risk, schedule and technical performance. When based on the EAC, the equation for the TCPI is (BAC - EV)/ (EAC - AC).

Performance reviews
Performance reviews offer a comparison of cost performance over time, schedule activities or work packages either over- or under-running the budget and the funds that have been estimated to be necessary for completing work in progress. When EVM is utilized, the information gained includes:
- Variance analysis:
  - ✓ The explanation, including cause, impact and corrective actions for cost (CV = EV - AC), schedule (SV = EV - PV) and variance at completion (VAC = BAC - EAC)
  - ✓ Most commonly analyzed measurements are cost and schedule variances
  - ✓ Through a comparison of planned against actual activity cost, similar variance analysis can be done for projects not using earned value management, with additional analysis done to establish cause/degree of variance relative to schedule baseline as well as any necessary corrective or preventative actions.
  - ✓ As more work is completed, acceptable variances' percentage range tend to decrease.
- Trend analysis:
  - ✓ To determine if performance is showing improvement or deterioration, trend analysis looks at project performance over time
- Earned value performance:
  - ✓ Provides a comparison of performance measurement baseline to actual schedule and cost performance
  - ✓ Analysis of the cost baseline vs actual costs for the work completed is utilized for cost performance comparisons when EVM is not being used.

For quick reference, terms, acronyms and formulas can be seen in table 8.1.

---

[88] Ibid., 221

Table 8.1. **Earned Value Management Terms and Formulas**

Term	Acronym	Formula	Description
Cost variance	CV	CV = EV - AC	CV provides the cost performance of the project to help in determining if the project is proceeding as planned. Subtracting AC from EV calculates the cost variance.
Schedule variance	SV	SV = EV - PV	SV indicates the project's schedule performance. This value can indicate whether or not the project work is proceeding as planned. Calculate the SV by subtracting the PV from the EV.
Cost performance index	CPI	CPI = EV/AC	For the CPI of individual budgets, divide EV by AC. For a cumulative CPI, divide the sum of all EV budgets by the sum of all ACs. A CPI of less than one indicates that the project is over budget while a CPI of over one indicates that the project will be completed under the estimated budget.
Schedule performance index	SPI	SPI = EV/PV	Project managers can use the SPI to make a prediction as to when their projects will be completed. To calculate the SPI, divide EV by PV. An SPI of one indicates the project is on schedule while greater than one indicates it is ahead of schedule and less than one indicates it is behind schedule.
Estimate at completion	EAC	EAC = BAC/CPI EAC = AC + ETC EAC = AC + (BAC - EV)	EAC is used by project managers to give their best estimate of the total costs of projects based on actual costs to date. The most frequently used formula for EAC is AC plus ETC, which is commonly utilized when previous assumptions regarding costs are proven to be incorrect.
Estimate to complete	ETC	ETC = EAC - AC	ETC is the expected cost necessary for the completion of all the remaining work for a scheduled activity, group of activities or the project itself. ETC assists project managers in the predication of the final cost of the project upon completion.
Variance at completion	VAC	VAC = BAC - EAC	VAC forecasts the difference between the Budget-at-Completion and the expected total costs to be accrued over the life of the project based on current trends.
Cumulative cost performance index	CPI^c	$CPI^c = \Sigma EV / \Sigma AC$	The Cumulative CPI Method forecasts the total amount to be spent by adding costs incurred to date to the remaining work to be earned, weighted against the current CPI performance value. This initiates from the 20 percent completion point.

Project management software

Project management software is frequently employed to monitor the three dimensions of EVM, PV, EV and AC, as well as to display graphical trends and forecast a range of potential final project results.

Reserve analysis

During the cost control process, in an effort to learn if the project's contingency and management reserves are still necessary or if a request for additional reserves should be submitted, reserve analysis can be used to monitor those reserves. There are several options for these reserves over the course of the project; they may be utilized as planned to cover the expense of risk mitigation events or other contingencies or, if it is deemed probable that risk events will not occur, they may be deleted from the project budget, thus making resources available for other projects or operations.

Outputs

Work performance information
Following calculation of the CV, SV, CPI, SPI and VAC values for WBS components, especially the work packages and control accounts, this information is documented and communicated to stakeholders.

Cost forecasts
Also documented and communicated to stakeholders, cost forecasts can be either a calculated EAC value or a bottom-up EAC value.

Change requests
These may comprise preventative or corrective actions involving the cost baseline or other project management plan components that were shown to be necessary by an analysis of project performance and are processed for review and disposition through the Perform Integrated Change Control process.

Project management plan updates
Updated elements can include (but are not limited to) changes to the cost baseline incorporated as a response to changes in scope, activity resources or cost estimates that have been approved. If cost variances are sufficiently severe, a revised cost baseline will be necessary to providing a basis for performance measurement that is realistic. In addition, as a response to stakeholders' feedback, changes to the cost management plan, e.g., revisions to control thresholds or specified accuracy levels necessary to managing the cost of the project, can be incorporated.

Project documents updates
Project documents updates may include (but are not limited to) cost estimates and basis of estimates.

Organizational process assets updates
These can include (but are not limited to) variance causes, corrective actions taken and the reasons for those actions, financial databases and other lessons learned.

Test What You've Learned

1) Which, if any, of the following is not an analytical technique utilized in the plan cost management process?
   a) Control thresholds
   b) Discounted cash flow
   c) Net present value
   d) Internal rate of return

2) Which units of measurement are most frequently used for comparisons during the Estimate Costs process?
   a) Staff hours
   b) Staff days
   c) Resource quantities
   d) Units of currency

3) Which, if any, of the following statements is/are true?
   a) It is only necessary to estimate project costs prior to the onset of a project.
   b) Cost estimates are reviewed over the course of a project.
   c) The accuracy of a cost estimate decreases throughout the project's life cycle.
   d) None of these statements are true.

4) _____ included in the scope baseline include:
   a) Work breakdowns
   b) Skilled resources
   c) Constraints
   d) Project budgets

5) Which of these techniques uses values from previous projects like the scope, cost and budget to estimate the parameters of a current project?
   a) Analogous estimating
   b) Parametric estimating
   c) Reserve analysis
   d) Three-point estimating

6) Reliability of models is most likely certain when they are:
   a) Grouped for the WBS's higher-level components
   b) Complex
   c) Scalable
   d) Reconciled with funding limits

7) Total and periodic funding requirements emerge from the:
   a) Project management plan
   b) Management reserve
   c) Cost baseline
   d) Expert judgment

8) Project funding requirements include:
   a) Project activity start and end dates
   b) Projected expenditures and anticipated liabilities
   c) Cost control rules and policies
   d) Stakeholder and project team input

9) _____ is the authorized budget assigned to scheduled work to be completed for an activity or work breakdown structure component.
   a) Earned value
   b) Planned value
   c) Budget at completion
   d) Cost baseline

10) _____ = AC + Bottom-up ETC is one of the equations used to calculate:
   a) Estimate at completion (EAC)
   b) Budget at completion (BAC)
   c) Schedule performance index (SPI)
   d) Schedule variance (SV)

Chapter 9: Project Quality Management

Project Quality Management encompasses the "processes and activities of the performing organization that determine quality policies, objectives, and responsibilities so that the project will satisfy the needs for which it was undertaken."[89] Essentially, this means that the project manager and the project team must, through a series of steps, ensure that the customer receives what they asked for and that the product, service, etc. is of the quality they expected it to be.

All projects, regardless of their anticipated deliverables, must be managed in terms of quality. However, the specific measures and techniques utilized in that process are tailored to the nature of those deliverables.

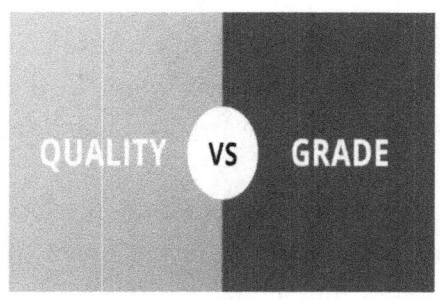

Another issue, *The PMBOK® Guide,* emphasizes is the difference between the concepts of *quality* and *grade*, quality being "the degree to which a set of inherent characteristics fulfill requirements" while a grade is a classification of "deliverables having the same functional use but different technical characteristics." Quality levels failing to meet requirements are perennial concerns, but a low level of quality may mean that a product is not of the highest grade (having no obvious defects) but is appropriate for general use. However, if what is intended and required to be high grade, i.e., having numerous features, is of low quality, its high-grade features would be useless.

All of this being said, it is clearly the project management team's task to determine what would be considered the product's appropriate level of accuracy (an assessment of correctness) and precision (a measure of exactness) for use in the project management plan. Keep in mind that these qualities are not interchangeable; a measurement being precise may not necessarily be accurate, and vice versa.

According to International Organization for Standardization (ISO) quality standards, current quality management approaches note the significance of:

- Customer satisfaction
  - ✓ With the goal of meeting customer expectations, product requirements must be understood, evaluated, defined and managed. This involves combining conformance to requirements, which will ensure that the product produces what it is created to produce, and fitness for use, i.e., the real needs must be satisfied by the product or service.
- Prevention over inspection
  - ✓ Rather than correcting mistakes uncovered by inspection or usage, which can be costly, quality must be planned, designed and built into the product, which is a considerably less expensive procedure.
- Continuous improvement

---

[89] Project Management Institute, *A Guide to the Project Management Body of Knowledge* (*The PMBOK® Guide*), 5th ed., p. 227

- ✓ As defined by Shewhart and modified by Deming, the basis for quality improvement is the PDCA (plan-do-check-act) cycle.
- ✓ Other continuous improvement initiatives include Total Quality Management (TQM), OPM3, Six Sigma, Kanban, Kaizen and Lean, which can improve both the management of the project and the quality of that project's product.
- o Management responsibility
    - ✓ Providing the appropriate resources at adequate capacities is a responsibility that falls into the category of managing quality. For example, Deming taught the auto industry that management actions were responsible for 85% of the issues related to quality.
- o Cost of quality (COQ)
    - ✓ Cost of quality "refers to the total cost of the conformance work and the nonconformance work that should be done as a compensatory effort because, on the first attempt to perform that work, the potential exists that some portion of the required work effort may be done or has been done incorrectly."[90]
    - ✓ While this phrase alludes to the total cost, it should be noted that this is not an expense that is incurred only at the end of the project; instead, it may crop up at any point in the deliverable's life cycle, or even post-project due to product returns, warranty claims or recall campaigns
    - ✓ To avoid post-project costs, sponsors may decide to make an investment into product quality improvement, particularly in the areas of conformance work, which is done to prevent defects or reduce their costs by inspecting out nonconforming units.
    - ✓ Program and portfolio management must utilize the appropriate reviews, templates and funding allocations to allay concerns about issues related to post-project COQ.

Figure 9.1 provides a roadmap to the relationships between the quality assurance and control quality processes and the IPECC, PDCA, cost of quality models and the project management process groups.

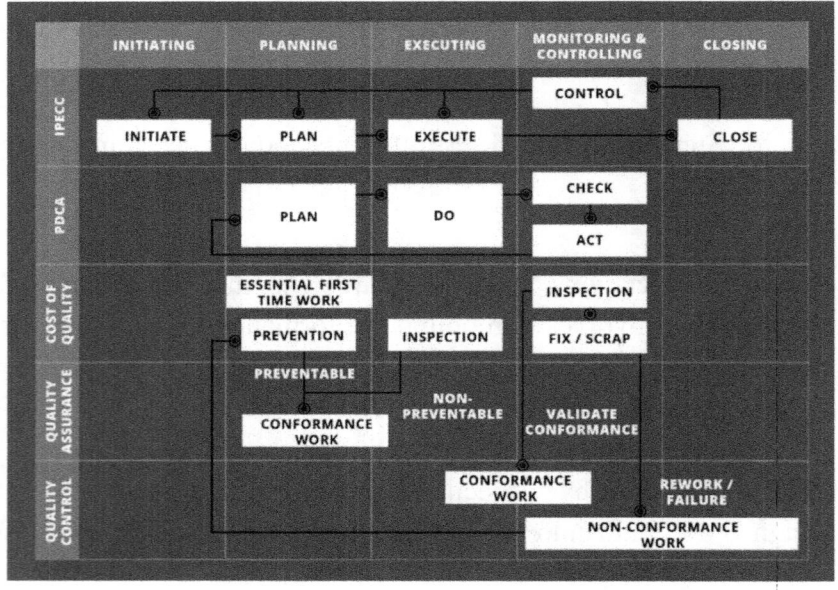

Figure 9.1. **Fundamental Relationships of Quality Assurance and Control Quality to the IPECC, PDCA, Cost of Quality Models and Project Management Process Groups**[91]

---

[90] Ibid., p. 229

[91] Ibid., p. 231

Plan Quality Management

Plan Quality Management is the "process of identifying quality requirements and/or standards for the project and its deliverables, and documenting how the project will demonstrate compliance with relevant quality requirements and/or standards."[92] Its central benefit is that it offers guidance and direction as to the way in which quality will be managed and confirmed over the course of the project.

This is a process that is performed concurrently with the other planning processes. An example would be that changes in deliverables proposed with the goal of meeting identified quality standards may require adjustments in cost or schedule as well as a detailed analysis of risk incurred by the impact of these changes on plans.

Figure 9.2. **Plan Quality Management Inputs, Tools and Techniques and Outputs**

Inputs	Tools & Techniques	Outputs
• Project management plan • Risk register • Requirements documentation • Enterprise environmental factors • Organizational process assets	• Cost-benefit analysis • Cost of quality • Seven basic quality tools • Benchmarking • Design of experiments • Statistical sampling • Additional quality planning tools • Meetings	• Quality management plan • Process improvement plan • Quality metrics • Quality checklists • Project documents updates

Inputs

Project management plan
Inputs to the quality management plan include (but are not limited to):

- o Scope baseline
    - ✓ Project scope statement
        - ➢ In addition to the project description, major project deliverables and acceptance criteria, frequently includes details concerning technical issues as well as other issues that can influence quality planning.
        - ➢ Of particular importance, acceptance criteria can increase/decrease quality costs and, hence, project costs, by a significant amount.
- o Work breakdown schedule (WBS)
    - ✓ Identifies deliverables and the work packages utilized in project performance measurement
- o WBS dictionary
- o Schedule baseline

---

[92] Ibid., p. 231

- ✓ Provides documentation of accepted schedule performance measures such as start and finish dates
- o Cost baseline
  - ✓ Provides the accepted time interval by which to measure cost performance
- o Other management plans

Stakeholder register
The stakeholder register assists with identifying which stakeholders have a role in project quality management.

Risk register
Information on threats/opportunities that can affect quality requirements.

Requirements documentation
Requirements documentation describes project requirements necessary to meeting stakeholder expectations, including (but not limited to) project (product) and quality requirements, all of which assist the management team in planning the means of implementing quality control on the project.

Enterprise environmental factors
Those that affect this process include (but are not limited to) governmental agency requirements, those rules, standards and guidelines that are specific to the application area, working/operating project conditions or its deliverables in such a way as to affect project quality, and cultural perceptions that could influence expectations about quality.

Organizational process assets
These include (but are not limited to):
- o Organizational quality policies, procedures and guidelines, which, with senior management's endorsement, establish the organization's expected direction in terms of implementation of its quality management approach
- o Historical databases
- o Lessons learned from earlier phases or projects.

Tools & Techniques

Cost-benefit analysis
A cost-benefit analysis of each quality activity provides a comparison of the quality steps' costs to their anticipated benefits, which include:
- o Less rework
- o Higher productivity
- o Lower costs
- o Increased stakeholder satisfaction
- o Greater profitability

Cost of quality (COQ)

Comprises all costs incurred over the product's life by investment into prevention of nonconformance, appraisal of the product or service as to conformance and rework (failure to meet requirements). Often sorted into internal, i.e., found by the produce, and external, i.e., found by the customer, failure costs are called cost of poor quality. External failure costs are typically the most expensive. Figure 9.3 offers clarity about this concept by providing examples of these costs.

Figure 9.3. Cost of Quality

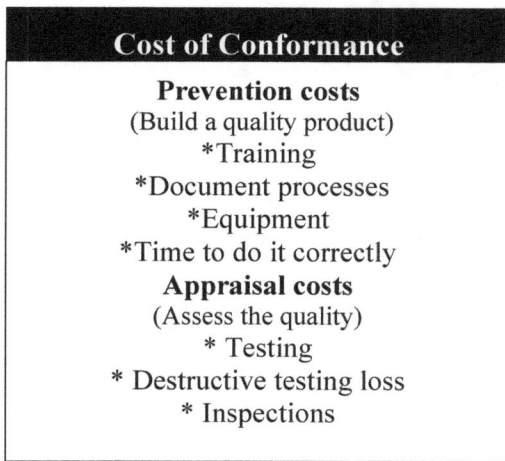

Seven basic quality tools

Figure 9.4. Seven basic quality tools - 7 QC Tools

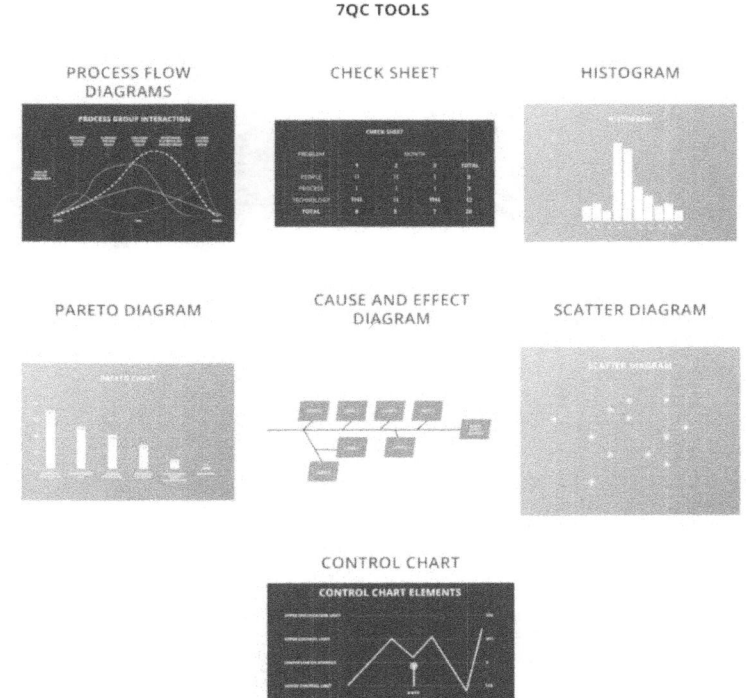

- Cause-and-effect diagrams (also known as fishbone or Ishikawa diagrams)
  - ✓ These are causal diagrams created by Kaoru Ishikawa
  - ✓ Illustrate the way in which various factors may be linked to a problem
  - ✓ Problem statement (gap to be closed or objective to be achieved) serves as a starting point to trace its source back to its actionable initial cause
  - ✓ Helpful to connecting undesirable effects to their cause, which can be eliminated through corrective action

Figure 9.5. **Fishbone Diagram**

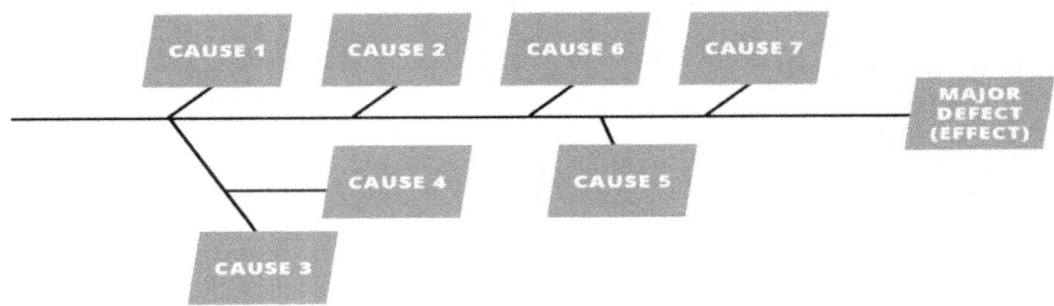

- Flowcharts (also known as process charts)
  - ✓ Display activities, decision points, branching loops, parallel paths and overall chain.

Figure 9.6. **Flowcharting**

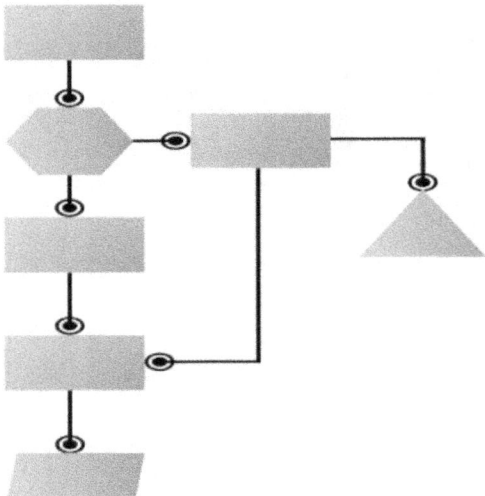

One example of a flowchart that is commonly used with Six Sigma projects is a SIPOC diagram or model, as seen below.

Figure 9.7. **The SIPOC Model**

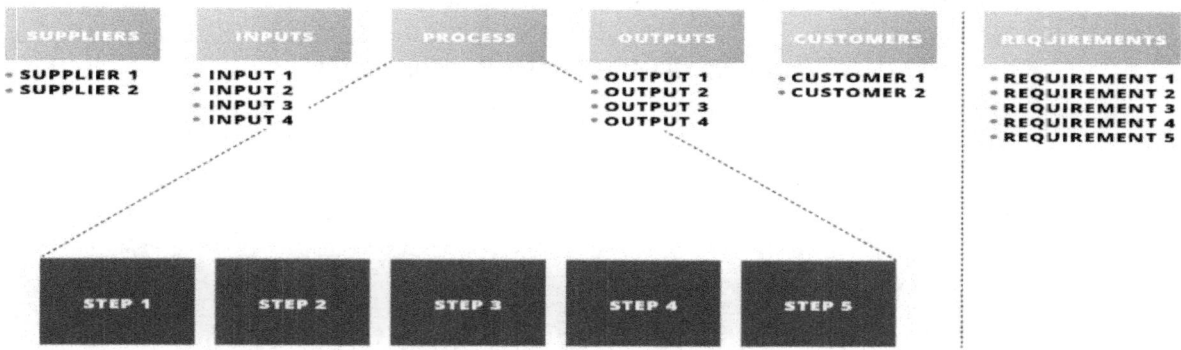

- ✓ Project's cost of quality can be obtained by utilizing "workflow branching logic and associated relative frequencies to estimate expected monetary value for the conformance and nonconformance work required to deliver the expected conforming output."[93]
- ✓ Another popular flowchart format are swimlanes in which the different lanes display the different participants, groups or processes.
o Check sheets (also known as tally sheets)
  - ✓ Used to organize facts to enable the effective collection of useful data about a possible problem in quality, particularly when attributes data are garnered during inspections to identify defects

Figure 9.8. **Example of a Check Sheet**

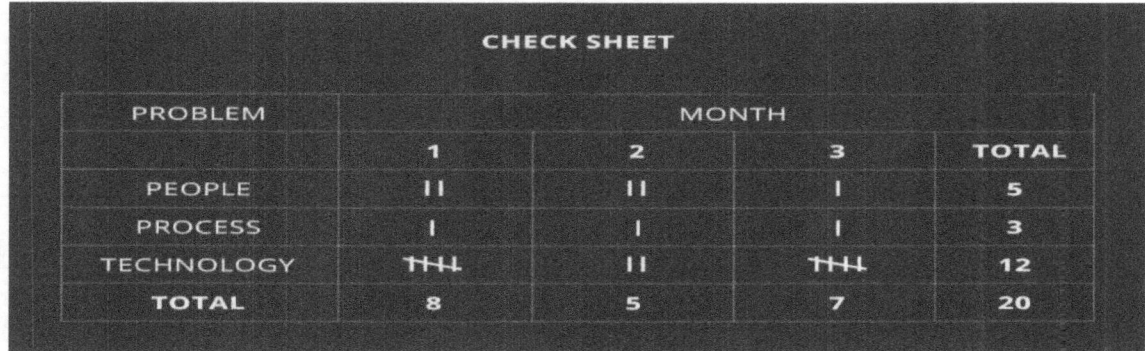

o Pareto diagrams (also known as 80-20 diagrams)
  - ✓ A special version of a vertical bar chart utilized in identification of the essential few sources that account for most of the effects of a problem; the Pareto diagram helps in prioritization
  - ✓ Created by management consultant Joseph Juran, who named it after Italian economist Vilfredo Pareto

---

[93] Ibid., p. 236

- ✓ Horizontal axis - categories serve as a probability distribution accounting for 100% of possible observations
- ✓ Each cause's relative frequency decreases in magnitude until the point at which the "other" source accounts for any causes not specified
- ✓ Categories will measure frequencies or consequences.

Figure 9.9. **Example of a Pareto Chart**

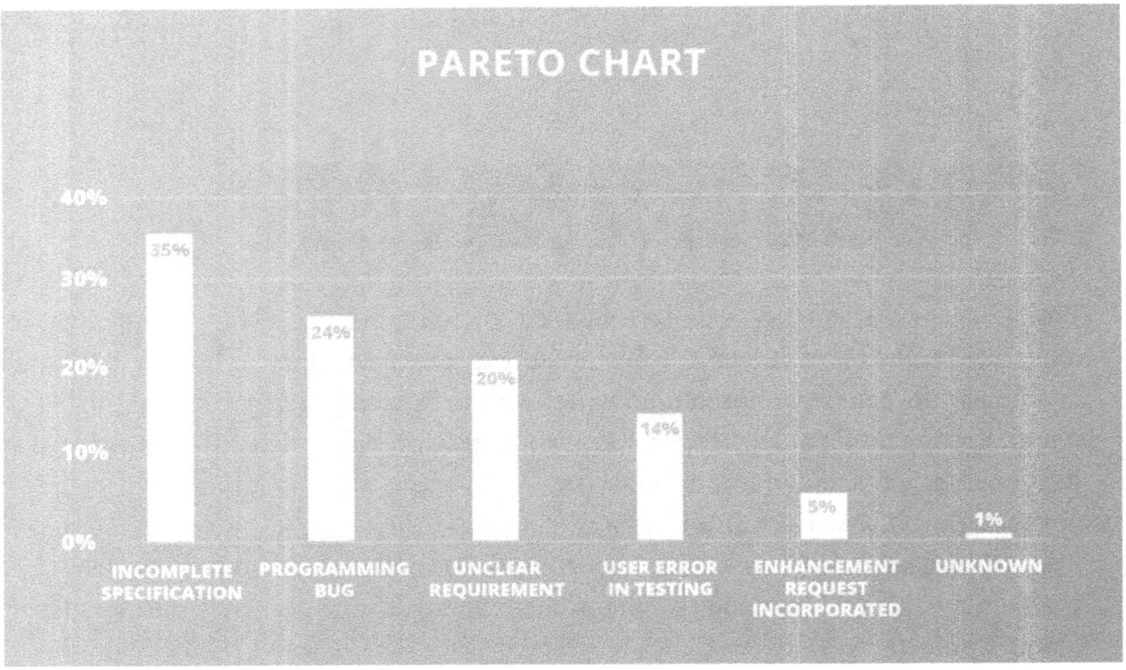

Figure 9.10. **Example of a Histogram**

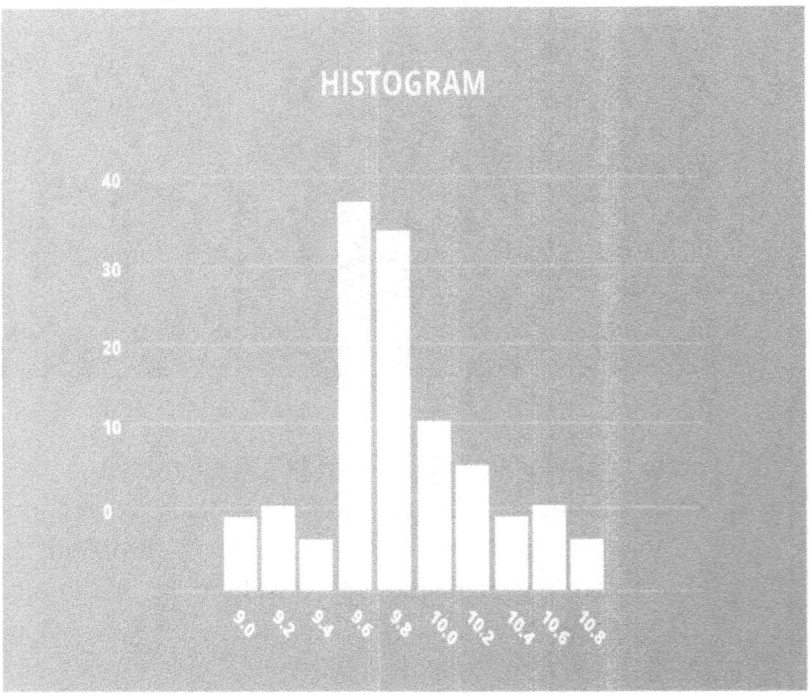

o Histograms
✓ Bar charts that describe a statistical variation's central tendency, dispersion and shape but do not take the influence of time on the variation existing within a distribution into consideration

- Control charts (also known as Process Behavior Charts)
  - ✓ Determine whether a process is/is not stable or does/does not have a predictable performance
  - ✓ Upper/lower specification limits based on agreed requirements reflect allowed maximum/minimum values
  - ✓ Control limits found with standard statistical calculations/principles are used to identify points at which corrective action may be taken to maintain a stable and capable process

Figure 9.11. **Elements of a Control Chart**

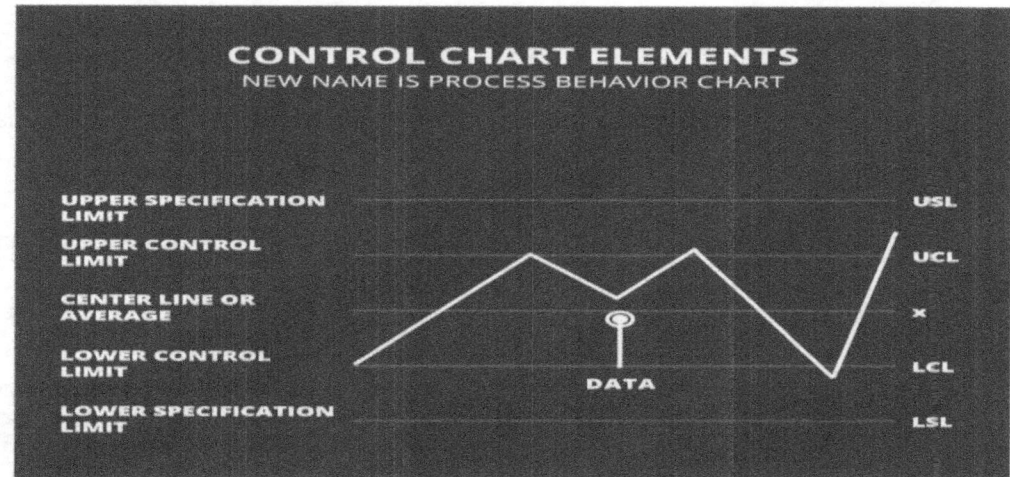

- ✓ Process is out of control when:
  - ➢ Data point exceeds a control limit
  - ➢ Seven consecutive plot points above or below the mean; this heuristic is known as The 'Rule of Seven.'

Figure 9.12. **The Rule of Seven**

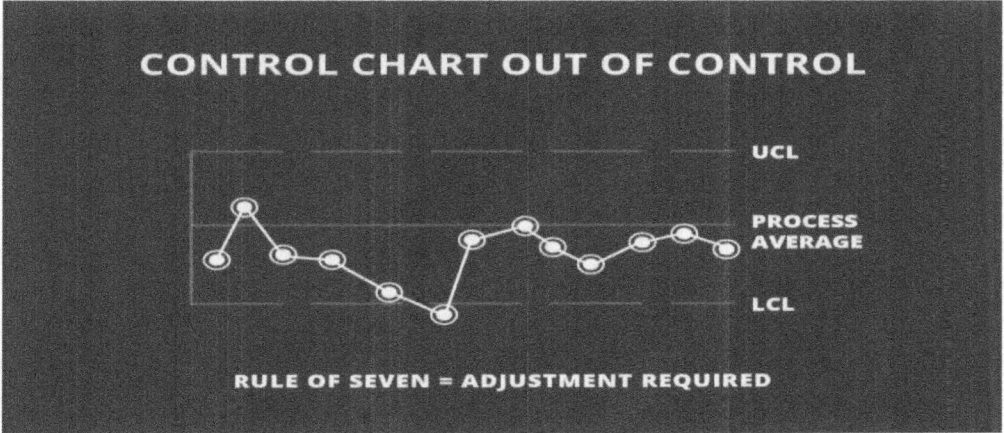

  - ➢ Another concern would be control chart hugging; when the points on the control chart seem to stick close to the center line or to a control limit line, it is called "hugging". This is an indication that something may not be right and needs to be investigated.

Figure 9.13. **Control Chart Hugging**

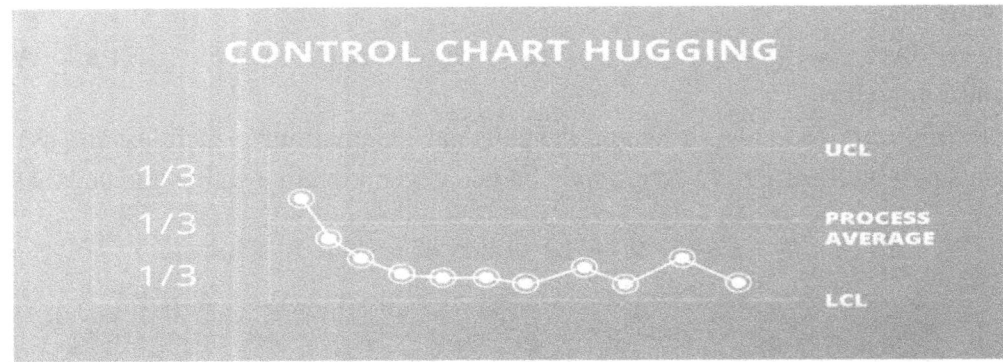

- ✓ Most often used in tracking repetitive processes necessary to produce manufactured lots, can be used to monitor cost/schedule variances, volume, frequency of scope change or other results to ascertain if project management processes are in control
- ✓ Control charts also help identify special causes versus common causes. Common causes are seen as normal, whereas special causes usually require some action.

Figure 9.14. **Process in Control**

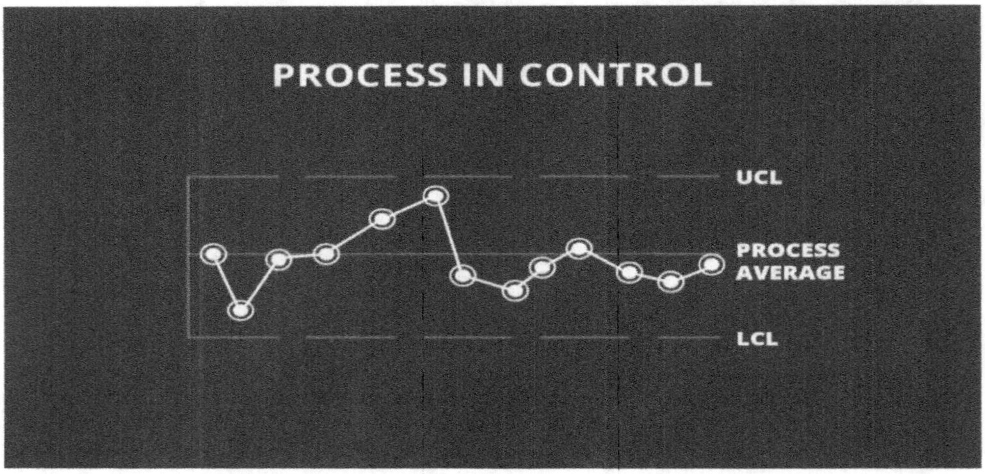

- o Scatter diagrams
    - ✓ Plot ordered pairs (X,Y)
    - ✓ Used to explain positive, inverse or no correlation between dependent variable Y and corresponding independent variable X
    - ✓ Using established correlation, a regression line can be calculated and utilized to determine an estimation of the way in which a change to the independent variable will alter the dependent variable's value.

Figure 9.15. **Example of a Scatter Diagram**

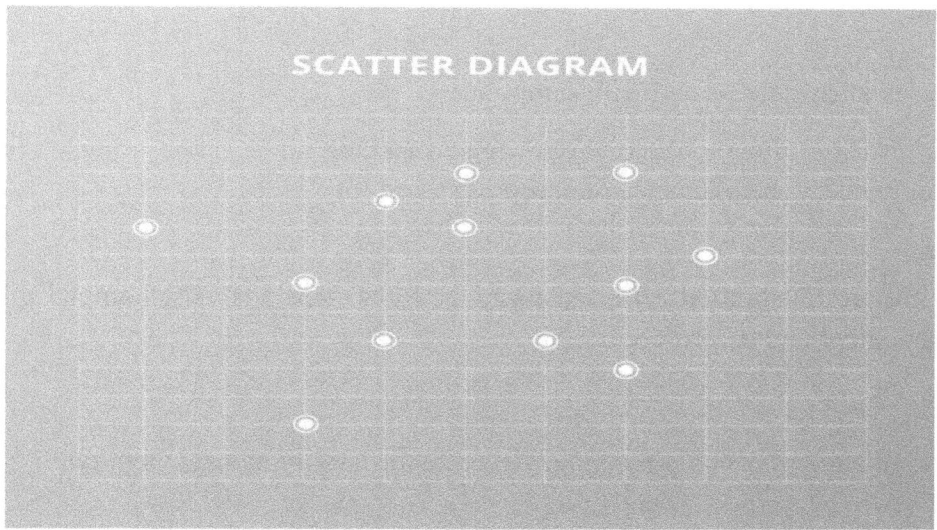

Benchmarking

Benchmarking is a comparison of actual/planned practices to those of similar projects (either within or external to the organization) with the goal of identifying best practices, generating improvement ideas and providing a basis for measuring performance.

Design of experiments

Design of experiments is a statistical method with which factors influencing specific product or process variables, whether under development or in production, can be identified. DOE has a role in the optimization of those products or processes by reducing product performance sensitivity to sources of variation caused by differences in environment or manufacturing. DOE offers a statistical framework whereby all important factors can be systematically altered simultaneously, rather than changing one at a time. Data analysis clarifies product/process ideal conditions, factors affecting the results and occurrence of interactions and synergy among factors

Figure 9.16. **Design of Experiments (DOE)**

EXAM PREPARATION GUIDE 165

Statistical sampling
Statistical sampling helps reduce cost and time. It is seen as a practical alternative to measuring the entire population.

There are two types of risk associated with sampling:
- o Producer's Risk - (alpha) chance of rejecting a good lot
- o Consumer's Risk - (beta) chance of accepting a bad lot

Additional tools
These include (but are not limited to) brainstorming, force field analysis, nominal group techniques and quality management and control tools.

Meetings
Relevant project team members hold meetings to create the quality management plan.

Outputs

Quality management plan
The quality management plan is a key component of the overall project management plan. The format and level of formality of the quality management plan will vary based on the requirements of the project.

Process improvement plan
Topics in the process improvement plan to consider include:
- o Process boundaries - Provide details about the process' purpose, start and end, inputs and outputs, owner and stakeholders
- o Process configuration - Provides a graph of processes that identifies interfaces and is utilized for analysis facilitation
- o Process metrics
- o Target for improved performance.

Quality metrics
These metrics specifically describe project/product attributes and the way in which the Control Quality process will measure them.
- o Tolerance - outlines allowable variations to the metrics
- o Examples - on-time performance, cost control, defect frequency, failure rate, availability, reliability and test coverage

Quality checklists
A quality checklist is a useful aid in a structured approach to ensure that key quality steps are performed.

Project documents updates
These can include (but are not limited to) the stakeholder register, the responsibility assignment matrix (discussed in chapter 10) and the WBS and WBS dictionary.

Perform Quality Assurance
Perform Quality Assurance is the "process of auditing the quality requirements and the results from quality control measurements to ensure that appropriate quality standards and operational definitions are used,"[94] with the main benefit being facilitation of quality processes' improvement.

The goal of this process is to increase confidence in the future or unfinished output's completion in a way that will meet the requirements and expectations that have been specified through prevention or inspecting out of defects during the work-in-progress stage of implementation. This execution process data are created during both Plan Quality Management and Control Quality processes.

PMI® recommends leveraging best practices from quality and management gurus such as Crosby, Deming and Juran.

Quality assurance prevention and inspection activities should have a noticeable influence on the project and provides an iterative way to improve the quality of all processes, limiting waste, eliminating activities that add no value and allowing enhanced levels of efficiency and effectiveness

Figure 9.17. **Perform Quality Assurance: Inputs, Tools and Techniques, and Outputs**

Inputs	Tools & Techniques	Outputs
•Quality management plan •Process improvement plan •Quality metrics •Quality checklists •Project documents	•Quality management and control tools •Quality audits •Process analysis	•Change requests •Project management plan updates •Project document updates •Organizational process assets updates

Inputs

Quality management plan

Process improvement plan

Quality metrics

Quality control measurements

---
[94] Ibid., p. 242

Project documents

Tools & Techniques

Quality management and control tools
- **Affinity diagrams**
  - Share qualities of mind-mapping techniques
  - Used in the generation of ideas that are then combined to produce organized patterns of thought concerning a problem
- **Process decision program charts (PDPC)**
  - Utilized to better comprehend a goal via the steps leading to that goal
  - Useful in that, when planning for contingencies, teams can anticipate intermediate steps that, if ignored, could prevent attainment of the goal
- **Interrelationship digraphs**
  - Offer a creative problem-solving process in scenarios that are moderately complicated and have intermingled logical relationship for up to 50 relevant items
  - May be developed via data attained from affinity, tree or fishbone diagrams
- **Tree diagrams (also known as systemic diagrams)**
  - Utilized for the representation of decomposition hierarchies, e.g., WBS, RBS (risk breakdown structure) and OBS (organizational breakdown structure)
  - Helpful in the visualization of parent-to-child relationships within any decomposition hierarchy using a systematic group of rules to define a nesting relationship
  - Can establish expected values for a limited number of dependent relationships that have been presented in a methodical illustration
- **Prioritization matrices**
  - Detect key issues and appropriate alternatives to be ordered as a set of implementation decisions
- **Activity network diagrams**
  - Network diagram formats are both the Activity on Arrow (AOA) and, most frequently, Activity on Node (AON)
  - Utilized with PERT, CPM and PDM
- **Matrix diagrams**
  - Reveal the strength of relationships between factors, causes and objectives existing between rows and columns forming the matrix
- **Quality audits**
  - Structured, independent processes undertaken to learn if project activities are in compliance with organizational and project policies, processes and procedures
  - Objectives may include:
    - Identification of all implemented good and best practices
    - Identification of all nonconformity, gaps and shortfalls
    - Sharing good practices introduced/implemented in similar organization or industry projects

- Offering assistance in a proactive manner to improve process implementation with the aim of helping the team increase productivity
- Emphasizing each audit's contribution to the organization's lessons learned repository
- Following quality audits, correction of deficiencies should result in the reduction of cost of quality and increases in sponsor/customer acceptance of project's product.
- May be scheduled or random and conducted by either internal or external auditors
- Can substantiate implementation of approved change requests, e.g., updates, corrective/preventative actions and defect repairs

o **Process analysis**
- Following steps outlined in the process improvement plan, identifies necessary improvements, examines problems and constraints experienced and non-value-added activities
- Includes root cause analysis to identify problems, their underlying causes and to develop preventative actions

Figure 9.18. **Examples of Control Tools**

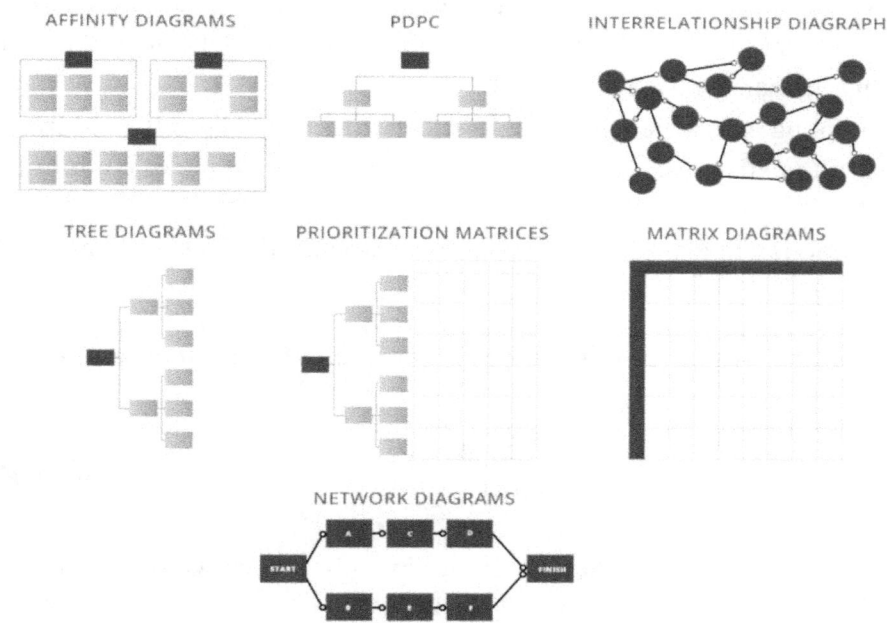

Outputs

Change requests
Change requests involve taking corrective or preventative action or performing defect repair.

Project management plan updates
These include (but are not limited to) elements of the quality, scope, schedule and cost management plans.

Organizational process assets updates

These may include (but are not limited to) the quality standards of the organization and the quality management system.

Control Quality

Control Quality is the "process of monitoring and recording results of executing the quality activities to assess performance and recommend necessary changes."[95] There are two gains made by this process: the identification of the causes of poor process or product quality and recommendations and/or actions to eliminate them and the validation of project deliverables and work meeting key stakeholders' requirements necessary for final acceptance.

To verify this, the process utilizes a set of operational techniques and tasks such as quality assurance (during the planning and executing phases) and quality control (during the executing and closing phases).

The project team's working knowledge of statistical control processes whereby the data contained in the control quality outputs can be evaluated should include knowing the differences between:
- Prevention (preventing errors from entering the process) AND inspection (preventing errors from reaching the hands of the customer)
- Attribute sampling (in which the result either does or does not conform) AND variables sampling (result rated on a continuous scale measuring the degree of conformity)
- Tolerances (specified range of acceptable results) AND control limits (identifying boundaries of common variation in a process or process performance that is statistically stable)

Figure 9.20. **Control Quality: Inputs, Tools and Techniques, and Outputs**

Inputs	Tools & Techniques	Outputs
• Project management plan • Quality metrics • Quality checklists • Work performance data • Approved change requests • Deliverables • Project documents • Organization process assets	• Seven basic quality tools • Statistical sampling • Approved change request review	• Quality control measurements • Validated changes • Verified deliverables • Work performance information • Change requests • Project management plan updates • Organizational process assets updates

---

[95] Ibid., p. 248

Inputs

Project management plan
The project management plans includes the project quality management plan.

Quality metrics
Described earlier in this chapter, in this context, examples include function points, mean time between failure (MTBF) and mean time to repair (MTTR).

Quality checklists
Quality checklists provide a structured approach to verifying quality.

Work performance data
Work performance data may comprise planned versus actual technical performance, planned versus actual schedule performance and planned versus actual cost performance.

Deliverables
The final project product, service or result is made of deliverables.

Project documents
Project documents may include (but are not limited to) agreements, quality audit reports and change logs, both supported by corrective action plans, training plans and effectiveness assessments, and process documentation as obtained using either the seven basic quality or quality management and control tools.

Tools & Techniques

Seven basic quality tools

Statistical sampling

Inspection
The examination of a work product aimed at determining if it does or does not conform to documented standards, an inspection usually includes measurements and can be done at any level.

Approved change requests review
All changes approved through Perform Integrated Change Control should be reviewed to ensure they were completed.

Outputs

Quality control measurements
The documented results of control quality activities, the quality control measurements should be prepared in the specified format as per the Plan Quality Management process.

Validated changes

Verified deliverables

Work performance information
In the context of this process, this includes information concerning project requirements fulfillment, e.g., causes for rejections, required rework or necessary process adjustments.

Change requests

Project management plan updates
This may include (but are not limited to) updates to the quality management and process improvement plans.

Project documents updates
Updated project documents include (but are not limited to) quality standards, quality audit reports and change logs backed by corrective action plans, training plans and effectiveness assessments
and process documentation, e.g., information gained through the use of the 7QC, quality management or control tools.

Organizational process assets updates
Facets of these updated assets may include (but are not limited to) completed checklists and lessons learned documentation, which can involve variance causes, reasoning behind corrective actions selected and other forms of lessons learned from quality control, all of which are documented to become part of the project's and performing organization's historical database.

Test What You've Learned

1) What is the difference between quality and grade?
   a) Quality is the degree to which a set of inherent characteristics fulfill requirements and grade is a classification of deliverables having the same functional use but different technical characteristics.
   b) Grade is the degree to which a set of inherent characteristics fulfill requirements and quality is a classification of deliverables having the same functional use but different technical characteristics.
   c) A correction of a product's grade is essential but a product's lack of quality just means it can be utilized for general use.
   d) Grade and quality are interchangeable.

2) The main benefit of _____ is that it provides guidance and direction as to the way the project team will manage and confirm quality over the course of the project.
   a) Using the seven basic quality tools
   b) The Plan Quality Management process
   c) Benchmarking
   d) Verifying deliverables

3) Cause-and-effect diagrams are also known as _____.
   a) Pareto diagrams
   b) Scatter diagrams
   c) Fishbone diagrams
   d) Process flow diagrams

4) The cost of conformance includes:
   a) Internal failure costs
   b) Rework and scrap
   c) Prevention and appraisal costs
   d) Liabilities and warranty work

5) A process is out of control when:
   a) A data point surpasses a control limit.
   b) There are ten consecutive plot points above or below the mean.
   c) A control limit exceeds a data point.
   d) A control limit is set at ±3.

6) A statistical method by which factors that influence specific product or process variables can be identified is termed:
   a) Statistical sampling
   b) Benchmarking
   c) Scatter plotting
   d) Design of experiments

7) Which, if any, of the following statements are true?
   a) The goal of the Perform Quality Assurance process to offer guidance and direction to the way quality will be managed and confirmed over the project's course.
   b) The process of auditing quality requirements and the results of quality control measurements is called the Perform Quality Assurance process.
   c) Quality audits reveal the strength of relationships between factors and causes impacting product or project quality.
   d) None of these statements are true.

8) _____ are very similar to _____.
   a) Interrelationship digraphs, prioritization matrices
   b) PDPC and PERT
   c) Activity on Arrow formats, Activity on Node formats
   d) Affinity diagrams, mind-mapping techniques

9) Benefits of the Control Quality process include:
   a) Identification of the causes of poor process or product quality
   b) Validation of project deliverables meeting key stakeholders' requirements
   c) Guidance as how quality will be managed over the course of the project
   d) Both a) and b)

10) Inputs to the Control Quality process include:
    a) Quality metrics
    b) Work performance information
    c) Approved change requests review
    d) Quality control measurements

Chapter 10: Project Human Resource Management

It is possible that you already have an understanding of what is involved in human resource management and the structure, formation and guidance of a team. However, as you prepare for the PMP® exam, you should also be aware of the way in which *The PMBOK® Guide* formally defines and details those processes.

Project Human Resource Management "includes the processes that organize, manage, and lead the project team" and "is comprised of the people with assigned roles and responsibilities for completing the project."[96]

Project Human Resource Management incorporates four distinct processes that guide project managers while they plan, acquire, develop and manage the project team. All of them interact, both with each other and with other Knowledge Area processes, and, due to these interactions, planning does not end once the team is assembled. Throughout the course of a project, this planning can involve the addition of new team members following the creation of a work breakdown schedule by the initial team, added risk planning to account for possible shortfalls in those individuals' skill levels, and alterations in activity durations when taking those levels of competency into account.

Project team management and leadership include (but are not limited to) factors such as team environment, team members' geographical locations, communications among stakeholders, politics (both internal and external), cultural issues and the uniqueness of the organization that can affect project performance. That being the case, the project manager must be attuned to and influence those factors. The project manager needs to also keep a close eye on issues of professional and ethical behavior, ensuring that all team members ascribe to the tenets of that behavior.

Plan Human Resource Management
Plan Human Resource Management is the "process of identifying and documenting project roles, responsibilities, required skills, reporting relationships, and creating a staffing management plan,"[97] the central benefits of which is that it institutes project roles, responsibilities and organization charts as well as a staffing management plan that includes a staff acquisition and release timetable.

Needless to say, the project manager wants the team to be comprised of individuals with the skills necessary to the success of the project; human resource planning provides the means to determine what those skills are and to identify human resources having those skills.

Other issues that must be addressed include training needs, team-building strategies, recognition and rewards programs, compliance considerations, safety issues and the staffing management plan's organ-

---

[96] Project Management Institute, *A Guide to the Project Management Body of Knowledge (The PMBOK® Guide)*, 5th ed., p. 255.

[97] Ibid., p. 258

izational impact, keeping in mind that all of these factors can affect project costs, schedules, risks, quality and other areas of a project.

Figure 10.1. **Plan Human Resource Management: Inputs, Tools and Techniques, and Outputs**

Inputs	Tools & Techniques	Outputs
• Project management plan • Activity resource requirements • Enterprise environmental factors • Organizational process assets	• Organizational charts & position descriptions • Networking • Organizational theiry • Expert judgment • Meetings	• Human resource management plan

Inputs

Project management plan

For this process, the project management plan provides information that includes (but is not limited to):
- o The project life cycle as well as the processes to be utilized for each phase
- o The way in which work will be done to achieve project objectives
- o A change management plan documenting the monitoring and controlling of changes
- o The means of maintaining project baselines' integrity
- o Stakeholders' needs and methods of communication

Activity resource requirements

Enterprise environmental factors

Enterprise environmental factors having an effect of this process include (but are not limited to) organizational culture and structure, existing human resources and their geographical dispersion, personnel administrative policies and marketplace conditions.

Organizational process assets

The assets affecting this process include (but are not limited to) organizational standard processes, policies and role descriptions, organizational charts and position description templates, lessons learned in previous projects and escalation procedures for dealing with issues both within the team and the performing organization.

Tools & Techniques

Organizational charts and position descriptions

Figure 10.2. **Example of an Organizational Chart**

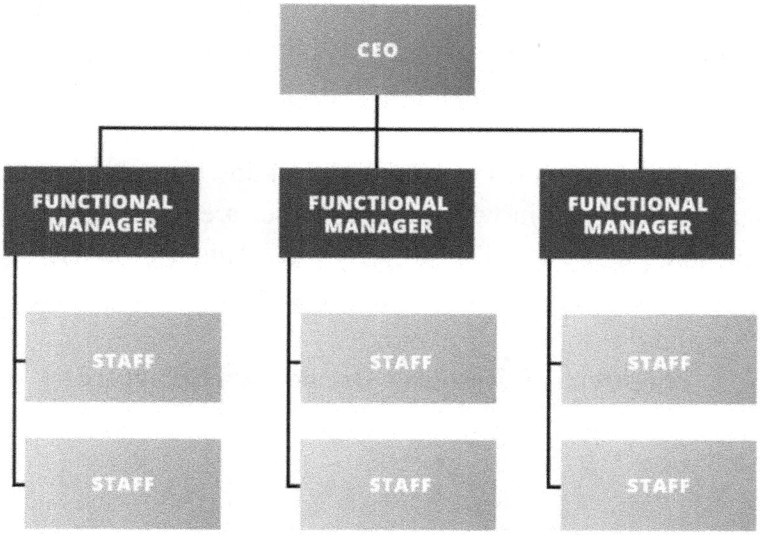

The formats that document team members' roles and responsibilities are most frequently one of three types: hierarchical, matrix and test-oriented. In addition, subsidiary plans, such as those for risk, quality or communications, may also list project assignments.

What is crucial, beyond the method used, is that there is an unambiguous owner of each and every work package and that every team member is cognizant of their own roles and responsibilities.

Hierarchical-type charts

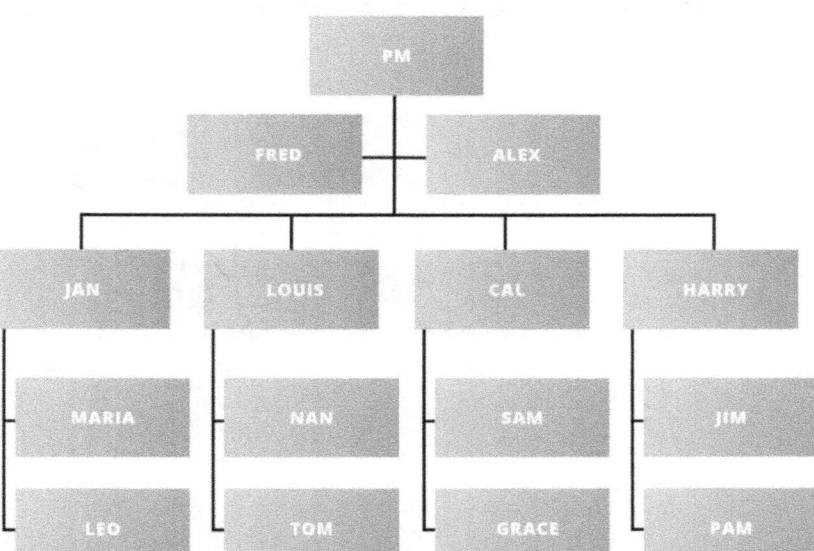

Figure 10.3. Organization Chart (Hierarchical)

These organization charts are traditional and are utilized to show positions and their respective responsibilities in a graphical, top-down format. Work breakdown structures designed in this way display the manner in which project deliverables are broken down into work packages as well as high-level areas of responsibility.

In contrast, an organizational breakdown structure (OBS) is organized as to the existing departments, units or teams of an organization, with project activities or work packages listed under each department.

Something else arranged in this fashion is the resource breakdown structure (RBS), which is a resource list organized according to a hierarchy in which the resources are related by category and type, used in the facilitation of the planning and control of project work. This can be useful when tracking project costs and can be used in conjunction with the accounting system of an organization.

Figure 10.4. **Resource Breakdown Structure**

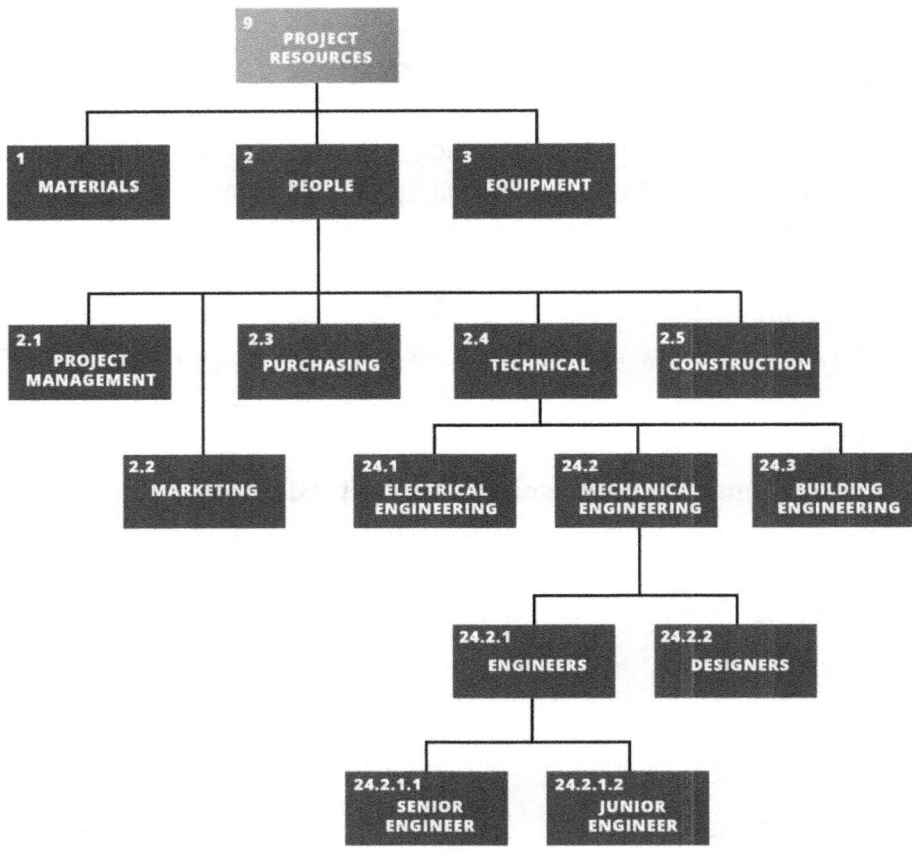

Matrix-based charts

Table 10.1. **RACI Matrix**

	ROLE 1	ROLE 2	ROLE 3	ROLE 4
TASK 1	R	C	I	A
TASK 2	I	I	R	A
TASK 3	C	R	A	I
TASK 4	A	R	I	
TASK 5	R	A	C	I
TASK 6	C	C	A+R	I

RACI MATRIX:
- **R** RESPONSIBLE PERSON WORKING ON ACTIVITY
- **A** ACCOUNTABLE PERSON WITH DECISION AUTHORITY
- **C** CONSULT-KEY STAKEHOLDER WHO SHOULD BE INCLUDED IN DECISION OR WORK ACTIVITY
- **I** INFORM-NEEDS TO KNOW OF DECISION OR ACTION

A grid displaying the project resources assigned to each work package, the responsibility assignment matrix (RAM) is utilized to illustrate the connections between work packages/activities and members of the project team.

These can be developed at various levels, dependent on the size of a project. For example, "a high-level RAM can define what a project team or group is responsible for within each component of the WBS, while lower-level RAMs are used within the group to designate roles, responsibilities and levels of authority for specific activities."[98]

The above table is a RACI (responsible, accountable, consult and inform) chart, listing the work to be completed in the left column (Activity), with the team members and their designated roles within each activity shown in the rest of the table. This form of chart can be very useful in those situations in which both internal and external resources comprise the team as it ensures clear classifications of roles and expectations.

---

[98] Ibid., p. 262

Text-oriented formats

Figure 10.5. Role Description (Text)

Role
Responsibilities
Authority

If detailed descriptions of team members' tasks, such as specific responsibilities, authority, competencies and qualifications are needed, they can be outlined in text-oriented formats such the one seen in figure 10.3. Also known as position descriptions and role-responsibility-authority forms, they can be utilized as templates for future projects, particularly when, throughout the current project, information updates are made by applying lessons learned.

Networking
The "formal and informal interaction with others in an organization, industry, or professional environment,"[99] networking is an excellent means of grasping the political and interpersonal elements that can influence the success of various staffing management options. Effective networking can improve human resource management by increasing knowledge of and access to assets such as strong competencies, specialized experience and opportunities for external partnerships. While it can be a helpful technique when used at a project's inception, it can continue to enhance project management professional development both during and after the close of a project.

Organizational theory
Information as to the ways people, teams and organizational units behave can be found in organizational theory. Its use can lessen the time, cost and effort necessary to the creation of the Plan Human Resource Management process outputs as well as increase planning efficiency. However, it is still important to understand that organizational structures are not all the same, having differing individual response, performance and personal relationship characteristics. In addition, as a team's maturity level increases over the course of a project life cycle, organizational theories may
suggest the exercise of a flexible style of leadership that adapts to those changes.

Expert judgment
In this context, expert judgment is utilized in the:

- Listing of the preliminary requirements for the necessary skills
- Based on standardized role descriptions within the organization, assessing the roles required for the project

---

[99] Ibid., p. 263

- Determining the preliminary level of effort and the number of resources necessary to meeting project objectives
- Based on the culture of the organization, determining the needed reporting relationships
- Providing guidelines on the lead time required for staffing, as based on lessons learned and market conditions
- Identifying risks associated with staff acquisition, retention and release plans
- Ascertaining and suggesting programs for compliance with applicable government and union contracts

Meetings

Outputs

Human resource management plan
Not surprisingly, the primary and in fact only output of the Plan Human Resources Management process is the human resource management plan, a part of the project management plan that "provides guidance on how project human resources should be defined, staffed, managed, and eventually."[100] This plan, as well as any later revisions, also serve as inputs to the Develop Project Management Plan process.

The human resource management plan comprises (but is not limited to):
- Roles and responsibilities
  - Role
    - The function taken by or assigned to a person involved in the project
    - Examples - public relations supervisor, business analyst and production coordinator
  - Authority
    - The right to make use of resources, make decisions, authorize approvals, and direct others as they complete the work of the project
  - Responsibility
    - Those duties and work to which a project team member has been assigned and that he/she is expected to perform to complete the activities of the project
  - Competency
    - The ability and skills necessary to completing activities to which a person has been assigned within the constraints of the project
    - Mismatches must be identified as they occur, followed by the initiation of proactive responses such as training, hiring and scheduling and scope changes.
- Project organization charts
- Staffing management plan
  - An element of the human resource management plan describing at what time and how project team members will be acquired, the length of time they will be needed and, specifically, the way in which human resource requirements will be met

---

[100] Ibid., p. 264

- ✓ Continuously updated during the project with the goal of directing ongoing acquisition and development of team members
- ✓ Varies by application and size of project, but may include:
  - ➢ Staff acquisition
    - Within or external to the organization
    - Central or distant locations
    - Costs for every level of expertise required for the project
    - Level of assistance to be provided by the organization's HR department and functional managers
- o Resource calendars
  - ✓ Provide information regarding working days/shifts during which resources are available
  - ✓ Individual and/or collective timeframes necessary for project team members
  - ✓ Timeframes for initiation of acquisition activities
- o Staff release plan
  - ✓ Releasing team members from a project means that those resource costs are no longer charged to that project, which reduces project costs.
  - ✓ Also mitigates human resource risks occurring during/at the end of a project
  - ✓ Improvement in morale caused by preplanned and smooth transitions to upcoming projects
- o Training needs
- o Recognition and rewards
- o Compliance
  - ✓ Strategies to achieve compliance with applicable government regulations, union contracts and other set human resource policies
- o Safety
  - ✓ Protection of team members from safety hazards must be addressed in the form of policies and procedures, information that should also be included in the risk register.

Acquire Project Team

Acquire Project Team is the "process of confirming human resource availability and obtaining the team necessary to complete project activities,"[101] that has the benefit of providing an outline of and guidance for the selection of a successful team and assignment of the responsibility to members of that team.

It should be kept in mind that the project management may not necessarily directly control team member selection due to collective bargaining agreements, the use of subcontractor personnel, matrix project environment, internal or external reporting relationships, etc.

Nevertheless, during the process of acquiring the team, certain factors must come under consideration, including:

- o The project manager/management team must effectively negotiate with (and persuade) those in the position to provide the human resources necessary to the project.

---

[101] Ibid., p. 267

- o Project schedules, budgets, customer satisfaction, quality and risks may all be affected by failing to acquire those human resources.
- o The assignment of alternative resources, even with lower competencies, may be necessary if the human resources are unavailable because of constraints such as economic factors or previous assignments to other projects, but only if this does not violate legal, regulatory, mandatory or other specific criteria.

Figure 10.6. **Acquire Project Team: Inputs, Tools and Techniques, and Outputs**

Inputs	Tools & Techniques	Outputs
• Human resource management plan • Enterprise environmental factors • Organizational process assets	• Pre-Assignment Negotiation • Acquisition • Virtual teams • Multi-criteria decision analysis	• Project staff assignments • Resource calendars • Project management plan updates

Inputs

Human resource management plan

Enterprise environmental factors
Enterprise environmental factors affecting the Acquire Project Team process include (but are not limited to) existing human resources information such as those resources' availability, levels of competency, prior experience, interest in working on the project and cost rate.

Organizational process assets
These include (but are not limited to) organizational standard policies, processes and procedures.

Tools & Techniques

Pre-assignment
The advance selection of project team members involves their pre-assignment, a situation that may be caused by the project being the result of the identification of specific individuals as part of a competitive proposal, the dependence of a project on the expertise of certain persons, or if, within the project charter, there are definitions of some staff assignments.

Negotiation
Negotiation of staff assignments is common to many projects. Examples include functional managers, who warrant that the project receives staff with the appropriate competencies and those staff members are able, willing and approved to work on the project until such time that they have met their responsi-

bilities as well as other project management teams within the performing organization and external organizations, vendors, suppliers, etc. to assign appropriate, scarce/specialized, qualified/certified or other specified human resources. External negotiating policies, practices, processes, guidelines, legal and other criteria must be taken into consideration.

Acquisition
The need for acquisition arises when the performing organization cannot supply the staff necessary to the completion of a project and services from outside sources must be acquired. That can necessitate hiring individual consultants or subcontracting elements of the project to another organization.

Virtual teams
Virtual teams are defined as "groups of people with a shared goal who fulfill their roles with little or no time spent meeting face to face"[102] This model makes the formation of teams from those in the same organization who reside in widespread geographic areas, who can provide specialized expertise but live at a distance, who work from home or on different shifts or who have mobility limitations/disabilities very feasible.

However, keep in mind that relying on virtual teams has some disadvantages, which include misunderstandings, feelings of isolation, problems sharing knowledge or experience among team members and technology costs. Taking the time to establish clear expectations, facilitate communication, develop conflict protocols, include everyone in the decision-making process, recognize and grasp cultural differences and share credit for success is essential.

Multi-criteria decision analysis
In this context, the use of this tool involves developing criteria based on the needs of the team, weighting those criteria in terms of the relative importance of those needs and selecting team members who will best meet them. Some examples include:
- o Availability (Will a potential team member be available to work over the course of the project timeline?)
- o Cost (Will the cost of retaining that team member fall within the prescribed budget?)
- o Experience (Is their experience relevant and will it contribute to the project?)
- o Ability (Are their competencies in line with project needs?)
- o Knowledge (Is the team member familiar with the customer, similar projects and the nuances of the project environment?)
- o Skills (Does the team member have the skills that enable them to utilize a project tool, implementation or training?)
- o Attitude (Can the member work with others as part of a cohesive team?)
- o International factors (In what geographical location and time zone does the member reside and what are their communication capabilities?)

---

[102] Ibid., p. 271

Outputs

Project staff assignments
Documenting these assignments can be done through the use of a project team directory, memos to team members and names included in the project management plan via project organization charts and schedules.

Resource calendars
Creation of a resource calendar requires knowledge about team members' availability and schedule constraints (time zones, work hours, vacation time, local holidays and commitments to other projects).

Project management plan updates

Develop Project Team
Develop Project Team is a fairly easy concept to understand; a project manager assembles the team and then develops them in a way that best serves the project objectives. The formal definition is that this is the "process of improving competencies, team member interaction, and overall team environment to enhance project performance,"[103] resulting in better teamwork, improved people skills and competencies, employees that are more motivated, reduction of staff turnover rates and improved project performance overall.

A primary responsibility of the project manager involves creating an environment that enables teamwork. Teams can be motivated through the use of challenges and opportunities, timely feedback and support as necessary, and recognition and providing rewards for good performance. The best team performance is gained through:

- Open and effective communication
- Team-building opportunities
- Building trust among team members
- Managing conflicts constructively
- Encouraging solving problems and decision making done collaboratively

All of this must be accomplished while keeping the diversity (language, experience, culture) of team members in mind and actually capitalizing on those cultural differences by focusing on the development and maintenance of the team and promoting working independently within a climate of mutual trust. This requires effective communication between team members over the entire life course of the project.

---

[103] Ibid., p. 273

Figure 10.7. **Develop Project Team: Inputs, Tools and Techniques, and Outputs**

Inputs	Tools & Techniques	Outputs
• Human resource management plan • Project staff assignments • Resource calendars	• Interpersonal skills • Training • Team-building activities • Ground rules • Colocation • Recognition and rewards • Personnel assessment tools	• Team performance assessments • Enterprise environmental factors updates

Inputs

Human resource management plan

The human resource management plan guides the definition, staffing, management, control of and eventual release of project human resources, identifying training strategies and as a result of ongoing team performance assessments, etc., adding elements such as rewards, feedback, additional training and disciplinary actions.

Project staff assignments

Resource calendars

Tools & Techniques

Interpersonal skills

Interpersonal skills, occasionally referred to as "soft skills," are "behavioral competencies that include proficiencies such as communication skills, emotional intelligence, conflict resolution, influence, team building, and group facilitation."[104]

Training

Training activities can be formal or informal, with methods that include classroom, online, computer-based, on-the-job provided by another project team member, mentoring and coaching. Skills development can be an element of the human resource management plan. Training does not always require planning; it can also occur due to observations, conversations, and appraisals of performance that occur during the controlling process. Costs of training can either be incorporated into the project budget or, if additional skills will add value to future projects, supported by the performing organization.

---

[104] Ibid., p. 275

Team-building activities

The goal of team-building activities is assisting individual team members in their efforts to effectively work together. These activities are especially useful when face-to-face contact is limited because team members are working from remote locations.

These activities are not limited to the initial phases of a project; instead, they should continue throughout that project's life cycle. It is the task of a project manager to continually monitor the functionality of the team and its performance to decide if any preventative or corrective actions are necessary.

The PMBOK® Guide cites what is known as the Tuckman model, which incorporates five development stages a team may pass through. However, it should not be assumed that these stages always occur in order; some teams remain in a particular stage, move forward only to return to an earlier stage or, in the case of team who have worked together previously, omit one stage altogether.

- Forming
    - ✓ The team members meet, learn about the project and their roles/responsibilities in the project and tend to be independent and not particularly open.
- Storming
    - ✓ As the team begins to attend to the project work, technical decisions and project management approach, they may not be open to differing ideas and perspectives and the environment may become counterproductive.
- Norming
    - ✓ As team members start working together and adjusting their work habits and behaviors in support of the team, they develop trust in each other.
- Performing
    - ✓ Teams attaining this stage are interdependent, easily work through problems and have become a well-organized unit.
- Adjourning
    - ✓ The work is finished and the team is moving on, which usually happens when, as deliverables are completed or as part of the Close Project or Phase process, the staff is released from the project.

Figure 10.8. **Team Development**

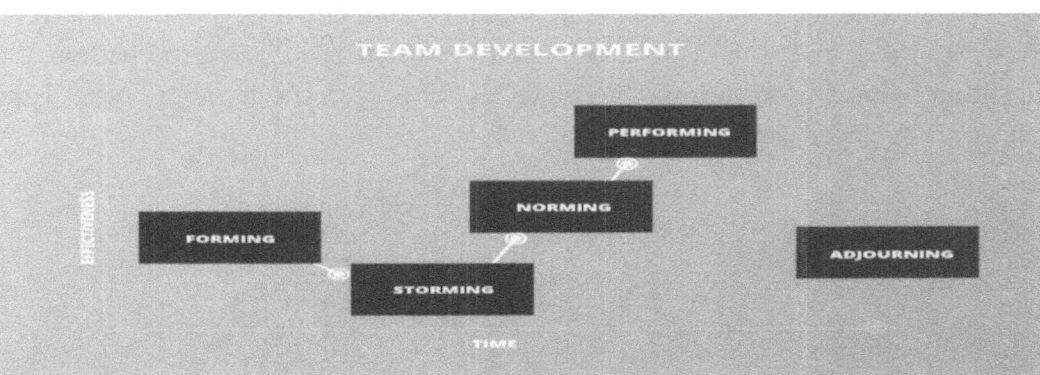

Ground rules
Ground rules comprise codes of conduct, communication, working together and observing etiquette and set clear expectations concerning acceptable team member behavior.

Colocation
As you can most likely surmise, colocation (or *tight matrix*) is the placement of many (or all) project team members actively working on a project in the same physical location, with the goal of improving their ability to work as a team. This can be limited to strategically crucial points in the project or can extend over the entire project.

While this can be a useful strategy, the benefits of virtual teams –more skilled resources, reduced costs, fewer travel and relocation expenses and team proximity to suppliers and stakeholders – should be kept in mind.

Recognition and rewards
The process of awarding of recognition and rewards is developed during the Plan Human Resource Management process and, to be effective, must involve providing individuals with rewards that satisfy their actual needs. Decisions to make such awards are made based on project performance appraisals and awards can be tangible, e.g., cash, or intangible, which some consider to be an even more effective motivation.

There are several Theories of Motivation. In human resource management plans, these theories are noted as recognition and reward systems. The best systems are those in which desired behaviors are acknowledged and rewarded.

The most beneficial system for team building has win-win rewards versus win-lose rewards. In win-lose reward systems, only one team member wins and others do not; this is detrimental to the sense of being a team and maintaining the team's optimal effectiveness.

Let us delve deeper into each of the theories.

Maslow's Hierarchy of Needs
All project managers should understand this basic theory. Abraham Maslow's theory groups human needs into five basic sections. Each section is a prerequisite for the next one to work. It is much like building blocks, as the foundation is needed to build each stage of a high structure. The needs of employees form an hierarchy, from lower needs to higher needs. The basic premise of this theory is that team members have needs and they interrelate.

Figure 10.9. Maslow's Hierarchy of Needs

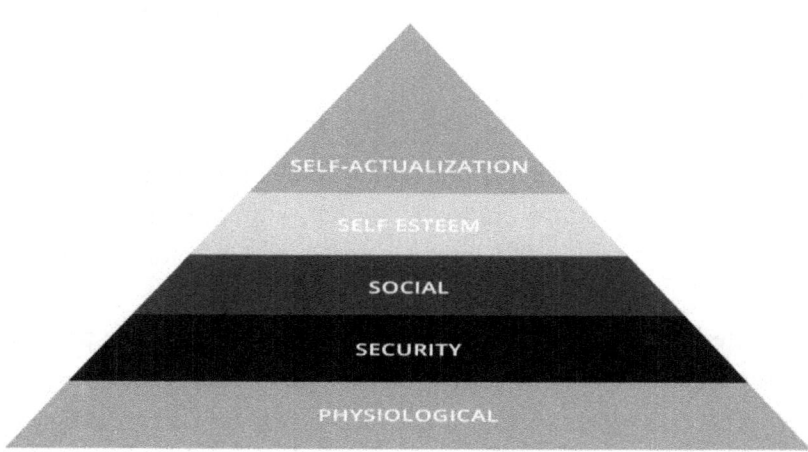

Expectancy Theory
Victor Vroom's motivational theory states that team members' choices are determined by the expected outcomes. If team members believe a goal is achievable, they will work towards it.

McGregor's Theory X and Theory Y
This theory states that people in a workplace can be categorized in two ways, Theory X and Theory Y.

Theory X states that team members only work to fulfill their personal goals. They do not like work and are unmotivated; therefore they must be forced to be productive. Desired results are achieved through constant supervision. For instance, assembly-line organizations often closely monitor and evaluate each action. Theory Y states that team members are self-motivated to work well to achieve the organization's or project's goals. Managers provide little external motivation to them. For instance, when organizations allow telecommuting and encourage it, managers trust that team members will continue to achieve desired results.

This theory is not used by organizations. Rather, managers use it regardless of the type of work.

Contingency Theory
Fred E. Fiedler developed this theory in the 1960s and 1970s. It states that a leader's effectiveness is determined by two sets of factors.

The first set of factors measure whether the leader is task-oriented or relationship-oriented. The second set of factors evaluates situational factors in the workplace, such as the existence of a stressful work environment. For instance, a task-oriented leader is more effective in a stressful environment; a relationship-oriented leader is more effective in a calm environment.

The opposite can also be true because a leader can be effective in one environment but not the other.

Herzberg's Motivation-Hygiene Theory

This theory was a result of studies conducted by Herzberg to determine which factors influence work satisfaction. The theory states that the presence of certain factors does not make someone satisfied, but the absence of particular factors makes someone unsatisfied. He categorized the factors into two groups, motivation factors and hygiene factors.

Hygiene factors must be present but they do not solely lead to motivation. Poor hygiene factors can diminish motivation. Hygiene factors are company policy, supervision, good relationship with boss, working conditions, paycheck, personal life, status, security, and relationship with coworkers.

Motivation factors motivate but are not effective unless hygiene factors are present. Motivation factors are achievement, recognition, work, responsibility, advancement, and growth.

McClelland's Theory of Needs

This theory is also known as Achievement Theory. It states that employees are motivated by three primary needs: achievement, power, and affiliation.

Team members who have a high need for achievement, or nAch, have a need to be visible. Although they prefer to work alone, they gravitate towards similar team members who have the same need. nAch team members do not prefer high risk projects because their individual effort may be affected by the project's risk. They also do not prefer low risk projects because their personal effort may not be recognized.

Team members who have a need for power, or nPow, mostly desire personal or institutional (social) power. Team members with social nPow are generally more effective than team members with personal nPow.

Humans with the need for affiliation (nAff) generally want to be part of a team, to uphold successful relationships, and to provide excellent face-to-face customer service. Effective project managers understand the needs of each team member, whether it be nAch, nPow, or nAff. They manage the different roles of each individual and motivate the team to achieve their maximum potential.

Figure 10.10. McClelland's Theory of Needs

Hersey and Blanchard Situational Leadership Theory

The situational leadership model is a leadership theory developed by Paul Hersey and Ken Blanchard. The fundamental concept of the situational leadership theory is that there is no single best style of leadership and successful leaders are those who adapt their leadership style to the maturity of the individual or group they are attempting to lead or influence. Effective leadership varies, not only with the person or group that is being influenced, but it also depends on the project, activity, or function that should be completed.

Figure 10.11. **Hersey and Blanchard Situational Leadership Theory**

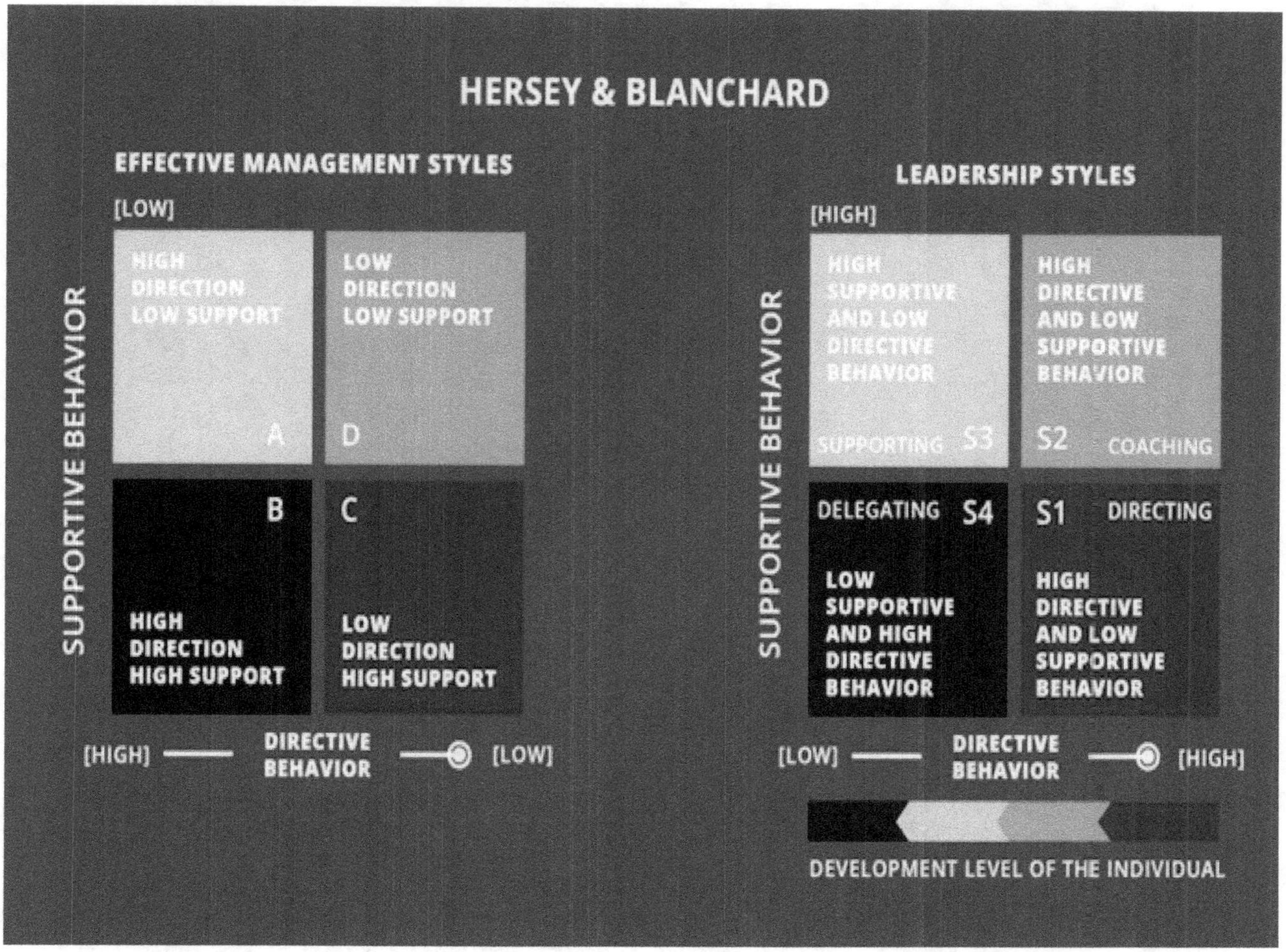

The table below summarizes the motivational theories that typically appear in the PMP® exam.

Table 10.1. **Motivational Theories**

MOTIVATIONAL THEORIES

THEORY	SOURCE	DESCRIPTION
HIERARCHY OF NEEDS	MASLOW	PSYCHOLOGICAL NEED, SECURITY, SOCIAL, SELF-ESTEEM, SELF-ACTUALIZATION
THEORY X	MACGREGOR	THE AVERAGE WORKER DISLIKES WORK AND AVOIDS WORK WHEN POSSIBLE. THE AVERAGE WORKER AVOIDS INCREASED RESPONSIBILITY AND SEEKS TO BE DIRECTED. MANAGEMENT STYLE: AUTHORITARIAN
THEORY Y	MACGREGOR	THE AVERAGE WORKER WANTS TO BE ACTIVE AND FINDS THE PHYSICAL AND MENTAL EFFORT ON THE JOB SATISFYING. MANAGEMENT STYLE: PARTICIPATORY
THEORY Z	OUCHI	THE SECRET TO JAPANESE SUCCESS AND QUALITY IS NOT TECHNOLOGY, BUT A SPECIAL WAY OF HANDLING PEOPLE: TRUST, RECOGNIZE EVER CHANGING RELATIONSHIPS AMONG PEOPLE AND INTIMACY.
	HERZBERG'S MOTIVATION HYGIENE THEORY	POOR HYGIENE DESTROYS MOTIVATION; IMPROVING HYGIENE WILL NOT MOTIVATE. HAVING AN OPPORTUNITY TO SUCCEED/ MOTIVATING AGENT WILL INCREASE MOTIVATION.
	FRED FIELDER'S CONTINGENCY THEORY	A LEADERS EFFECTIVENESS IS CONTINGENT UPON TWO FACTORS; FIRST FACTOR MEASURES WHETHER LEADER IS RELATION-ORIENTED OR TASK-ORIENTED; SECOND FACTOR EVALUATES SITUATIONAL FACTORS IN THE WORKPLACE.
	VICTOR VROOM	PEOPLE ARE MOTIVATED IF THERE IS AN EXPECTATION OF A FAVORABLE OUTCOME.
LIFE CYCLE THEORY	HIERARCHY AND BLANCHARD	LEADERSHIP STYLE MUST CHANGE WITH THE MATURITY OF INDIVIDUAL EMPLOYEES.

Personnel assessment tools

Tools such as attitudinal surveys, specific assessments, structured interviews, ability tests and focus groups provide both the project manager and the team with insights into team members' areas of strength and weakness.

Outputs

Team performance assessments

Measurement of a successful team's performance is done in consideration of "technical success according to agreed-upon project objectives (including quality levels), performance on project schedule (finished on time), and performance on budget (finished within financial constraints)."[105]

Indicators of a team's effectiveness include improvements in skills and competencies that facilitate more effective completion of assignments and assist the individuals in performing better as a team, reductions in staff turnover rate and increases in team cohesiveness through which members openly share both experiences and information, thus improving overall project performance.

Performance evaluations allow improvements to be made through the identification of what is required in the areas of training, coaching, mentoring or necessary changes, as well as the resources needed to implement these activities and achieve improvements in performance. All of this must be documented and forwarded to relevant parties.

Enterprise environmental factors updates

These include (but are not limited to) personnel administration, employee training records and skill assessments.

Manage Project Team

Manage Project Team is the "process of tracing team member performance, providing feedback, resolving issues, and managing team changes to optimize project performance,"[106] that provides the benefits of influencing team behavior, managing conflict, resolving issues and appraising the performance of team members.

Management of the project team results in the submission of change requests, updating of the human resources management plan and resolution of issues, with input provided for performance appraisals and lessons learned added to the organization's database.

Project managers need a variety of skills with which to foster teamwork and integrate team members' efforts, with the goal of creating highly effective teams. Special emphasis is placed on communication, conflict management, negotiation and leadership as project managers offer challenging assignments to team members as well as recognition for high performance.

---

[105] Ibid., p. 278

[106] Ibid., p. 279

Figure 10.12. **Manage Project Team: Inputs, Tools and Techniques, and Outputs**

Inputs	Tools & Techniques	Outputs
• Human resource management plan • Project staff assignments • Team performance assessments • Issue log • Work performance reports • Organization process assets	• Observation and conversation • Project performance appraisals • Conflict management • Interpersonal skills	• Change requests • Project management plan updates • Project documents updates • Enterprise environmental factors updates • Organizational process assets updates

Inputs

Human resource management plan

In this context, the human resource management plan offers guidance on definition, staffing, management, control and eventual release of project human resources, including (but not limited to) rules and responsibilities, project organization and the staffing management plan.

Project staff assignments

Team performance assessments

Issue log

Because issues are bound to arise when managing the project team, this log is utilized to document and monitor whoever is responsible for the timely resolution of those issues.

Work performance reports

These reports document comparisons between the current project status and project forecasts and can be helpful to project managers in the areas of schedule, cost and quality control and scope validation.

Information gained from both performance reports and related forecasts can facilitate the determination of future human resource requirements, recognition and rewards and staffing management plan updates.

Organizational process assets

Organizational process assets affecting the Manage Project Team process comprise (but are not limited to) certificates of appreciation, newsletters, websites, bonus structures, corporate apparel and other organizational perquisites.

Tools & Techniques

Observation and conversation

As mentioned previously, project managers can remain attuned to the work and attitudes of project team members through observation and conversation as the team monitors progress toward attainment of project deliverables, accomplishments and interpersonal issues.

Project performance appraisals

Project performance appraisals are opportunities for providing constructive feedback, clarifying roles, identifying new issues, and working towards ensuring there are clear and specific goals for the way forward.

Conflict management

There can be no doubt that conflict, emerging from scarce resources, scheduling priorities and personal work styles, is inevitable in a project environment. That is not always negative, as the successful management of conflict and even differences of opinion can result in increased productivity, more positive working relationships, greater creativity and improved decision making.

Usually, factors that affect methods of conflict resolution include a conflict's relative significance and intensity, time pressure for resolving the conflict, the position assumed by involved parties and the degree of motivation to resolve the conflict, either on a long- or short-term basis.

Conflict resolution techniques include (in no particular order):

- Withdraw/Avoid, which involves postponing action on the issue to be better prepared or to let someone else resolve it
- Smooth/Accommodate, which places emphasis on areas of agreement instead of areas of disagreement and granting concessions to maintain harmony
- Compromise/Reconcile, which is a search for solutions that bring some satisfaction to all parties with the goal of temporarily or partially resolving the conflict
- Force/Direct, by which one pushes their own viewpoints with no regard for others, providing only win-lose solutions that are most frequently enforced via a power position to handle an emergency
- Collaborate/Problem Solve, that incorporates multiple viewpoints and ideas from differing perspectives, requiring a cooperative attitude and the use of open dialogue, usually ending in consensus and commitment

Interpersonal skills

Correctly analyzing situations and appropriately interacting with team members require a project manager to utilize a combination of technical, personal and conceptual skills with the gain of ultimately allowing that manager to benefit from the strengths of all team members.

These can include:

- o Leadership, a skill that is crucial throughout the phases of the project life cycle and is particularly relevant to communicating the vision and inspiring the project team to high performance.
- o Influencing, which requires the ability to be convincing and to articulate points and positions very clearly
- o Effective decision making, guidelines for which include a focus on goals to be met, following a decision-making process, studying environmental factors, analysing information that is available, developing team members' personal qualities, stimulating team creativity and managing risk.

Outputs

Change requests
Keeping in mind that staffing changes, made either by choice or due to uncontrollable events, can influence the rest of the project management plan as can issues related to staffing. Those issues can actually be disruptive, making it necessary to extend the schedule or exceed the budget, change requests that must be processed via the Perform Integrated Change Control process.

Preventative actions also require change requests, but are developed with the aim of reducing the probability and/or impact of problems prior to their occurrence.

Project management plan updates
These updates include (but are not limited to) the human resource management plan.

Project documents updates
These are updated indirectly and include (but are not limited to) the issue log, roles descriptions and project staff assignments.

Enterprise environmental factors updates
The Manage Team process can result in updates that include (but are not limited to) input to organizational performance appraisals and personnel skill updates.

Organizational process assets updates
These updates may include (but are not limited to) historical information and lessons learned documentation, template and organizational standard processes.

Test What You've Learned

1) Which, if any, of the following statements are false?
   a) Hierarchical-type organization charts display positions and respective responsibilities in a bottom-down format.
   b) Organizational breakdown structures are organized in terms of existing departments, units or teams and include project activities or work packages listed under each department.
   c) Lists arranged in the order in which resources are related by category and type are referred to as resource breakdown structures.
   d) Each work package cited in an organizational chart must have an unambiguous owner.

2) A _____ is utilized to illustrate connections between work packages and activities and project team members.
   a) Text-oriented table
   b) Resource breakdown schedule
   c) Hierarchical chart
   d) Resource list

3) _____ is the formal/informal interaction with other in an organization, industry or professional environment.
   a) Social media
   b) Meetings
   c) Networking
   d) Negotiation

4) The element of the human resource management plan that outlines, among other things, at what time and how project team members will be acquired is called: _____.
   a) The resource calendar
   b) The project organization chart
   c) The staffing management plan
   d) The acquisitions plan

5) Misunderstandings, problems with information and experience sharing and technology costs are drawbacks of _____.
   a) Acquisition
   b) Colocation
   c) Project staff assignments
   d) Virtual teams

6) Documenting project staff assignments can be accomplished through the use of:
   a) Project team directories
   b) Emails
   c) Websites
   d) Breakroom message boards

7) Good communication, emotional intelligence and group facilitation are all _____.
   a) Training skills
   b) Managerial skills
   c) Norming skills
   d) Interpersonal skills

8) During the storming team development stage:
   a) Teams meet to learn about the project and their roles in that project.
   b) The team may not be open to others' ideas.
   c) Team members begin to develop trust in one another.
   d) Teams have become well-organized units.

9) The other phrase that refers to colocation is a _____.
   a) Performing phase
   b) Loose matrix
   c) Tight matrix
   d) Team placement

10) The conflict resolution technique in which a search for solutions takes place is called:
    a) Compromise/Reconcile
    b) Smooth/Accommodate
    c) Collaborate/Problem Solve
    d) Suggest/Capitulate

Chapter 11: Project Communications Management

It is easy to understand why, for project managers, communication is crucial. While team members communicate with both you and other team members, project managers communicate with everyone involved in the project – team members, stakeholders, upper management, etc.

Project Communications Management is defined as including the "processes that are required to ensure timely and appropriate planning, collection, creation, distribution, storage, retrieval, management, control, monitoring, and the ultimate disposition of project information."[107] These processes can be both internal or external to the organization and can create a meeting point between stakeholders from differing cultural and/or organizational backgrounds, having various levels of expertise and a variety of perspectives, all of which can impact the execution and outcome of the project.

Modes of communication can include (but are not limited to):
- Internal, taking place within the project
- External, involving customers, vendors, other projects and organizations and the public
- Vertical, moving up and down the organization
- Horizontal, to and among peers
- Official, via newsletters or annual reports
- Unofficial, meaning off the record communications
- Written, oral, verbal (voice inflections) and nonverbal (body language

Communication skills common to both general and project management include effective listening, questioning and probing for details, educating, fact-finding, the setting and management of expectations, persuading, motivating, coaching, negotiating, conflict resolution, summarizing what has been done and identification of the next steps to take.

Plan Communications Management

Plan Communications Management is the "process of developing an appropriate approach and plan for project communications based on stakeholders' information and needs and available organizational assets,"[108] This process is crucial to any project's success, eliminating problems like message delivery delays, information sent to the wrong recipients, failed communication with stakeholders and possible misunderstandings. Its chief advantage is the identification and documentation of the most effective and efficient mode of communication with stakeholders.

---

[107] Project Management Institute, *A Guide to the Project Management Body of Knowledge* (*The PMBOK® Guide*), 5th ed., p. 287.

[108] Ibid., p. 289

Generally, communication planning takes place early in the project, preferably during development of the project management plan, which permits the allocation of time and budget to communication activities. To be of value, information must be provided in the right format at the right time to the right people and have the right impact.

With this in mind, issues that must be considered include (but are not limited to):

- What information is needed, who needs it and who is authorized to have it?
- When will it be needed?
- Where will it be stored and in what format?
- How can it be retrieved?
- Are there barriers such as time zones, language and cross-cultural considerations that must be considered?

The answers to all of these questions must be regularly reviewed and, if necessary, revised throughout the project to account for any changes that have occurred.

Figure 11.1. **Plan Communications Management: Inputs, Tools and Techniques, and Outputs**

Inputs	Tools & Techniques	Outputs
• Project management plan • Stakeholder register • Enterprise environmental factors • Organization process assets	• Communication requirements analysis • Communication technology • Communication models • Communication methods • Meetings	• Communications management plan • Project documents updates

Inputs

Project management plan

Stakeholder register

Enterprise environmental factors
Because an organization's structure affects the project's communication requirements in a major way, there is a strong connection between this process and all enterprise environmental factors. As was noted in chapter 3, these can include organizational culture, structure and governance, geographic distribution of facilities and resources, government or industry standards, infrastructure, available human resources, personnel administration, company work authorization systems, marketplace conditions, the risk tolerance of stakeholders, the political climate, the established communication channels of an organization, available commercial databases and the project management information system.

Organizational process assets

Of all possible organizational process factors, those that are most crucial to communications are lessons learned and historical information, which can offer information on previous projects' communication issues and their mode of resolution.

Tools & Techniques

Communications requirements analysis

This analysis provides help in determining project stakeholders' communication needs by merging information type and format with an estimation of the value of that information. This is necessary to limiting the use of project resources to the communication of information furthering the project's success or in cases when a lack of communication can lead to the project's failure.

The complexity of a project's communication can be seen in the number of potential communication channels, which can be derived with $n(n-1)/2$ (n representing the number of stakeholders). This allows the project manager to both determine and limit who is communicating with whom and who receives what information.

Information sources utilized in the identification and definition of project communication requirements include (but are not limited to):

- Organizational charts
- Project organization and stakeholder responsibility relationships
- Disciplines, departments and specialties encompassed by the project
- Logistical information concerning the number of individuals involved and their locations
- Internal (communications within the organization) and external (communications with the media, public or contractors) needs
- Stakeholder information and communication requirements gained from the stakeholder register

Communication technology

Methods can significantly vary in terms of techniques, which can include everything from short conversations to lengthy meetings and simple notes to schedules, databases and websites. Factors influencing communication technology selection include the urgency, frequency and format of the information to be shared, the technology's compatibility, availability and accessibility for all stakeholders over the entire course of the project, the ease of its use, project environment (face-to-face, virtual, one or multiple time zones, one or more than one language, cultural factors), and the information's sensitivity/confidentiality.

Communication models

Figure 11.2 displays a basic communication model that comprises two parties, the sender and the receiver. In a simple model such as this, the sequence of steps includes 1) encode, in which the sender translates (encodes) thoughts or ideas; 2) transmit message, which may be compromised by distance, unfamiliar technology, an infrastructure that is inadequate, differences in culture or the absence of background information;

3) decode, in which the receiver converts the message into significant thoughts or ideas; 4) acknowledge, in which the receiver indicates their receipt of the message (which does not imply agreement with or an understanding of that message); and 5) feedback/response.

Figure 11.2 **Basic Communication Model**[109]

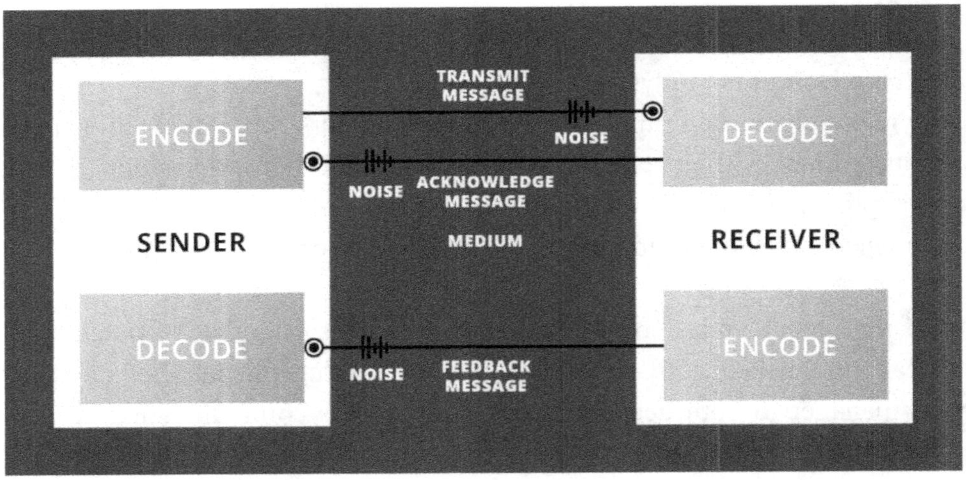

During the communication process, the sender's responsibilities are to ascertain that the message is indeed transmitted, the information is clear, correct and complete and confirmation that the information communicated is understood. The receiver must be sure that all of the information has been received, that it is understood and appropriately acknowledged.

Communication methods
Communication methods can be classified as interactive (a multidirectional exchange of information between two or more parties that is efficient and includes meetings, phone conversations,
instant messaging, Skype, etc.), push communication (information sent to those who need it with no assurance that it was received or understood that includes letters, memos, reports, etc.) and pull communication (utilized for large volumes of information or large audiences, necessitating that recipients are responsible for accessing that information and includes intranet sites, e-learning, lessons learned databases, etc.).

Meetings

Outputs

Communication management plan
The communication management plan, a component of the project management plan, comprises the way in which communication will be planned, structured, monitored and controlled over the course of the project. Information contained in the plan includes:

---

[109] Ibid., p. 294

- Stakeholder communication requirements
- Information transmitted, comprising its language, format, content and level of detail, as well as the reasons for communicating that information
- Required information distribution and acknowledge of receipt's timeframe and frequency
- Person(s) with the responsibility of communicating the information and authorizing its release (if confidential)
- Recipient(s) of the information
- Methods/technologies for conveyance of the information
- Resources (including time and budget) allocated
- If issues cannot be resolved at a lower level, escalation process that identifies time frames and the names of those in the management chain
- Updating/refining methods to be used on the plan over the project's progress and development
- Glossary of common terminology
- Information flow charts including workflows with possible authorization sequence, list of reports, meeting plans, etc.
- Communication constraints, most frequently the result of specific legislation or regulation, technology, organizational policies, etc.

Project documents updates
These include (but are not limited to) the project schedule and the stakeholder register.

Manage Communications
Manage Communications is the "process of creating, collecting, distributing, storing, retrieving, and the ultimate disposition of project information in accordance to the communications management plan,"[110] with the most important gain being that the communication flow between project stakeholders is both efficient and effective.

This process is not limited to the distribution of meaningful information. Its additional goal is that the information is generated appropriately, is both received and understood by recipients and offers stakeholders the ability to request additional information, clarification and, if necessary, discussion.

Techniques and concerns involved in effective management of communication include (but are not limited to) sender-receiver models, choice of media, writing style, techniques for meeting management, presentation (body language and visual aids design), facilitation (building a consensus and overcoming obstacles) and listening (acknowledging, clarifying and confirming understanding) techniques.

---

[110] Ibid., p. 297

Figure 11.3. **Manage Communications Management: Inputs, Tools and Techniques, and Outputs**

Inputs	Tools & Techniques	Outputs
• Communications management plan • Work performance reports • Enterprise environmental factors • Organization process assets	• Communication technology • Communication models • Communication methods • Information management systems • Performance reporting	• Projects communications • Project management plan updates • Project documents updates • Organizational process assets updates

Inputs

Communications management plan

Work performance reports
If information concerning project performance and status is comprehensive, accurate and available in a timely fashion, it can be utilized in the facilitation of discussions and creation of communications.

Enterprise environmental factors
Factors specific to this process include (but are not limited to) organizational culture and structure, government/industry standards and regulations and the project management information system.

Organizational process assets
This process involves organizational process assets such as procedures, policies, processes and guidelines in terms of communication management.

Tools & Techniques

Communication technology

Communication models
In selecting a communication model, it is crucial that the choice is project-appropriate and any barriers (noise) are identified and managed.

Communication methods
The three communication methods are interactive, push and pull. Push is also known as active, whereas pull is also known as passive.

Information management systems

There are a number of tools with which project information is managed and distributed, which include letters, memos, reports and press releases (hard-copy document management), email, fax, voice mail, phone, video/web conferencing, websites and web publishing (electronic communications management) and web interfaces with scheduling/project management software, meeting and virtual office support software, portals and collaborative work management tools (electronic project management tools).

Performance reporting

Keeping in mind that when reporting performance, information must be given at a level appropriate for each audience, formats can extend from simple status reports to those that are more complex and can be prepared on a regular or exception basis. While simple status reports might be comprised of information such as percent complete or the scope, schedule, cost and quality for each area, more elaborate reports can include analyzes of past performance and project forecasts (such as time and cost), risks' and issues' current status, work completed and/or to be completed, summary of changes approved within the period and other relevant information to be reviewed and discussed.

Outputs

Project communications

Managing communications involves actions having to do with information being created, distributed, acknowledged and understood. This can include (but is not limited to) performance reports, status of deliverables, schedule progress and cost incurred. All project communications are not the same; they can vary and be influenced by the urgency and impact of the message, the mode of its delivery and its level of confidentiality, among others.

Project management plan updates

Project documents updates

These can include (but are not limited to) stakeholder notifications concerning issues that have been resolved, changes that have been approved and general project status, project reports, project presentations, project records (correspondence, memos, meeting minutes and other documents that describe the project), feedback from stakeholders that can be utilized in the modification of improvement of the project's future performance, and lessons learned documentation, e.g., causes of issues, reasoning on which corrective action was based and other types of lessons learned.

Control Communications

Control communications is the "process of monitoring and controlling communications throughout the entire project life cycle to ensure the information needs of the project stakeholders are met,"[111] which has the key benefit of ensuring the project stakeholders' information needs are met. Iterations of either/or the Plan and Manage Communication processes be initiated by the Control Communications

---

[111] Ibid., p. 303

process, illustrating the Project Communication Management processes' continuous nature. Certain elements, e.g., issues or key performance indicators such as actual vs planned schedule, cost and quality, may serve as triggers for immediate revisions but others may not. The effect and consequences of project communications must be carefully measured and controlled so that the right message is delivered to the correct audience at the appropriate time.

Figure 11.4 **Control Communications Management: Inputs, Tools and Techniques, and Outputs**

Inputs	Tools & Techniques	Outputs
• Project management plan • Project communications • Issue log • Work performance data • Organization process assets	• Information management systems • Expert judgment • Meetings	• Work performance information • Change requests • Project management plan updates • Project documents updates • Organizational process assets updates

Inputs

Project management plan
Information found in the project management plan that can impact the Control Communications process includes (but is not limited to) the communication requirements of the stakeholders, reasons for, the timeframe and frequency of the distribution of required information, the individual/group responsible for that distribution and the individual/group in receipt of that information.

Project communications
Project communications used in the Control Communications process may include (but are not limited to) deliverables status, schedule process and cost incurred.

Issue log
Because the log stipulates the person responsible for resolving issues by a target date as well as details concerning issue resolution, it serves as a reference for what has occurred in the past as well as a platform for the subsequent delivery of communications.

Work performance data
In this context, significant work performance data includes information about communications already delivered as well as feedback on those communications, communication effectiveness survey results and/or other raw observations that have been identified.

Organizational process assets

These include (but are limited to) report templates, policies, standards and procedures that provide communication definitions, what is available in terms of specific communication technologies, permitted communication media, policies concerning record retention and security requirements.

Tools & Techniques

Information management systems

The organization's information management system may include software packages useful for consolidating reports and simplifying distribution of reports to shareholders and can comprise table reporting, spreadsheet analysis and visual representations.

Expert judgment

Meetings

Discussions with team members can allow them to decide on the best ways to update and communication information about project performance in addition to how to respond to shareholders' requests for information.

Outputs

Work performance information

Change requests

Change requests, which are processed via the Perform Integrated Change Control process, may cause new/revised cost estimates, activity sequences, schedule dates, resource requirements, risk response alternatives analyzes; changes to the project management plan and documents; and recommendations as to corrective action to bring expected future performance back in line with the project management plan as well as actions that will prevent the occurrence of future negative project performance.

Project documents updates

These include (but are not limited to) forecasts, performance reports and the issue log.

Organizational process assets updates

These include (but are not limited to) report formats and lessons learned documentation that may be integrated into the historical database, including the causes of issue, reasons that the corrective action was selected and other forms of lessons learned.

Test What You've Learned

1) What barriers to communication must be considered during the Plan Communications Management process?
   a) Time zones, language and cross-cultural issues
   b) Technology and staff availability
   c) Formats and language
   d) Working hours and language

2) _____ that affect the Plan Communications Management process include the political climate and personnel administration.
   a) Organizational process assets
   b) Enterprise environmental factors
   c) Elements of the project management plan
   d) Stakeholder characteristics

3) The number of potential communication channels can be derived with:
   a) $n/2$
   b) $(n - 1)/2$
   c) $n(n - 2)/2$
   d) $n(n - 1)/2$

4) During the communication process, it is the _____ responsibility to ensure that the information has been received, is understood and acknowledged properly.
   a) Sender's
   b) Project manager's
   c) Receiver's
   d) Communications officer's

5) Which, if any, of the following statements is false?
   a) The Manage Communications process only involves the distribution of important information.
   b) The Manage Communications process involves the development of the correct approach to project communications based on stakeholder needs.
   c) As part of the Manage Communication process, it must be ensured that stakeholders are given the opportunity to request additional information.
   d) None of these statements are false.

6) _____ are inputs into the Control Communications Management process.
   a) Work performance information and change requests
   b) Meetings and issue logs
   c) Work performance data and issue logs
   d) Information management systems and expert judgment

7) Which, if any, of the following statements are false?
   a) Issue logs only contain details concerning resolution of those issues.
   b) Change requests are processed during the Perform Integrated Change Control process.
   c) An organization's information management system may include software that can format and consolidate reports for distribution.
   d) All of these statements are false.

8) _____ communication involves customers, vendors, other projects and organizations and the public.
   a) Vertical
   b) Horizontal
   c) Internal
   d) External

9) The most significant benefit of the Manage Communications process is that it:
   a) Identifies and documents the most effective way to communicate with stakeholders.
   b) Certifies that the communication flow between project stakeholders is both efficient and effective throughout the project life cycle.
   c) Ensures that project stakeholders' information needs are met throughout the project life cycle.
   d) Provides information as to communications sensitivity and confidentiality.

10) As an output of the Manage Communications process, project communications can be influenced by the:
    a) Status of deliverables
    b) Schedule progress
    c) Message's urgency and impact
    d) Time zones and language barriers

Chapter 12: Project Risk Management

Project Risk Management encompasses the processes of planning risk management, identifying and analyzing risk, planning risk responses and controlling risk. Its objectives "are to increase the likelihood and impact of positive events, and decrease the likelihood and impact of negative events in the project."[112] This may seem a bit puzzling because, according to the dictionary, the word *risk* implies "the possibility that something bad or unpleasant (such as an injury or a loss) will happen,"[113] while in project management parlance, a risk to a project can actually present an opportunity.

A risk may:
- Have one or more causes, which can be an expected or potential requirement, assumption or condition creating the chance for a positive or negative outcome
- Have one or more impacts
- Occur under conditions contributed to by aspects of the project's or organization's environment, which include:
  - ✓ Project management practices that are immature
  - ✓ A lack of management practices that are integrated
  - ✓ Multiple projects running concurrently
  - ✓ Relying on external players outside the project's direct control

Every project involves a degree of uncertainty from which project risk originates. Known risks have been both identified and analyzed, which makes planning for them possible, although some cannot be proactively managed and must therefore be assigned a contingency reserve. Obviously, there is no way to proactively managed unknown risks and they may be assigned a management reserve.

There are differences between individual and overall project risks. Overall risk:
- Embodies uncertainty's effect on the entire project
- As it comprises all sources of project uncertainty, it is greater than the sum of all individual risks with a project.
- Represents stakeholders' exposure to implications of project negative and positive outcome variations

Dependent on their risk attitude, organizations and stakeholders who view risk as the effect of uncertainty on project and organizational objectives are willing to accept varying degrees of risk. There are a number of factors that influence those attitudes, which *The PMBOK® Guide* sorts according to three themes, *risk appetite* (the degree of uncertainty an entity is willing to assume in anticipation of a reward), *risk tolerance* (the degree, amount or volume of risk withstood by an organization or individual), and *risk threshold* (which refers to the measures along the levels of uncertainty or impact

---

[112] Project Management Institute, *A Guide to the Project Management Body of Knowledge* (*The PMBOK® Guide*), 5th ed., p. 309.
[113] *Merriam-Webster Dictionary*, 11th ed., p. 1076.

at which a stakeholder might have a specific interest). The parameters of risk threshold are such that below that threshold, the risk will be accepted by the organization while above that threshold, risk will not be tolerated. This is tied to the concept of Utility Theory or Utility Function.

The way in which individuals and groups respond to risks is influenced by their attitudes towards those risks. Perceptions, tolerances and other biases (which must, whenever possible, be made explicit) drive risk attitudes. For every project, a consistent approach must be established while communication about risk and the manner in which it is handled should be frank and candid. What organization perceives as a balance between risk taking and risk avoidance should be reflected in its risk responses. A successful organization is committed to proactively and consistently addressing the management of risk at every level.

Plan Risk Management

Plan Risk Management is the "process of defining how to conduct risk management activities for a project," that "ensures that the degree, type, and visibility of risk management are commensurate with both the risks and the importance of the project to the organization."[114] This process must initiate at the conception of the project and should be completed early while the project is being planned.

Figure 12.1. **Plan Risk Management: Inputs, Tools and Techniques, and Outputs**

Inputs	Tools & Techniques	Outputs
• Project management plan • Project charter • Stakeholder register • Enterprise environmental factors • Organization process assets	• Analytical techniques • Expert judgment • Meetings	• Risk management plan

---

[114] Ibid., p. 313

Inputs

Project management plan
Because the risk management plan must be consistent with the all subsidiary management plans and their baselines, especially risk-affected areas such as scope, schedule and cost, the risk management planning must include that information.

Project charter
Inputs like high-level risks, project descriptions and requirements can be gleaned from the project charter.

Stakeholder register

Enterprise environmental factors
Risk attitudes, thresholds and tolerances (among other possible factors) all affect the Plan Risk Management process.

Organizational process assets
Those that can influence this process include (but are not limited to) risk categories and statement formats, common definitions of concepts and terms, standard templates, roles and responsibilities, decision-making authority levels and lessons learned.

Tools & Techniques

Analytical techniques
When compiling the risk management plan, the context merges stakeholder risk attitudes and a given project's strategic risk exposure. Thus, one useful activity would be to analysis stakeholder risk profiles to measure their risk appetite and tolerance.

Expert judgment

Meetings
Discussions can involve the definition of high-level plans for conducting risk management activities as well as setting or reviewing risk contingency application approaches and tailoring general organizational templates for risk categories, term definitions, e.g., risk levels, probability by type of risk, impact by objective type and the probability and impact matrix.

Outputs

Risk management plan
Describing the way in which risk management activities will be structured and performed, the risk management plan includes:

- Methodology, defining the approaches, tools and data utilized to perform risk management on the project
- Roles and responsibilities, defining and clarifying the responsibilities of risk management team members for each type of activity in the risk management plan
- Budgeting, based on assigned resources, estimating funds required for inclusion in the cost baseline and establishing protocols for application of contingency and management reserves
- Timing, defining when and how frequently risk management processes will be performed over the project life cycle and establishing both the protocols for application of schedule contingency reserves and risk management activities to be included in the project schedule
- Risk categories, offering a means to group potential causes of risk. In a risk identification exercise, the project team can utilize a risk breakdown structure (RBS) to examine many sources from which project risk might emerge. An RBS, which is a hierarchical representation of risks according to their categories, can be seen in figure 12.2.

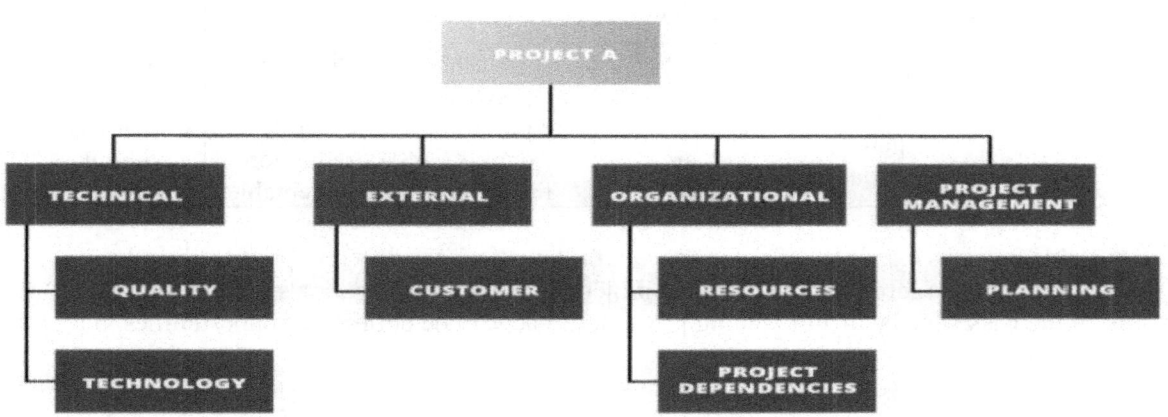

Figure 12.2. **Risk Breakdown Structure (RBS)**

- Risk probability and impact definitions, different levels of which must be developed specific to the project context to allow for risk analysis' quality and credibility.

Table 12.1. **Definition of Impact Scales for Four Project Objectives**

Project objective	Defined Conditions for Impact Scales of a Risk on Major Project Objectives (Examples are shown for negative impacts only.)				
	Relative or numerical scales are shown.				
	Very low/0.05	Low/ 0.10	Moderate/0.20	High/0.40	Very high/0.80
Cost	Insignificant cost increase	< 10% cost increase	10 - 20% cost increase	20 - 40% cost increase	> 40% cost increase
Time	Insignificant time increase	< 5% time increase	5 - 10% time increase	10 - 20% time increase	> 20% time increase
Scope	Barely noticeable scope increase	Minor aspects of scope affected	Major aspects of scope affected	Sponsor deems scope reduction unacceptable.	Project end item effectively without value.
Quality	Barely noticeable quality degradation	Only very demanding applications are affected.	Sponsor approval required for quality reduction.	Sponsor deems quality reduction unacceptable.	Project end item effectively without value.

This table presents examples of risk impact definitions for four different project objectives which should be tailored to the individual project and to the organization's risk thresholds during the Risk Management Planning process. Impact can be defined for opportunities in a similar manner.

- o Probability and impact matrix, which serves as a grid for mapping each risk occurrence's probability and impact on project objectives
- o Revised stakeholders' tolerances
- o Reporting formats
- o Tracking

Identify Risks

Identify risks is the "process of determining which risks may affect the project and documenting their characteristics," the main benefit of which is "the documentation of existing risks and the knowledge and ability it provides to the project team to anticipate events."[115]

Project managers, project team members, the risk management (if it has been assigned), customers, subject matter experts external to the project team, end users, other project managers, stakeholders and risk management experts can all participate in risk identification activities.

---

[115] Ibid., p. 319

Further, this is an ongoing process, with iteration frequency and participation varying by situation. As the project moves through its life cycle, new risks may evolve or be discovered, but the format of risk statements should remain consistent to allow for clear and unambiguous understanding of each risk. This will increase the ability to measure the relative effect on the project of one risk compared to another risk.

Figure 12.3. **Identify Risks: Inputs, Tools and Techniques, and Outputs**

Inputs	Tools & Techniques	Outputs
• Risk management plan • Cost management plan • Schedule managment plan • Quality management plan • Human resource management plan • Scope baseline • Activity duration estimates • Stakeholder register • Project documents • Procurement documents • Enterprise environmental factors • Organizational process assets	• Documentation reviews • Information gathering techniques • Checklist analysis • Assumptions analysis • Diagramming techniques • SWOT analysis • Expert judgment	• Risk register

Inputs

Risk management plan
In the context of identifying risks, the assignment of roles and responsibilities, provision within the budget and schedule for risk management activities and categories of risk are the important elements from the risk management plan that are utilized.

Cost management plan
This supplies the processes and controls used to assist in the identification of risks across the project.

Schedule management plan
Information about the project time/schedule objectives and expectations that could be affected by both known and unknown risks are found in the schedule management plan.

Quality management plan
To identify risks, the project team can use the baseline of quality measures and metrics from the quality management plan.

Human resources management plan

Activity Cost Estimates
Reviews of activity cost estimates can be helpful when identifying risks due to the quantitative assessment of the likely costs to complete scheduled activities which, ideally, are expressed as a range with the degree(s) of risk indicated by the width of that range. This can provide projections that indicate the sufficiency or insufficiency of the estimate in terms of completing the activity which can pose a risk to the project.

Activity duration estimates
Reviews of these estimates can assist in the identification of risk in terms of the time allowances for the activities or for the entire project, which, once again, reveals the relative degree(s) of risk by the width of the range of such estimates.

Stakeholder register
Reviewing stakeholder information can provide inputs to the Identify Risks process because, as a result, key stakeholders, particularly the sponsor and the customer, will be interviewed or in some way participate in this process.

Project documents
With the use of project documents such as the project charter and schedule, schedule network diagrams, the issue log, the quality checklist and other information, the project team can better identify project risks.

Procurement documents
These will be discussed in detail in the next chapter but for now, you should be aware that if external procurement of resources is required by the project, procurement documents provide a crucial input to the Identify Risks process.

Enterprise environmental factors
Those that can affect this process are comprised by (but are not limited to) published information (including commercial databases), academic and industry studies, published checklists, benchmarking and risk attitudes.

Organizational process assets
Those that can influence this process include (bat are not limited to) project files, organizational and project process controls, risk statement formats or templates and lessons learned.

Tools & Techniques

Documentation reviews
Plans, assumptions, previous project files, agreements and other information can be included in a structured review of project documentation. Indicators of risk in the project include plans' consistency in addition to consistency between those plans and the project requirements and assumptions.

Information gathering techniques
- Brainstorming, which, in this context, is used to produce a comprehensive list of project risks using categories of risk, such as those found in a risk breakdown structure that is then utilized in the identification and categorization by type of risk as well as refinement of those definitions
- Delphi technique
- Interviewing
- Root cause analysis

Checklist analysis
The lowest level of the RBS, historical information and knowledge and other sources of information are used to compile risk identification checklists. *The PMBOK® Guide* points out that despite the simplicity and speed of a checklist, "it is impossible to build an exhaustive one, and care should be taken to ensure the checklist is not used to avoid the effort of proper risk identification."[16] Exploration of items not appearing on the checklist is necessary as well as periodic pruning to remove or archive related items.

Assumptions analysis
Assumptions' inaccuracy, instability, inconsistency or incompleteness can be utilized to identify risks to the project.

Diagramming techniques
These may include cause and effect diagrams (fishbone or Ishikawa), system or process flow charts, and influence diagrams (as seen in figure 12.4).

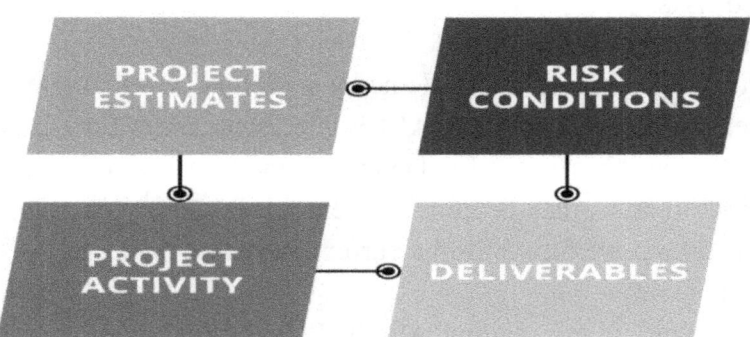

Figure 12.4 **Influence Diagram**[117]

---

[116] Ibid., p. 325
[117] Ibid., p. 326

SWOT analysis

SWOT analysis begins with the identification of strengths and weaknesses of the organization that focuses on either the project, organization or the general business area and then highlights any opportunities arising from organizational strengths or threats emerging from organizational weaknesses. It also identifies opportunities for overcoming weaknesses as well as the degree to which organizational strengths counteract threats.

Figure 12.5. **SWOT Analysis**

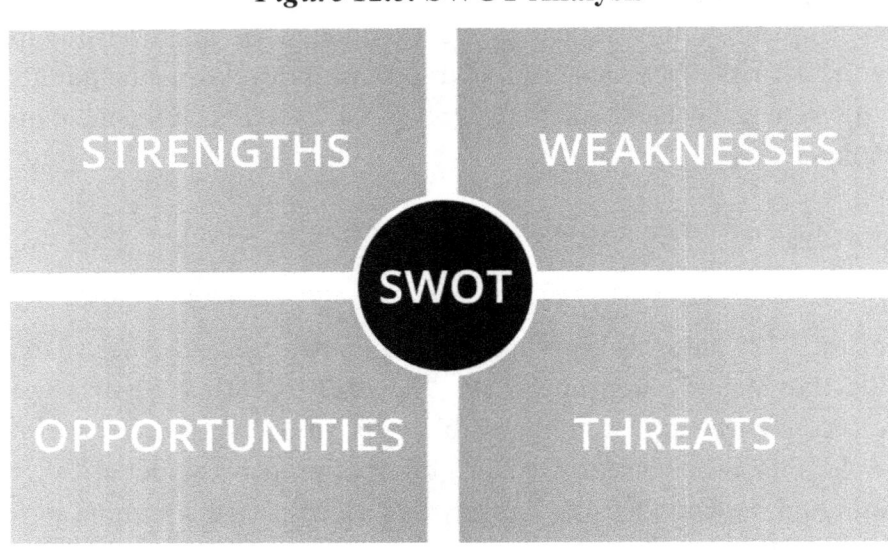

Expert judgment

Outputs

Risk register

The initial entry into the risk register, a document into which risk analysis and risk response planning results are recorded, serves as the primary output from the Identify Risks process. Preparing the risk register starts with the following information, which is then available to other project and risk management processes.

- List of identified risks
    - ✓ Provides as much detail as is reasonable
    - ✓ May be structured utilizing risk statements such that, for example, an EVENT may occur which causes an IMPACT or, if a CAUSE is present, an EVENT may occur that leads to an EFFECT. Risk root causes, the fundamental conditions/events that may cause one or more identified risks to arise, may become clearer and should be recorded and used in support of risk identification in the future for the current and other projects.
- List of potential responses
    - ✓ If identified, should be used as inputs to the Plan Risk Responses process

Perform Qualitative Risk Analysis

Perform Qualitative Risk Analysis is the "process of prioritizing risks for further analysis or action by assessing and combining their probability of occurrence and impact,"[118] which offers the primary gain of enabling project managers to reduce uncertainty levels and focus on high priority tasks.

Employing the relative probability/likelihood of occurring, the corresponding impact on project objectives if they do occur and other factors like the response time frame and the organization's risk tolerance associated with project cost, scope and quality constraints , Perform Qualitative Risk Analysis assesses the priority of identified risks. The project team and other stakeholders' risk attitudes are reflected by such assessments, which therefore require explicit identification and management of the risk approaches of key participants in the Perform Qualitative Risk Analysis process to be effective.

Risk approaches can introduce bias into these assessments so attention must be paid to recognizing and correcting such bias. In addition, the establishment of definitions of probability and impact levels can reduce the effect of bias. Generally, Perform Qualitative Risk Analysis is a quick and cost-effective way to establish priorities for Plan Risk Responses and sets the ground rules for Perform Quantitative Risk Analysis. As defined in the project's risk management plan, this process is performed on a regular basis over the project life cycle and can move into Perform Quantitative Risk Analysis or directly into the Plan Risk Responses process.

Figure 12.6. **Perform Qualitative Risk Analysis: Inputs, Tools and Techniques, and Outputs**

Inputs	Tools & Techniques	Outputs
• Risk management plan • Scope baseline • Risk register • Enterprise environmental factors • Organizational process assets	• Risk probability and impact assessement • Probability and impact matrix • Risk data quality assessment • Risk categorization • Risk urgency assessment • Expert judgment	• Project documents update

Inputs

Risk management plan

Usually, risk management plan components used here were adapted to the project during risk management planning. If not, they can be developed during the Perform Qualitative Risk analysis and include:

---

[118] Ibid., p. 328

- Roles and responsibilities for performing risk management
- Schedule activities for risk management
- Budgets
- Risk categories
- Probability and impact definitions
- The probability and impact matrix
- Revised stakeholders' risk tolerances

Scope baseline
Risks encountered during common or recurrent projects are often thoroughly understood while projects that utilize state-of-the-art or highly innovative technology as well as highly complex projects tend to have more uncertainly, which can be evaluated by examining the scope baseline.

Risk register

Enterprise environmental factors
This process can utilizes industry studies of like projects by risk specialists and risk databases that may be located within industry or proprietary sources.

Organizational process assets
These are comprised of information on prior completed project similar to the current project.

Tools & Techniques

Risk probability and impact assessment
Examining the likelihood that every specific risk will occur involves risk probability assessment. Investigations of the potential effect of risks on project objectives like schedule, cost, quality or performance (including both negative effects, i.e., threats, and positive effects, i.e., opportunities) are risk impact assessments.

- Risks
  - Assessed via interviews/meetings with those who are familiar with agenda risk categories
  - Details that expand explanations, including assumptions that justify the levels assigned are also recorded.
  - According to definitions from the risk management plan, probabilities and impacts are rated, with risks rated low in terms of probability and impact included in the risk register's watch list for monitoring in the future.

Probability and impact matrix
A probability and impact matrix is used to evaluate each risk's importance and priority with some risks, based on a risk rating based on assessed probability and impact that allows risks to be prioritized for additional quantitative analysis and planning risk responses. After every risk is rated on its probability of occurrence and impact should it occur, the organization must decide which groupings of

probability and impact form the meanings of high, moderate and low risk, a process that is done prior to the inception of the project and added to organizational process assets. The following table is an example of a matrix based on these calculations and decisions.

Keep in mind that risk scores guide responses to those risks; obviously, if a risk is deemed to have a negative impact on an objective (a threat) and also appears in the matrix's high-risk zone, proactive management action going beyond placing it in the risk register or adding a contingency reserve is called for.

Table 12.2. **Probability and Impact Matrix**[119]

PROBABILITY	THREATS					OPPORTUNITIES				
0.90	0.05	0.09	0.18	0.36	0.72	0.72	0.36	0.18	0.09	0.05
0.70	0.04	0.07	0.14	0.28	0.56	0.56	0.28	0.14	0.07	0.04
0.50	0.03	0.05	0.10	0.20	0.40	0.40	0.20	0.10	0.05	0.03
0.30	0.02	0.03	0.06	0.12	0.24	0.24	0.12	0.06	0.03	0.02
0.10	0.01	0.01	0.02	0.04	0.08	0.08	0.04	0.02	0.01	0.01
	0.05	0.10	0.20	0.40	0.80	0.80	0.40	0.20	0.10	0.05

IMPACT (NUMERICAL SCALE) ON AN OBJECTIVE (EG. COST, TIME, SCOPE OR QUALITY)

EACH RISK IS RATED ON ITS PROBABILITY OF OCCURRING AND IMPACT ON AN OBJECTIVE IF IT DOES OCCUR. THE ORGANIZATION'S THRESHOLDS FOR LOW, MODERATE OR HIGH RISKS ARE SHOWN IN THE MATRIX AND DETERMINE WHETHER THE RISK IS SCORED AS HIGH, MODERATE OR LOW FOR THAT OBJECTIVE.

Risk data quality assessment

The definition of this technique is quite straightforward; clearly, in this step, the "degree to which the data about risks is useful for risk management"[120] is carefully considered, which involves looking at how well the risk is understood as well as the data's accuracy, quality, reliability and integrity. Data that are of low quality can adversely affect qualitative risk analysis and may make gathering better quality data necessary, a process that can use more time and resources than was originally planned.

Risk categorization

Risk categorization:

- o Involves using the RBS to classify sources of risk, the WBS to sort the area of the project affected or other helpful categories such as project phase
- o Can also be done through the use of common root causes
- o Allows project teams to decide which areas of the project are most likely to encounter risk
- o Assists in determining work packages, activities, project phases or roles
- o Provides the means of developing effective risk responses

---

[119] Ibid., p. 331
[120] Ibid., p. 332

Risk urgency assessment
Priority indicators include:

- Probability of risk detection
- Time to affect a risk response
- Symptoms and warning signs
- Risk rating

When performing a qualitative analysis, the risk rating (obtained from the probability and impact matrix) added to the risk urgency assessment can provide a final risk severity rating.

Expert judgment

Outputs

Project documents updates
Documents updated include (but are not limited to):

- The risk register
  - Assessments of probability and impacts of each risk
  - Risk rankings or scores
  - Risk urgency information or categorization
  - Watch list of low probability risks or those needing further analysis
- Assumptions log updates
  - Change with new information gained through analysis process which may be combined with project scope statement or placed in a separate assumptions log

Perform Quantitative Analysis
Perform Quantitative Analysis is the "process of numerically analyzing the effect of identified risks on overall project objectives."[121] Aiming to reduce project uncertainty, this process provides quantitative information concerning risk that can support decision making. In this process, risks already prioritized via the Perform Qualitative Risk Analysis because they could potentially and substantially impact the project's competing objectives. Perform Quantitative Analysis examines those effects on project objectives with the goal of evaluating all risks' aggregate effect on the project, sometimes assigning an individual numerical priority rating to each risk. This may not always be possible because of a lack of adequate data to develop appropriate models; it is up to the project manager's expert judgment to determine the viability of and actual need for the Perform Quantitative Analysis process. However, even if the process takes place, it may be necessary to repeat it during the Control Risks process to be certain that the overall project risk has been sufficiently curtailed.

---

[121] Ibid., p. 333

Figure 12.7. **Perform Quantitative Risk Analysis: Inputs, Tools and Techniques, and Outputs**

Inputs	Tools & Techniques	Outputs
• Risk management plan • Cost management plan • Schedule management plan • Risk register • Enterprise environmental factors • Organizational process assets	• Data gathering and representation techniques • Quantitative risk analysis and modeling techniques • Expert judgment	• Project documents update

Inputs

Risk management plan

Cost management plan
Guidelines for the establishment and management of risk reserves can be found in the cost management plan.

Schedule management plan
This also offers risk reserve management and establishment guidelines.

Risk register

Enterprise environmental factors
These factors offer the risk analysis insight and context, including industry studies of similar projects by risk specialists and risk databases that may be attained from industry/proprietary sources.

Organizational process assets

Tools & Techniques

Data gathering and representative techniques

Interviewing
- Capitalizes on experience and historical data for the quantification of the probability and impact of risks on project objectives
- Information gathered on the optimistic or *low*, pessimistic or *high*, or most likely scenarios for some distributions that are commonly utilized
- An important element that offers insights on the analysis' reliability and credibility is the documentation of rationale of risk ranges and the assumptions on which they are based.

Table 12.3. Range of Project Cost Estimates Collected During the Risk Interview

Range of Project Cost Estimates			
WBS Element	Low	Most Likely	High
Design	$4 M	$6 M	$10 M
Build	$16 M	$20 M	$35 M
Test	$11 M	$15 M	$23 M
Total Project	$31 M	$41 M	$68 M

Probability distributions
- o The uncertainty in values, e.g., schedule activities' durations and project components' costs, are represented by continuous probability distributions.
- o Uncertain events, e.g., test outcomes or possible decision tree scenarios, are represented by discrete distributions.
- o If there is no obvious, more likely value falling between specified high and low bounds, uniform distributions can be utilized.

Figure 12.8. Beta Distribution[122]

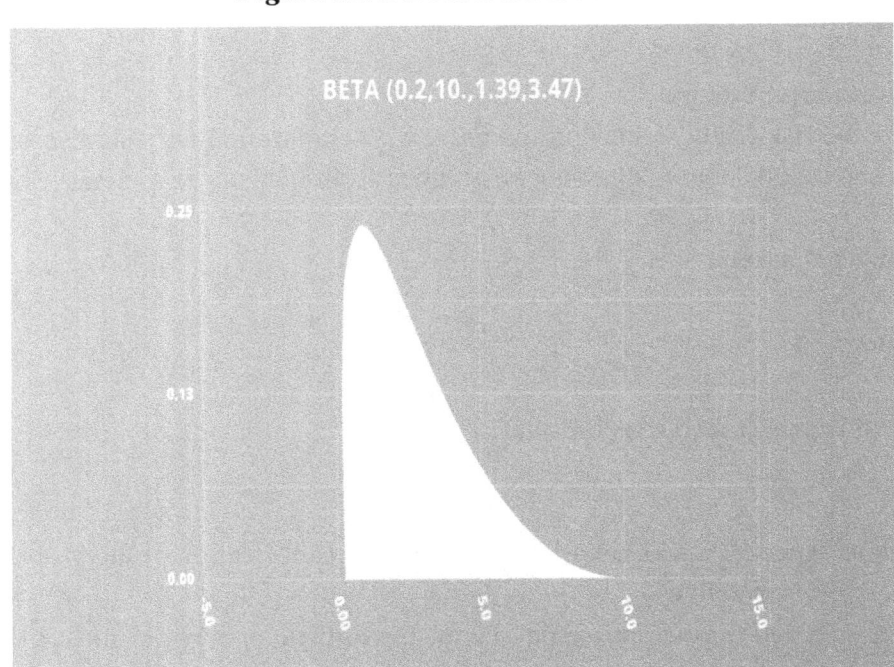

---

[122] Scott Baird, *"processmodel,"* https://www.processmodel.com/blog/faq-items/beta-distribution/

Figure 12.9. **Triangular Distribution**[123]

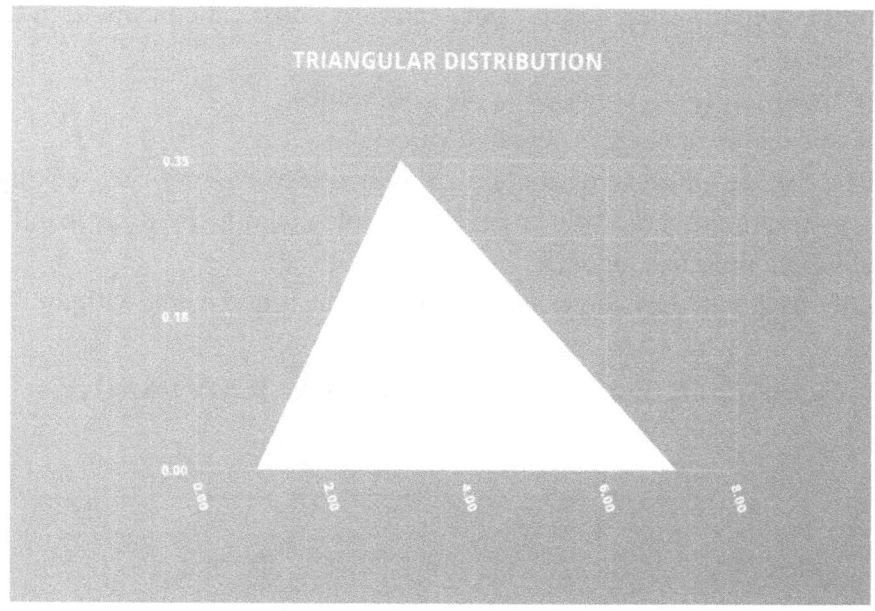

Quantitative risk analysis and modeling techniques

Both event- and project-oriented analysis approaches are frequently utilized, which include:

- Sensitivity analysis
    - ✓ Utilized in the determination of which risks have the greatest potential impact on a project
    - ✓ Checks on the extent to which each project element's uncertainty influences the objective under scrutiny when all other uncertain elements are kept at their baseline values
    - ✓ Typically, results are displayed as a tornado diagram, as seen in the figure below.

Figure 12.10. **Tornado Diagram**

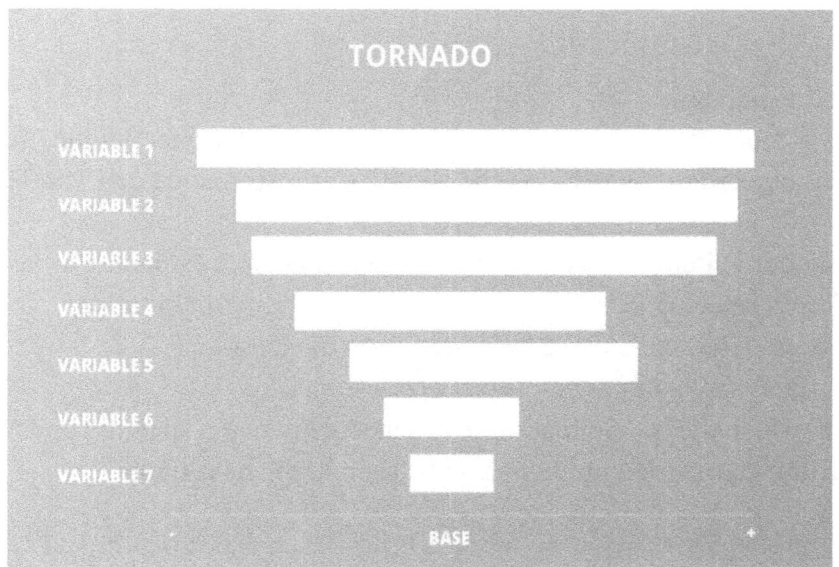

- Expected monetary value analysis
  ✓ When future scenarios may or may not occur is a statistical concept used to calculate the average outcome.
  ✓ EMV of opportunities - expressed as positive values
  ✓ EMV of threats - expressed as negative values
  ✓ Requires a risk-neutral assumption, i.e., neither risk-averse nor risk-seeking
  ✓ Derived by multiplying the value of each possible outcome by its probability of occurence then adding the products together
  ✓ Commonly used in a decision tree analysis, as shown in the below figure

Figure 12.11. **Expected Monetary Value (EMV) Analysis**

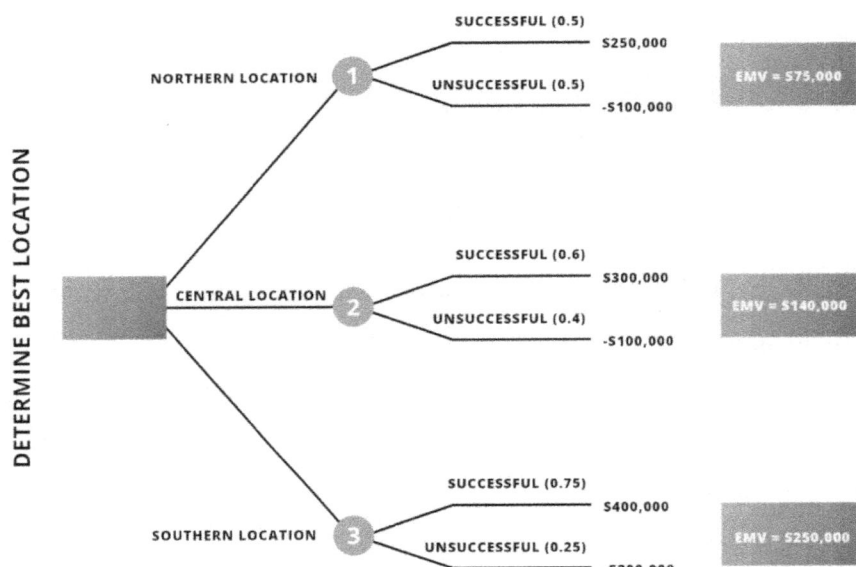

- Modeling and simulation
  ✓ Employs a model translating specified, detailed project uncertainties into potential impact on project objectives, usually via the Monte Carlo technique or Latin Hypercube Sampling (LHS)
  ✓ Project model is iterated with input values such as cost estimates or activity durations that are randomly selected from these variables' probability distributions
  ✓ Total cost/completion date is determined from the iterations.
  ✓ Cost risk analysis - simulation utilizes cost estimates
  ✓ Schedule risk analysis - simulation uses schedule network diagram and risk ranges
  ✓ Output from a cost risk simulation can be seen in the next figure.

Figure 12.12. **Cost Risk Simulation Results**[124]

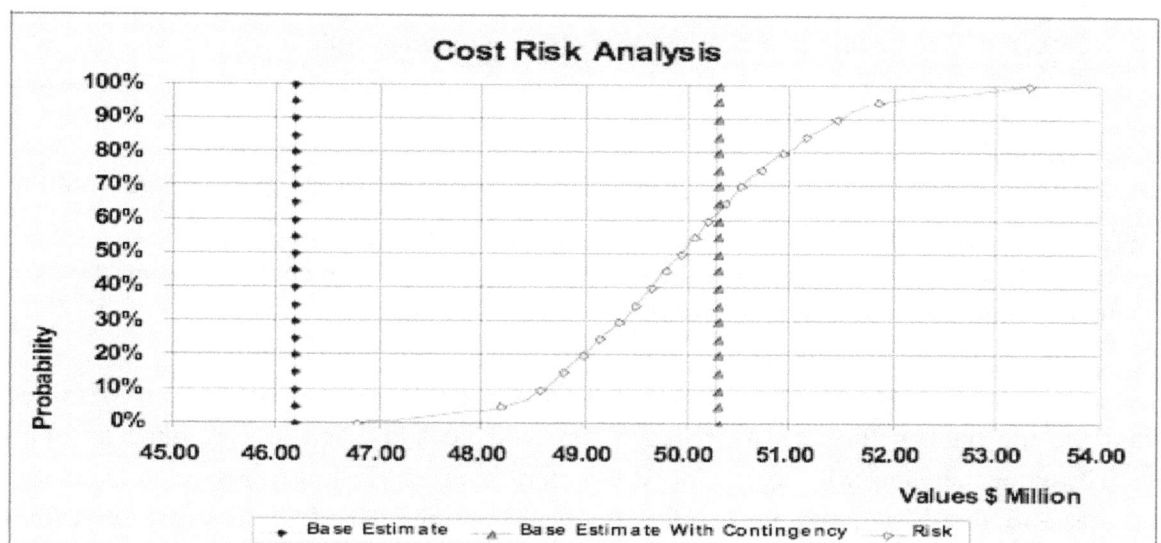

Expert judgment
Expert judgment may be necessary to determine potential impacts of schedule and cost, in the evaluation of probability and the definition of inputs like probability distributions into the tools, as well as the interpretation of data, e.g., weaknesses and strengths of tools and the appropriate use of specific tools.

Outputs

Project documents updates

Probabilistic analysis of the project
- o Estimates of potential project schedule and cost outcomes
    - ✓ Possible completion dates and costs as well as associated confidence levels
    - ✓ Frequently expressed as a cumulative frequency distribution
    - ✓ Utilized with stakeholder risk tolerances to allow quantification of cost and time contingency reserves necessary to bringing risk of overrunning project objectives to acceptable levels
- o Probability of achieving cost and time objectives
- o Prioritized list of quantified risks
    - ✓ Comprises risks posing greatest threat or offering greatest opportunity, including those having greatest effects on cost or the critical path
- o Trends in quantitative risk analysis results
    - ✓ Can lead to conclusions that affect risk responses

---

[124] Scott Cullen, "Risk Management," https://www.wbdg.org/project/riskmanage.php

✓ New insights reflected in organizational historical information as to project schedule, cost, quality and performance
✓ Presented as a quantitative risk analysis report, either separate from or connected to the risk register

Plan Risk Responses

Plan Risk Responses is the "process of developing options and actions to enhance opportunities and to reduce threats to project objectives." The most important benefit gained from this process is that it speaks to risks in terms of priority and, as is necessary, incorporates resources and activities into the budget, schedule and project management plan.

Adhering to the Perform Quantitative Risk Analysis process (if it was utilized), it is necessary to understand the mechanism through which each risk will be addressed to formulate an appropriate response. Those mechanisms will be employed to determine if the risk response plan is achieving the desired effect and should incorporate identification and assignment of the one person who will be responsible for each risk response that has been agreed upon and funded. It is crucial that responses to risk:

o Are correct in terms of the risk's significance
o Cost-effective
o Practical within the context of the project
o Agreed upon by all involved parties
o Owned by a conscientious individual

Figure 12.13. **Plan Risk Responses: Inputs, Tools and Techniques, and Outputs**

Inputs	Tools & Techniques	Outputs
• Risk management plan • Risk register	• Strategies for negative risks or threats • Strategies for positive risks or opportunities • Contingent response strategies • Expert judgment	• Project management plan updates • Project documents update

Inputs

Risk management plan
o Risk management plan elements include:
o Roles and responsibilities
o Risk analysis definitions
o Timeline for reviews and for deleting risks from review
o Low, moderate and high risk thresholds, which help pinpoint risks in need of specific responses

Risk register

This is in reference to:

- Identified risks
- Risks' root causes
- Potential responses list
- Risks in need of near term responses
- Risks requiring additional analysis and response
- Trends seen qualitative analysis results
- Watch list - a compilation of low-priority risks within the risk register

Tools & Techniques

Strategies for negative risks or threats

Three strategies for handling threats or risks with the potential of having a negative impact on project objectives – *avoid*, *transfer* and *mitigate* – have differing and unique effects on the risk condition. An additional strategy, *accept*, can be utilized for both negative risks/threats and positive risks/opportunities. Each strategy should be selected to coordinate with probability and impact on the project's overall objectives of each risk. "Avoid" and "mitigate" work well for high-impact, critical risks, while "transfer" and "accept" are useful for less critical threats with a low overall impact.

- Avoid:
    - ✓ Strategy by which the project team works to eliminate the threat/protect the project from its impact
    - ✓ Requires entirely eliminating the threat by revising the project management plan, isolating project objectives from the impact or altering the objective that is in jeopardy
    - ✓ Avoiding risks appearing early in the project necessitates requirements clarification, obtaining information, communication improvement or acquiring expertise.
    - ✓ Examples
        - ➢ Schedule extension
        - ➢ Strategy revision
        - ➢ Reduction of scope
        - ➢ Entirely shutting down the project (the most radical avoidance strategy)
- Transfer:
    - ✓ Strategy by which the project team moves a threat's impact and the ownership of a response to a 3rd party
    - ✓ Gives responsibility to another person without eliminating the threat
    - ✓ Does not indicate the risk is disowned via a transfer to a later project or to another person without their knowledge and consent
    - ✓ Most effective when dealing with exposure to financial risk
    - ✓ Transference tools are diverse and include (but are not limited to):
        - ➢ Insurance
        - ➢ Performance bonds
        - ➢ Warranties

- Guarantees
- Examples
  - Contractually transferring some work and its risk back to the buyer if that party has capabilities not possessed by the seller
  - Cost-plus contract may transfer the cost risk to the buyer.
  - Fixed-rate contracts may transfer risk to the seller.
- Mitigate:
  - A strategy in which the project team attempts to reduce the occurrence probability or a risk's impact
  - Probability or impact reduction must be within acceptable threshold limits.
  - Often more effective to take early action rather than attempting to repair damage once the risk has occurred
  - Examples:
    - Adoption of simpler processes
    - Conducting additional tests
    - Selection of a more reliable supplier
  - Reducing risk of scaling up from a bench-scale model of a process/product may require prototype development.
  - If probability reduction is impossible, may address impact by focusing on linkages that determine severity, e.g., impact of a failure of an original component may be lessened by redundancy designed into the system
- Accept:
  - A strategy in which the project team acknowledges the risk but takes no action unless it occurs
  - Adopted when addressing a specific risk in any other manner is either impossible or not cost-effective
  - Indicates that, in dealing with the risk, the team has chosen not to alter the project management plan or cannot identify another appropriate response strategy
  - Passive acceptance
    - Requires no action beyond documenting the strategy
    - Risks will be dealt when they occur.
    - Threat must be periodically reviewed to be certain that no significant change has occurred.
  - Active acceptance
    - Establishes a contingency reserve to handle risks with amounts of time, money or resources necessary to do so

Strategies for positive risks or opportunities

There are three strategic responses – *exploit*, *enhance* and share –aimed at dealing with risks having impacts on project objectives that are potentially positive and a fourth, *accept*, that can be utilized for both positive and negative risks.

- Exploit:
  - ✓ Used when the organization intends to ensure the realization of an opportunity gained through a risk with a positive impact
  - ✓ Aimed at eliminating uncertainty of an upside risk by ascertaining that the opportunity occurs
  - ✓ Examples:
    - ➤ Assignment of most talented resources to the project to reduce time to completion
    - ➤ Reducing cost or duration necessary to achieving project objectives by utilizing new or upgraded technology
- Enhance:
  - ✓ Increases the opportunity's probability and/or positive impact
  - ✓ Key risk drivers' identification and maximization may increase their probability.
  - ✓ Example:
    - ➤ Increasing resources to an activity to finish more quickly
- Share:
  - ✓ Involves allocation of some/all ownership to a 3rd party best able to capitalize on the opportunity to benefit the project
  - ✓ Example:
    - ➤ Formation of risk-sharing partnerships, team, special-purpose companies or joint ventures to take advantage of the opportunity so that all parties experience a gain
- Accept:
  - ✓ Willingness to take advantage of the opportunity should it arise but not actively pursuing it

Contingent response strategies

These are formulated to only be implemented if certain events occur. Responses are triggered by events such as missing intermediate milestones or attaining a greater supplier priority and those events must be defined and tracked. When this technique identifies risk responses, they are frequently referred to as contingency or fallback plans and incorporate identified triggering events that activate those plans.

Expert judgment

Outputs

Project management plan updates
Updates include (but are not limited to):
- Schedule management plan - changes/updates in resource loading/leveling in addition to schedule strategy updates
- Cost management plan - changes in cost accounting, tracking, reports, budget strategy and the consumption of contingency reserves
- Quality management plan - changes/updates in requirements, quality assurance or control and updates to requirements documentation

- Procurement management plan - changes/updates in strategy, e.g., revisions in make-or-buy decisions or contract type(s)
- Human resource management plan - changes/updates in project organizational structure, resource applications, staff allocation and resource loading
- Scope baseline - changes/updates due to new or omitted work
- Schedule baseline - changes/updates due to new or omitted work
- Cost baseline - changes/updates due to new or omitted work

Project documents updates

Risk register updates, including (but not limited to):
- Risk owners and assigned responsibilities
- Response strategies that have been agreed upon
- Specific actions implementing selected response strategy
- Risk occurrence trigger conditions, symptoms and warnings
- Budget and schedule activities
- Contingency plans and triggers for their activation
- Fallback plans in cases of the primary response proving to be inadequate for a risk that has occurred
- Residual risks remaining following planned responses and those that were deliberately accepted
- Secondary risks directly resulting from a risk response
- Contingency reserves (based on project quantitative risk analysis and organizational risk thresholds)

Assumptions log updates - account for changes in assumptions due to new information becoming available through risk response application

Technical documentation updates

Change requests

Control Risks
Control Risks is the "process of implementing risk response plans, tracking identified risks, monitoring residual risks, and evaluating risk process effectiveness throughout the project,"[125] thereby improving risk approach efficiency throughout the project life cycle with the goal of continually optimizing risk responses.

While, over the life cycle of a project, planned risk responses incorporated in the risk register are executed, continuous monitoring of project work for new, changing or outdated risk is crucial. Information generated during project execution is used when the Control Risk process utilizes techniques such as variance and trend analysis. In addition, the Control Risk process ascertains if

---

[125] Ibid., p. 349

project assumptions are still valid; analysis has revealed an assessed risk has changed or can be retired; adherence to risk management policies or procedures is being maintained; and modifications in contingency reserves for cost or schedule are necessary to align with the current risk assessment.

Figure 12.14. **Control Risks: Inputs, Tools and Techniques, and Outputs**

Inputs	Tools & Techniques	Outputs
• Project management plan • Work performance data • Work performance reports	• Risk assessment • Risk audits • Variance and trend analysis • Technical performance measurement • Reserve analysis • Meetings	• Work performance information • Change requests • Project management plan updates • Project documents update • Organizational process assets updates

Inputs

Project management plan
As it includes the risk management plan, the project management plan offers guidance in terms of risk monitoring and controlling.

Risk register

Work performance data
This includes data associated with performance results that may be impacted by risks, including (but not limited to) deliverable status, schedule progress and costs incurred.

Work performance reports
Using information from performance measurements, these reports
do an analysis to provide work performance information such as variance analysis, earned value and forecasting data, all of which can impact controlling performance-related risks.

Tools & Techniques

Risk reassessment
The identification of new risks, the reassessment of current risks and closure of outdated risks often result from the Control Risks process.

Risk audits
- Both examine and document risk response effectiveness in terms of dealing with identified risks and their root causes and the risk management process
- Appropriate frequency of audits (defined in the risk management plan) is the project manager's responsibility.
- May be included in routine review meetings or in separate risk audit meetings
- Audit and its objective format must be clearly defined prior to the audit.

Variance and trend analysis

Technical performance measurement
- A comparison of technical accomplishments to the schedule of technical achievement
- Necessitates definitions of objective, quantifiable measures of technical performance used to compare actual results to targets
- May include weight, transaction times, number of delivered defects, storage capacity, etc.
- Deviations, e.g., demonstrating more/less functionality than planned, assist in forecasting the degree of success in achieving project scope.

Reserve analysis
With the goal of determining the adequacy of contingency reserves still available, this compares that amount to the amount of risk remaining at any time during the project.

Meetings
Frequently meeting to discuss risks increases the chances that people will identify both risks and opportunities.

Outputs

Work performance information

Change requests
Change requests are sometimes caused by the implementation of contingency plans or workarounds and must be prepared and submitted to the Perform Integrated Change process. These can include recommended corrective actions that adjust the performance of the project work to coincide with the project management plan and include both contingency plans and workarounds or recommended preventative actions that guarantee future project work performance will align with the project management plan.

Project management plan updates

Project documents updates
Although updates include (but are not limited to) the risk register, risk register updates can include outcomes of risk reassessments, audits and periodic reviews, as well as outcomes such as closing risks that are no longer applicable and release of their associated reserves and actual outcomes of the project's risks and of responses to those risks.

Organizational process assets updates
These include (but are not limited to) risk management plan templates, including the probability and impact matrix and risk register, risk breakdown structure and lessons learned.

Test What You've Learned

1) Which, if any, of the following statements is false?
    a) A risk usually has only one cause.
    b) Project risk originates in the degree of uncertainty seen in every project.
    c) Unknown risks cannot be actively managed.
    d) Overall risk is greater than the sum of all individual risks with a project.

2) A/an _____ may be assigned to an unknown risk.
    a) Tolerance rating
    b) Degree of uncertainty
    c) Management reserve
    d) Unknown unknown

3) The degree, amount, or volume of risk withstood by an organization or individual is their _____.
    a) Risk appetite
    b) Risk tolerance
    c) Risk threshold
    d) Risk limit

4) A/an _____ is a grid that maps the probability of each risk occurrence and its impact on project objectives should it occur.
    a) Impact scale
    b) Risk breakdown structure (RBS)
    c) Checklist analysis
    d) Probability and impact matrix

5) Outputs of the Identify Risk process include:
    a) Risk management plan
    b) Documentation reviews
    c) Risk register
    d) Change requests

6) Which, if any, of the following statements is false?
    a) A checklist analysis is the lowest level of the risk breakdown schedule (RBS).
    b) Further examination of any item not appearing on a risk identification checklist is unnecessary.
    c) A checklist should not be used to avoid the work of proper risk identification.
    d) It is important to periodically remove or archive items on the risk checklist.

7) Establishing definitions of probability and impact levels can decrease the effect of _____.
   a) Risk uncertainty
   b) Poor judgment
   c) Risk tolerance
   d) Bias

8) When one is creating probability distributions, a/an _____ can be utilized when there is no obvious, more likely value between specified low and high bounds.
   a) Cost distribution
   b) Uniform distribution
   c) Beta distribution
   d) Triangular distribution

9) An example of an "avoid" strategy is to _____.
   a) Produce a performance bond
   b) Adopt a simpler process
   c) Choose a more reliable supplier
   d) Reduce scope

10) Inputs to the Control Risks process include:
    a) Risk assessment, risk audits and change requests
    b) Reserve analysis, work performance reports and organizational process assets
    c) Project management plan, work performance data and work performance reports
    d) Change requests, project management plan and risk assessments

Chapter 13: Project Procurement Management

Project Procurement Management is comprised of the "processes necessary to purchase or acquire products, services, or results needed from outside the project team."[126] Much of this activity includes the use of contracts and purchase offers, the development, management and administration of which are the responsibility of authorized project team members.

Project Procurement Management is not a one-way street; it also involves the control of agreements entered into by the buyer, an outside organization that is acquiring deliverables from the seller, i.e., the performing organization. It is important for you to understand the definition and other information about procurement contracts. Contracts:

- Are also called agreements, understandings, subcontracts or purchase orders
- Are inclusive of terms and conditions as well as other buyer specifications as to what the seller is obligated to perform or provide
- Are the responsibility of the project management team in terms of meeting the project's specific needs while maintaining adherence to organizational procurement policies
- Are subject to an extensive approval and review processes because they are legally binding
- Are sometimes worded in such a way that some identifiable project risks can be shared with or transferred to the seller
- Can be managed either simultaneously or in sequences, with the possibility of each contract life cycle ending during any phase of the project life cycle
- Involve sellers (contractors, subcontractors, vendors, service providers, or suppliers) and buyers (clients, customers, prime contractors, acquiring organizations, service requestors or purchasers)

In situations in which the acquisition is not limited to shelf material, goods or common products, the work is usually managed by the seller, in which case:

- The buyer becomes the customer/key project stakeholder.
- Project management team is in charge of all project management processes rather than only those of this Knowledge Area.
- Contract terms and conditions serve as key inputs to these processes; in fact, the contract may actually include those inputs such as major deliverables, key milestones and cost objectives or constrain project team options, e.g., require buyer approval of staffing decisions in design projects.

---

[126] Project Management Institute, *A Guide to the Project Management Body of Knowledge* (*The PMBOK® Guide*), 5th ed., p. 355.

Plan Procurement Management

Plan Procurement Management is the "process of documenting project procurement decisions, specifying the approach, and identifying potential sellers."[127] Benefits include the determination of outside support must be acquired and what, how much and when is to acquired. In this process, project needs that can or should be met by an entity outside of the organization versus those that can be accomplished by the project team are identified. It should be kept in mind that, for every product, service or result acquired from an external source, the team must perform the processes from Plan Procurement Management through Close Procurements. The evaluation of potential sellers must also be completed; this is particularly crucial if buyers aim to have a degree of influence/control over decisions involving acquisitions.

In addition, the person responsible for obtaining/holding applicable permits or professional licenses must be determined. The project schedule can be affected by any decisions made during this process and those decisions must coordinate with Develop Schedule, Estimate Activity Resources and make-or-buy analyzes.

Figure 13.1. **Control Risks: Inputs, Tools and Techniques, and Outputs**

Inputs	Tools & Techniques	Outputs
• Project management plan • Work performance data • Work performance reports	• Risk assessment • Risk audits • Variance and trend analysis • Technical performance measurement • Reserve analysis • Meetings	• Work performance information • Change requests • Project management plan updates • Project documents update • Organizational process assets updates

Inputs

Project management plan
Outlining the project's need, justification, requirements and current boundaries, the project management plan includes (but is not limited to) the contents of the scope baseline:

- o Project scope statement
    - ✓ Descriptions of the product scope, service and result
    - ✓ Deliverables list
    - ✓ Acceptance criteria
    - ✓ Information about technical concerns/issue that could affect cost estimating

---
[127] Ibid., p. 358

- ✓ Constraints such as required deliver dates, available skilled resources and organizational policies
- o WBS, which holds work components that may be externally resources and the WBS dictionary, which identifies deliverables as well as work in each WBS component necessary to producing those deliverables

Requirements documentation
These include contractual/legal implications such as health, safety, security, performance, environmental, insurance, intellectual property rights, equal employment opportunity, licenses and permits.

Risk register

Activity resource requirements
Prior to planning to fulfil the procurement needs of a project, it must be understood what those needs entail in terms of people, equipment and location.

Project schedule
Consulting the project schedule is necessary to determining when project needs must be fulfilled, i.e., required timelines or mandated delivery dates.

Activity cost estimates
These assist in evaluating the appropriateness of potential sellers' bids or proposals.

Stakeholder register

Enterprise environmental factors
These include marketplace conditions and the products, services and results available in that marketplace, suppliers (especially their past performance/reputation), products', services' and results' usual terms and conditions or those that exist for a specific industry and any local requirements that are unique.

Organizational process assets
The forms of contractual agreements utilized by the organization as well as formal procurement policies, procedures and guidelines, management systems and the multi-tier supplier system comprised of sellers that are prequalified based on prior experiences are the assets used when planning project procurements.
Legal contractual agreements include:
- o Fixed-price
  - ✓ Agreements setting the fee to be paid for a defined scope of work regardless of the cost or effort to deliver it

- ✓ Can integrate financial incentives predicated on the achievement or exceeding of such things as schedule delivery dates, cost, technical performance (or any quantifiable and measurable feature)
- ✓ Exact specification of product or services being procured by the buyer is required.
  - ➢ Firm fixed price contracts (FFP):
    - ▪ Most frequently used contract type because prices set at the onset cannot change except in the event of a scope change
    - ▪ Adverse performance can lead to price increases, which are the sellers' responsibility
    - ▪ Exact specification of product or services being procured by the buyer is required, who is responsible for any changes that increase costs.
  - ➢ Fixed price incentive fee contracts (FPIF):
    - ▪ Allow for deviation from performance but provide financial incentives linked to the achievement of agreed upon metrics (cost, schedule or seller's technical performance)
    - ▪ Final price set based on seller's performance after completion of all work
    - ▪ With the price ceiling set, the seller, who is obligated to complete the work, is responsible for all costs over that ceiling.
  - ➢ Fixed price with economic price adjustment (FP-EPA):
    - ▪ Seen in many long-term buyer/seller relationships in which seller's performance period extends over many years
    - ▪ Although price is fixed, includes a special provision (EPA clause) to permit predefined contract price adjustments if conditions (inflation, cost increases/decreases) change for specific commodities
    - ▪ EPA clause must allow for precise adjustment of final price related to a reliable financial index.
    - ▪ Provide buyer/seller protection from uncontrollable external conditions
- o Cost-reimbursable contracts:
  - ✓ Are comprised of payments, aka, cost reimbursements, to seller for all valid actual costs earned for work that has been completed in addition to a fee indicative of the profit of that seller
  - ✓ In the event that a seller exceeds or fails to attain defined objectives (costs, schedule, technical performance), these contracts can include financial incentive clauses.
  - ✓ Provide flexibility by allowing redirection of the seller in the event that precise definition of the work's scope cannot be provided at the project's inception or when there are high risks
    - ➢ Cost plus fixed fee contracts (CPFF)
      - ▪ All allowable costs of contract work performance reimbursed to the seller
      - ▪ As set out in the contract, seller receives a fixed fee calculated as a percentage of project costs as initially estimated.
      - ▪ Fee does not adjust unless project scope changes, is not altered due to seller performance and is only paid for completed work.
    - ➢ Cost plus incentive fee contracts (CPIF)

- All allowable costs of contract work performance reimbursed to the seller as well as a predetermined incentive fee according to performance objectives established in the contract
- In the event that final costs are less than or exceed estimates, buyer and seller share overages/underages according a pre-negotiated cost-sharing formula.
  - Cost plus award fee contracts (CPAF)
    - Although seller receives reimbursement for all legitimate costs, the bulk of the earned fee is founded on meeting broad, subjective performance criteria as defined by and incorporated into the contract, as judged by the buyer.
    - Usually, fee is not subject to appeals.
- Time and material contracts (T&M):
  - Hybrids with features of both:
    - Cost-reimbursable contracts, i.e., can remain open-ended and may incur a cost increase to the buyer, can increase in value and sometimes include not-to-exceed values/time limits to prevent unlimited increases in cost
    - Fixed-rate contracts, i.e., some parameters (e.g., unit labor, material costs, seller profit) are specified in the contract
      - When an exact statement of work cannot be developed in a timely manner, used for staff augmentation, acquisition of experts and any other outside support

Table 13.1. **Contractual Agreements and Contingent Risks**

CONTRACT TYPE	PRIMARY BEARER OF RISK	EXPLANATION
Fixed Price	Seller	Since the price is fixed, cost overruns may not be passed on to the buyer and must be borne by the seller.
Cost Plus Fixed Fee	Buyer	Since all costs must be reimbursed to the seller, the buyer runs the risk of cost overruns.
Cost Plus Incentive Fee	Buyer and Seller	The buyer bears most of the risk, but the seller's incentive fee motivates that the seller keep costs down.
Time and Material	Buyer	The buyer pays the seller for all time and materials utilized by the seller, hence, the buyer must bear the greatest risk of overruns.

Tools & Techniques

Make-or-buy analysis

As can be easily seen from the term, make-or-buy analysis is a technique utilized "to determine whether particular work can best be accomplished by the project team or should be purchased from outside sources."[128] Even when the organization's resources are capable of producing an item or service, they may be fully involved with other projects and are hence unavailable.

There are a number of other issues to be considered when making this decision:
- Budget constraints
- Buy or lease?
- Risk sharing between the buyer and the seller
- Specific contract terms and conditions

Expert judgment

In the process, expert judgment can be employed to either develop or modify the evaluation criteria used to assess seller proposals or, in terms of legal expertise, to deal with unique issues having to do with procurement.

Market research

This would include looking at industry and vendor-specific capabilities, frequently leveraging information attained through conferences, online reviews and other sources. In addition, this can involve refinement of certain procurement objectives to "leverage maturing technologies while balancing risk associated with the breadth of vendors who can provide the materials and services desired."[129]

Meetings

Outputs

Procurement management plan

As part of the project management plan, the procurement management plan, from development of the procurement documents through contract closure, lays out the way in which the team will obtain goods and services from sources external to the performing
organization. It can be formal, informal, detailed or broad, but is always based on each project's needs and can include valuable information concerning:

- Contract types
- Issues concerning risk management
- The possible use of independent estimates and if they will be utilized as evaluation criteria

---

[128] Ibid., p. 365
[129] Ibid., p. 365

- Unilateral actions taken by the project management team in the case of the performing organization having a prescribed procurement, contracting or purchasing department
- If necessary, standardized procurement documents
- Management of multiple suppliers
- Coordination of procurement with other aspects of the project, e.g., scheduling and performance reporting
- The presence of constraints/assumptions that may influence planned procurements
- Managing lengthy lead times to purchase some items from suppliers and adjustment of the necessary additional time in terms of project schedule development
- Making make-or-buy decisions and coordinating them with the Estimate Activity Resources and Develop Schedule processes
- Establishing each contract's deliverable schedule dates and synchronizing the schedule development and control processes
- Identification of performance bonds' or insurance contracts' requirements with the goal of project risk mitigation
- Creating the direction for sellers on the development and maintenance of a work breakdown schedule (WBS)
- Providing the form/format to be utilized for procurement/contract statements of work
- If prequalified sellers are to be used, identifying them
- Procurement metrics for the management of contracts and evaluation of seller

Procurement statement of work (SOW)
Created from the project scope baseline, each procurement's SOW provides a definition limited to that specific element of the project scope comprised by the related contract. In the case of procurement items, the procurement SOW provides an item's description that is detailed to an extent allowing prospective sellers to decide whether they have the capability to provide that item, be it a product, service or result. The item's nature, the buyer's needs or the expected contract form can all influence how much detail is sufficient.

While each individual procurement item requires a SOW, multiple products/services can be combined into one procurement item within a single SOW. In addition, revision and refinement of a procurement SOW can occur during the time it travels through the process until it is incorporated into a signed agreement. A SOW can include:

- Specifications
- Desired quantity
- Quality levels
- Performance data
- Period of performance
- Work location
- Description of any required collateral services, e.g., performance reporting, post-project operational support
- Other requirements

Procurement documents

Utilized to solicit proposals from prospective sellers, procurement documents generally use terms like *bid*, *tender* or *quotation* when decisions about the selection of sellers will center on price, e.g., purchasing commercial or standard items, while *proposal* is used when considerations such as technical capability or approach are of utmost importance. Dependent on the industry and location of the procurement, various types of procurement documents use terms such as:

- Request for information (RFI)
- Invitation for bid (IFB)
- Request for proposal (RFP)
- Request for quotation (RFQ)
- Tender notice
- Invitation for negotiation
- Invitation for seller's initial response

The buyer's goal in structuring procurement documents is to make it easier to receive sellers' responses that are accurate, complete and simple to evaluate; in addition, they should be sufficiently flexible to allow for sellers' suggestions as to improved ways to meet the same requirements.

Documents include descriptions of the responses' desired form, applicable procurement SOWs and any contractual provisions that are required and should include a complexity and level of detail that coincide with the value of and risks associated with the procurement that has been planned.

Source selection criteria

Developed and utilized in the rating of seller proposals, source selection criteria can be either subjective or objective and are frequently included in procurement documents. For readily available items, this may be limited to the purchase price, which, in this context, includes both the item's cost and all additional expenses, e.g., delivery.

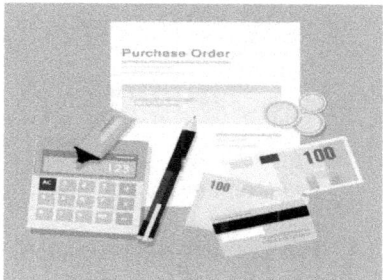

Criteria that will support an assessment for products, services or results that are more complex include:

- Understanding of need, i.e., to what degree does the seller's proposal address the procurement SOW?
- Overall or life-cycle cost
- Technical capability
- Risk, i.e., what degree of risk is set in the SOW, how much will be assigned to the seller and how does that seller mitigate risk?
- Managerial and technical approaches
- Warranty, i.e., what is warranted and for how long?
- Financial capacity
- Production capacity and interest
- Size and type of business (small, disadvantaged, involved in a specific program)

- o   Sellers' past performance
- o   Intellectual property and/or proprietary rights, i.e., will the seller assert those rights?

Make-or-buy decisions

Change decisions

Project documents updates
This may include (but are not limited to) requirements documentation and traceability matrix and the risk register.

Conduct Procurements
Conduct Procurements is the "process of obtaining seller responses, selecting a seller, and awarding a contract"[130] which offers the key benefit of providing alignment of internal and external stakeholders' expectation via set agreements. In the course of this process, bids or proposals will be received by the team, who will then employ previously defined selection criteria to choose one or more acceptable sellers. This process can be repeated for major procurement items, in which case a short list of qualified sellers can be developed followed by those sellers' providing more specific and comprehensive documents with which a detailed evaluation can be conducted using tools and techniques such as a weighting system.

Figure 13.2. **Conduct Procurements: Inputs, Tools and Techniques, and Outputs**

Inputs	Tools & Techniques	Outputs
• Procurement management plan • Procurement documents • Source selection criteria • Seller proposals • Project documents • Make-or-buy decisions • Procurement statement of work • Organizational process assets	• Bidder conference • Proposal evaluation techniques • Independent estimates • Expert judgment • Advertising • Analytical techniques • Procurement negotiations	• Selected sellers • Agreements • Resource calendars • Change requests • Project management plan updates • Project documents updates

---

[130] Ibid., p. 371

Inputs

Procurement management plan

Procurement documents

Source selection criteria

Seller proposals
Compiled as a response to a procurement document package, these put forth the information to be used by evaluators to choose one or more successful sellers.

Project documents

Make-or-buy decisions
Make-or-buy decisions can be based on the organization's core capabilities, value to be delivered by sellers, risks involved in meeting needs cost effectively, and internal capability in comparison to vendors.

Procurement statement of work
Procurement SOWs may include (but are not limited to) specifications, desired quantity, levels of quality, performance data, performance period, work location and other requirements.

Organizational process assets
These include (but are not limited to) lists of prospective and previously qualified sellers, information on both positive and negative relevant past experience with sellers and prior agreements.

Tools & Techniques

Bidder conferences
Held prior to bid or proposal submission, bidder conferences (sometimes referred to as contractor, vendor and pre-bid conferences) are meetings between the buyer and all prospective sellers that are utilized to be certain that all prospective sellers have an understanding of the procurement requirements that is both clear and common to all of them and that there is no preferential treatment. Questions from bidders can be collected and/or field visits arranged, all in advance of the bidder conference.

Proposal evaluation techniques

Independent estimates

Independent estimates can take two forms; they can be done in-house by the procuring organization or through a professional estimator who is external to the organization. These estimates are intended for use as a benchmark of proposed responses. Any significant differences can be a red flag indicating deficiencies, ambiguities and/or misunderstandings on the part of the seller.

Expert judgment
A multidisciplinary review team with expertise in areas such as contracting, legal, finance, accounting, engineering, design, research, development, sales and manufacturing can be utilized to evaluate seller proposals.

Advertising
Placing advertisements in newspapers, specialty trade publications and internet venues can greatly expand an already existing list of potential sellers. This may be required by government jurisdictions, particularly in the case of pending government contracts.

Analytical techniques

Procurement negotiations
Through procurement negotiations, mutual agreement can be attained as to purchases' structure, requirements and other terms before the contract is formalized and signed. Topics discussed should include:

- Responsibilities
- Authority to make revisions
- Applicable terms and governing law
- Methods of technical and business management
- Proprietary rights
- Contract financing
- Technical solutions
- Overall schedule
- Payments and price

Although the project manager is not necessarily the lead negotiator in this process, both the manager and team members may assist and, if called upon to do so, clarify the project's technical, quality and management requirements.

Outputs

Selected sellers

Agreements
Although there will be variations in agreement document components, they may include:

- SOW or deliverables
- Schedule baseline
- Performance reporting
- Roles and responsibilities

- Place of performance for the seller
- Pricing, payment terms, fees, retainer, penalties and incentives
- Criteria for inspection and acceptance
- Warranty and product support
- Liability limitation(s)
- Insurance and performance bonds
- Subordinate subcontractor approvals
- Handling of change requests
- Mechanisms for Alternative dispute resolution (ADR)
- Termination clause

Resource calendars

Change requests

Project management plan updates
Project management plan updates include (but are not limited to) cost, scope and schedule baselines and communications and procurement management plans.

Control Procurements
Control Procurements is the "process of managing procurement relationships, monitoring contract performance, and making changes and corrections to contracts as appropriate"[131] thus ensuring that the performance of both the seller and the buyer meet procurement requirements as per the legal agreement. It also comprises the component of financial management, monitoring payments and ascertaining that tenets of the contract, i.e., payment terms and the linkage of seller compensation with seller progress, are fully realized.

Administration of the procurement contract is undertaken by both the buyer and seller, each certifying that the other party is meeting obligations as noted in the contract and that the legal rights of both are protected. In the case of larger projects having multiple providers, the management of interfaces among those providers is key. In some cases, contract administration is a separate function from the project organization itself, with the person in charge
reporting to a supervisor from another department; this is frequently true when the organization is also selling to an external customer.

---

[131] Ibid., p. 379

Figure 13.3. **Control Procurements: Inputs, Tools and Techniques, and Outputs**

Inputs	Tools & Techniques	Outputs
• Project management plan • Procurement documents • Agreements • Approved change requests • Work performance reports • Work performance data	• Contract change control system • Procurement performance reviews • Inspections and audits • Performance reporting • Payment systems • Claims administration • Records management system	• Work performance information • Change requests • Project management plan updates • Project documents updates • Organizational process assets updates

Inputs

Project management plan

Procurement documents
Complete supporting records for the administration of the procurement processes, including contract awards and the statement of work, are contained within the documents utilized in this process.

Agreements

Approved change requests
Revisions to the contract's terms and conditions, e.g., procurement SOW, pricing and product, service or result descriptions, all of which must be formally documented and approved, are included in change requests.

Work performance reports
These include technical documentation and work performance information indicating which deliverables have or have not been completed.

Work performance data
Data include:

- o The degree to which quality standards are being met
- o Incurred or committed costs
- o Identification of paid seller invoices

Tools & Techniques

Contract change control system
This is integrated with the integrated change control system and is employed to define the process used to modify the procurement and includes the paperwork, systems for tracking, procedures for the resolution of disputes and approval levels required to authorize changes.

Inspections and audits

Performance reporting
Performance reporting involves the comparison of work performance data and sellers' reports to the agreement requirements. The work performance information obtained from this evaluation is then reported as being appropriate.

Payment systems
The buyer's accounts payable system usually processes payments to the seller after an authorized team member certifies that the work is satisfactory, with all payments both made and documented as per the terms of the contract.

Claims administration
In cases in which the buyer and seller are unable to come to an agreement on compensation for the change or even that the change has occurred, what are variously called claims, disputes or appeals must be documented, processed, monitored and managed over the contract life cycle. All of this must be in accordance with the terms of the contract. Negotiation is the preferred means of settling all such claims and disputes, sometimes through alternative dispute resolution (ADR) that adheres to procedures established in the contract.

Records management system
Comprised of a specific set of processes, related control functions and automation tools, this system is employed by the project manager in the management of contract and procurement documentation and records.

Outputs

Work performance information
This information offers the ability to identify current or potential problems that will support later claims or new procurements. This can be a circular process, with the organization gaining knowledge about the procurement's performance, thus supporting better forecasting, risk management and decision making, as well as being helpful if there is a dispute with the vendor.

Information includes compliance of contracts, providing a mechanism with which specific deliverables expected/received from vendors can be tracked and that supports better communication with vendors. This ensures that any potential issues are quickly addressed and results satisfy all parties.

Change requests
In addition to those described previously, these can also be changes requested but as yet unresolved and should include the direction provided by the buyer or actions taken by the seller. Of course, in because these changes can be disputed by one party, leading to the other party's claim, these changes must be uniquely identified and fully documented.

Project management plan updates
These include (but are not limited to) the procurement management plan, updates of which should indicate change requests impacting costs or schedules, and the schedule and cost baselines.

Project documents updates
These comprise (but are not limited to) procurement documentation that include:

- o The procurement contract with all supporting schedules
- o Requested as yet unapproved contract changes
- o Approved change requests
- o Seller-developed technical documentation and work performance information
    - ✓ Deliverables
    - ✓ Seller performance reports and warranties
    - ✓ Financial documents such as invoices and payment records
    - ✓ Results of inspections related to contracts

Organizational process assets updates
These updates include (but are not limited to):

- o Correspondence providing written documentation of aspects of buyer/seller communication
    - ✓ Necessary warnings of unsatisfactory performance
    - ✓ Contract changes/clarification requests
    - ✓ Reported results of buyer audits and inspections that may be indicative of seller weaknesses to be corrected
- o Payment schedules and requests
- o Seller performance evaluation documentation
    - ✓ Prepared by the buyer
    - ✓ May provide the basis for early contract termination or the administration of contract penalties, fees or incentives.
    - ✓ Documents seller's ability to continue performing project work
    - ✓ Informs as to whether the seller will be allowed to work on future projects
    - ✓ Provides a rating of the seller's performance on the current project

Close Procurements
As you might expect, Close Procurements is "the process of completing each procurement"[132] with the goal of documenting agreements and other information to be used in the future. The finalization of open claims, updating of records to show final results and including such information in organization

---

[132] Ibid., p. 386

archives are administrative activities that are involved in this process. Although Close Procurements attends to each contract that applies to the project or project phase, it should be kept in mind that, in the case of multiphase projects, a contract's term may only relate to a given phase of the project. In this case, the process only closes those procurement(s) applicable to that phase. Additionally, even following closure, unresolved claims can remain subject to litigation in which case, contract terms and conditions can provide specific guidelines to agreement closure.

This process also addresses early contract termination as the result of mutual agreement, one party's default or for the buyer's convenience (if noted in the contract). Buyer's and seller's rights in these circumstances can be found in the terminations clause of the contract. Although, as based on those terms and conditions, the buyer may be able to terminate the contract at any time for cause or convenience and both as a whole or in part, the seller may be compensated for their preparations and for any work completed and accepted.

Figure 13.4. **Close Procurements: Inputs, Tools and Techniques, and Outputs**

Inputs
- Project management plan
- Procurement documents

Tools & Techniques
- Procurement audits
- Procurement negotiations
- Records management system

Outputs
- Closed procurements
- Organizational process assets updates

Inputs

Project management plan

Procurement documents
Closing a contract requires the collection, indexing and filing of all procurement documentation with the goal of providing information
for lessons learned and to serve as the foundation for the evaluation of contractors in future. This include information on the contract:

- Schedule
- Scope
- Quality
- Cost performance
- Payment records
- Inspection results

Tools & Techniques

Procurement audits

Procurement negotiations

Records management system

Outputs

Closed procurements
Most frequently via an authorized procurement administrator, the buyer provides formal written notice as to the completion of the project to the seller. The terms and conditions of the contract usually offer a definition of the requirements for formal procurement closure, which also appear in the procurement management plan.

Organizational process assets updates
The elements updated may include (but are not limited to) the procurement file, which is a complete set of indexed contract documentation, deliverable acceptance and documentation of lessons learned.

Test What You've Learned

1) Which, if any, of the following statements is true?
   a) The only type of contracts included in project procurement management involve the performing organization (the seller).
   b) This process encompasses the control of any contract issued by the outside organization (the buyer).
   c) Contracts sometimes include the means by which project risks can be shared by or transferred to the seller.
   d) All of these statements are false.

2) What contractual and legal elements are included in requirements documentation?
   a) Insurance and equal opportunity employment
   b) Security and scope
   c) Intellectual property rights and activity resources
   d) Product service and results

3) A _____ is the most frequently used type of contract.
   a) Fixed price incentive fee contract (FFP)
   b) Fixed price with economic price adjustment (FP-EPA)
   c) Firm fixed price contract (FFP)
   d) Cost-reimbursable contract

4) _____ are frequently used when a buyer/seller relationship is of considerable duration.
   a) Firm fixed price contracts
   b) Fixed price incentive fee contracts (FPIF)
   c) Cost-reimbursable contracts
   d) Fixed price with economic price adjustment contracts (FP-EPA)

5) Which, if any, of the following statements is false?
   a) In CPIF contracts, when final costs are less or more than estimates, buyers and sellers share overages or underages.
   b) In CPFF contracts, all allowable costs of contract work performance are reimbursed to the buyer.
   c) Cost-reimbursable contracts permit redirection of sellers if the work scope's exact definition is not provided at the project's inception.
   d) In CPAF contracts, fees are not subject to appeals.

6) Issues to be considered in doing a _____ include risk sharing between the buyer and seller and budget constraints.
   a) Market research
   b) Procurement SOW

EXAM PREPARATION GUIDE 255

c) Source selection
  d) Make-or-buy

7) A _____ can include desired quantity, work location and period of performance.
  a) Statement of work (SOW)
  b) Procurement document
  c) Tender notice
  d) Project document update

8) A bidder conference is a technique utilized in the _____ process.
  a) Plan Procurement Management
  b) Close Procurements
  c) Conduct Procurements
  d) Control Procurements

9) Work performance data employed in the Control Procurements process include:
  a) The degree to which quality standards are being met
  b) Systems for tracking deliverables
  c) The buyer's accounts payable system
  d) Technical documentation

10) Source selection criteria can include:
  a) Seller's proposals
  b) Audit trails
  c) Supplier's capacity and life-cycle cost
  d) Competitive ranges of bids

Chapter 14: Project Stakeholder Management

Project Stakeholder Management is comprised of the "processes required to identify the people, groups, or organizations that could impact or be impacted by the project, to analyze stakeholder expectations and their impact on the project, and to develop appropriate management strategies for effectively engaging stakeholders in project decisions and execution."[133]

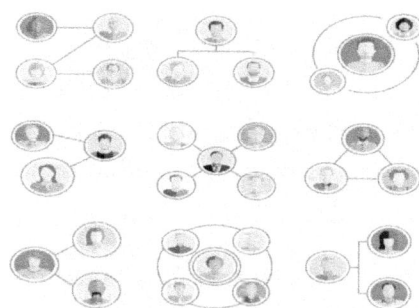

In addition, this process centers on understanding stakeholders' needs and expectations via continuous communication, speaking to issues when they arise, handling interests that may conflict and encouraging stakeholder involvement in project decisions and activities when appropriate.

Stakeholders are effected by or can affect a project in either a positive or negative way. The identification and management of these stakeholders by the project manager is of great importance; failure to do so appropriately can cause the failure of a project. Figure 14.1 illustrates this process.

Figure 14.1. **Stakeholder Management**

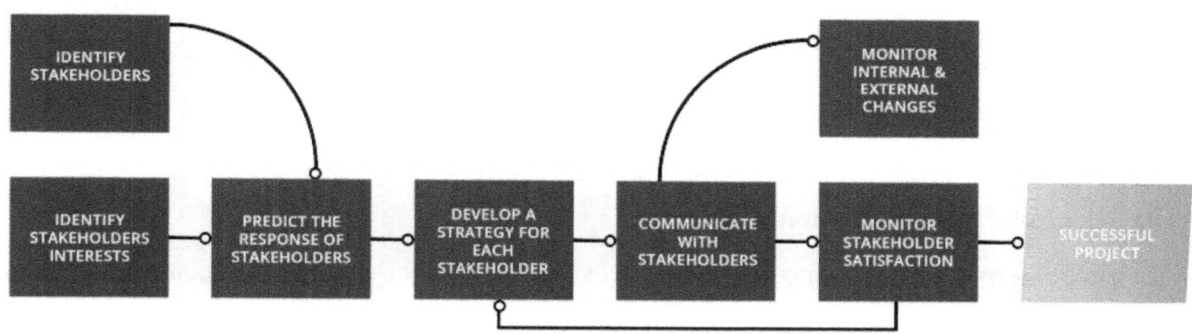

Identify Stakeholders

Identify Stakeholders is the "process of identifying the people, groups, or organizations that could impact or be impacted by a decision, activity, or outcome of a project, analyzing and documenting relevant information regarding their interests, involvement, interdependencies, influence, and potential impact on a project."[134] This process aids the project by allowing the identification of the appropriate focus for each individual, group or organization who "may affect, be affected by, or perceive themselves to be affected by a decision, activity, or outcome of a project."[135]

---

[133] Project Management Institute, *A Guide to the Project Management Body of Knowledge* (*The PMBOK® Guide*), 5th ed., p. 391.

[134] Ibid., p. 393
[135] Ibid., p. 394

Stakeholders:

- o Include customers, sponsors, the performing organization and the public
- o Have interests that may be positively or negatively affected by a project's execution or completion
- o May influence the project and its deliverables
- o Can be at various organizational levels or have different levels of authority
- o Should be categorized in terms of their interest and involvement in and influence on the project, keeping in mind that their effect/influence may not emerge until a project or phase is in its later stages

Figure 14.2. **Identify Stakeholders: Inputs, Tools and Techniques, and Outputs**

Inputs

Project charter

The project charter offers information concerning:

- o Internal/external parties related to and affected by the project's result or execution
- o Project sponsors
- o Customers
- o Team members
- o Groups/departments participating in the project
- o Other people/organizations affected by the project

Procurement documents

Information can be obtained from these documents if the project results from a procurement activity or is founded on an established contract because the parties in that contract are key stakeholders.

Enterprise environmental factors

Those that influence this process include (but are not limited to) organizational culture and structure, governmental or industry standards such as regulations and product standards and global, regional or local trends, practices or habits.

Organizational process assets

These are comprised of (but not limited to) stakeholder register templates, lessons learned from previous projects or phases and previous projects' stakeholder registers.

Tools & Techniques

Stakeholder analysis

Stakeholder analysis is a "technique of systematically gathering and analyzing quantitative and qualitative information to determine whose interests should be taken into account throughout the project."[136] This is comprised of the identification of stakeholders' interests, expectations, influence and possible support or non-support of the project as well as relationships with the project and with other stakeholders that could potentially leveraged for coalition building and partnerships, thus increasing the likelihood of project success. Of course, all of this information is examined to determine the way in which it relates to the project at its various stages or phases.

Classification models utilized for stakeholders analysis include those that group them according to their levels of authority, i.e., power, and concern (interest); power and active involvement (influence); influence and ability to affect project planning and/or execution (impact); and salience, which combines power, urgency (need for immediate attention) and legitimacy (appropriate involvement). Figure 14.3 below provides an example of a stakeholder power/interest grid, which is equally applicable to all of the other grid types.

Figure 14.3. **Power/Interest Grid with Stakeholders**

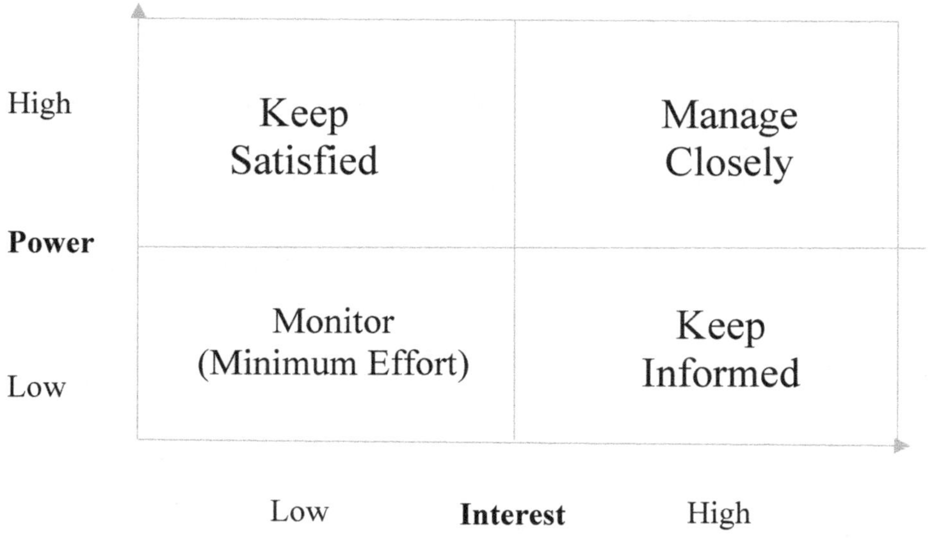

Power	Low Interest	High Interest
High	Keep Satisfied	Manage Closely
Low	Monitor (Minimum Effort)	Keep Informed

---

[136] Ibid., p. 395

Expert judgment
Information assisting in the identification and classification of stakeholders can be obtained through individual consultations or panels with senior management, other organizational units, key stakeholders already identified, project managers who have completed projects in the same area, subject matter experts, industry groups/consultants, professional/ technical associations, regulatory bodies and nongovernmental organizations.

Outputs

Stakeholder register
At this point, the stakeholder register includes (but is not limited to) the name, position within the organization, location, project role, contact information, major requirements and expectations and possible influence of project stakeholders. In addition, the life cycle phase on which their interest is centered and their classification (internal/external, supporter/neutral/ resistor, etc.) should be noted. Keep in mind that, as stakeholders may change or new ones may be identified, the register must be regularly updated throughout the course of the project.

Plan Stakeholder Management
Plan Stakeholder Management is the "process of developing appropriate management strategies to effectively engage stakeholders throughout the project life cycle, based on the analysis of their needs, interests, and potential impact on project success."[137] The gain attained by this process is that project interests are supported because the project manager obtains a clear and actionable plan to guide interactions with stakeholders.

This plan offers information as to the project's effect on stakeholders, allowing effective engagement with those stakeholders and the means to manage their expectations and to improve communication. However, what is most important about stakeholder management is the creation and maintenance of relationships that can meet their needs and requirements within project boundaries. Further, this process must be ongoing; as mentioned previously, both the composition of the stakeholder community and their required level of engagement can change as the project progresses.

Figure 14.4. **Plan Stakeholder Management: Inputs, Tools and Techniques, and Outputs**

Inputs	Tools & Techniques	Outputs
• Project management plan • Stakeholder register • Enterprise environmental factors • Organizational process assets	• Expert judgment • Meetings • Analytical techniques	• Stakeholder management plan • Project documents updates

---

[137] Ibid., p. 399

Inputs

Project management plan
The information from the project management plan includes (but is not limited to) the project life cycle and the processes involved in each phase, descriptions of the way in which work will be executed and human resources requirements met to attain project objectives, how roles, responsibilities and staffing management will be addressed and structured, documentation of change monitoring and control found in the change management plan and stakeholder communication needs and techniques.

Stakeholder register

Enterprise environmental factors
Although all of these factors serve as inputs here, the most significant include organizational culture and structure and political climate as they assist in the determination of the best options with which to support the most appropriate stakeholder management process.

Tools & Techniques

Expert judgment

Meetings

Analytical techniques
In this process, it is necessary to analyze stakeholder engagement levels as compared to the planned levels of engagement necessary to the successful completion of the project. Stakeholder engagement levels are classified as *unaware*, i.e., unaware of project and potential impacts, *resistant*, i.e., cognizant of project and potential impacts and resistant to change, *neutral*, i.e., neither supportive not resistant but aware of the project, *supportive*, i.e., which combine awareness of project and potential impacts with support of change and *leading*, those that are aware of both project and potential impacts and who actively engage in guaranteeing project success. This process is utilized to identify gaps between current and desirable engagement levels, which can be addressed by the use of expert judgment by the project team.

Table 14.1 illustrates the engagement levels of several project stakeholders.

Table 14.1. **Stakeholders' Engagement Assessment Matrix**[138]

Stakeholder	Unaware	Resistant	Neutral	Supportive	Leading
Stakeholder 1	C			D	
Stakeholder 2			C	D	
Stakeholder 3				D C	

Outputs

Stakeholder management plan
Appropriate precautions should be taken when distributing the information found in the stakeholder management plan, particularly in the case of those stakeholders who are resistant to the project. Further, to ensure ongoing accuracy and relevancy, the project manager should regularly review the validity of underlying assumptions incorporated in the plan.

In addition to data from the stakeholder register, the stakeholder management plan frequently offers:

- Desired/current key stakeholder engagement levels
- Scope/impact of change to stakeholders
- Potential overlap and interrelationships between stakeholders
- Language, format, content, level of detail of information to be provided to stakeholders, as well as the reasons for and anticipated impact of that information
- Information distribution time frame and frequency
- Method(s) to be used to update and refine the plan over the course of the project

Project documents updates
These include (but are not limited to) project schedule and stakeholder register.

Manage Stakeholder Engagement
Manage Stakeholder Engagement is the "process of communicating and working with stakeholders to meet their needs/expectations, address issues as they occur, and foster appropriate stakeholder engagement in project activities throughout the project life cycle."[139]

This process makes it possible for the project manager to enhance active support, reduce resistance and ensure that stakeholders have a clear understanding of the goals, objectives, benefits and risks involved in the project, all of which increase the likelihood of project success by a significant degree.

---

[138] Ibid., p. 403

[139] Ibid., p. 404

It should also be kept in mind that stakeholders' ability to influence the project is usually highest at the time of the initial stages and progressively lessens over the course of the project.

Figure 14.5. **Manage Stakeholder Engagement: Inputs, Tools & Techniques, and Outputs**

Inputs	Tools & Techniques	Outputs
• Stakeholder management plan • Communications management plan • Change log • Organizational process assets	• Communication methods • Interpersonal skills • Management skills	• Issue log • Change requests • Project management plan updates • Project documents updates • Organizational process assets updates

Inputs

Stakeholder management plan

Communications management plan
With the goal of managing stakeholder expectations, this information includes (but is not limited to) stakeholder communications requirement, the language, format, content, level of detail of information to be provided to stakeholders as well as the reasons for distribution of information, persons/groups to receive the information and escalation process.

Change log
Because this is utilized to document any changes occurring during a project, information about those changes and their impact on issues such as time, cost and risk must be communicated to the stakeholders.

Organizational process assets
These include (but are not limited to) organizational communication requirements, issue management and change control procedures and historical information concerning previous projects.

Tools & Techniques

Communication methods
These methods were discussed in detail in chapter 10. In this process, methods are dependent on stakeholders' communication requirement that indicate how, when and which method should be used in a project.

Interpersonal skills
These include the project manager's ability to build trust, resolve conflicts, overcome resistance to change and engage in active listening.

Management skills
These are aimed facilitating consensus as to project objectives, encouraging support of the project, engaging in negotiation to fulfil project needs and modification of organizational behavior to accept the outcomes of the project.

Outputs

Issue log
The issue log may require updating if and when new issues arise and/or current issues attain resolution.

Change requests

Project management plan updates
The project management plan may need to updated due to the identification of or changes in stakeholder requirements. This can include alterations in communication methods and the results of addressing concerns and issue resolution.

Project documents updates
Although these updates may include other documents, they are mostly comprised of the stakeholder register with the identification of new stakeholders or when those already in the register are no longer involved with and/or impacted by the project.

Organizational process assets updates
These may include (but are not limited to) stakeholder notifications, both formal and informal project reports noting project status, lessons learned, issue logs, project closure reports and outputs from other Knowledge areas. Project presentations, stakeholder feedback and documentation of lessons learned may also be updated.

Control Stakeholder Engagement
Control Stakeholder Engagement is the "process of monitoring overall project stakeholder relationships and adjusting strategies and plans for engaging stakeholders."[140] This process is aimed at maintaining or increasing stakeholder activities' efficiency and effectiveness as the project evolves and its environment changes.

---

[140] Ibid., p. 409

Figure 14.6 **Control Stakeholder Engagement: Inputs, Tools and Techniques, and Outputs**

Inputs	Tools & Techniques	Outputs
• Project management plan • Issue log • Work performance data • Project documents	• Information management systems • Expert judgment • Meetings	• Work performance information • Change requests • Project management plan updates • Project documents updates • Organizational process assets updates

Inputs

Project management plan

This process uses information included in the project management plan that includes (but is not limited to) the project life cycle and the processes to be utilized during each phase, the way in which the work necessary to accomplishing project objectives will be executed, the means used to meet human resources requirements and the ways in which roles, responsibilities, reporting relationships and staffing management will be addressed and organized, documentation of the monitoring and control of changes, and needs and techniques for stakeholder communication.

Issue log

Work performance data

Examples include:

- Reported percentage of completed work
- Technical performance measures
- Schedule activities' start and finish dates
- Number of change requests
- Actual costs and durations

Project documents

These include (but are not limited to) the project schedule, stakeholder register, issue and change logs and project communications.

Tools & Techniques

Information management systems

In this process, these systems are utilized for the capture, storage and distribution of information to stakeholders which includes project costs, schedule progress and performance.

Expert judgment

Meetings

Outputs

Work performance information
While raw data cannot be used in the decision-making process, work performance information that has been correlated and contextualized can form the basis of those decisions. Examples include deliverables' status, status of change request implementation and forecasted estimates to complete.

Change requests
Processed via the Perform Integrated Change Control process, these can include recommended corrective actions to be taken to allow the project's expected future performance to coincide with the project management plan as well as preventative measures to reduce the possibility of future negative project performance.

Project management plan updates
As the need for changes in strategies or approaches become apparent, project management plan updates may include (but are not limited to) alteration of the change, communications, cost human resource, quality, requirements, risk, schedule, scope and stakeholder management plans.

Project documents updates
These can include (but are not limited to) the stakeholder register and the issue log.

Organizational process assets updates
Updates may include (but are not limited to) stakeholder notifications, project reports, project presentations and records, stakeholder feedback and lessons learned documentation.

Test What You've Learned

1) Vital information about stakeholders includes:
   a) Interests, involvement and influence
   b) Influence, political affiliation and potential impact
   c) Interdependencies and organizational roles
   d) Influence and income

2) As an input to the Identify Stakeholders process, the _____ provides information about internal and external parties related to and affected by the result or execution of the project.
   a) Stakeholder analysis
   b) Organization process assets
   c) Enterprise environmental factors
   d) Project charter

3) Classification models used in stakeholder analysis group stakeholders according to:
   a) Involvement in and detachment from the project
   b) Power and interest
   c) Legitimacy and awareness
   d) Management role and salience

4) Outputs of the Plan Stakeholder Management process include:
   a) Project management plan updates
   b) Organizational process assets updates
   c) Stakeholder register updates
   d) Project documents updates

5) A stakeholder's level of engagement is classified as leading if they are:
   a) Aware of project and potential impacts and actively involved in ensuring project success
   b) Neither supportive nor resistant
   c) Aware of potential impacts
   d) Supportive of change

6) Inputs to the Manage Stakeholder Engagement process include:
   a) Issue log
   b) Change requests
   c) Change log
   d) Enterprise environmental factors

7) An element of the project management plan utilized in the Control Stakeholder Engagement process is:
   a) Expert judgment
   b) Work performance data
   c) Work performance information
   d) The project life cycle

8) Which, if any, of the following statements are true?
   a) The correlation and contextualization of work performance information make it suitable for use in decision making.
   b) Forecasted completion estimates are elements of work performance data.
   c) The decision-making process utilizes work performance data.
   d) None of these statements are true.

9) Change requests are just one of the outputs of _____.
   a) The Identify Stakeholders process
   b) The Plan Stakeholder Management process
   c) The Manage Stakeholder Engagement process
   d) The Control Stakeholder Engagement process

10) Information used to identify stakeholders can be obtained from _____ if the project is founded on an established contract.
   a) Stakeholder analysis
   b) Enterprise environmental factors
   c) Procurement documents
   d) Project charter

Appendices

Appendix A. Project Management Formulas

PURPOSE	FORMULA
NET PRESENT VALUE	$PV = FV/(1+r)^n$
INTERNAL RATE OF RETURN	Discount rate at which net present value = 0
EXPECTED MONETARY VALUE (EMV)	Σ products of probabilities & corresponding values
INCENTIVE FEE	The target fee adjusted by the seller's share ration as a percentage of the cost variance from the target cost.
TRIANGULAR DISTRIBUTION	Mean = (a+m+b) / 3
VARIANCE	$v = (a^2+m^2+b^2-am-ab-mb) / 18$
STANDARD DEVIATION	$\sigma = \sqrt{variance}$
BETA DISTRIBUTION	Mean = (a+4m+b) / 6
VARIANCE	$v = [(b-a)/6]^2$
STANDARD DEVIATION	$\sigma = (b-a)/6 = \sqrt{variance}$
TOTAL TRIANGULAR & BETA	
MEAN	Σ [Individual means]
VARIANCE	$v = \Sigma$ [Individual variance]
STANDARD DEVIATION	$\sigma = \sqrt{Total\ variance}$
COMMUNICATION PATHS	n(n-1)/2
EARNED VALUE	CV = EV – AC
	SV = EV - PV
	CPI = EV / AC
	SPI = EV / PV
	ETC = EAC – AC
	VAC = BAC – EAC
	TCPI = (BAC - EV) / (BAC - AC)
EAC DO NOT EXTRAPOLATE VARIANCES	BAC + AC – EV
EAC IGNORE EXISTING BUDGET	AC + ETC
EAC VARIANCES WILL CONTINUE	BAC / CPI
EAC WORST CASE	BAC/(CPI * SPI)
EAC PMBOK® FORMULA	AC + (BAC - EV) /CPI
POINT OF TOTAL ASSUMPTION (PTA)	((Ceiling Price - Target Price) / Buyer's Share Ratio) + Target Cost

Appendix B: Chapter Quiz Answer Key

Chapter 2: The Basics

1) Which, if any, of these statements is true?
   c) The term "temporary" in the context of a project indicates that it has a definite beginning and fixed end.
2) A _____ is a collection of projects, programs, subportfolios and operations managed as a group to achieve strategic objectives.
   d) Portfolio
3) Organizational planning affects projects in terms of _____.
   a) Project prioritization
4) Competing project constraints do not include:
   d) Communication
5) Projects within a program are related through:
   c) A common outcome
6) Which, if any, of these statements is false?
   a) Projects/programs in a portfolio must be interdependent or directly related.
7) A project management office (PMO) that has a low degree of control and serves as a consultant to projects is:
   b) Supportive
8) The integration of data and information from corporate strategic projects is the task of:
   d) The project management office
9) The focus of the _____ is on specified project objectives.
   b) The project manager
10) Business value is:
    d) Both a) and c)

Chapter 3: Organization Influences & Project Life Cycle

1) Which, if any, of the following is true?
   e) As an enterprise environmental factor, organizational structure can affect resource availability.
2) James only reports to one superior. Thus, he works within a _____ organization.
   d) Functional
3) A _____ structure intermingles functional and projectized characteristics and is classified by the relative level of power and influence between functional and project managers.
   c) Matrix
4) As a project expediter, Alicia:
   e) Serves as a staff assistant.
5) Tim is a project manager in a projectized organization and thus:
   d) Has a great deal of independence and authority.
6) The Initiating and Planning process includes:
   b) Specific organizational policies such as those associated with human resources and safety

7) Alan is trying to deal with an outdated project management information system, which should be considered to be a constraint imposed by _____.
   e) An enterprise environmental factor.
8) Enterprise environmental factors:
   d) May either enhance or restrain project management options.
9) Issue and defect management procedures fall into the category of _____ processes:
   b) Executing, Monitoring and Controlling
10) Stakeholders:
    d) Include both customers and sellers.

Chapter 4: Project Management Processes

1) Which, if any, of the following statements are true?
   d) Both b) and c) are true.
2) What is/are not identified during the Initiating Process Group?
   b) Project team members
3) Reviewing and assessing detail project requirements, constraints and assumptions with stakeholders is a task related to:
   b) The Planning Performance Domain
4) The coordination of people and resources, management of stakeholder expectations and the integration and performance of project activities takes place during the:
   d) The Executing Performance Domain
5) James is working within the Executing Process Group and has acquired and managed project resources and implemented the quality management plan. Which task, if any, has James skipped?
   a) Managing task execution by leading and developing the project team to achieve project deliverables.
6) The widget being produced by Thomas' project, which has moved to the Closing phase, may or may not fit the customer's sprocket. What should Thomas do?
   d) Revisit task 1 of the Monitoring and Controlling Process Group.
7) Stakeholder buy-in and engagement are much easier to attain if:
   a) The delineation of strategy, tactics and a course of action is carefully done as part of the Planning Process Group.
8) Knowledge and skills required in the Executing Process Group include:
   d) Managing flow of information and vendor management techniques
9) When closing a project, you must:
   c) Transfer ownership of deliverables to assigned shareholders
10) _____ is performance data collected from various controlling processes, analyzed in context and integrated based on relationships across areas.
    b) Work performance information

EXAM PREPARATION GUIDE 271

Chapter 5: Project Integration Management

1) Which, if any, of the following statements are true?
   c) The project statement of work is provided by the project sponsor.
2) What offers the information that will determine if undertaking a project is worth the investment it will require?
   d) The business case
3) Utilized throughout project integration process, _____ include(s) brainstorming and problem solving.
   a) Facilitation techniques
4) _____ are scheduled and implemented by the project team and may be either corrective or preventative.
   b) Approved change requests
5) Standardized guidelines and work instructions are included in:
   a) Organizational process assets
6) Which, if any, of the following statements are false?
   a) Preventative action is completed to realign project work performance with the project management plan.
7) Outputs of the Monitor and Control Project Work process include:
   a) Change requests
8) _____ are updated and reissued based on work performance information provided as the project is executed.
   b) Schedule forecasts
9) The Performing Integrated Change Control process is undertaken:
   d) Throughout the entire course of a project.
10) Which of these processes are in the order in which they are completed?
    c) Develop Project Charter, Develop Project Management Plan, Direct and Manage Project Execution

Chapter 6: Project Scope Management

1) The work performed to deliver a product, service or result with the features and functions that have been specified is the _____.
   b) Project scope
2) Enterprise environmental factors that can affect the Plan Scope Management process include:
   c) Infrastructure
3) _____ provides the foundation for defining and managing the project, including product scope.
   a) Collect Requirements
4) Which, if any, of the following statements is true?
   c) One element of the project scope statement is project exclusion, which helps to manage stakeholder expectations.
5) _____ is the process of subdividing project deliverables and project work into smaller, easier to manage components.

b) Create WBS
6) What is defined as a technique utilized to divide and subdivide project scope and deliverables into smaller, more manageable parts?
   d) Decomposition
7) Tools utilized in the Validate Scope process include:
   c) Inspection
8) In the Control Scope process, work performance information includes:
   c) Impact of variances on schedule and cost
9) Frequently, _____ is used in the analysis of information necessary to decomposing deliverables into smaller components when creating a WBS.
   a) Expert judgment
10) Acceptance criteria is included in the:
    c) Project scope statement

Chapter 7: Project Time Management

1) Where are the Project Time Management processes and the tools and techniques utilized in those processes documented?
   a) Schedule management plan
2) If you were working to complete a representation of the plan for executing the project's duration, dependencies and other planning information, what document would you be producing?
   c) Schedule model
3) Tools and techniques utilized in the Define Activities process include:
   b) Decomposition, rolling wave planning and expert judgment
4) Which, if any, of the following statement is true?
   a) A schedule management plan includes the rules of performance measurement.
5) A/an _____ is the amount of time whereby a successor activity can be advanced with respect to a predecessor activity and a/an _____ is the amount of time whereby a successor activity will be delayed with respect to a predecessor activity.
   c) Lead, lag
6) _____ are included in duration estimates, are occasionally referred to as buffers and are used to account for schedule uncertainty.
   d) Contingency reserves
7) _____ utilizes most likely, optimistic and pessimistic estimates to describe an activity's duration's approximate range.
   b) PERT
8) Which, if any, of the following statements are false?
   a) There is little difference between the critical path and critical chain methods.
9) _____ are non-work schedule activities that are added to manage scheduling uncertainty.
   d) Duration buffers
10) When a resource has been assigned to two or more activities during the same time period, _____ can be used to balance supply with demand.
    c) Resource leveling

Chapter 8: Project Cost Management

1) Which, if any, of the following is not an analytical technique utilized in the plan cost management process?
   a) Control thresholds
2) Which units of measurement are most frequently used for comparisons during the estimate costs process?
   d) Units of currency
3) Which, if any, of the following statements is true?
   b) Cost estimates are reviewed throughout the project's life cycle.
4) _____ included in the scope baseline include:
   c) Constraints
5) Which of these techniques uses values from previous projects like the scope, cost and budget to estimate the parameters of a current project?
   a) Analogous estimating
6) Reliability of models is most likely certain when they are:
   c) Scalable
7) Total and periodic funding requirements emerge from the:
   c) Cost baseline
8) Project funding requirements include:
   b) Projected expenditures and anticipated liabilities
9) _____ is the authorized budget assigned to scheduled work to be completed for an activity or work breakdown structure component.
   b) Planned value
10) *AC + Bottom-up ETC* is one of the equations used to calculate:
    a) Estimate at completion (EAC)

Chapter 9: Project Quality Management

1) What is the difference between quality and grade?
   a) Quality is the degree to which a set of inherent characteristics fulfil requirements and grade is a classification of deliverables having the same functional use but different technical characteristics.
2) The main benefit of _____ is that it provides guidance and direction as to the way the project team will manage and confirm quality over the course of the project.
   b) The Plan Quality Management process
3) Cause-and-effect diagrams are also known as _____.
   c) fishbone diagrams
4) The cost of conformance includes:
   c) Prevention and appraisal costs
5) A process is out of control when:
   a) A data point surpasses a control limit.

6) A statistical method by which factors that influence specific product or process variables can be identified is termed:
   d) Design of experiments
7) Which, if any, of the following statements are true?
   b) The process of auditing quality requirements and the results of quality control measurements is called the Perform Quality Assurance process.
8) _____ are very similar to _____.
   d) Affinity diagrams, mind-mapping techniques
9) Benefits of the Control Quality process include:
   d) Both a) and b)
10) Inputs to the Control Quality process include:
    a) Quality metrics

Chapter 10: Project Human Resource Management

1) Which, if any, of the following statements are false?
   a) Hierarchical-type organization charts display positions and respective responsibilities in a bottom-down format.
2) A _____ is utilized to illustrate connections between work packages and activities and project team members.
   b) Resource breakdown schedule
3) _____ is the formal/informal interaction with other in an organization, industry or professional environment.
   c) networking
4) The element of the human resource management plan that outlines, among other things, at what time and how project team members will be acquired is called _____.
   c) Staffing management plan
5) Misunderstandings, problems with information and experience sharing and technology costs are drawbacks of _____.
   d) Virtual teams
6) Documenting project staff assignments can be accomplished through the use of:
   a) Project team directories
7) Good communication, emotional intelligence and group facilitation are all _____.
   d) Interpersonal skills
8) During the storming team development stage:
   b) Teams may not be open to others' ideas.
9) The other phrase that refers to colocation is a _____.
   c) Tight matrix
10) The conflict resolution technique in which a search for solutions takes place is called:
    a) Compromise/Reconcile

EXAM PREPARATION GUIDE 275

Chapter 11: Project Communications Management

1) What barriers to communication must be considered during the Plan Communications Management process?
   a) Time zones, language and cross-cultural issues
2) _____ that affect the Plan Communications Management process include the political climate and personnel administration.
   b) Enterprise environmental factors
3) The number of potential communication channels can be derived with:
   d) $n(n - 1)/2$
4) During the communication process, it is the _____ responsibility to ensure that the information has been received, is understood and acknowledged properly.
   c) Receiver
5) Which, if any, of the following statements is true?
   c) As part of the Manage Communication process, it must be ensured that stakeholders are given the opportunity to request additional information.
6) _____ are inputs into the Control Communications Management process.
   c) Work performance data and issue logs
7) Which, if any, of the following statements are false?
   a) Issue logs only contain details concerning resolution of those issues.
8) _____ communication involves customers, vendors, other projects and organizations and the public.
   d) External
9) The most significant benefit of the Manage Communications process is that it:
   b) Certifies that the communication flow between project stakeholders is both efficient and effective throughout the project life cycle.
10) As an output of the Manage Communications process, project communications can be influenced by the:
    c) Message's urgency and impact

Chapter 12: Project Risk Management

1) Which, if any, of the following statements is false?
   a) A risk usually has only one cause.
2) A/an _____ may be assigned to an unknown risk.
   c) Management reserve
3) The degree, amount, or volume of risk withstood by an organization or individual is their _____.
   b) Risk tolerance
4) A/an _____ is a grid that maps the probability of each risk occurrence and its impact on project objectives should it occur.
   d) Probability and impact matrix

5) Outputs of the Identify Risk process include:
   c) Risk register
6) Which, if any, of the following statements is false?
   b) Further examination of any item not appearing on a risk identification checklist is unnecessary.
7) Establishing definitions of probability and impact levels can decrease the effect of _____.
   d) Bias
8) When creating probability distributions, a/an _____ can be utilized when there is no obvious, more likely value between specified low and high bounds.
   b) Uniform distribution
9) An example of an "avoid" strategy is to _____.
   d) Reduce scope
10) Inputs to the Control Risks process include:
    c) Project management plan, work performance data and work performance reports

Chapter 13: Project Procurement Management

1) Which, if any, of the following statements is true?
   b) This process encompasses the control of any contract issued by the outside organization (the buyer).
2) What contractual and legal elements are included in requirements documentation?
   a) Insurance and equal opportunity employment
3) A _____ is the most frequently used type of contract.
   c) Firm fixed price contract (FFP)
4) _____ are frequently used when a buyer/seller relationship is of considerable duration.
   d) Fixed price with economic price adjustment contracts (FP-EPA)
5) Which, if any, of the following statements is false?
   a) In CPIF contracts, when final costs are less or more than estimates, buyers and sellers share overages or underages.
6) Issues to be considered in doing a _____ include risk sharing between the buyer and seller and budget constraints.
   d) Make-or-buy analysis
7) A _____ can include desired quantity, work location and period of performance.
   a) Statement of work (SOW)
8) A bidder conference is a technique utilized in the _____ process.
   c) Conduct Procurements
9) Work performance data employed in the Control Procurements process include:
   a) The degree to which quality standards are being met

EXAM PREPARATION GUIDE   277

10) Source selection criteria can include:
    c) Supplier's capacity and life-cycle cost

Chapter 14: Project Stakeholder Management

1) Vital information about stakeholders includes:
   e) Interests, involvement and influence
2) As an input to the Identify Stakeholders process, the _____ provides information about internal and external parties related to and affected by the result or execution of the project.
   d) Project charter
3) Classification models used in stakeholder analysis group stakeholders according to:
   b) Power and interest
4) Outputs of the Plan Stakeholder Management process include:
   d) Project documents updates
5) A stakeholder's level of engagement is classified as leading if they are:
   e) Aware of project and potential impacts and actively involved in ensuring project success
6) Inputs to the Manage Stakeholder Engagement process include:
   a) Issue log
7) An element of the project management plan utilized in the Control Stakeholder Engagement process is:
   d) The project life cycle
8) Which, if any, of the following statements are true?
   e) The correlation and contextualization of work performance information make it suitable for use in decision making.
9) Change requests are just one of the outputs of _____.
   d) The Control Stakeholder Engagement process\
10) Information used to identify stakeholders can be obtained from _____ if the project is founded on an established contract.
    c) Procurement documents

Appendix C: Sample Exam One

QUESTION NO: 1
_____ is an element of the project scope statement.
A. Acceptance criteria
B. A stakeholder list
C. A summary budget
D. Detailed risks analysis

QUESTION NO: 2
Which document contains the necessary information to determine if a project is worth the requested investment?
A. Cost baseline

B. Service level agreement
C. Letter agreement
D. Business case

QUESTION NO: 3
Which input to the Plan Risk Management process provides information on high-level risks?
A. Project charter
B. Enterprise environmental factors
C. Stakeholder register
D. Organizational process assets

QUESTION NO: 4
Which of the terms below is an example of personnel assessment?
A. Resource leveling
B. Tight matrix
C. Team-building activity
D. Focus group

QUESTION NO: 5
Which input to the Manage Stakeholder Engagement process provides guidance on how stakeholders can best be involved in a project?
A. Feedback loop
B. Stakeholder analysis
C. Communication management plan
D. Stakeholder management plan

QUESTION NO: 6
Which input to the Identify Stakeholders process provides information about internal or external participants related to the project?
A. Procurement documents
B. Communications plan
C. Project charter
D. Stakeholder register

QUESTION NO: 7
In which Process Group is the Identify Stakeholders process found?
A. Initiating
B. Monitoring and Controlling
C. Planning
D. Executing

QUESTION NO: 8

A/an _____ serves as an input to Develop Project Charter.

A. Business case
B. Activity list
C. Project management plan
D. Cost forecast

QUESTION NO: 9

Which Knowledge Area involves identifying the people, groups, or organizations that may be impacted by or impact a project?

A. Project Risk Management
B. Project Human Resource Management
C. Project Scope Management
D. Project Stakeholder Management

QUESTION NO: 10

Which input to Collect Requirements is used to identify stakeholders who can assist with identifying requirements?

A. Stakeholder register
B. Scope management plan
C. Stakeholder management plan
D. Project charter

QUESTION NO: 11

In which Knowledge Area is the project charter developed?

A. Project Cost Management
B. Project Scope Management
C. Project Time Management
D. Project Integration Management

QUESTION NO: 12

In which stages of a project is the ability to influence cost the greatest?

A. Early
B. Middle
C. Late
D. Completion

QUESTION NO: 13

Which process involves developing an approximation of the monetary resources needed to complete project activities?

A. Estimate Costs
B. Control Costs

C. Determine Budget
D. Plan Cost Management

QUESTION NO: 14
Which tool or technique is used in the Develop Project Management Plan process?
A. Pareto diagram
B. Performance reporting
C. SWOT analysis
D. Expert judgment

QUESTION NO: 15
The organization's perceived balance between risk taking and risk avoidance is reflected in risk:
A. Responses
B. Appetite
C. Tolerance
D. Attitude

QUESTION NO: 16
_____ is an output of the Manage Stakeholder Engagement process.
A. change requests
B. enterprise environmental factors
C. the stakeholder management plan
D. the change log

QUESTION NO: 17
Which process numerically analyzes the effect of identified risks on overall project objectives?
A. Plan Risk Management
B. Plan Risk Responses
C. Perform Quantitative Risk Analysis
D. Perform Qualitative Risk Analysis

QUESTION NO: 18
Which Collect Requirements output links the product requirements to the deliverables that satisfy them?
A. Requirements documentation
B. Requirements traceability matrix
C. Project management plan updates
D. Project documents updates

QUESTION NO: 19
A temporary endeavor that creates a unique product or service is called a:
A. Project
B. Plan

C. Program
D. Portfolio

QUESTION NO: 20
The process of prioritizing risks for further analysis or action is known as:
A. Plan Risk Management
B. Plan Risk Responses
C. Perform Qualitative Risk Analysis
D. Perform Quantitative Risk Analysis

QUESTION NO: 21
Stakeholder satisfaction should be managed as a key project:
A. Benefit
B. Initiative
C. Objective
D. Process

QUESTION NO: 22
Which cost is associated with non-conformance?
A. Liabilities
B. Inspections
C. Training
D. Equipment

QUESTION NO: 23
Which Process Group is Identify Risks part of?
A. Planning
B. Executing
C. Closing
D. Initiating

QUESTION NO: 24
The business needs, assumptions, constraints and the understanding of the customers' needs and high-level requirements are documented in the:
A. Project management plan
B. Project charter
C. Work breakdown structure
D. Stakeholder register

QUESTION NO: 25
Which Process Group and Knowledge Area include the Sequence Activities process?
A. Executing Process Group and Project Time Management
B. Executing Process Group and Project Cost Management

C. Planning Process Group and Project Time Management
D. Planning Process Group and Project Cost Management

QUESTION NO: 26
In the Plan Stakeholder Management process, expert judgment is used to:
A. Provide information needed to plan appropriate ways to engage project stakeholders
B. Ensure comprehensive identification and listing of new stakeholders
C. Analyze the information needed to develop the project scope statement
D. Decide the level of engagement of the stakeholders at each required stage

QUESTION NO: 27
Which document defines how a project is executed, monitored and controlled, and closed?
A. Strategic plan
B. Project charter
C. Project management plan
D. Service level agreement

QUESTION NO: 28
Which tool or technique is used in the Plan Scope Management process?
A. Document analysis
B. Observations
C. Product analysis
D. Expert judgment

QUESTION NO: 29
Which tool or technique is an examination of industry and specific vendor capabilities?
A. Independent estimates
B. Market research
C. Analytical techniques
D. Bidder conferences

QUESTION NO: 30
An input used in developing the communications management plan is:
A. Communication models
B. Enterprise environmental factors
C. Organizational communications
D. Organizational cultures and styles

QUESTION NO: 31
Which process is enterprise environmental factors an input to?
A. Control Scope
B. Define Scope

C. Plan Scope Management
D. Collect Requirements

QUESTION NO: 32
Which process develops options and actions to enhance opportunities and reduce threats to project objectives?
A. Identify Risks
B. Control Risks
C. Plan Risk Management
D. Plan Risk Responses

QUESTION NO: 33
The process of establishing the policies, procedures and documentation for planning, developing, managing, executing and controlling the project schedule is known as:
A. Plan Schedule Management
B. Develop Project Charter
C. Develop Schedule
D. Plan Scope Management

QUESTION NO: 34
_____ is an input to the Plan Stakeholder Management process.
A. The project charter
B. The stakeholder analysis
C. A communication management plan
D. A stakeholder register

QUESTION NO: 35
_____ is/are input(s) to the Plan Cost Management process.
A. Cost estimates
B. Resource calendars
C. The project charter
D. The risk register

QUESTION NO: 36
The process of identifying and documenting project roles, responsibilities, required skills, reporting relationships and creating a staffing management plan is known as:
A. Develop Project Team
B. Manage Project Team
C. Acquire Project Team
D. Plan Human Resource Management

QUESTION NO: 37
A project in which the scope, time, and cost of delivery are determined as early as possible is following a life cycle that is:
A. Adaptive
B. Predictive
C. Incremental
D. Iterative

QUESTION NO: 38
Which quality management and control tool is useful in visualizing parent-to-child relationships in a decomposed hierarchy that uses a systematic set of rules to define a nesting relationship?
A. Interrelationship digraphs
B. Tree diagram
C. Affinity diagram
D. Network diagram

QUESTION NO: 39
The only Process Group that comprises processes that typically occur throughout the project life cycle is:
A. Planning
B. Executing
C. Monitoring and Controlling
D. Closing

QUESTION NO: 40
In which Project Human Resource Management process is Organizational theory used as a tool?
A. Manage Project Team
B. Acquire Project Team
C. Develop Project Team
D. Plan Human Resource Management

QUESTION NO: 41
Which tools or techniques are used in the Plan Schedule Management process?
A. Benchmarking, expert judgment, and analytical techniques
B. Statistical sampling, benchmarking, and meetings
C. Negotiations, pre-assignment, and multi-criteria decision analysis
D. Expert judgment, analytical techniques, and meetings

QUESTION NO: 42
A project manager is appointed full-time to a project and is given full-time administrative staff and full-time project team members. Which type of organizational structure is described by this scenario?
A. Projectized
B. Weak matrix

C. Functional
D. Balanced matrix

QUESTION NO: 43
To which Process Group does the Plan Stakeholder Management process belong?
A. Executing
B. Initiating
C. Planning
D. Monitoring and Controlling

QUESTION NO: 44
A method of obtaining early feedback on requirements by providing a working model of the expected product before actually building is known as:
A. Benchmarking
B. Context diagrams
C. Brainstorming
D. Prototyping

QUESTION NO: 45
Which stakeholder classification model groups stakeholders based on their level of authority and their active involvement in the project?
A. Power/influence grid
B. Power/interest grid
C. Influence/impact grid
D. Salience model

QUESTION NO: 46
Which Plan Schedule Management tool or technique may involve choosing strategic options to estimate and schedule the project?
A. Facilitation techniques
B. Expert judgment
C. Analytical techniques
D. Variance analysis

QUESTION NO: 47
Which of the 7 basic quality control tools is most useful when gathering attributes data in an inspection to identify defects?
A. Control charts
B. Pareto diagrams
C. Ishikawa diagrams
D. Checksheets

QUESTION NO: 48
_____ is the process of estimating the type and quantity of material, human resources, equipment, or supplies required to perform each activity.
A. Collect Requirements
B. Conduct Procurements
C. Estimate Activity Durations
D. Estimate Activity Resources

QUESTION NO: 49
Which item is a formal proposal to modify any document, deliverable, or baseline?
A. Change request
B. Requirements documentation
C. Scope baseline
D. Risk urgency assessment

QUESTION NO: 50
Which process determines the risks that may affect the project and documents their characteristics?
A. Control Risks
B. Plan Risk Management
C. Plan Risk Responses
D. Identify Risks

QUESTION NO: 51
An example of a group decision-making technique is:
A. Nominal group technique
B. Unanimity
C. Affinity diagram
D. Multi-criteria decision analysis

QUESTION NO: 52
Which risk management strategy seeks to eliminate the uncertainty associated with a particular upside risk by ensuring that the opportunity is realized?
A. Enhance
B. Share
C. Exploit
D. Accept

QUESTION NO: 53
Payback period, return on investment, internal rate of return, discounted cash flow, and net present value are all examples of:
A. Expert judgment
B. Analytical techniques
C. Earned value management
D. Group decision-making techniques

QUESTION NO: 54
The definition of when and how often the risk management processes will be performed throughout the project life cycle is included in which risk management plan component?
A. Timing
B. Methodology
C. Risk categories
D. Budgeting

QUESTION NO: 55
Using values such as scope, cost, budget, and duration or measures of scale such as size, weight, and complexity from a previous similar project as the basis for estimating the same parameter or measurement for a current project describes which type of estimating?
A. Bottom-up
B. Parametric
C. Analogous
D. Three-point

QUESTION NO: 56
Sending letters, memos, reports, emails, and faxes to share information is an example of which type of communication?
A. Direct
B. Interactive
C. Pull
D. Push

QUESTION NO: 57
Which process involves defining, preparing, and coordinating all subsidiary plans and integrating them into a comprehensive plan?
A. Direct and Manage Project Work
B. Develop Project Management Plan
C. Plan Quality Management
D. Monitor and Control Project Work

QUESTION NO: 58
Inputs to the Plan Schedule Management process include:
A. Organizational process assets and the project charter
B. Enterprise environmental factors and schedule tools
C. Time tables and Pareto diagrams
D. Activity attributes and resource calendars

QUESTION NO: 59
In which process is a Strengths, Weaknesses, Opportunities, and Threats (SWOT) analysis used as a tool or technique?

A. Identify Risks
B. Control Risks
C. Perform Quantitative Risk Analysis
D. Perform Qualitative Risk Analysis

QUESTION NO: 60
Which process identifies whether the needs of a project can best be met by acquiring products, services, or results outside of the organization?
A. Plan Procurement Management
B. Control Procurements
C. Collect Requirements
D. Plan Cost Management

QUESTION NO: 61
The planned work contained in the lowest level of work breakdown structure (WBS) components is known as:
A. Work packages
B. Accepted deliverables
C. The WBS dictionary
D. The scope baseline

QUESTION NO: 62
When should quality planning be performed?
A. While developing the project charter
B. In parallel with the other planning processes
C. As part of a detailed risk analysis
D. As a separate step from the other planning processes

QUESTION NO: 63
In which process is risk categorization a tool or technique?
A. Plan Risk Responses
B. Plan Risk Management
C. Perform Qualitative Risk Analysis
D. Perform Quantitative Risk Analysis

QUESTION NO: 64
A regression line is used to estimate:
A. Whether or not a process is stable or has predictable performance
B. How a change to the independent variable influences the value of the dependent variable
C. The upper and lower specification limits on a control chart
D. The central tendency, dispersion, and shape of a statistical distribution

QUESTION NO: 65
Units of measure, level of precision, level of accuracy, control thresholds, and rules of performance measurement are examples of items that are established in the:
A. Cost management plan
B. Work performance information
C. Quality management plan
D. Work breakdown structure

QUESTION NO: 66
When does the project team determine which dependencies are discretionary?
A. Before the Define Activities process
B. During the Define Activities process
C. Before the Sequence Activities process
D. During the Sequence Activities process

QUESTION NO: 67
Which process involves subdividing project deliverables and project work into smaller, more manageable portions?
A. Develop Schedule
B. Create VVBS
C. Estimate Activity Resources
D. Define Scope

QUESTION NO: 68
In a project, float measures the:
A. Ability to shuffle schedule activities to lessen the duration of the project
B. Amount of time an activity can be extended or delayed without altering the project finish date
C. Cost expended to restore order to the project schedule after crashing the schedule
D. Estimate of the total resources needed for the project after performing a forward pass

QUESTION NO: 69
Project deliverables that have been completed and checked for correctness through the Control Quality process are known as:
A. Verified deliverables
B. Validated deliverables
C. Acceptance criteria
D. Activity resource requirements

QUESTION NO: 70
Which quality tool may prove useful in understanding and estimating the cost of quality in a process?
A. Checksheets
B. Histograms
C. Flowcharts
D. Control charts

QUESTION NO: 71
A graphic display of project team members and their reporting relationships is known as a:
A. Resource calendar
B. Project organization chart
C. Resource breakdown structure (RBS)
D. Responsibility assignment matrix (RAM)

QUESTION NO: 72
Which items are components of a project management plan?
A. Change management plan, process improvement plan, and scope management plan
B. Agreements, procurement management plan, and work performance information
C. Schedule management plan, project schedule, and resource calendars
D. Scope baseline, project statement of work, and requirements traceability matrix

QUESTION NO: 73
Which Project Time Management process includes bottom-up estimating as a tool or technique?
A. Estimate Activity Resources
B. Sequence Activities
C. Estimate Activity Durations
D. Develop Schedule

QUESTION NO: 74
A graphic display of project team members and their reporting relationships is known as a:
A. Resource calendar
B. Project organization chart
C. Resource breakdown structure (RBS)
D. Responsibility assignment matrix (RAM)

QUESTION NO: 75
Which changes occur in risk and uncertainty as well as the cost of changes as the life cycle of a typical project progresses?
A. Risk and uncertainty increase; the cost of changes increases
B. Risk and uncertainty increase; the cost of changes decreases
C. Risk and uncertainty decrease; the cost of changes increases
D. Risk and uncertainty decrease; the cost of changes decreases

QUESTION NO: 76
Regression analysis, failure mode and effect analysis (FMEA), fault tree analysis (FTA), and trend analysis are examples of which tool or technique?
A. Expert judgment
B. Forecasting methods
C. Earned value management
D. Analytical techniques

QUESTION NO: 77

The Perform Quality Assurance process occurs in the _____ Process Group.

A. Executing
B. Monitoring and Controlling
C. Initiating
D. Planning

QUESTION NO: 78

_____ is an input to the Manage Project Team process.

A. Work performance reports
B. Change requests
C. Activity resource requirements
D. Enterprise environmental factors

QUESTION NO: 79

Which input provides suppliers with a clear set of goals, requirements, and outcomes?

A. Procurement statement of work
B. Purchase order
C. Source selection criteria
D. Bidder conference

QUESTION NO: 80

A large portion of a projects budget is typically expended on the processes in which Process Group?

A. Executing
B. Planning
C. Monitoring and Controlling
D. Closing

QUESTION NO: 81

A project manager providing information to the right audience, in the right format, at the right time is an example of which type of communication?

A. Efficient
B. Effective
C. Push
D. Pull

QUESTION NO: 82

A project charter is an output of the _____ Process Group.

A. Executing
B. Planning
C. Initiating
D. Closing

QUESTION NO: 83
Which tool or technique is effective in a project in which the deliverable is not a service or result?
A. Inspection
B. Variance analysis
C. Decomposition
D. Product analysis

QUESTION NO: 84
The process of confirming human resource availability and obtaining the team necessary to complete project activities is known as:
A. Plan Human Resource Management
B. Acquire Project Team
C. Manage Project Team
D. Develop Project Team

QUESTION NO: 85
An input to Conduct Procurements is:
A. Independent estimates
B. Selected sellers
C. Seller proposals
D. Resource calendars

QUESTION NO: 86
What are the Project Procurement Management processes?
A. Conduct Procurements, Control Procurements, Integrate Procurements, and Close Procurements
B. Estimate Procurements, Integrate Procurements, Control Procurements, and Validate Procurements
C. Plan Procurement Management, Conduct Procurements, Control Procurements, and Close Procurements
D. Plan Procurement Management, Perform Procurements, Control Procurements, and Validate Procurements

QUESTION NO: 87
Which tool or technique is used to develop the human resource management plan?
A. Ground rules
B. Expert judgment
C. Team-building activities
D. Interpersonal skills

QUESTION NO: 88
Processes in the Planning Process Group are typically carried out during which part of the project life cycle?
A. Only once, at the beginning
B. At the beginning and the end

C. Once during each phase
D. Repeatedly

QUESTION NO: 89
The basis of identification for current or potential problems to support later claims or new procurements is provided by:
A. A risk urgency assessment
B. The scope baseline
C. Work performance information
D. Procurement audits

QUESTION NO: 90
Typical outcomes of a project include:
A. Products, services, and improvements
B. Products, programs, and services
C. Improvements, portfolios, and services
D. Improvements, processes, and products

QUESTION NO: 91
Which grid shows which resources are tied to work packages?
A. Work breakdown structure (WBS)
B. Responsibility assignment matrix (RAM)
C. Project assignment chart
D. Personnel assignment matrix

QUESTION NO: 92
The iterative process of increasing the level of detail in a project
management plan as greater amounts of information become available is known as:
A. Continuous improvement
B. Predictive planning
C. Progressive elaboration
D. Quality assurance

QUESTION NO: 93
Status of deliverables, implementation status for change requests, and forecasted estimates to complete are examples of:
A. Earned value management
B. Enterprise environmental factors
C. Organizational process assets
D. Work performance information

QUESTION NO: 94
Which item is an output of Plan Quality Management and an input to Perform Quality Assurance?

A. Organizational process updates
B. Quality metrics
C. Change requests
D. Quality control measurements

QUESTION NO: 95
A project manager managing a cross-cultural virtual project team across several time zones should be concerned about the impacts of which communication technology factor?
A. Urgent information need
B. Sensitivity of information
C. Project environment
D. Ease of use

QUESTION NO: 96
The number of potential communication channels for a project with 5 stakeholders is:
A. 10
B. 12
C. 20
D. 24

QUESTION NO: 97
Which tool or technique of the Define Activities process allows for work to exist at various levels of detail depending on where it is in the project life cycle?
A. Historical relationships
B. Dependency determination
C. Bottom-up estimating
D. Rolling wave planning

QUESTION NO: 98
An output of the Create WBS process is:
A. Scope baseline
B. Change requests
C. Accepted deliverables
D. Variance analysis

QUESTION NO: 99
A tool or technique used in the Control Procurements process is:
A. Expert judgment
B. Performance reporting
C. Bidder conferences
D. Reserve analysis

QUESTION NO: 100
Which type of project management office (PMO) supplies templates, best practices, and training to project teams?
A. Supportive
B. Directive
C. Controlling
D. Instructive

QUESTION NO: 101
Which Define Activities output extends the description of the activity by identifying the multiple components associated with each activity?
A. Project document updates
B. Activity list
C. Activity attributes
D. Project calendars

QUESTION NO: 102
An input to the Identify Stakeholders process is:
A. The project management plan
B. The stakeholder register
C. Procurement documents
D. Stakeholder analysis

QUESTION NO: 103
What is the estimate at completion (EAC) if the budget at completion (BAC) is $100, the actual cost (AC) is $50, and the earned value (EV) is $25?
A. $50
B. $100
C. $125
D. $200

QUESTION NO: 104
Job satisfaction, challenging work, and sufficient financial compensation are values related to which interpersonal skill?
A. Influencing
B. Motivation
C. Negotiation
D. Trust building

QUESTION NO: 105
A project manager should communicate to stakeholders about resolved project issues by updating the:
A. project records
B. project reports

C. stakeholder notifications
D. stakeholder register

QUESTION NO: 106
A disadvantage associated with virtual teams is that they:
A. Require communication technology that is not readily available
B. Create difficulties when including people with disabilities
C. Often cannot accommodate teams that work different hours or shifts
D. Create the possibility for misunderstandings to arise

QUESTION NO: 107
In which phase of team building activities do team members begin to work together and adjust their work habits and behavior to support the team?
A. Performing
B. Storming
C. Norming
D. Forming

QUESTION NO: 108
The Project Human Resource Management process that involves confirming human resource availability and obtaining the team necessary to complete project activities is:
A. Acquire Project Team
B. Plan Human Resource Management
C. Manage Project Team
D. Develop Project Team

QUESTION NO: 109
For a stakeholder with low interest and high power, the project manager should:
A. Monitor the stakeholder
B. Manage the stakeholder closely
C. Keep the stakeholder satisfied
D. Keep the stakeholder informed

QUESTION NO: 110
In a typical project, project managers spend most of their time:
A. Estimating
B. Scheduling
C. Controlling
D. Communicating

QUESTION NO: 111
Which schedule method allows the project team to place buffers on the project schedule path to account for limited resources and project uncertainties?

A. Critical path method
B. Critical chain method
C. Resource levelling
D. Schedule network analysis

QUESTION NO: 112
Correlated and contextualized information on how closely the scope is being maintained relative to the scope baseline is contained within:
A. project documents updates
B. project management plan updates
C. change requests
D. work performance information

QUESTION NO: 113
The most appropriate project life cycle model for an environment with a high level of change and extensive stakeholder involvement in projects is:
A. adaptive
B. reflexive
C. predictive
D. iterative

QUESTION NO: 114
Variance and trend analysis is a tool and technique used in which process?
A. Perform Qualitative Risk Analysis
B. Perform Quantitative Risk Analysis
C. Control Risks
D. Plan Risk Responses

QUESTION NO: 115
An intentional activity to modify a nonconforming product or product component is called:
A. defect repair
B. work repair
C. corrective action
D. preventive action

QUESTION NO: 116
Which quality tool incorporates the upper and lower specification limits allowed within an agreement?
A. Control chart
B. Flowchart
C. Checksheet
D. Pareto diagram

QUESTION NO: 117
Analytical techniques are a tool and technique of which process in Project Procurement Management?

A. Plan Procurement Management
B. Control Procurements
C. Conduct Procurements
D. Close Procurements

QUESTION NO: 118
The process of obtaining seller responses, selecting a seller, and awarding a contract is called:
A. Close Procurements
B. Control Procurements
C. Plan Procurements
D. Conduct Procurements

QUESTION NO: 119
Impacts to other organizational areas, levels of service, and acceptance criteria are typical components of which document?
A. Business case
B. Work breakdown structure
C. Requirements documentation
D. Risk register

QUESTION NO: 120
Which Process Group includes the Manage Stakeholder Engagement process?
A. Executing
B. Planning
C. Monitoring and Controlling
D. Initiating

QUESTION NO: 121
In complex projects/ initiating processes should be completed:
A. Within a work package
B. In each phase of the project
C. To estimate schedule constraints
D. To estimate resource allocations

QUESTION NO: 122
A project manager requesting industry groups and consultants to recommend project intervention is relying on:
A. Communication models
B. Stakeholder participation
C. Expert judgment
D. Enterprise environmental factors

QUESTION NO: 123
Tools and techniques used in Direct and Manage Project Work include:
A. Process analysis and expert judgment
B. Analytical techniques and a project management information system
C. Performance reviews and meetings
D. Expert judgment and meetings

QUESTION NO: 124
Which of the Perform Quality Assurance tools and techniques may enhance the creation of the work breakdown structure (WBS) to give structure to the decomposition of the scope?
A. Activity network diagrams
B. Affinity diagrams
C. Matrix diagrams
D. Interrelationship digraphs

QUESTION NO: 125
Which type of communication is a project manager using who communicates to the project team though email?
A. Formal
B. Informal
C. Horizontal
D. Unofficial

QUESTION NO: 126
An input to the Perform Integrated Change Control process is:
A. expert judgment
B. seller proposals
C. the project charter
D. the project management plan

QUESTION NO: 127
Managing on-going production of goods and services to ensure business continues efficiently describes which type of management?
A. Portfolio
B. Project
C. Program
D. Operations

QUESTION NO: 128
Which type of manager is assigned by the performing organization to lead the team that is responsible for achieving the project objectives?
A. Program
B. Functional

C. Project
D. Portfolio

QUESTION NO: 129
Which of the seven basic quality tools is particularly useful for gathering attribute data while performing inspections to identify defects?
A. Histograms
B. Scatter diagrams
C. Flowcharts
D. Checksheets

QUESTION NO: 130
The most commonly used type of precedence relationship in the precedence diagramming method (PDM) is:
A. start-to-start (SS)
B. start-to-finish (SF)
C. finish-to-start (FS)
D. finish-to-finish (FF)

QUESTION NO: 131
Which technique is used in Perform Quantitative Risk Analysis?
A. Sensitivity analysis
B. Probability and impact matrix
C. Risk data quality assessment
D. Risk categorization

QUESTION NO: 132
Which illustrates the connection between work that needs to be done and its project team members?
A. Work breakdown structure (WBS)
B. Network diagrams
C. Staffing management plan
D. Responsibility assignment matrix (RAM)

QUESTION NO: 133
Which tools or techniques will a project manager use for Develop Project Team?
A. Negotiation
B. Roles and responsibilities
C. Recognition and rewards
D. Prizing and promoting

QUESTION NO: 134
Which of the following is an input to Direct and Manage Project Execution?
A. Requested changes

B. Approved change requests
C. Work performance information
D. Implemented defect repair

QUESTION NO: 135
Which input to the Manage Stakeholder Engagement process is used to document changes that occur during the project?
A. Issue log
B. Change log
C. Expert judgment
D. Change requests

QUESTION NO: 136
A technique used to determine the cause and degree of difference between baseline and actual performance is:
A. Product analysis
B. Variance analysis
C. Document analysis
D. Decomposition

QUESTION NO: 137
Scope, schedule, and cost parameters are integrated in the:
A. Performance measurement baseline
B. Analysis of project forecasts
C. Summary of changes approved in a period
D. Analysis of past performance

QUESTION NO: 138
What is the schedule performance index (SPI) if the planned value (PV) is $100, the actual cost (AC) is $150, and the earned value (EV) is $50?
A. 0.50
B. 0.67
C. 1.50
D. 2.00

QUESTION NO: 139
Which item is an input to the Define Activities process?
A. Schedule data
B. Activity list
C. Risk register
D. Scope baseline

QUESTION NO: 140
Which process involves monitoring the status of the project to update the project costs and managing changes to the cost baseline?
A. Estimate Costs
B. Control Costs
C. Determine Budget
D. Plan Cost Management

QUESTION NO: 141
Which group is formally chartered and responsible for reviewing, evaluating, approving, delaying, or rejecting changes to the project and for recording and communicating decisions?
A. Project team
B. Focus group
C. Change control board
D. Project stakeholders

QUESTION NO: 142
Plan Schedule Management is a process in which Knowledge Area?
A. Project Scope Management
B. Project Human Resource Management
C. Project Integration Management
D. Project Time Management

QUESTION NO: 143
An output of the Validate Scope process is:
A. A requirements traceability matrix
B. The scope management plan
C. Work performance reports
D. Change requests

QUESTION NO: 144
The Perform Integrated Change Control process occurs in which Process Group?
A. Initiating
B. Executing
C. Monitoring and Controlling
D. Planning

QUESTION NO: 145
Which input may influence quality assurance work and should be monitored within the context of a system for configuration management?
A. Work performance data
B. Project documents
C. Scope baseline
D. Requirements documentation

QUESTION NO: 146
Change requests are processed for review and disposition according to which process?
A. Control Quality
B. Control Scope
C. Monitor and Control Project Work
D. Perform Integrated Change Control

QUESTION NO: 147
The review of a sellers progress toward achieving the goals of scope and quality within cost and schedule compared to the contract is known as:
A. Work performance information
B. Inspections and audits
C. Payment systems
D. Procurement performance reviews

QUESTION NO: 148
The iterative and interactive nature of the Process Groups creates the need for the processes in which Knowledge Area?
A. Project Communications Management
B. Project Integration Management
C. Project Risk Management
D. Project Scope Management

QUESTION NO: 149
Market conditions and published commercial information are examples of which input to the Estimate Costs process?
A. Scope baseline
B. Organizational process assets
C. Enterprise environmental factors
D. Risk register

QUESTION NO: 150
An output of the Develop Project Team process is:
A. Organizational process assets
B. Enterprise environmental factors updates
C. Project staff assignments
D. Organizational charts and position descriptions

QUESTION NO: 151
A risk response strategy in which the project team shifts the impact of a threat, together with ownership of the response, to a third party is called:
A. mitigate
B. accept

C. transfer
D. avoid

QUESTION NO: 152
An output of the Plan Quality Management process is:
A. A process improvement plan
B. Quality control measurements
C. Work performance information
D. The project management plan

QUESTION NO: 153
A project manager should document the escalation path for unresolved project risks in the:
A. Change control plan
B. Stakeholder register
C. Risk log
D. Communications management plan

QUESTION NO: 154
Which process in Project Time Management includes reserve analysis as a tool or technique?
A. Estimate Activity Resources
B. Sequence Activities
C. Estimate Activity Durations
D. Develop Schedule

QUESTION NO: 155
Which earned value management (EVM) metric is a measure of the cost efficiency of budgeted resources expressed as a ratio of earned value (EV) to actual cost (AC)?
A. Cost variance (CV)
B. Cost performance index (CPI)
C. Budget at completion (BAC)
D. Variance at completion (VAC)

QUESTION NO: 156
Which tool or technique is used to manage change requests and the resulting decisions?
A. Change control tools
B. Expert judgment
C. Delphi technique
D. Change log

QUESTION NO: 157
A key benefit of the Manage Communications process is that it enables:
A. The best use of communication methods
B. An efficient and effective communication flow

C. Project costs to be reduced
D. The best use of communication technology

QUESTION NO: 158
The ways in which the roles and responsibilities, reporting relationships, and staffing management will be addressed and structured within a project is described in the:
A. Human resource management plan
B. Activity resource requirements
C. Personnel assessment tools
D. Multi-criteria decision analysis

QUESTION NO: 159
An input to the Plan Procurement Management process is:
A. Source selection criteria
B. Market research
C. A stakeholder register
D. A records management system

QUESTION NO: 160
Reserve analysis is a tool and technique used in which process?
A. Plan Risk Management
B. Plan Risk Responses
C. Identify Risks
D. Control Risks

QUESTION NO: 161
Which type of dependency is established based on knowledge of best practices within a particular application area or some unusual aspect of the project in which a specific sequence is desired, even though there may be other acceptable sequences?
A. External
B. Internal
C. Mandatory
D. Discretionary

QUESTION NO: 162
The Monitoring and Controlling Process Group includes processes that:
A. Establish the scope, objectives, and course of action of a project
B. Define a new project or a new phase of an existing project
C. Track, review, and regulate the progress and performance of a project
D. Complete the work defined in the project management plan

QUESTION NO: 163
Which Control Quality tool is also known as an arrow diagram?
A. Matrix diagram

B. Affinity diagram
C. Tree diagram
D. Activity network diagram

QUESTION NO: 164
An effective technique for resolving conflict that incorporates multiple viewpoints from differing perspectives to achieve consensus and commitment is:
A. smooth/accommodate
B. force/direct
C. collaborate/problem solve
D. compromise/reconcile

QUESTION NO: 165
Which tool or technique is used in validating the scope of a project?
A. Facilitated workshops
B. Interviews
C. Inspection
D. Meetings

QUESTION NO: 166
Configuration identification, configuration status accounting, and configuration verification and audit are all activities in which process?
A. Perform Quality Assurance
B. Direct and Manage Project Work
C. Monitor and Control Project Work
D. Perform Integrated Change Control

QUESTION NO: 167
Which tool or technique is used in the Estimate Costs process?
A. Acquisition
B. Earned value management
C. Vendor bid analysis
D. Forecasting

QUESTION NO: 168
Which tool or technique is used in the Perform Integrated Change Control process?
A. Decomposition
B. Modeling techniques
C. Resource optimization
D. Meetings

QUESTION NO: 169
A logical relationship in which a successor activity cannot start until a predecessor activity has finished is known as:
A. Start-to-start (SS)
B. Start-to-finish (SF)
C. Finish-to-start (FS)
D. Finish-to-finish (FF)

QUESTION NO: 170
Which type of contract gives both the seller and the buyer flexibility to deviate or not from performance with financial incentives?
A. Cost Plus Incentive Fee (CPIF)
B. Fixed Price Incentive Fee (FPIF)
C. Cost Pius Award Fee (CPAF)
D. Time and Material (T&M)

QUESTION NO: 171
The degree, amount, or volume of risk that an organization or individual will withstand is known as its risk:
A. Analysis
B. Appetite
C. Tolerance
D. Response

QUESTION NO: 172
An output of the Perform Integrated Change Control process is:
A. Deliverables
B. Validated changes
C. The change log
D. The requirements traceability matrix

QUESTION NO: 173
During which process does the project team receive bids and proposals?
A. Conduct Procurements
B. Plan Procurements
C. Estimate Costs
D. Control Budget

QUESTION NO: 174
The process of monitoring the status of the project and product scope as well as managing the changes to the scope baseline is known as:
A. Validate Scope
B. Plan Scope Management

C. Control Scope
D. Define Scope

QUESTION NO: 175
Which output is the approved version of the time-phased project budget?
A. Resource calendar
B. Scope baseline
C. Trend analysis
D. Cost baseline

QUESTION NO: 176
The purpose of the Project Communications Management Knowledge Area is to:
A. Monitor and control communications throughout the entire project life cycle
B. Maintain an optimal flow of information among all project participants
C. Develop an appropriate approach for project communications
D. Ensure timely and appropriate collection of project information

QUESTION NO: 177
Processes in the Initiating Process Group may be completed at the organizational level and be outside of the project's:
A. Level of control
B. Communication channels
C. Scope
D. Strategic alignment

QUESTION NO: 178
Specification of both the deliverables and the processes is the focus of:
A. Change control
B. Configuration control
C. Project monitoring and control
D. Issue control

QUESTION NO: 179
Which output of Project Cost Management consists of quantitative assessment of the likely costs for resources required to complete the activity:
A. A cost estimate
B. Earned value management
C. Cost management plan
D. Cost baseline

QUESTION NO: 180
While processes in the Planning Process Group seek to collect feedback and define project documents to guide project work, organizational procedures dictate when the project planning:
A. ends

B. begins
C. delays
D. deviates

QUESTION NO: 181
Which item is a cost of conformance?
A. Training
B. Liabilities
C. Lost business
D. Scrap

QUESTION NO: 182
Which key interpersonal skill of a project manager is defined as the strategy of sharing power and relying on interpersonal skills to convince others to cooperate toward common goals?
A. Collaboration
B. Negotiation
C. Decision making
D. Influencing

QUESTION NO: 183
Activity cost estimates and the project schedule are inputs to which Project Cost Management process?
A. Estimate Costs
B. Control Costs
C. Plan Cost Management
D. Determine Budget

QUESTION NO: 184
Which change request is an intentional activity that realigns the performance of the project work with the project management plan?
A. Update
B. Preventive action
C. Defect repair
D. Corrective action

QUESTION NO: 185
Which type of dependency is legally or contractually required or inherent in the nature of work and often involves physical limitations?
A. Mandatory
B. Discretionary
C. Internal
D. External

QUESTION NO: 186
During which process does a project manager review all prior information to ensure that all project work is completed and that the project has met its objectives?
A. Monitor and Control Project Work
B. Perform Quality Assurance
C. Close Project or Phase
D. Control Scope

QUESTION NO: 187
When alternative dispute resolution (ADR) is necessary, which tool or technique should be utilized?
A. Interactive communication
B. Claims administration
C. Conflict management
D. Performance reporting

QUESTION NO: 188
What type of float is caused when a backward pass is calculated from a schedule constraint that is later than the early finish date set
during a forward pass calculation?
A. Negative
B. Zero
C. Positive
D. Free

QUESTION NO: 189
A reward can only be effective if it is:
A. Given immediately after the project is completed
B. Something that is tangible
C. Formally given during project performance appraisals
D. Satisfying a need valued by the individual

QUESTION NO: 190
Which tool or technique allows a large number of ideas to be classified into groups for review and analysis?
A. Nominal group technique
B. Idea/mind mapping
C. Affinity diagram
D. Brainstorming

QUESTION NO: 191
Lessons learned are created and project resources are released in which Process Group?
A. Planning
B. Executing

C. Closing
D. Initiating

QUESTION NO: 192
The process of identifying and documenting relationships among the project activities is known as:
A. Control Schedule
B. Sequence Activities
C. Define Activities
D. Develop Schedule

QUESTION NO: 193
Conditions that are not under the control of the project team that influence, direct, or constrain a project are called:
A. Enterprise environmental factors
B. Work performance reports
C. Organizational process assets
D. Context diagrams

QUESTION NO: 194
Updates to organizational process assets such as procurement files, deliverable acceptances, and lessons learned documentation are typical outputs of which process?
A. Close Project or Phase
B. Conduct Procurements
C. Control Procurements
D. Closed Procurements

QUESTION NO: 195
Sensitivity analysis is typically displayed as a/an:
A. Decision tree diagram
B. Tornado diagram
C. Pareto diagram
D. Ishikawa diagram

QUESTION NO: 196
A project manager builds consensus and overcomes obstacles by employing which communication technique?
A. Listening
B. Facilitation
C. Meeting management
D. Presentation

QUESTION NO: 197
An input to Close Project or Phase is:
A. Accepted deliverables

B. Final products or services
C. Document updates
D. Work performance information

QUESTION NO: 198
An output of the Direct and Manage Project Work process is:
A. Deliverables
B. Activity lists
C. A work breakdown structure
D. A scope statement

QUESTION NO: 199
External organizations that have a special relationship with the enterprise and provide specialized expertise are called:
A. Customers
B. Business partners
C. Sellers
D. Functional managers

QUESTION NO: 200
Which Knowledge Areas include processes from the Closing Process Group?
A. Project Quality Management and Project Time Management
B. Project Scope Management and Project Risk Management
C. Project Stakeholder Management and Project Cost Management
D. Project Integration Management and Project Procurement Management

Appendix D: Answer Key/ Sample Exam One

1	A
2	D
3	A
4	D
5	D
6	C
7	A
8	A
9	D
10	A
11	D
12	A
13	A
14	D
15	A
16	A

17	C
18	B
19	A
20	C
21	C
22	A
23	A
24	B
25	C
26	D
27	C
28	D
29	B
30	B
31	C
32	D
33	A
34	D
35	C
36	D
37	B
38	B
39	A
40	D
41	D
42	A
43	C
44	D
45	A
46	C
47	D
48	D
49	A
50	D
51	B
52	C
53	B
54	A
55	C
56	D
57	B
58	A
59	A
60	A
61	A
62	B
63	C
64	B

65	A
66	D
67	B
68	B
69	A
70	C
71	B
72	A
73	A
74	B
75	C
76	D
77	A
78	A
79	A
80	A
81	B
82	C
83	D
84	B
85	C
86	C
87	B
88	D
89	C
90	A
91	B
92	C
93	D
94	B
95	C
96	A
97	D
98	A
99	B
100	A
101	C
102	C
103	D
104	B
105	C
106	D
107	C
108	A
109	C
110	D
111	B
112	D

113	A
114	C
115	A
116	A
117	C
118	D
119	C
120	A
121	B
122	C
123	D
124	B
125	B
126	D
127	D
128	C
129	D
130	C
131	A
132	D
133	C
134	B
135	B
136	B
137	A
138	A
139	D
140	B
141	C
142	D
143	D
144	C
145	B
146	D
147	D
148	B
149	C
150	B
151	C
152	A
153	D
154	C
155	B
156	A
157	B
158	A
159	C
160	D

161	D
162	C
163	D
164	C
165	C
166	D
167	C
168	D
169	C
170	B
171	C
172	C
173	A
174	C
175	D
176	D
177	A
178	B
179	A
180	A
181	A
182	D
183	D
184	D
185	A
186	C
187	B
188	C
189	D
190	C
191	C
192	B
193	A
194	D
195	B
196	B
197	A
198	A
199	B
200	D

Appendix E: Sample Exam Two

QUESTION NO: 1

Power, urgency, and legitimacy are attributes of which stakeholder classification model?

A. Salience

B. Influence/impact

C. Power/interest
D. Power/influence

QUESTION NO: 2
Through whom do project managers accomplish work?
A. Consultants and stakeholders
B. Stakeholders and functional managers
C. Project team members and consultants
D. Project team members and stakeholders

QUESTION NO: 3
A stakeholder expresses a need not known to the project manager. The project manager most likely missed a step in which stakeholder management process?
A. Plan Stakeholder Management
B. Identify Stakeholders
C. Manage Stakeholder Engagement
D. Control Stakeholder Engagement

QUESTION NO: 4
Skills necessary for project management such as motivating to provide encouragement; listening actively; persuading a team to perform an action; and summarizing, recapping, and identifying next steps are known as:
A. organizational skills
B. technical skills
C. communication skills
D. hard skills

QUESTION NO: 5
When a project is undertaken to reduce defects in a product or service, the objective of the project is to create a/an:
A. improvement
B. program
C. result
D. portfolio

QUESTION NO: 6
The degree of uncertainty an entity is willing to take on in anticipation of a reward is known as its risk _____.
A. management
B. response
C. tolerance
D. appetite

QUESTION NO: 7
The zero duration of milestones in project planning occurs because milestones:
A. Are unpredictable and challenge the Plan Schedule Management process.
B. Occur at random times in the project plans.
C. Represent a moment in time such as a significant project point or event.
D. Represent both significant and insignificant points in the project and are difficult to anticipate.

QUESTION NO: 8
The component of the human resource management plan that includes ways in which team members can obtain certifications that support their ability to benefit the project is known as:
A. recognition and rewards
B. compliance
C. staff acquisition
D. training needs

QUESTION NO: 9
Stakeholders can be identified in later stages of the project because the Identify Stakeholders process should be:
A. Continuous
B. Discrete
C. Regulated
D. Arbitrary

QUESTION NO: 10
In project management, a temporary project can be:
A. Completed without planning
B. A routine business process
C. Long in duration
D. Ongoing to produce goods

QUESTION NO: 11
Which document in the project management plan can be updated in the Plan Procurement Management process?
A. Budget estimates
B. Risk matrix
C. Requirements documentation
D. Procurement documents

QUESTION NO: 12
Which type of probability distribution is used to represent uncertain events such as the outcome of a test or a possible scenario in a decision tree?
A. Uniform
B. Continuous

C. Discrete
D. Linear

QUESTION NO: 13
Which stakeholder approves a project's result?
A. Customer
B. Sponsor
C. Seller
D. Functional manager

QUESTION NO: 14
Which process involves determining, documenting, and managing stakeholders' needs and requirements to meet project objectives?
A. Collect Requirements
B. Plan Scope Management
C. Define Scope
D. Define Activities

QUESTION NO: 15
Plan Communications Management develops an approach and plan for project communications based on stakeholders' needs and requirements and:
A. Available organizational assets
B. Project staff assignments
C. Interpersonal skills
D. Enterprise environmental factors

QUESTION NO: 16
What is the risk rating if the probability of occurrence is 0.30 and the impact if it does occur is moderate (0.20)?
A. 0.03
B. 0.06
C. 0.10
D. 0.50

QUESTION NO: 17
A complete set of concepts, terms, and activities that comprise an area of specialization is known as:
A. a Knowledge Area
B. a Process Group
C. program management
D. portfolio management

QUESTION NO: 18
The risk response strategy in which the project team acts to reduce the probability of occurrence or impact of a risk is known as:
A. exploit
B. avoid
C. mitigate
D. share

QUESTION NO: 19
Which process is conducted from project inception through completion and is ultimately the responsibility of the project manager?
A. Control Quality
B. Monitor and Control Project Work
C. Control Scope
D. Perform Integrated Change Control

QUESTION NO: 20
Project management processes ensure:
A. Alignment with organizational strategy
B. An efficient means to achieve the project objectives
C. Performance of the project team
D. An effective flow of the project throughout its life cycle

QUESTION NO: 21
Which project risk listed in the table below is most likely to occur?

Project Risks	Probability	Impact
Risk 1	L	M
Risk 2	H	H
Risk 3	L	L
Risk 4	M	L

A. 1
B. 2
C. 3
D. 4

QUESTION NO: 22
Which of these is an enterprise environmental factor?
A. Marketplace conditions
B. Policies and procedures
C. Project files from previous projects
D. Lessons learned from previous projects

QUESTION NO: 23
Project Stakeholder Management focuses on:
A. project staff assignments
B. project tea m acquisition
C. managing conflicting interests
D. communication methods

QUESTION NO: 24
A risk that arises as a direct result of implementing a risk response is called a _____ risk.
A. contingent
B. residual
C. potential
D. secondary

QUESTION NO: 25
The purpose of developing a project scope management plan is to:
A. Manage the timely completion of the project.
B. Ensure that the project includes all of the work required.
C. Make sure the project will satisfy the needs for which it was begun.
D. Reduce the risk of negative events in the project.

QUESTION NO: 26
A tool or technique used in the Develop Project Charter process is/are:
A. Change control tools
B. Expert judgment
C. Meetings
D. Analytical techniques

QUESTION NO: 27
Which items are components of a project management plan?
A. Change management plan, process improvement plan, and scope management plan
B. Agreements, procurement management plan, and work performance information
C. Schedule management plan, project schedule, and resource calendars
D. Scope baseline, project statement of work, and requirements traceability matrix

QUESTION NO: 28
Which project document is updated in the Control Stakeholder Engagement process?
A. Project reports
B. Issue log
C. Lessons learned documentation
D. Work performance information

QUESTION NO: 29
Which Project Time Management process includes bottom-up estimating as a tool or technique?
A. Estimate Activity Resources
B. Sequence Activities
C. Estimate Activity Durations
D. Develop Schedule

QUESTION NO: 30
Progressively elaborating high-level information into detailed plans is performed by the:
A. Project management office
B. Portfolio manager
C. Program manager
D. Project manager

QUESTION NO: 31
One of the key benefits of the Plan Human Resource Management process is that it:
A. outlines team selection guidelines and team member responsibilities.
B. establishes project roles and responsibilities.
C. improves teamwork, interpersonal skills, and competencies.
D. provides an accurate appraisal of team member performance.

QUESTION NO: 32
Which Define Activities tool or technique is used for dividing and subdividing the project scope and project deliverables into smaller, more manageable parts?
A. Decomposition
B. Inspection
C. Project analysis
D. Document analysis

QUESTION NO: 33
In the Define Activities process, the schedule management plan is used to:
A. Capture the lessons learned from other projects for comparison.
B. Contain the standard activity list.
C. Document and support the project change requests.
D. Prescribe the level of detail needed to manage the work.

QUESTION NO: 34
A project team attempts to produce a deliverable and finds that they have neither the expertise nor the time to complete the deliverable in a timely manner. This issue could have been avoided if
they had created and followed a:
A. risk management plan
B. human resource management plan

C. scope management plan
D. procurement management plan

QUESTION NO: 35
A benefit of using virtual teams in the Acquire Project Team process is the reduction of the:
A. cultural differences of team members
B. possibility of communication misunderstandings
C. costs associated with travel
D. costs associated with technology

QUESTION NO: 36
A special type of bar chart used in sensitivity analysis for comparing the relative importance of the variables is called a:
A. triangular distribution
B. tornado diagram
C. beta distribution
D. fishbone diagram

QUESTION NO: 37
A full-time project manager with low to moderate authority and part-time administrative staff is working in an organizational structure with which type of matrix?
A. Strong
B. Weak
C. Managed
D. Balanced

QUESTION NO: 38
Project Scope Management is primarily concerned with:
A. Developing a detailed description of the project and product.
B. Determining how requirements will be analyzed, documented, and managed.
C. Defining and controlling what is and is not included in the project.
D. Formalizing acceptance of the completed project deliverables.

QUESTION NO: 39
The lowest level normally depicted in a work breakdown structure (WBS) is called a/an:
A. work package
B. deliverable
C. milestone
D. activity

QUESTION NO: 40
The scope management plan and scope baseline are contained in:
A. organizational process assets

B. a requirements traceability matrix
C. the project charter
D. the project management plan

QUESTION NO: 41
Which Manage Communications tool or technique focuses on identifying and managing barriers?
A. Communication methods
B. Information technology
C. Communication models
D. Information management systems

QUESTION NO: 42
Which type of organizational structure is displayed in the diagram provided?
A. Balanced matrix
B. Projectized
C. Strong matrix
D. Functional

QUESTION NO: 43
Outputs of the Control Communications process include:
A. expert judgment and change requests.
B. work performance information and change requests.
C. organizational process asset updates and an issue log.
D. project management plan updates and an issue log.

QUESTION NO: 44
In the Plan Procurement Management process, which source selection criteria analyzes if the seller's proposed technical methodologies, techniques, solutions, and services meet the
procurement documents requirements?
A. Technical approach
B. Technical capability
C. Business size and type
D. Production capacity and interest

QUESTION NO: 45
Stakeholder communication requirements should be included as a component of:
A. enterprise environmental factors
B. organizational process assets
C. the project management plan
D. the stakeholder register

QUESTION NO: 46
Which group creativity technique asks a selected group of experts to answer questionnaires and provide feedback regarding the responses from each round of requirements gathering?
A. The Delphi technique
B. Nominal group technique
C. Affinity diagram
D. Brainstorming

QUESTION NO: 47
At which point of the project is the uncertainty the highest and the risk of failing the greatest?
A. Final phase of the project
B. Start of the project
C. End of the project
D. Midpoint of the project

QUESTION NO: 48
What type of project structure is a hierarchically organized depiction of the resources by type?
A. Organizational breakdown structure (OBS)
B. Resource breakdown structure (RBS)
C. Work breakdown structure (WBS)
D. Project breakdown structure (PBS)

QUESTION NO: 49
The primary benefit of the Plan Schedule Management process is that it:
A. provides guidance to identify time or schedule challenges within the project.
B. tightly links processes to create a seamless project schedule.
C. guides how the project schedule will be managed throughout the project.
D. creates an overview of all activities broken down into manageable subsections.

QUESTION NO: 50
Grouping the stakeholders based on their level of authority and their level of concern regarding project outcomes describes which classification model for stakeholder analysis?
A. Influence/impact grid
B. Power/influence grid
C. Power/interest grid
D. Salience model

QUESTION NO: 51
Funding limit reconciliation is a tool and technique of which Project Cost Management process?
A. Estimate Costs
B. Control Costs
C. Plan Cost Management
D. Determine Budget

QUESTION NO: 52
What is the definition of Direct and Manage Project Execution?
A. Integrating all planned activities
B. Performing the activities included in the plan
C. Developing and maintaining the plan
D. Execution of deliverables

QUESTION NO: 53
What name(s) is (are) associated with the Plan-Do-Check-Act cycle?
A. Pareto
B. Ishikawa
C. Deming
D. Delphi

QUESTION NO: 54
Which tool or technique is required in order to determine the project budget?
A. Cost of quality
B. Historical relationships
C. Project management software
D. Forecasting

QUESTION NO: 55
Requirements documentation will typically contain at least:
A. Stakeholder requirements, staffing requirements, and transition requirements.
B. Business requirements, the stakeholder register, and functional requirements.
C. Stakeholder impact, budget requirements, and communications requirements.
D. Business objectives, stakeholder impact, and functional requirements.

QUESTION NO: 56
Which process involves the creation of a document that provides the project manager with the authority to apply resources to a project?
A. Define Activities
B. Direct and Manage Project Work
C. Develop Project Management Plan
D. Develop Project Charter

QUESTION NO: 57
The process of identifying and documenting the specific actions to be performed to produce the project deliverables is known as:
A. Define Activities
B. Sequence Activities
C. Define Scope
D. Control Schedule

QUESTION NO: 58
Which document includes the project scope, major deliverables, assumptions, and constraints?
A. Project charter
B. Project scope statement
C. Scope management plan
D. Project document updates

QUESTION NO: 59
When an activity cannot be estimated with a reasonable degree of confidence, the work within the activity is decomposed into more
detail using which type of estimating?
A. Bottom-up
B. Parametric
C. Analogous
D. Three-point

QUESTION NO: 60
Definitions of probability and impact, revised stakeholder tolerances, and tracking are components of which subsidiary plan?
A. Cost management plan
B. Quality management plan
C. Communications management plan
D. Risk management plan

QUESTION NO: 61
Which component of the human resource management plan describes when and how project team members are acquired and how long they will be needed?
A. Resource breakdown structure
B. Staffing management plan
C. Project organizational chart
D. Scope management plan

QUESTION NO: 62
What is an objective of the Develop Project Team process?
A. Feelings of trust and improved cohesiveness
B. Ground rules for interaction
C. Enhanced resource availability
D. Functional managers becoming more involved

QUESTION NO: 63
When is a Salience Model used?
A. In a work breakdown structure (WBS)
B. During quality assurance

C. In stakeholder analysis
D. During quality control (QC)

QUESTION NO: 64
Which of the following is contained within the communications management plan?
A. An organizational chart
B. Glossary of common terminology
C. Organizational process assets
D. Enterprise environmental factors

QUESTION NO: 65
Which of the following is a tool and technique for Estimate Activity Durations?
A. Parametric estimating
B. Monte Carlo analysis
C. Alternatives analysis
D. Bottom-up estimating

QUESTION NO: 66
Projects can be divided into phases to provide better management control. Collectively, what are these phases known as?
A. Complete project phase
B. Product life
C. The project life cycle
D. Project cycle

QUESTION NO: 67
Which of the following statements correctly characterizes pull communication?
A. It includes letters, memos, reports, emails, and faxes
B. It requires recipients to access communication content at their own discretion
C. It is the most efficient way to ensure a common understanding among all participants
D. It is primarily used when the volume of information to be transferred is minimal

QUESTION NO: 68
Which Knowledge Area is concerned with the processes required to ensure timely and appropriate generation, collection, distribution, storage, retrieval, and ultimate disposition of project information?
A. Project Integration Management
B. Project Communications Management
C. Project Management Information System (PMIS)
D. Project Scope Management

QUESTION NO: 69
Which of the following tools or techniques is used for Estimate Activity Durations?

A. Critical path method
B. Rolling wave planning
C. Precedence diagramming method
D. Parametric estimating

QUESTION NO: 70
Which tool or technique of Plan Quality involves comparing actual or planned practices to those of other projects to generate ideas for improvement and provide a basis by which to measure performance?
A. Histogram
B. Quality audits
C. Benchmarking
D. Performance measurement analysis

QUESTION NO: 71
Taking out insurance in relation to risk management is called what?
A. Transference
B. Avoidance
C. Exploring
D. Mitigation

QUESTION NO: 72
During which process group is the quality policy determined?
A. Initiating
B. Executing
C. Planning
D. Controlling

QUESTION NO: 73
In an organization with a projectized organizational structure, who controls the project budget?
A. Functional manager
B. Project manager
C. Program manager
D. Project management office

QUESTION NO: 74
Who, along with the project manager, is supposed to direct the performance of the planned project activities and manage the various technical and organizational interfaces that exist within the project?
A. The customer and functional managers
B. The risk owners and stakeholders
C. The sponsors and stakeholders
D. The project management team

QUESTION NO: 75
Status of deliverables, implementation status for change requests, and forecasted estimates to complete are examples of:
A. Earned value management
B. Enterprise environmental factors
C. Organizational process assets
D. Work performance information

QUESTION NO: 76
Which item is an output of Plan Quality Management and an input to Perform Quality Assurance?
A. Organizational process updates
B. Quality metrics
C. Change requests
D. Quality control measurements

QUESTION NO: 77
A project manager managing a cross-cultural virtual project team across several time zones should be concerned about the impacts of which communication technology factor?
A. Urgent information need
B. Sensitivity of information
C. Project environment
D. Ease of use

QUESTION NO: 78
The number of communication channels for a project with 5 stakeholders is:
A. 10
B. 12
C. 20
D. 24

QUESTION NO: 79
Which tool or technique of the Define Activities process allows for work to exist at various levels of detail depending on where it is in the project life cycle?
A. Historical relationships
B. Dependency determination
C. Bottom-up estimating
D. Rolling wave planning

QUESTION NO: 80
An output of the Create WBS process is:
A. Scope baseline
B. Change requests
C. Accepted deliverables
D. Variance analysis

QUESTION NO: 81
A tool or technique used in the Control Procurements process is:
A. Expert judgment
B. Performance reporting
C. Bidder conferences
D. Reserve analysis

QUESTION NO: 82
Which type of project management office (PMO) supplies templates, best practices, and training to project teams?
A. Supportive
B. Directive
C. Controlling
D. Instructive

QUESTION NO: 83
Which Define Activities output extends the description of the
activity by identifying the multiple components associated with each activity?
A. Project document updates
B. Activity list
C. Activity attributes
D. Project calendars

QUESTION NO: 84
An input to the Identify Stakeholders process is:
A. The project management plan
B. The stakeholder register
C. Procurement documents
D. Stakeholder analysis

QUESTION NO: 85
What is the estimate at completion (EAC) if the budget at completion (BAC) is $100, the actual cost (AC) is $50, and the earned value (EV) is $25?
A. $50
B. $100
C. $125
D. $200

QUESTION NO: 86
Job satisfaction, challenging work, and sufficient financial compensation are values related to which interpersonal skill?
A. Influencing
B. Motivation

C. Negotiation
D. Trust building

QUESTION NO: 87
A project manager should communicate to stakeholders about resolved project issues by updating the:
A. project records
B. project reports
C. stakeholder notifications
D. stakeholder register

QUESTION NO: 88
A disadvantage associated with virtual teams is that they:
A. Require communication technology that is not readily available
B. Create difficulties when including people with disabilities
C. Often cannot accommodate teams that work different hours or shifts
D. Create the possibility for misunderstandings to arise

QUESTION NO: 89
In which phase of team building activities do team members begin to work together and adjust their work habits and behavior to support the team?
A. Performing
B. Storming
C. Norming
D. Forming

QUESTION NO: 90
The Project Human Resource Management process that involves confirming human resource availability and obtaining the team necessary to complete project activities is:
A. Acquire Project Team
B. Plan Human Resource Management
C. Manage Project Team
D. Develop Project Team

QUESTION NO: 91
For a stakeholder with low interest and high power, the project manager should:
A. Monitor the stakeholder
B. Manage the stakeholder closely
C. Keep the stakeholder satisfied
D. Keep the stakeholder informed

QUESTION NO: 92
In a typical project, project managers spend most of their time:

A. Estimating
B. Scheduling
C. Controlling
D. Communicating

QUESTION NO: 93
Which schedule method allows the project team to place buffers on the project schedule path to account for limited resources and project uncertainties?
A. Critical path method
B. Critical chain method
C. Resource levelling
D. Schedule network analysis

QUESTION NO: 94
Correlated and contextualized information on how closely the scope is being maintained relative to the scope baseline is contained within:
A. project documents updates
B. project management plan updates
C. change requests
D. work performance information

QUESTION NO: 95
The most appropriate project life cycle model for an environment with a high level of change and extensive stakeholder involvement in projects is:
A. adaptive
B. reflexive
C. predictive
D. iterative

QUESTION NO: 96
Variance and trend analysis is a tool and technique used in which process?
A. Perform Qualitative Risk Analysis
B. Perform Quantitative Risk Analysis
C. Control Risks
D. Plan Risk Responses

QUESTION NO: 97
An intentional activity to modify a nonconforming product or product component is called:
A. defect repair
B. work repair
C. corrective action
D. preventive action

QUESTION NO: 98
Which quality tool incorporates the upper and lower specification limits allowed within an agreement?
A. Control chart
B. Flowchart
C. Checksheet
D. Pareto diagram

QUESTION NO: 99
Analytical techniques are a tool and technique of which process in Project Procurement Management?
A. Plan Procurement Management
B. Control Procurements
C. Conduct Procurements
D. Close Procurements

QUESTION NO: 100
The process of obtaining seller responses, selecting a seller, and awarding a contract is called:
A. Close Procurements
B. Control Procurements
C. Plan Procurements
D. Conduct Procurements

QUESTION NO: 101
Impacts to other organizational areas, levels of service, and acceptance criteria are typical components of which document?
A. Business case
B. Work breakdown structure
C. Requirements documentation
D. Risk register

QUESTION NO: 102
Which Process Group includes the Manage Stakeholder Engagement process?
A. Executing
B. Planning
C. Monitoring and Controlling
D. Initiating

QUESTION NO: 103
In complex projects/ initiating processes should be completed:
A. Within a work package
B. In each phase of the project
C. To estimate schedule constraints
D. To estimate resource allocations

QUESTION NO: 104
A project manager requesting industry groups and consultants to recommend project intervention is relying on:
A. Communication models
B. Stakeholder participation
C. Expert judgment
D. Enterprise environmental factors

QUESTION NO: 105
Tools and techniques used in Direct and Manage Project Work include:
A. Process analysis and expert judgment
B. Analytical techniques and a project management information system
C. Performance reviews and meetings
D. Expert judgment and meetings

QUESTION NO: 106
Which of the Perform Quality Assurance tools and techniques may enhance the creation of the work breakdown structure (WBS) to give structure to the decomposition of the scope?
A. Activity network diagrams
B. Affinity diagrams
C. Matrix diagrams
D. Interrelationship digraphs

QUESTION NO: 107
A project manager who communicates to the project team though email is using which type of communication?
A. Formal
B. Informal r
C. Horizontal
D. Unofficial

QUESTION NO: 108
An input to the Perform Integrated Change Control process is:
A. expert judgment
B. seller proposals
C. the project charter
D. the project management plan

QUESTION NO: 109
Managing ongoing production of goods and services to ensure business continues efficiently describes which type of management?
A. Portfolio
B. Project

C. Program
D. Operations

QUESTION NO: 110
Which type of manager is assigned by the performing organization to lead the team that is responsible for achieving the project objectives?
A. Program
B. Functional
C. Project
D. Portfolio

QUESTION NO: 111
Which of the seven basic quality tools is especially useful for gathering attributes data while performing inspections to identify defects?
A. Histograms
B. Scatter diagrams
C. Flowcharts
D. Checksheets

QUESTION NO: 112
The most commonly used type of precedence relationship in the precedence diagramming method (PDM) is:
A. start-to-start (SS)
B. start-to-finish (SF)
C. finish-to-start (FS)
D. finish-to-finish (FF)

QUESTION NO: 113
Which technique is used in Perform Quantitative Risk Analysis?
A. Sensitivity analysis
B. Probability and impact matrix
C. Risk data quality assessment
D. Risk categorization

QUESTION NO: 114
Which illustrates the connection between work that needs to be done and its project team members?
A. Work breakdown structure (WBS)
B. Network diagrams
C. Staffing management plan
D. Responsibility assignment matrix (RAM)

QUESTION NO: 115
Which tools or techniques will a project manager use for Develop Project Team?

A. Negotiation
B. Roles and responsibilities
C. Recognition and rewards
D. Prizing and promoting

QUESTION NO: 116
Which of the following is an input to Direct and Manage Project Execution?
A. Requested changes
B. Approved change requests
C. Work performance information
D. Implemented defect repair

QUESTION NO: 117
When would resource leveling be applied to a schedule model?
A. Before constraints have been identified
B. Before it has been analyzed by the critical path method
C. After it has been analyzed by the critical path method
D. After critical activities have been removed from the critical path

QUESTION NO: 118
While implementing an approved change, a critical defect was introduced. Removing the defect will delay the product delivery. What is the MOST appropriate approach to managing this situation?
A. Utilize the change control process
B. Crash the schedule to fix the defect
C. Leave the defect in and work around it
D. Fast-track the remaining development

QUESTION NO: 119
Which tool and technique identifies inefficient and ineffective policies, processes, and procedures?
A. Scope audits
B. Scope reviews
C. Quality audits
D. Control chart

QUESTION NO: 120
Which type of analysis would be used for the Plan Quality process?
A. Schedule
B. Checklist
C. Assumption
D. Cost-Benefit

QUESTION NO: 121
The integrative nature of project management requires which Process Group to interact with the other Process Groups?
A. Planning
B. Executing
C. Monitoring and Controlling
D. Project Management

QUESTION NO: 122
Which Process Group typically consumes the bulk of a project's budget?
A. Monitoring and Controlling
B. Executing
C. Planning
D. Initiating

QUESTION NO: 123
Which of the following involves making information available to project stakeholders in a timely manner?
A. Plan Communications
B. Performance reporting
C. Project status reports
D. Manage Communications

QUESTION NO: 124
What is the name of a graphic display of project team members and their reporting relationships?
A. Role dependencies chart
B. Reporting flow diagram
C. Project organization chart
D. Project team structure diagram

QUESTION NO: 125
Which of the following consists of the detailed project scope statement and its associated WBS and WBS dictionary?
A. Scope plan
B. Product scope
C. Scope management plan
D. Scope baseline

QUESTION NO: 126
Activity resource requirements and the resource breakdown structure (RBS) are outputs of which Project Time Management process?
A. Control Schedule
B. Define Activities

C. Develop Schedule
D. Estimate Activity Resources

QUESTION NO: 127
A change log for communications can be used to communicate to
the appropriate stakeholders that there are changes:
A. To the project management plan
B. To the risk register
C. In the scope verification processes
D. And their impact to the project in terms of time, cost, and risk

QUESTION NO: 128
A procurement management plan is a subsidiary of which other type of plan?
A. Resource plan
B. Project management plan
C. Cost control plan
D. Expected monetary value plan

QUESTION NO: 129
To which process is work performance information an input?
A. Administer Procurements
B. Direct and Manage Project Work
C. Create WBS
D. Perform Qualitative Risk Analysis

QUESTION NO: 130
Which defines the portion of work included in a contract for items being purchased or acquired?
A. Procurement management plan
B. Evaluation criteria
C. Work breakdown structure
D. Procurement statement of work

QUESTION NO: 131
The Human Resource Management processes are:
A. Develop Human Resource Plan, Acquire Project Team, Develop Project Team, and Manage Project Team
B. Acquire Project Team, Manage Project Team, Manage Stakeholder Expectations, and Develop Project Team
C. Acquire Project Team, Develop Human Resource Plan, Conflict Management, and Manage Project Team
D. Develop Project Team, Manage Project Team, Estimate Activity Resources, and Acquire Project Team

QUESTION NO: 132
What are the formal and informal policies, procedures, and guidelines that could impact how the project's scope is managed?
A. Organizational process assets
B. Enterprise environmental factors
C. Project management processes
D. Project scope management plan

QUESTION NO: 133
Organizational planning impacts projects by means of project prioritization based on risk, funding, and an organizations:
A. Budget plan
B. Resource plan
C. Scope plan
D. Strategic plan

QUESTION NO: 134
A project management office manages a number of aspects including the:
A. Project scope, schedule, cost, and quality of the products of the work packages
B. Central coordination of communication management across projects
C. Assignment of project resources to best meet project objectives
D. Overall risk, overall opportunity, and interdependencies among projects at the enterprise level

QUESTION NO: 135
An input to the Control Quality process is:
A. Activity attributes
B. Quality control measurements
C. Enterprise environmental factors
D. Deliverables

QUESTION NO: 136
The chart below is an example of a:

ID	Requirements Description	Project Objectives	WBS Deliverables	Product Design	Product Development	Test Cases
001						
002						
003						

A. Responsibility assignment matrix (RAM)
B. Work breakdown structure (WBS)
C. RACI chart
D. Requirements traceability matrix

QUESTION NO: 137
Which Perform Quality Assurance tool or technique is used to identify a problem, discover the underlying causes that lead to it, and develop preventative actions?
A. Inspection
B. Quality audits
C. Design of experiments
D. Root cause analysis

QUESTION NO: 138
The following chart contains information about the tasks in a project.
Based on the chart, what is the cost performance index (CPI) for Task 2?

Task	PV	AC	EV
1	10,000	10,000	10,000
2	10,000	8,000	10,000
3	10,000	8,000	8,000
4	9,000	12,000	10,000
5	10,000	12,000	12,000
6	10,000	10,000	12,000
7	12,000	12,000	10,000
8	10,000	8,000	9,000
9	12,000	10,000	11,000

A. 0.8
B. 1
C. 1.25
D. 1.8

QUESTION NO: 139
The following chart contains information about the tasks in a project.
Based on the chart, what is the schedule variance (SV) for Task 8?

Task	PV	AC	EV
1	10,000	10,000	10,000
2	10,000	8,000	10,000
3	10,000	8,000	8,000
4	9,000	12,000	10,000
5	10,000	12,000	12,000
6	10,000	10,000	12,000
7	12,000	12,000	10,000
8	10,000	8,000	9,000
9	12,000	10,000	11,000

A. -2,000

B. -1,000
C. 1,000
D. 2,000

QUESTION NO: 140
The following chart contains information about the tasks in a project.
Based on the chart, what is the cost variance (CV) for Task 6?

Task	PV	AC	EV
1	10,000	10,000	10,000
2	10,000	8,000	10,000
3	10,000	8,000	8,000
4	9,000	12,000	10,000
5	10,000	12,000	12,000
6	10,000	10,000	12,000
7	12,000	12,000	10,000
8	10,000	8,000	9,000
9	12,000	10,000	11,000

A. -2,000
B. 0
C. 1,000
D. 2,000

QUESTION NO: 141
The following chart contains information about the tasks in a project. Based on the chart, what is the schedule performance index (5PI) for Task 4?

Task	PV	AC	EV
1	10,000	10,000	10,000
2	10,000	8,000	10,000
3	10,000	8,000	8,000
4	9,000	12,000	10,000
5	10,000	12,000	12,000
6	10,000	10,000	12,000
7	12,000	12,000	10,000
8	10,000	8,000	9,000
9	12,000	10,000	11,000

A. 0.83
B. 0.9
C. 1.11
D. 1.33

EXAM PREPARATION GUIDE   343

QUESTION NO: 142
Which type of analysis is used to determine the cause and degree of difference between the baseline and actual performance?
A. Schedule network analysis
B. Reserve analysis
C. Alternative analysis
D. Variance analysis

QUESTION NO: 143
Which items are an output of the Perform Integrated Change Control process?
A. Work performance reports
B. Accepted deliverables
C. Project management plan updates
D. Organizational process assets

QUESTION NO: 144
Which term describes an assessment of correctness?
A. Accuracy
B. Precision
C. Grade
D. Quality

QUESTION NO: 145
The cost baseline and project funding requirements are outputs of which process in Project Cost Management?
A. Estimate Costs
B. Control Costs
C. Plan Cost Management
D. Determine Budget

QUESTION NO: 146
At the start of a typical project life cycle, costs are:
A. low, peak as work is carried out, and drop as the project nears the end.
B. low, become steady as work is carried out, and increase as the project nears the end.
C. high, drop as work is carried out, and increase as the project nears the end.
D. high, become low as work is carried out, and drop as the project nears the end.

QUESTION NO: 147
Success is measured by benefits realization for a:
A. strategic plan
B. project
C. portfolio
D. program

QUESTION NO: 148
Organizational process assets, a lessons-learned database, and historical information are all inputs to which process?
A. Plan Cost Management
B. Plan Scope Management
C. Plan Stakeholder Management
D. Plan Schedule Management

QUESTION NO: 149
A project team member agrees to change a project deliverable after a conversation with an external stakeholder. It is later discovered that the change has had an adverse effect on another deliverable. This could have been avoided if the project team had implemented:
A. Quality assurance
B. A stakeholder management plan
C. Project team building
D. Integrated change control

QUESTION NO: 150
Whose approval may be required for change requests after change control board (CCB) approval?
A. Functional managers
B. Business partners
C. Customers or sponsors
D. Subject matter experts

QUESTION NO: 151
A project requires a component with well-understood specifications. Performance targets are established at the outset, and the final contract price is determined after completion of all work based on the seller's performance. The most appropriate agreement with the supplier is:
A. Cost Plus Incentive Fee (CPIF)
B. Fixed Price Incentive Fee (FPIF)
C. Cost Plus Award Fee (CPAF)
D. Fixed Price with Economic Price Adjustment (FP-EPA)

QUESTION NO: 152
Which enterprise environmental factors may influence Plan Schedule Management?
A. Cultural views regarding time schedules and professional and ethical behaviors
B. Historical information and change control procedures
C. Risk control procedures and the probability and impact matrix
D. Resource availability and organizational culture and structure

QUESTION NO: 153
Which type of dependency used in the Sequence Activities process is sometimes referred to as preferred logic, preferential logic, or soft logic?

A. Internal
B. External
C. Discretionary
D. Mandatory

QUESTION NO: 154
When the business objectives of an organization change, project goals need to be:
A. realigned
B. performed
C. improved
D. controlled

QUESTION NO: 155
The approaches, tools, and data sources that will be used to perform risk management on a project are determined by the:
A. Methodology
B. Risk category
C. Risk attitude
D. Assumption analysis

QUESTION NO: 156
An input of the Plan Procurement Management process is:
A. Make-or-buy decisions
B. Activity cost estimates
C. Seller proposals
D. Procurement documents

QUESTION NO: 157
Outputs of the Control Communications process include:
A. expert judgment and change requests
B. work performance information and change requests
C. project management plan updates and work performance information
D. issue logs and organizational process assets updates

QUESTION NO: 158
A measure of cost performance that is required to be achieved with the remaining resources in order to meet a specified management goal and is expressed as the ratio of the cost needed for finishing the outstanding work to the remaining budget is known as the:
A. budget at completion (BAC)
B. earned value management (EVM)
C. to-complete performance index
D. cost performance index

QUESTION NO: 159

A collection of projects managed as a group to achieve strategic objectives is referred to as a:

A. plan
B. process
C. program
D. portfolio

QUESTION NO: 160

Which Process Group's purpose is to track, review, and regulate the progress and performance of the project; identify any areas in which changes to the plan are required; and initiate the corresponding changes?

A. Monitoring and Controlling
B. Initiating
C. Planning
D. Executing

QUESTION NO: 161

Work performance information and cost forecasts are outputs of which Project Cost Management process?

A. Estimate Costs
B. Plan Cost Management
C. Determine Budget
D. Control Costs

QUESTION NO: 162

An output of Control Schedule is:

A. A project schedule network diagram
B. A schedule management plan
C. Schedule data
D. Schedule forecasts

QUESTION NO: 163

What is the name of the statistical method that helps identify which factors may influence specific variables of a product or process under development or in production?

A. Failure modes and effects analysis
B. Design of experiments
C. Quality checklist
D. Risk analysis

QUESTION NO: 164

What cost control technique is used to compare actual project performance to planned or expected performance?

A. Cost aggregation

B. Trend analysis
C. Forecasting
D. Variance analysis

QUESTION NO: 165
What is the term assigned to products or services having the same functional use but different technical characteristics?
A. Scope
B. Quality
C. Specification
D. Grade

QUESTION NO: 166
Which schedule network analysis technique modifies the project schedule to account for limited resources?
A. Human resource planning
B. Fast tracking
C. Critical chain method
D. Rolling wave planning

QUESTION NO: 167
Which of the following is an output of the Monitor and Control Project Work process?
A. Change requests
B. Performance reports
C. Organizational process assets
D. Project management plan

QUESTION NO: 168
Which estimating technique uses the actual costs of previous similar projects as a basis for estimating the costs of the current project?
A. Analogous
B. Parametric
C. Bottom-up
D. Top-down

QUESTION NO: 169
What is the difference between the critical path and the critical chain?
A. Scope changes
B. Resource limitations
C. Risk analysis
D. Quality audits

QUESTION NO: 170
Which enterprise environmental factors are considered during Estimate Costs?
A. Market conditions and published commercial information
B. Company structure and market conditions
C. Commercial information and company structure
D. Existing human resources and market conditions

QUESTION NO: 171
An input of the Control Schedule process is the:
A. resource calendar
B. activity list
C. risk management plan
D. organizational process assets

QUESTION NO: 172
Which Develop Schedule tool and technique produces a theoretical early start date and late start date?
A. Critical path method
B. Variance analysis
C. Schedule compression
D. Schedule comparison bar charts

QUESTION NO: 173
Perform Quality Control is accomplished by:
A. Identifying quality standards that are relevant to the project and determining how to satisfy them
B. Monitoring and recording the results of executing the quality activities to assess performance and recommend necessary changes
C. Ensuring that the entire project team has been adequately trained in quality assurance processes
D. Applying Monte Carlo, sampling, Pareto analysis, and benchmarking techniques to ensure conformance to quality standards

QUESTION NO: 174
Which type of estimating can produce higher levels of accuracy, depending upon the scphistication and underlying data built into the model?
A. Bottom-up
B. Three-point
C. Parametric
D. Analogous

QUESTION NO: 175
Cost baseline is an output of which of the following processes?
A. Control Costs
B. Determine Budget
C. Estimate Costs
D. Estimate Activity Resources

QUESTION NO: 176
Change requests are an output from which Project Integration Management process?
A. Direct and Manage Project Execution
B. Develop Project Management Plan
C. Close Project
D. Develop Project Charter

QUESTION NO: 177
Which process involves aggregating the estimated costs of the individual schedule activities or work packages?
A. Estimate Costs
B. Estimate Activity Resources
C. Control Costs
D. Determine Budget

QUESTION NO: 178
The CPI is .92, and the EV is US$172,500. What is the actual cost of the project?
A. US$158,700
B. US$172,500
C. US$187,500
D. US$245,600

QUESTION NO: 179
Which type of analysis is used to examine project results through time to determine if performance is improving or deteriorating?
A. Control chart
B. Earned value
C. Variance
D. Trend

QUESTION NO: 180
Which is one of the major outputs of Sequence Activities?
A. Responsibility assignment matrix (RAM)
B. Work breakdown structure (WBS) update
C. Project schedule network diagram
D. Mandatory dependencies list

QUESTION NO: 181
When does Monitor and Control Risks occur?
A. At project initiation
B. During work performance analysis
C. Throughout the life of the project
D. At project milestones

QUESTION NO: 182
Which process occurs within the Monitoring and Controlling Process Group?
A. Control Costs
B. Plan Quality
C. Perform Quantitative Risk Analysis
D. Determine Budget

QUESTION NO: 183
Which of the following processes audits the quality requirements and the results from quality control measures to ensure appropriate quality standards and operational definitions are used?
A. Perform Quality Control
B. Quality Metrics
C. Perform Quality Assurance
D. Plan Quality

QUESTION NO: 184
How the schedule variance is calculated using the earned value technique?
A. EV less AC
B. AC less PV
C. EV less PV
D. AC less EV

QUESTION NO: 185
At the completion of a project, a report is prepared that details the outcome of the research conducted on a global trend during the project. Which item did this project create?
A. Result
B. Product
C. Service
D. Improvement

QUESTION NO: 186
Retreating from an actual or potential conflict or postponing the issue to be better prepared or to be resolved by others describes which of the five general techniques for managing conflict?
A. Smooth/accommodate
B. Withdraw/avoid
C. Compromise/reconcile
D. Force/direct

QUESTION NO: 187
Which tools or techniques are used during the Close Project or Phase process?
A. Reserve analysis and expert judgment
B. Facilitation techniques and meetings

C. Expert judgment and analytical techniques
D. Performance reviews and meetings

QUESTION NO: 188
An example of a group decision-making technique is:
A. nominal group technique
B. majority
C. affinity diagram
D. multi-criteria decision analysis

QUESTION NO: 189
Which tool or technique used in the Control Procurements process can be conducted during the execution of the project to verify compliance with deliverables?
A. Procurement documents
B. Inspection and audits
C. Estimate budget
D. Risk register

QUESTION NO: 190
Those who enter into a contractual agreement to provide services necessary for a project are:
A. buyers
B. sellers
C. business partners
D. product users

QUESTION NO: 191
When closing a project or phase, part of the process may require the use of which type of analysis?
A. Reserve analysis
B. Regression analysis
C. Document analysis
D. Product analysis

QUESTION NO: 192
Completion of the product scope is measured against the product:
A. prototypes
B. requirements
C. analyses
D. benchmarks

QUESTION NO: 193
Which organizational process assets update is performed during the Close Procurements process?
A. Procurement audit
B. Lessons learned

C. Performance reporting
D. Payment requests

QUESTION NO: 194
The individual or group that provides resources and support for a project and is accountable for success is the:
A. sponsor
B. customer
C. business partners
D. functional managers

QUESTION NO: 195
Sharing good practices introduced or implemented in similar projects in the organization and/or industry is an example of:
A. quality audits
B. process analysis
C. statistical sampling
D. benchmarking

QUESTION NO: 196
Project or phase closure guidelines or requirements, historical information, and the lessons learned knowledge base are examples of which input to the Close Project or Phase process?
A. Organizational process assets
B. A work breakdown structure
C. The project management plan
D. Enterprise environmental factors

QUESTION NO: 197
Which technique should a project manager use in a situation in which a collaborative approach to conflict management is not possible?
A. Coaching
B. Avoidance
C. Consensus
D. Influencing

QUESTION NO: 198
The procurement process that documents agreements and related documentation for future reference is known as:
A. Plan Procurements
B. Control Procurements
C. Close Procurements
D. Conduct Procurements

QUESTION NO: 199
The links between the processes in the Process Groups are often:
A. Intuitive
B. Iterative
C. Measured
D. Monitored

QUESTION NO: 200
The process of formalizing acceptance of the completed project deliverables is known as:
A. Validate Scope
B. Close Project or Phase
C. Control Quality
D. Verify Scope

Appendix F: Answer Key/ Sample Exam Two

1	A
2	D
3	A
4	C
5	A
6	D
7	C
8	D
9	A
10	C
11	C
12	C
13	A
14	A
15	A
16	B
17	A
18	C
19	D
20	D
21	B
22	A
23	C
24	D
25	B
26	B
27	A
28	B
29	A
30	D

31	B
32	A
33	D
34	D
35	C
36	B
37	D
38	C
39	A
40	D
41	C
42	B
43	B
44	A
45	C
46	A
47	B
48	B
49	C
50	C
51	D
52	B
53	C
54	B
55	D
56	D
57	A
58	B
59	A
60	D
61	B
62	A
63	C
64	B
65	A
66	C
67	B
68	B
69	D
70	C
71	A
72	C
73	B
74	D
75	D
76	B
77	C
78	A

79	D
80	A
81	B
82	A
83	C
84	C
85	D
86	B
87	C
88	D
89	C
90	A
91	C
92	D
93	B
94	D
95	A
96	C
97	A
98	A
99	C
100	D
101	C
102	A
103	B
104	C
105	D
106	B
107	B
108	D
109	D
110	C
111	D
112	C
113	A
114	D
115	C
116	B
117	C
118	A
119	C
120	D
121	C
122	B
123	D
124	C
125	D
126	D

127	D
128	B
129	B
130	D
131	A
132	A
133	D
134	D
135	D
136	D
137	D
138	C
139	B
140	D
141	C
142	D
143	C
144	A
145	D
146	A
147	D
148	C
149	D
150	C
151	B
152	D
153	C
154	A
155	A
156	B
157	B
158	C
159	D
160	A
161	D
162	D
163	B
164	D
165	D
166	C
167	A
168	A
169	B
170	A
171	D
172	A
173	B
174	C

175	B
176	A
177	B
178	C
179	D
180	C
181	C
182	A
183	C
184	C
185	A
186	B
187	C
188	B
189	B
190	B
191	B
192	B
193	B
194	A
195	A
196	A
197	B
198	C
199	B
200	A

Index

Locators in **'bold'** refers to diagrams, "*t*" refers to tables.

100 percent rule, 95
7 QC Tools, **159**

accepted deliverables, 98
Achievement Theory, 190
acquire project team process, 182–183, 183*t*
activities list, 110, 115, 123
activity attributes, 109, 115, 119, 123
activity cost estimates, 115, 142, 143, 145, 240
   risk identification and, 216
activity duration estimates, 118, 122, 124
   risk identification and, 216
activity identifier (ID), 109
activity list, 109, 118
activity network diagrams, 168
activity resource requirements, 117, 119
activity resource requirements, 123, 129, 240
activity-on-node (AON), 111
advertisements, 248
affinity diagrams, **86**, 168
agile projects, 85
agreements, 58, 143, 248–249
alternative analysis, 116
alternatives generation, 90
analogous estimating technique, 120, 140–141
analytical techniques, 77, 106, 137
   70, 70
  risk management process and, 212
  stakeholders management plan and, 261
AON, 111
approved change requests, 75. *see also* change request
acquisition if project team, 184

assets, process, 29–30, 61
assumption logs, updates, and risk management plan, 232
assumptions analysis, 217

bandwagon effect, 98
basic communication model, **202**
benchmarking, 87, 165
benefits realization, 58
beta distributions, **224**
bidder conferences, 247–248
Blanchard, Ken, 191
bottom-up estimating process, 116, 141
budget at completion (BAC), 69
buffers, 121, 126
burnup or burndown charts, 74,
business case, 57–58
business partners, 32
business value, 23

cause-and-effect diagrams, 160
CCM, 125–126
change control board (CCB), 64, 72, 75
change control meetings. *see also* meetings
change control process, 99
change control tools, 75
change logs, 75
   stakeholders management and, 263
change request, 98, 132, 152, 169
   approval of, 75, 171, 250
   and the change control board (CCB), 64, 72
   communication and, 207
   and contingency plans, 234
   control scope and, 100
   determining, 69
   and the monitor and control project work process, 74

Index

and procurement management, 252
   reasons for, 71
   responsibility for, 72
   and staffing requirements, 196
   stakeholders management and, 266
change requests reviews, 171
changes
   request for, 69
   validated, 69
check sheets, 161
checklist analysis, 217
checklists, quality, 166, 171
claims administration, 251
classification models, 259
close procurements process, 252–253
close project or phase, 76, 76t
   deliverables, 77
   inputs, 77
   and organizational process assets, 77
   project management plan, 77
closing process group, 49–50
Code of Accounts, 95
collect requirements process, 83–84, 83t, 89
collect requirements process, and requirements management plan, 84
communication, modes of, 199
communication management, 205
communication management plan, 202–203
communication methods, 202, 204
   stakeholders management and, 263
communication models, 201–202
communication technology, 201
communication tool, 93
communications management plan, stakeholders management and, 263
conducts procurements process, 246
configuration management activities, 73
conflict resolution techniques, 195
context diagrams, 87

contingency reserves, 121, 145, 233
Contingency Theory, 189
contingent response strategies, and risks, 231
contract change control system, 251
contract termination, 253
contractual agreements and contingent risks, 242t
contractual agreements, types of, 240–242
control chart hugging, 163–164, **164**
control charts, 163
control communications process, 205–206, 206t
control cost process, 145–146, 146t
control procurements, 249–250, 250t
control quality process, 97, 167
control risks process, 222, 232–233, 233t, 239t
control schedule process, 129–130, 130t
control scope, 99
control stakeholder engagement process, 264–265
control tools, **169**
COQ, 141, 156, **159**, 159–164
cost aggregation, 144
cost baselines, 144–145
   managing, 145
cost estimate, basis of, 142
cost forecasts, 69, 152
cost management plan, 137–138, 139, 143
   and cost estimating, 142
   risk identification and, 215
   risk reserves management and, 223
cost management processes, 137
cost of quality (COQ), 141, 156, **159**, 159–164
cost performance index, 69
cost risk simulation analysis, **227**
cost variance (CV), 69

Index

cost-benefit analysis, 158
CPM, 124–125
Create WBS, 92–93, 93*t*
critical chain method (CCM), 125–126
Critical Path Diagramming Method, **125**
Critical path method (CPM), 124–125
cultures, organizational, and projects, 26
customers, 32

decision analysis, multi-criteria, 184
decomposition, 94–95, 108
define activities, 107, 107*t*, 108
   expert judgment and, 108
define scope, 89, 89*t*
deliverables, 66–67, 91, 171
   acceptance of, 96–98
   and close project or phase, 77
   as an input, 77
   as an output, 66–67
   verified, 97
Delphi technique, the, 98
dependency determination, 112–113
design of experiments (DOE), 165, **165**
determine budget process, 142, 143*t*
develop project management plan, 104
develop project management plan process, 60–61, 105, 181
develop project team concept, 185–186
develop schedule process, 118, 122–123, 123*t*
   and schedule baseline, 127
diagramming techniques, 217
digraphs, interrelationship, 168
Direct and Manage Project work process, 65
document analysis, 87
documentation reviews, risk management and, 217
DOE, 165
duration estimate, 119

duration estimate information, 120

EAC, 149
earned value management, 68
earned value management (EVM), 147–149, 150–151, 151*t*
earned value management (EVM) reports, 74
enterprise environmental factors, 30–31, **31**, 58, 60–61, 65, 69, 74, 82, 105–106, 108, 119, 124, 158, 176, 204
   and Acquire Project Team process, 183
   communication requirements and, 200
   cost management plan and, 140
   and Estimate Activity Resources, 116
   and marketplace conditions, 240
   Project Stakeholder Management processes and, 258
   risk management and, 212, 216, 220
   risk management plan, 223
   Sequence Activities, 111
   and stakeholder management process, 261
   and the WBS, 93
environmental factors, enterprise, 30–31, 60–61, 69, 74, 82, 105–106, 108, 119, 124, 158, 176
   and acquire project team process, 183
   communication requirements and, 200
   cost management plan and, 140
   and marketplace conditions, 240
   project stakeholder management processes and, 259
   risk management and, 212, 216, 220
   risk management plan, 223
   and stakeholder management process, 261
   and the WBS, 93
estimate activity durations process, 118, 118*t*

Index

estimate activity resources process, 114–115, 116
estimate at completion (EAC), 69, 149
estimate costs, 138–139, 139t
estimate to complete (ETC), 68
estimates, basis of, 143
estimates to complete (ETC), 69
EVM, 147–149, 150–151
executing process group, 46–47
Expectancy Theory, 189
experiments, design of, 165
expert judgement, sellers proposals evaluation, 248
expert judgment, 59, 65, 70, 75, 77, 90, 180–181
   and budget costs, 137, 144
   define activities and, 108
   and duration estimate, 120
   and estimate activity resources, 116
   plan schedule management and, 106
   and probability, 227
   and procurement, 243
   and scope management plan, 82
   stakeholder identification/classification, 260
   and WBS, 94

facilitated workshops, 85, 90
facilitation techniques, 59
feasibility study, 57
   elements of, **58**
feedback, 44, 87
Fiedler, Fred E., 189
Fishbone Diagram, **160**
flowcharts, 160–161
focus groups, 85
forecasts
   cost, 69, 149, 152
   schedule, 68, 132
functional managers, 33

funding requirements, project, 145, 146

Gantt or Bar Chart Example, **128**
gold plating, 92, 99
governance, project, 32
grade vs. quality, 155
ground rules, and the project team, 188
group creativity techniques, 86–87
group decision-making techniques, 87, 98, 121, 142
groups, organizational, 32–33

Hersey, Paul, 191
Herzberg's Motivation-Hygiene Theory, 190
histograms, 162, **162**
historical information, 78
historical relationships, 144
human resource management plan, 139, 181–182
   soft kills, 186
human resource management process, 175

identify risks process, 214–215, 215t
independent estimates, 247–248
information, historical, 78
information gathering techniques, 217
information management system, and communication management, 205, 207
initiating process group, 42–43
inspection, 98, 171
interactive communication, 202
interpersonal skills, 195–196
   stakeholders and, 264
interrelationship digraphs, 168
interviews, 85
issue log, 194

Index

and communication management, 206
stakeholders management and, 264

JAD session, 85
joint application design/development (JAD) session, 85

knowledge areas
   mapping diagram, 52*t*
   role of, 51–52

lags, 113–114, 127, 131
leads, 113–114, 127, 131
leads and lags, **114**
life cycle, project, 34–37
limit reconciliation, 144
logical relationships, 109–110, 114, 123, 128

make-or-buy analysis, 243
make-or-buy decisions, 247
manage communications process, 203–204, 204*t*
manage project team process, 194*t*
manage stakeholder engagement process, 262–263
management, forms of, **19**, 19–20
management reserves, 122
management skills, 264
managers, functional, 33
market research, 243
Maslow, Abraham, 188
Maslow's Hierarchy of Needs, 188–189,
matrix diagrams, 168
McClelland's Theory of Needs, **190**, 190
McGregor's Theory X and Theory Y, 189

meetings. *see also* change control meetings
   attendees at, 66, 70, 75, 166
   and communication management, 207
   and cost management, 137
   risk management plan and, 212, 234
   and scope management plan, 82
   types of, 77
metrics, quality, 166
Milestone Chart Example, **128**
milestone list, 109, 110
mind mapping, **86**
modeling techniques, 126–127, 131
monitor and control project work
   process, 67–68, 68*t*, 74
   enterprise environmental factors and, 69
   organizational process assets and, 69–70
monitoring and controlling processes, 41, 44, 47–48
motivation, theories of, 188–192

negotiation, and staff assignments, 183–184
networking, 180

OBS, 178
observation and conversation, by project managers, 195
observations, 87
operations and operations management, linkage between, 21–22
OPM, 18
organization, strong matrix, **27**
organizational breakdown structure (OBS), 178
organizational chart, **177**
organizational cultures, 26

Index

organizational groups, 32–33
organizational process assets, 61, 65, 74–75, 90, 100, 119, 158, 183, 254
  and Close Project or Phase, 77
  and communication management, 204, 207
  communication requirements and, 201
  cost management plan and, 140
  and the Estimate Activity Resources process, 116
  and human resource management, 176
  and manage project team process, 194
  and the monitor and control project work process, 69–70
  and the perform integrated change control process, 74–75
  and plan scope management, 82
  and procurement contracts, 240–241
  and project costs, 144
  project costs and, 147
  project stakeholder management processes and, 259
  risk management and, 212, 216, 220
  and schedule control process, 130
  sellers and, 247
  stakeholders management and, 263, 264
  updates of, 77–78, 101, 152, 170, 172, 207
    and procurement management, 252
    risk management plan and, 235
    stakeholders management and, 266
organizational project management (OPM), 18
organizational structures, 26–29
organizational styles, 26
organizational theory, 180
organizations
  and business case, 57
  definition of, 26
  and project management, 22
  project management and, 26
outputs, 59–60, 61–63, 66–67
  and scope management plan, 82

parametric estimating technique, 120, 141
Pareto diagrams, 161, **162**
partners, business, 32
payment systems, 251
PBOs, 22
PDM, 111–112
PDPC, 168
perform integrated change control process, 64, 65, 69, 72–73, 98, 99, 132
  and change request, 100
  and change requests, 152
  and organizational process assets, 74–75
perform integrated change process, 145
perform quality assurance process, 167
perform quantitative analysis process, 218-219222–223, 223t
performance, reporting, 205
performance domain I, initiating, 43t
performance domain II, planning, 45–46t
performance domain III, executing, 47t
performance domain IV, monitoring and controlling, 48t
performance domain V, closing, 49–50t
performance reporting, 251
performance reviews, 131, 150
personnel assessment tools, 192
PERT, 120
plan communications management process, 199–200, 200t
plan cost management process, 135
Plan Human Resource Management process, 175–176
plan human resource management process, 180

Index

Plan Human Resource Management process, recognition and reward program, 188
plan procurement management process, 239
plan quality management inputs, 157t
plan quality management process, 157, 167
plan risk management process, 211
plan risk responses process, 228
plan schedule management process, 105
  and analytical techniques, 106
plan scope management, 81,
plan stakeholder management process, 260, 261
planned expenditures, 144
planning process group, activities of, 44t
planning risk management, 210
PMBOK Guide, The, 16, 55, 81, 104, 120, 155
  and checklists, 217
PMIS, 66, 70, 74
PMI's Management Systems, **73**
portfolio management, 23
  definition of, 18
portfolios, 17
position descriptions, 180
potential outcomes, forecast of, 70
Power/Interest Grid with Stakeholders, **259**
precedence diagramming method (PDM), 111–112
precedence relationships, 112,
prioritization matrices, 168
probability and impact matrix, **221**
  project risks and, 220–221
probability distributions, 224
  and expert judgment, 227
process analysis, 169
process assets, organizational, 29–30, 59, 61, 74–75, 77, 82, 90, 101, 119, 158, 170, 183, 204
  and communication management, 207
  control scope and, 100
  cost management plan and, 140
  and human resource management, 176
  and manage project team process, 194
  and project costs, 144
  project costs and, 147
  Project Stakeholder Management processes and, 259
  risk management and, 212, 216, 220
  and Schedule Control Process, 130
  sellers and, 247
  stakeholders management and, 264
  updates of, 152, 172, 207
process decision program charts (PDPC), 168
process groups
  closing processes, 49–50
  initiating processes, 42–43
  mapping diagram, 52t
  monitoring and controlling processes, 41, 44
  planning, 44
process groups interaction, **40**, **42**
process improvement plan, 166
process in control, **164**
process outputs, 60
procurement contracts, 238
  and organizational process assets, 240–241
procurement documents, 245, 250, 254, 258
  updates of, and procurement documents, 246
procurement management, 238
procurement management plan, and procurement management, 243–244
procurement negotiations, 248
procurement statement of work (SOW), 244, 247

Index

product analysis and, 90
product performance sensitivity, 165
program management, 23
  definition of, 18
programs, 17
project
  definition of, 16
  description of, 89
project budget, 145*t*
project calendars, 129, 130
project change, 99
project charter, 55*t*, 59, 82, 90, 92
  development of, 55–56
  elements of, 92*t*
  and project requirements, 85
  and project schedules, 105
  risk management and, 212
  stakeholders and, 258
project communications management
  process, 199, 205, 206
project completion, 76
project coordinator, 17
project cost management process, 135
project data flow diagram, **51**
project deliverables, 91
project documents
  communication management and, 205
  and quality management, 171
  risk identification and, 216
  stakeholders management and, 265
  updates of, 71, 75, 92, 96, 98, 101, 114, 117, 122, 129, 132, 142, 145, 152, 167, 172, 203, 205, 207
    and procurement management, 252
    risk management plan, 222
    and the risk register, 235
    stakeholders management and, 262, 264, 266
  vs. project management plan, 63*t*
project expeditor, 17
project funding requirements, 145, 146

project governance, 32
project information, 50–51
project integration management, 55
  knowledge area, 104
project life cycle, 34–37
project management, 23
  definition of, 17
  influence of organizations on, 26
  organizational (OPM), 18
  process groups and, 17
  terminology of, 50–51
project management certification
  application process, 13–14
  eligibility requirements, 13
  the examination, 14–15
project management information system (PMIS), 66, 70, 74
Project Management Office (PMO), the, 20–21
project management plan, 61–62, 99, 157–158, 171, 176, 249
  and the control communications process, 206
  development of, 59–60
  as an input, 64, 68, 74, 81
  and project costs, 146
  risk management and, 212
  and risk monitoring, 233
  and schedule management plan, 105, 110, 130
  and the scope baseline, 239–240
  stakeholders management and, 265
  updates of, 71, 76, 101, 129, 132, 152, 169, 172, 231-232
    and procurement management, 252
    stakeholders management and, 266
    stakeholders requirements and, 264
  validate scope process and, 97
  vs. project documents, 63*t*
project management processes, 17, 40
project management software, 116, 131

Index

and cost estimating, 142
and earned value management (EVM), 151
project managers
and human resource management, 175
   managing stakeholders' expectations, 31–32
   and project completion, 76
   responsibility of, 185
   role of, 23, 58, 76
Project Objective - "SMART", **88**
project performance appraisals, 195
project procurement management process, 238
project quality management process, 155
project risk management process, 210
project schedule, 104, 127–128, 130, 143, 240
   and cost management, 140
   creating, 110
project schedule model, 122
project schedule network diagrams, 114, 123, 128
project scope, definition of, 81
project scope management, 81
project scope statement, 91, 93, 110
   and activity durations, 119
   elements of, 92t
   information in the, 91–92
   and project schedule, 124
project staff assignments, 124
Project Stakeholder Management processes, 257
project stakeholders and governance, 31–32. *see also* stakeholders
project statement of work (SOW), 56
project team, 34
   develop, 185–186
   developmental stages of, 187
   ground rules for, 188
   location of, 188
   performance assessments for, 193
   recognition and reward program for, 188
project team members, acquisition of, 184
project team members, pre-assignment of, 183
Project Time Management, 104
project-based organizations (PBOs), 22
projectized organization, **29**
projects, 17
   directing and managing, 63–64, **64**
   probabilistic analysis of, 227–228
   successful, 33, 89
prototypes, 87
published estimating data, 116
pull communication, 202
push communication, 202

QFD, 85
quality assurance, **156**
quality assurance prevention, 167
quality audits, 168–169
quality checklists, 166, 171
quality control, 170, 170t
quality control measurements, 172
Quality Function Deployment (QFD), 85
quality management and control tools, 168–169
quality management approaches, 155–156
quality management plan, 166
   risk management and, 215
quality metrics, 166, 171
quality tools, 159–160
quality verification, 171
quality vs grade, 155
quantitative risk analysis and modeling techniques, 225–227
questionnaires and surveys, 87

Index

RACI matrix, 179
range of project cost estimates, 224*t*
RBS, 213
recognition and reward program, 188
records management system, 251
register, stakeholder, 85
requirements
   collect, 83–84
   project funding, 145
   and scope management plan, 84
   types of, 84
requirements documentation, 88, 90, 93, 97, 100, 158, 240
   as an output, 88
requirements management plan, 83, 84
requirements traceability matrix, 89, 97, 100
reserve analysis, 121–122, 141, 144, 151, 234
resource breakdown structure, **117**, 117, 119
   and Develop Schedule process, 124
resource breakdown structure (RBS), 178
resource calendars, 115, 119, 124, 143, 185
resource cost, 115
resource leveling, 126, 131
resource optimization techniques, 126, 131
resource smoothing, 126, 131
resources, assignment of, 127
reviews. *see* inspection
risk
   examples of, 210
   identification of, 214
   management of, 211
   overall, 210
   themes of, 210
risk assessment, 233
risk attitude, 210–211
risk audits, 234

risk breakdown structure (RBS), 213
risk categorization, 221
risk data quality assessment, 221
risk impact definitions, 214*t*
risk management plan, 212–213, 215, 219–220, 228
   project documents updates and, 222
   project risks and, 220
risk management process, project charter and, 212
risk probability assessment, 220
risk register, 115, 119, 124, 158, 218, 229
   and project cost, 140
   and project costs, 143
   updates, 232
risk reserves management
   cost management plan and, 223
   schedule management plan and, 223
risk scores, 221
risk urgency assessment, 222
risks
   how to handle, 229–230
   negative, 229–230
   positive, 230–231
rolling wave planning, 89, **108**, 108
rule of seven, the, **163**

sampling
   risks of, 166
   statistical, 166
scatter diagrams, 164–165
schedule baseline, and Develop Schedule process, 127
schedule compression, 127, 132
schedule data, 129
schedule forecasts, 68, 132
schedule management plan, 104, 106–107, 107, 115, 118
   risk management and, 215

Index

risk reserves management and, 223
schedule model, 104, 127
schedule network analysis, 124
schedule performance index (SPI), 68
schedule variance (SV), 68
scheduling assumptions, 129
scheduling management plan, 123
scheduling overview, 104*t*
scheduling tools, 127, 132
scope, project, 81
scope baseline, 96, 99, 108, 139–140, 143
   risk management and, 220
scope creep, 92, 99
scope management plan, 90
   as an input, 84
   as an output, 82
   requirements for, 84
   and the WBS, 93
scope models, 87. *see also* context diagrams
seller proposals, and procurement documents, 247
sellers, 32
sellers proposals, review of, 248
Sequence Activities, 109, 110*t*
   and organizational process assets, 111
single-point activity duration estimates, 120
SIPOC Model, the, **161**
Situational Leadership Theory, 191
slack, 125
source selection criteria, 245–246
SOW, 56
SPI, 132
sponsors, 32, 57
staff assignments
   negotiation and, 183–184
   project, 124, 185
stakeholder analysis, 259
stakeholder engagement levels, analysis of, 261
stakeholder management, **257**
stakeholder management plan, 84, 262
   and project requirements, 84
stakeholder register, 85, 260
   risk identification and, 216
stakeholder requirements, and budgeting, 135
stakeholders, **33**
   expectations, 158, 257, 263
   identification of, 260
   identifying, 257–258
   involvement of, 83
   management plan of, 84
   project, 31–32
   types of, 32–33
stakeholders' communication, 201
Stakeholders' Engagement Assessment Matrix, **262**
stakeholders register, 158
statistical sampling, 166
strong matrix organization, **27**
structures, organizational, 26–29
styles, organization, and projects, 26
surveys and questionnaires, 87
SV, 132
SWOT analysis, 218

TCPI, 150
team, selection of, 182
team development, **187**
team management, project, 175
team performance assessments, 193
team-building activities, 187
technical performance measurement, 234
three-point estimating technique, 120–121, 141
time performance indicators, 132
time reserves, 121
to-complete performance index (TCPI),

Index

150
tools and techniques
  advertisements, 248
  alternative analysis, 116
  alternatives generation and, 90
  analogous estimating technique and, 120, 140–141
  analytical techniques, 70, 77, 106, 261
  analytical techniques and, 137, 212
  and benchmarking, 87
  bidder conferences, 247
  bottom-up estimating process, 141
  change requests reviews, 171
  checklist analysis, 217
  claims administration, 251
  communication methods and, 204
  communication methods, stakeholders management and, 263
  communications requirements analysis, 201
  and context diagrams, 87
  contract change control system, 251
  cost aggregation and, 144
  cost-benefit analysis, 158
  critical chain method (CCM), 125
  Critical path method (CPM), 124–125
  and decomposition, 94–95
  decomposition of, 108
  and document analysis, 87
  documentation reviews, 217
  expert judgment, 61, 65, 70, 75, 77, 82, 94, 120, 243
  expert judgment and, 59, 90, 106, 116, 137, 144
  facilitated workshops and, 85, 90
  facilitation techniques, 59, 61
  focus groups and, 85
  group creativity techniques, 86–87
  and group decision-making techniques, 87, 121
  group decision-making techniques, 142
  historical relationships and, 144
  independent estimates, 247–248
  information gathering techniques, 217
  information management system, 265
  information management systems, 205
  inspection, 98, 171
  interpersonal skills, 186
    stakeholders and, 264
  issue log, stakeholders management and, 264
  leads and lags, 132
  make-or-buy analysis, 243
  management skills, 264
  market research, 243
  modeling techniques, 126–127, 131
  observation and conversation, 195
  and observations, 87
  organizational chart, 177–178
  parametric estimating technique, 120
  parametric estimating technique and, 141
  payment systems, 251
  performance reporting, 251
  performance reporting and, 205
  performance reviews and, 131
  pre-assignment of team members, 183
  precedence diagramming method (PDM), 111–112
  probability distributions, 224
  procurement negotiations, 248
  product analysis and, 90
  project, 59
  project management plan, stakeholders requirements and, 264
  project management software, 131, 142
  and prototypes, 87
  quality management and control tools, 168–169
  questionnaires and surveys, 87
  records management system, 251
  reserve analysis, 121, 141

Index

reserve analysis and, 144
resource optimization techniques, 126
risk assessment, 233
risk probability assessment, 220
risks handling strategies, 229–230
schedule compression, 132
schedule network analysis, 124
stakeholder analysis, 259
stakeholder identification/classification, 260
team-building activities, 187
technical performance measurement, 234
three-point estimating technique, 120–121, 141
training and project team, 186
using interviews, 85, 223
variance analysis, 100
vendor bid analysis, 142
total float, 125
training needs, 186
tree diagrams, 168
triangular distributions, **225**
Tuckman model, 187

user stories, 85
users, 32
Utility Theory/Function, 211

validate scope, 96–97, 97*t*
Validate Scope process, and the project management plan, 97
validated changes, 69
validation and acceptance, 97
variance analysis, 100
variances, 68, 69
vendor bid analysis, 142
verified deliverables, 97
virtual teams, 184, 188

Vroom, Victor, 189

WBS, 92–93, 132
  decomposition of, 95
  Define activities and, 107
  structuring, 94–95, **95**
WBS dictionary, 96
WBS ID, 95, 109
work breakdown structure (WBS), 92–93, 96
work packages, 93, 94, 107, 117
work performance data, 98, 100, 130, 250
  and communication management, 206
  stakeholders management and, 265
work performance information, 69, 98, 132, 146, 152, 171, 172, 251, 266. *see also* work performance reports
  Control scope and, 100
work performance reports, 71, 74, 233, 250. *see also* work performance information
  and communication, 204
  use of, 194

www.ingramcontent.com/pod-product-compliance
Lightning Source LLC
Chambersburg PA
CBHW081757300426
44116CB00014B/2149